Young Catholic America

Young Catholic America

*Emerging Adults In, Out of,
and Gone from the Church*

CHRISTIAN SMITH
KYLE LONGEST
JONATHAN HILL
and
KARI CHRISTOFFERSEN

OXFORD
UNIVERSITY PRESS

OXFORD
UNIVERSITY PRESS

Oxford University Press is a department of the University of Oxford.
It furthers the University's objective of excellence in research, scholarship,
and education by publishing worldwide.

Oxford   New York

Auckland   Cape Town   Dar es Salaam   Hong Kong   Karachi
Kuala Lumpur   Madrid   Melbourne   Mexico City   Nairobi
New Delhi   Shanghai   Taipei   Toronto

With offices in

Argentina   Austria   Brazil   Chile   Czech Republic   France   Greece
Guatemala   Hungary   Italy   Japan   Poland   Portugal   Singapore
South Korea   Switzerland   Thailand   Turkey   Ukraine   Vietnam

Oxford is a registered trade mark of Oxford University Press
in the UK and certain other countries.

Published in the United States of America by
Oxford University Press
198 Madison Avenue, New York, NY 10016

Cataloging data is on file with the Library of Congress.

9780199341078

3   5   7   9   8   6   4   2

Printed in the United States of America on acid-free paper

CONTENTS

ACKNOWLEDGMENTS

Many thanks to Chris Coble and Craig Dykstra of Lilly Endowment Inc. for their financial and moral support of our research. Work for this book was also supported by the Deur Endowment of the Department of Sociology and Social Work at Calvin College. We must also thank Robert Brenneman, Brian Starks, Neil Carlson, Tim Matovina, Jim Heft, Mary Ellen Konieczny, Robert Sullivan, Nicole Garnett, Rick Garnett, Brad Gregory, Bradley Wright, Michael Heintz, John Cavadini, John McGreevy, Mike Hout, Melissa Wilde, Trish Snell, Peter Steinfels, Lisa Menendez, and Terri Clark for their various sorts of valuable help on this project. Anna Williams provided extremely helpful copy editing services. And Missy Petrelius of the Notre Dame Center for Social Research also helped provide valuable statistics on divorce, for which we are grateful. As always, many thanks as well to Cynthia Read.

Young Catholic America

Introduction

What happens in the religious and spiritual lives of American Catholic teenagers when they grow up, graduate from high school, and start leaving home to launch their own new adult lives? What is the shape of the religious and spiritual lives of American Catholic 18- to 23-year-olds? What are the social influences that form the lives of young Catholics during this phase of life? And how do young adult Catholics change or not change religiously, spiritually, and otherwise as they leave their teenage years behind and head into their 20s? Does attending a Catholic school make a difference in religious outcomes? And who becomes Catholic between their teenage and emerging adult years? Those are the questions that this book answers.

Tracking Catholic Teenagers as They Become Emerging Adults

In the following chapters, we analyze and interpret data collected in the third wave of a research project on the faith lives of American youth, the National Study of Youth and Religion (NSYR), in order to better understand the religious and spiritual lives of Catholic "emerging adults."[1] We and our colleagues have been studying the sample of young people on whom this study is based since they were 13 to 17 years old, when we first conducted a nationally representative telephone survey with 3,290 of them in 2002 and 2003, and then personally interviewed 267 of them in 45 states around the country.[2] One of us (Christian Smith) published the book *Soul Searching: The Religious and Spiritual Lives of American Teenagers* in 2005, based on what we learned from that first wave of data collected.[3] In 2005, we also conducted a second telephone survey with most of the same subjects and re-interviewed 122 of the same respondents.[4] Between 2002 and 2007, we continued systematically to stay in touch with and track the locations of as many of our study respondents as was humanly possible. In 2007 and 2008 we conducted a third wave of surveys and interviews with them.[5] Our respondents in this third wave were by then 18 to 23 years old. They had passed beyond the high school stage and were entering emerging adulthood. One of us (Smith) published another book, *Souls in Transition: The Religious and Spiritual Lives of Emerging Adults*, in 2009, based on what we learned from this third wave of data collection.[6] Two of us (Smith and Christoffersen) were also co-authors on another book about the troubles of emerging adult life and culture generally.[7]

The present book examines the same sample of Catholic youth, spanning the ages of 13 to 23, focusing on the third measured point of their ongoing life trajectories. That enables us to study them at that moment, in 2007 and 2008, but also to look back and see how their life conditions in previous years have shaped their current lives as emerging adults. Our Catholic respondents in this third wave of the NSYR have transitioned to a new phase of life, are striking out on their own, and are encountering many new challenges and experiences. We want to know what happens in the midst of those transitions to their religious faith, practices, beliefs, associations, and commitments. How much do they change and why? Answering such questions well is the central purpose of this book.[8]

Better understanding the religious and spiritual lives of emerging adult Catholics will tell us many valuable things. It will first of all improve our general knowledge about this fairly recently developed stage of the life course called "emerging adulthood" (about which more details below). What are the major strengths and problems of emerging adults today? What is it like to be an 18- to 23-year-old in America? How are they faring in their journey to full adulthood? Understanding the religious and spiritual lives of Catholic emerging adults better will also provide an important angle on the nature of basic life course changes, both religious and otherwise, as youth transition out of their teenage years into adulthood.[9] What does it mean to shift from one life phase to the other? How are Catholics changed by undergoing that process? What implications does that transition have for the different way Catholic youth's lives turn out? How do different features of American culture and society facilitate or complicate the transition to adulthood for Catholics?

Furthermore, the present study promises to broaden and deepen our understanding of American religion itself, particularly of American Catholicism. How important is religion for young people today? Are there generational changes afoot that seem to be strengthening or weakening Catholic faith and practice in the U.S.? What factors present in Catholics' lives at young ages appear to form religious and spiritual outcomes later in life? Why and how do some young Catholics abandon or grow in their faith, or convert to new religions? What effect, if any, does attending a Catholic school or college have on life outcomes? What are the major social and cultural forces influencing the contours and texture of American religion, particularly Catholicism, today?

Relation to Previous Research

This book builds on and extends beyond previous studies of Catholic youth and emerging adults. Sociologists Patrick McNamara, Dean Hoge, James Davidson, Bill D'Antonio, and their colleagues have previously published numerous works on the religious lives of young adult Catholics.[10] Most of these studies—which collected data between the late 1970s and the early 2000s—reported similar findings and drew parallel conclusions. Social and cultural changes in U.S. society, the American religious system, and the Catholic Church itself, they reported, profoundly affected American Catholics, such that younger American Catholics ("post–Vatican II" and "Millennials") are quite different in many ways from older generations ("Vatican II"– and "pre–Vatican II"–era Catholics). As a result, young American Catholics were found by these studies to be:

- less well-educated and knowledgeable about their Catholic faith, reporting that they do not understand it well enough to explain it to any children they might have;
- more individualistic in their approach to religious authority and beliefs, viewing their own personal subjective experiences and sensibilities, rather than Church teachings, as the arbiters of truth and value;
- therefore very selective in what parts of their tradition they decide to believe and practice (e.g., adhering to core doctrinal truths about Jesus' resurrection and the Eucharist, but discarding Church teachings on sex, birth control, abortion, etc.);
- more tentative and weak in their affiliation with the Church ("loosely tethered");
- less involved in the Church as an institution (by regularly attending Mass, making Confession, etc.);
- more liberal-minded about and tolerant of non-Catholic faiths and non-religion, viewing the Catholic Church as only one denomination among many in a larger religious system of voluntary participation;
- still largely adhering to a general Catholic identity, yet retaining the right to define that as they wish;
- less likely to place their Catholic identity at the center of their personal identity structures, but rather viewing it as one among many other competing identities;
- unable to articulate a coherent account of what it means to be Catholic.

The story of most previous research on young Catholics, in short, is largely one of decline and loss.

These previous studies were valuable pieces of scholarship that contributed to our understanding of young adult Catholics. Yet we believe it is still worth pushing harder on the question of emerging adult Catholics, for a few reasons. First, some of the data on which the prior studies were based are dated by now. In fact, some of those researched in certain of these studies could nearly be the parents of the emerging adults we examine in this book. If generational change matters, as surely it does, then we need to continue to follow successive generations of Catholics to track possible developments in their faith and lives. The evidence upon which this book is based was collected much more recently than that of prior studies, and so provides a much more contemporary view of Catholic emerging adults.

Second, some of the studies cited above were justly criticized by other scholars for serious problems in their data-collection methodologies.[11] We have good reasons to think that sampling biases and systematic non-response biases could have misrepresented in their findings the population of young adult Catholics. The data upon which the present study is based, by contrast, are well established as nationally representative and of the highest quality.

Third, all but one of the studies above[12]—as valuable as they might have been—were based on cross-sectional data, collected as a "snapshot" picture at one point in time. Cross-sectional evidence can tell us a lot. But it cannot help us to see changes over time in the same lives. It cannot reveal developmental trajectories. And studies that focus on respondents who as adults identify as Catholic fail to include those raised Catholic but who have since exited the Church. By contrast, the data we examine in our analysis for this book come from a longitudinal or "panel" study, collected over time in three separate waves, as described above. That research design and data structure will enable us to observe changes across time that previous studies could not.

Fourth, most of the previous studies noted above offer generalizations about *all* young adult Catholics, often comparing them to older Catholics. That can be good and valuable. But there are other good ways to "slice the pie." In this book, instead of generalizing about emerging adult Catholics as a whole, we often make comparisons between different kinds of emerging adult Catholics. Rather than seeing how younger Catholics are different from older Catholics, we examine here how some young Catholics are different from other young Catholics and why they might be so. That can go a long way toward revealing interesting distinctions between Catholics of the same generation, which can tell a lot about the influences of different earlier-life factors on later outcomes.

On Emerging Adulthood

We said above that we will in this book be calling the Catholic young people that this study examines "emerging adults" and we want to explain here why.[13] In the last several decades, a number of macro social changes have combined to create a new phase in the American life course. Seven have been particularly important.

First is the dramatic growth of higher education. The GI Bill, changes in the American economy, and government subsidizing of community colleges and state universities led, in the second half of the last century, to a dramatic rise in the number of high school graduates going on to college and university. More recently, many feel pressured—in pursuit of the American dream—to pursue years of graduate school education after receiving a bachelor's degree. As a result, a huge proportion of American youth no longer finish school and begin stable careers at age 18, but extend their formal schooling well into their 20s. And those who are aiming to join America's professional and knowledge classes—those who most powerfully shape our culture and society—are continuing in graduate and professional school programs often up until or beyond the age of 30.

A second and related social change crucial to the rise of emerging adulthood is the delay of marriage by American youth over the last several decades. Between 1950 and 2006, the median age of first marriage for women rose from 20.3 to 25.9 years old. For men during that same time the median age rose from 22.8 to 27.5 years old. The sharpest increase for both took place after 1970.[14] Half a century ago, many young people were anxious to get out of high school, marry, settle down, have children, and start a long-term career. But many today spend almost a decade between high school graduation and marriage exploring life's many options as singles, with unprecedented freedom.[15]

A third major social transformation contributing to the rise of emerging adulthood as a distinct life phase concerns changes in the American and global economy that undermine stable, life-long careers and replace them instead with careers of lower security, more frequent job changes, and an ongoing need for new training and education. Most young people today know they need to approach their careers with a variety of skills, maximal flexibility, and readiness to re-tool as needed. That itself pushes youth toward extended schooling, delay of marriage, and, arguably, a general psychological orientation of maximizing options and postponing commitments. Far from being happy to graduate high school and take the factory job their father or uncle arranged for them—which likely does not exist anymore—many young people today spend five to ten years experimenting with different jobs before finally deciding on a long-term career direction.

Fourth, and partly as a response to all of the above, parents of today's youth, aware of the resources it often takes to succeed, seem increasingly willing to extend financial and other support to their children, well into their 20s and perhaps early 30s. According to the best estimates, American parents spend an average of $38,340 per child in total material assistance (cash, housing, educational expenses, food, etc.) over the 17-year period between ages 18 and 34.[16] These resources subsidize the freedom that emerging adults enjoy to take a good, long time before settling down into full adulthood, as culturally defined by completing one's education, attaining a stable career, achieving financial independence, and forming a new family.

Fifth, the widespread availability of the Pill and other relatively reliable forms of artificial contraception fostered a culture, especially after the 1960s, in which sexual intercourse was radically separated in people's minds from fertility and parenthood. Increasingly it was assumed that one could have sex as one wished without the worry and risk of getting pregnant or getting someone else pregnant. After 1973, too, legalized abortion came increasingly to be understood as a way to terminate unplanned and inconvenient pregnancies, further extending the cultural disconnect between sex and parenthood. Moreover, in response to the growing threat of AIDS and other sexually transmitted diseases in the 1980s, a public health regime taught young people how to have "safe sex," primarily through the regular use of condoms. All of this helped create an atmosphere in which youth treated sex as a normal, perhaps recreational, part of a romantic relationship, maybe even a casual relationship, which need have no consequences that might force one to settle down and take on parental responsibilities.

The sixth change that has contributed to shaping today's emerging adult culture is the spread and influence of postmodern theory. Postmodern thought in its current expression originated in "high theory" among humanities scholars in literary theory and related fields. But in recent decades, a vulgar version of postmodernism has disseminated through much of American culture. Previous generations of Americans would likely have believed in reason, progress, science, universal rationality, the nation, and truth. Popular postmodernism debunks those beliefs, however, teaching instead that "absolute truth" does not exist, that reason is only one parochial form of knowledge, that truth claims are typically masked assertions of power, that morality is relative, that nothing is universal, and that nobody can really know anything for certain. That too has profoundly influenced emerging adults, including, we will see, young Catholics.

Finally, seventh, America's material prosperity has shaped emerging adult culture. The post–World War II economic boom, which has largely continued to the present (despite the temporary setbacks of multiple economic recessions), has inundated the lives of all but the poorest Americans with immense amounts of material goods, consumer choice, visual media images, new luxury items, and sophisticated technologies and gadgets. Since the Depression era, Americans' expectations for increasingly comfortable material lifestyles and improved forms of media consumption have grown as fast as or faster than the mass-consumer economy could meet them. Personal savings have declined. Consumer debt has increased. Houses have grown in size. And pressures to succeed financially have increased. Emerging adults today have grown up in a society awash in a sea of material products, media images, and purchased experiences that have inflated their expectations and sense of entitlement. It is all they have ever known and it is what they expect.

These seven social transformations together have dramatically altered the experience of American life between the ages of 18 and 29. Studies agree that the transition to adulthood today is as a result more complex, disjointed, and confusing than it was in past decades. The steps through and to schooling, a long-term job, marriage, and parenthood are simply less organized and coherent today than they were in generations past. At the same time, these years are marked by a historically unparalleled freedom to roam, experiment, learn, move on, and try again. This new situation has been variously labeled "extended adolescence," "youthhood," "adultolescence," "the twixter years," "young adulthood," the "twenty-somethings," and "emerging adulthood."

We find persuasive the psychologist Jeffrey Arnett's argument that, of all of these labels, "emerging adulthood" is the most appropriate.[17] That is because, rather than viewing these years as just the last hurrah of adolescence or an early stage of real adulthood, it recognizes the unique characteristics of this new and particular phase of life. The features marking this stage are intense identity exploration, instability, a focus on self, feeling in limbo or in transition or in-between, and a sense of possibilities, opportunities, and hope. These, of course, are also often accompanied—as we will see in this book—by large doses of transience, confusion, anxiety, self-obsession, melodrama, conflict, disappointment, and sometimes emotional devastation. Many popular television shows of the last few decades—*Beverly Hills 90210*, *Dawson's Creek*, *Seinfeld*, and *Friends*—reflect through Hollywood's lens the character and challenges of this recently developing, in-between stage of life.

To grasp the significance of emerging adulthood, it is necessary to realize that life stages are not natural, immutable phases of existence. Rather, they are cultural constructions that interact with biology and material production, and are profoundly shaped by the social and institutional conditions that generate and sustain them. So "the teenage years" or "adolescence" as a distinct stage of life was very much a twentieth-century invention, brought into being by changes in education, child labor laws, urbanization and suburbanization, mass consumerism, and the media. Similarly, a new, distinct, and important stage in life, emerging adulthood, situated between the teenage years and full-fledged adulthood, has emerged in our culture in recent decades—reshaping the meaning of self, youth, relationships, and life commitments as well as a variety of behaviors and dispositions among the young. As a result, life for many today between ages 18 and 29, roughly, has morphed into a new experience quite different from that of previous generations. The purpose of this book is to investigate what happens to the religious and spiritual lives of Catholic youth in particular as they enter and begin to move through emerging adulthood.

A related note on terminology. In the scholarly literature, emerging adulthood refers to 18- to 29-year-olds. The sample of Americans that this book investigates and reports on, however, represents only the first half of emerging adulthood, ages 18 to 23. As a consequence, this book's cases, findings, and interpretations do not actually speak for or about all emerging adults in the U.S. today but rather those in the beginning portion of this life course stage. However, rather than consistently recognizing this qualification by adding another adjective to every mention of emerging adult—such as "*new* emerging adult," and then perhaps using the clumsy acronym NEA for short—we will instead use the term "emerging adult." Readers should keep in mind throughout, however, that this is shorthand for convenience' sake to represent only the first half of emerging adulthood. Americans 24 to 29 years old could prove to look and sound quite different, though only more research will tell.[18]

What Follows

Chapter 1 places all that follows in historical context, by examining momentous changes in American Catholicism across the twentieth century. Chapter 2 focuses more specifically on changes (or lack thereof) among American Catholic emerging adults between the years 1972 and 2008. Chapter 3 uses NSYR survey data to present a statistical portrait of the religious faith and practice of different kinds of emerging adult Catholics today. Chapter 4 then explores NSYR interview data on emerging adult Catholics to parse out a typology of different kinds of Catholic young adults and the various ways they approach their faith and life. We then step aside with a somewhat technical but conceptually very important excursus on the larger methodological question of who in a panel survey should actually be counted as "Catholic," given the various characteristics that might be thought of as counting for or indicating respondents' Catholicism. Chapter 5 examines the different trajectories of religious faith and practice observable among our NSYR sample from the teenage to the emerging adult years, exploring the types and seeming causes of differences in trajectories across these years. Chapter 6 examines the associations between different kinds of Catholic faith among American youth and variance in life course outcomes, answering the question of whether Catholic faith and practice make a significant difference in the outcomes of these young people's lives. Finally, Chapter 7 concludes with a brief analysis of the extent to which Catholic schooling make perceptible differences in the faith and practice of American Catholic emerging adults, and differences we observe between Latino versus white Catholic young people in the U.S. Before getting to those analyses and findings, however, we believe it best to set what follows in the context of American Catholic history in the twentieth century, to which we now turn.

|| 1 ||

Catholic Emerging Adults in Historical Context: 1945 to 1970

The sociological imagination tells us that if we wish to make sense of any particular fact or event, we need to view it in its larger social and historical context. Since we wish here to understand contemporary Catholic emerging adults, we must begin with the larger social and historical context into which they have been born and raised. Taking note of important features of the history, culture, and social conditions of American Catholicism broadly will help us better understand and explain what we find about Catholic young people today in the rest of this book. Doing so requires that we examine changes to the demographics of American Catholics in the second half of the twentieth century, social and cultural changes happening *around* the Catholic Church, and changes *within* the Catholic Church itself during the same time period.[1]

Changing American Catholic Demographics

First, let us think about ages, cohorts, and generations. The young Catholics (and ex-Catholics) whom we study in this book were born between 1985 and 1990, placing them in the larger generation sometimes labeled "Millennials," "Echo Boomers," "Generation Next," and the "Net Generation." They were children during the George H.W. Bush and Bill Clinton presidential administrations, and teenagers during the George W. Bush years. Their parents are mostly Baby Boomers, born between the mid-1950s and mid-1960s. Importantly, they (the parents) were the first generation of American Catholics to come of age during their teenage years *after* the Second Vatican Council (1962–1965). Most of the *grand*parents of our emerging adults were born between the mid-1920s and the late 1940s. They (the grandparents) belong(ed) mainly to the so-called "Silent Generation," wedged between the cohort who fought World War II (the "Greatest Generation") and the Baby Boomers, though some were early

Boomers themselves. The grandparents came of age and were formed religiously well before the Second Vatican Council. These generational differences have significant implications for making sense of the emerging adults we are studying in this book, as we see in what follows.[2]

The American economy grew rapidly in the decades after the Second World War, expanding the ranks of the American middle class and spreading material prosperity and consumption more broadly than ever before. The American system of higher education also expanded dramatically during this period: ever-larger numbers of young people enrolled in colleges, universities, and graduate and professional schools. Residential patterns in these decades also shifted, with much of the population moving from urban areas to newly constructed subur-ban sub developments.[3] These three developments—economic, educational, and residential—had particularly large impacts on American Catholicism. After World War II, American Catholics experienced more upward economic mobil-ity and participated more in higher education than their non-Catholic counter-parts. Although American Catholics remained in urban areas longer than Protes-tants and Jews did, they too eventually moved from inner-city to suburban settings at a rate similar to or higher than those of other Americans during these decades.[4] These forms of educational, socioeconomic, and residential mobility dramatically affected the character of American Catholicism.[5]

Until the mid–twentieth century, Catholics in America were predominantly immigrants who lived in urban areas and were of European "ethnicity," whether Irish, Italian, Polish, French, or southern or western German. (Since the 1980s, Hispanic immigrants have come to represent a large proportion of the American Catholic population, but they are less important for the mid-century period on which we focus here, so we pay them less attention.)[6] American Catholics at the time mostly belonged to the working class and were sometimes poor or near poor. Many lived in neighborhoods that were densely populated with other Catholics, sometimes in neighborhoods so segregated by religion that they were experi-enced as urban Catholic ghettos.[7] Catholicism was a distinct minority in the field of American religion, and Catholics were a minority in the American population.[8] Attending not public schools but Catholic elementary and secondary schools run by priests, religious brothers, and nuns was normative for very many American Catholics.[9] Church authorities were generally revered in Catholic communities, the Church was generally viewed as the one true Christian Church, and participa-tion in Church liturgies and other activities was typically high.[10] Catholics tended strongly to marry other Catholics, especially those within their own ethnic group, rather than non-Catholics, and "inter denominational" marriages were actively discouraged.

In part because of these factors, Catholicism was also culturally marginal in the U.S., the target of much mainstream prejudice and vilification. In the nineteenth and early twentieth centuries, Catholics intermittently faced persecution from hostile groups like the "Know Nothings," the Ku Klux Klan, and other nativist, protectionist, and anti-"papist" movements and organizations. In various episodes during the nineteenth century, American Protestants attacked and damaged Catholic Church buildings and harassed and even rioted against Catholics in the streets.[11] Catholic political power was strong in places, but was only local and regional in extent, at best: national politics were still in the hands of the Protestant establishment.[12] In short, until the mid–twentieth century, American Catholicism was notably peculiar and marginal, yet important to most of its members, who lived it out in a "parochial/tribal style" of faith.[13]

The decades after World War II changed much of that. Some of the trends discussed here had already begun in the 1920s, 1930s, and 1940s.[14] Yet in a relatively short period after World War II, American Catholics for the first time became for the most part socially, religiously, demographically, and politically normalized and accepted. Much of this process was driven by the remarkable rates of Catholic educational achievement, upward socioeconomic mobility, and suburbanization in the second half of the twentieth century.[15] Some of it was prompted by the horizons-expanding experience of Catholic soldiers fighting the war in Europe and the Pacific. Also relevant was a revival of "liberal Catholicism" among many Catholic intellectuals and educators in the 1950s and 1960s, which displaced the "Catholic revival" outlook that so dominated U.S. Church culture in the 1930s and 1940s.[16] As a result of these causes, American Catholics became no longer immigrant outsiders but regular Americans. Their formerly distinct ethnicities melted into the generic category of "white."[17] They went to college and worked in middle-class occupations. They lived among Protestants and other non-Catholic Americans in suburban neighborhoods. And their children increasingly attended public and non-Catholic private schools. They opposed communism during the Cold War. And in 1960, one of their own, John Kennedy, was elected president of the U.S. "All of this produced a sizeable class of 'professional' Catholics ready and willing to share in the sub-urban American dream of tolerance and affluence."[18]

This "mainstreaming" of American Catholicism in the second half of the twentieth century was also the result of changes in the society and culture *surrounding* the Catholic Church. The atrocities of World War II, particularly the Nazi concentration camps and the Holocaust, spurred the development in American culture of increasing tolerance of and civil rights for minority groups.[19] That theme was vividly advanced in new spheres of life by the black civil rights movement of the 1950s and 1960s, but it affected broader thinking in America about Jews, Asians, and Catholics as well.[20] The dominant Protestant establishment was in this era also giving way to a more inclusive cultural conceptualization of the American religious field centered around the notion of a "Protestant-Catholic-Jew" form of

American faith.[21] Evangelical and fundamentalist Protestantism had in the late 1920s mostly receded into the background of American public life and, with few exceptions (such as the high visibility of the evangelist Billy Graham), would not re-emerge on the national public stage until the mid-1970s. Meanwhile, mainline Protestantism, which enjoyed a brief post-war revival in numerical strength, was becoming ever more theologically, culturally, and morally accommodating to its surroundings. A new wave of religious ecumenism was gaining momentum in the U.S. and beyond. In a sense, then, much of denominational mainline Protestantism was becoming sufficiently organizationally open and internally secularized that it held little stake anymore in opposing Catholicism as theologically, culturally, or ecclesiologically "dangerous."

In the political sphere, too, Catholics were no longer marginalized but assimilated into the mainstream. The Vatican proved to be a reliable opponent of Marxism and communism during the Cold War.[22] President Kennedy, as he had promised, did not impose Catholic religious and moral dictates on national policy. In fact, he gained admiration and respect and was seen by some as positively refreshing and inspiring and, later, as a noble American martyr. The American Catholic population was also growing significantly in size, both absolutely and relatively—from numbering 12 million in 1900, to 29 million in 1950 and 48 million in 1970, representing, respectively, 16, 19, and 24 percent of the total U.S. population.[23] More generally, American identity was becoming reorganized around not Anglo culture and religious affiliations but the shared experiences of capitalist consumerism and national media consumption, the latter particularly in the form of network television programming. In such a climate, the previous non-Catholic orientation of distrusting, disdaining, marginalizing, and attacking the Catholic Church and American Catholics made less sense. That was a welcome change for most American Catholics.

The consequence of all of these trends is that American Catholics entered—fully, dramatically, and often with something of a "chip on the shoulder" to prove themselves worthy and respectable—into mainstream American culture and society. Rather suddenly, American Catholics were no longer poor, different, discriminated-against outsiders. Catholics had rapidly moved up and inside. They had "arrived."[24]

As part of that process of upward mobility and social acceptance, they inevitably also became highly acculturated. Mid- to late twentieth-century American Catholics entered into and began enjoying mainstream American culture and lifestyles with few reservations or restraints. After centuries of insisting that they were good, loyal, patriotic Americans, they finally gained the opportunity to embrace all that a prosperous America had to offer. Important for present purposes, that included major doses of material prosperity, educational broadening, ecumenical tolerance, moral diversity, and liberal individualism.[25]

All these facts about American Catholics' upward mobility, social acceptance, and mainstream acculturation are crucial to understanding emerging adult Catholics and ex-Catholics today.

Changes within the Catholic Church

There is, however, another context to take into account in order to understand contemporary emerging adult Catholics. So far, we have focused on key socio-economic and demographic transformations within the American Catholic population, and on other social and cultural changes that happened around the Catholic Church in the early decades of the second half of the twentieth century. Other contextual changes need to be recognized before we are ready to move on.

The first is profound changes within the Catholic Church itself, some triggered and others only accelerated by the Second Vatican Council (1962–1965). Other commentators have discussed the effects of Vatican II on the Church and we need not repeat all their observations here.[26] Most broadly, Vatican II opened up the Catholic Church to a new appreciation for and dialogue with the modern, non-Catholic world and to reforms within the Church that many believed were needed.[27] While it reiterated in new forms traditional Catholic teachings on many central theological and ecclesiological matters, Vatican II also promulgated numerous reforms in and for the Church, emphasizing the importance of the laity, the integrity of conscience, worship in the vernacular, ecumenical dialogue, religious freedom, human rights, and more. We do not here take a particular interpretive stand on Vatican II as a whole—whether liberal, traditionalist, or otherwise—since ongoing debates about how the Second Vatican Council should be rightly interpreted themselves have consequences for our present concerns. It is enough to make a few observations here.

First, to overstate the point only somewhat, Vatican II meant that American Catholics, many of whose leaders had previously worked to shut out, denounce, and resist modern culture[28], needed "in one frantic decade" to assimilate many features of modernity.[29] Certainly, American Catholics had for decades enjoyed religious freedom and rubbed shoulders with Protestants and Jews. Various movements of engagement and renewal were at work in the Church before Vatican II, including Catholic Action, the liturgical movement, the Cursillo movement, and more.[30] Catholics used many modern technologies, despite their often anti-modern rhetoric. And many progressive American Catholic leaders had long advocated an open engagement with modernity prior to the council.[31] Still, Catholicism's relative marginality in American culture during the late nineteenth and early twentieth century had served to shield the Church from many of the secularizing forces that ravaged American Protestantism during that time period.[32] But in some ways, and at the risk of exaggeration, Vatican II marked a kind of "cold turkey" break with Tridentine Catholicism (that is, Catholic faith as defined by the Council of Trent of 1545 to 1563), or, to use a different image, for a kind of "polar plunge" into modernity.[33] Protestantism had been at the heart of modernity from the start and so had centuries to more gradually interpret and assimilate modern culture. "Catholicism, on the other hand, has really for the first time tried to absorb the effects of this whole vast modern development from the Enlightenment to the present in the short period between 1963 and 1973!"[34] That proved an overwhelming challenge.[35]

Seen from another perspective, Vatican II effectively removed the restraints on progressive Catholics who had in previous years been agitating for significant change. Numerous Catholic leaders, particularly in Catholic higher education, had through the 1950s become increasingly critical of what they saw as the Church's separatism, clericalism, ghetto mentality, authoritarianism, intolerance of diversity, moralism, complacency, indoctrination, defensiveness, smugness, and triumphalism. They had grown discontent with the "scholastic synthesis" of the neo-Thomistic revival that had dominated Catholic intellectual life in the prior decades, and were calling for a more open-minded engagement with modern philosophy, social theory, and theology.[36] These progressive Catholics engaged with increasing boldness in what they believed was healthy self-criticism—but which others thought bordered on "self-flagellation."[37] These progressives saw the Church as newly "coming of age" in a way that would demand "a considerable reorientation of Catholic life."[38] In the first half of the twentieth century, after the papal condemnations of Americanism and Modernism, such arguments met great opposition. The spirit and culture fomented by Vatican II, however, gave progressive activists room to mobilize and criticize. "The barriers against which the forces of change had been building up through the fifties gave way entirely," in historian Philip Gleason's words. "The results were so dramatic that they took even the proponents of reform by surprise."[39]

Whatever the implications of the immediate teachings of Vatican II, it seems that after the council ended, the Church in the U.S. did a less than ideal job of instructing the faithful in the pews about its teachings and their implications. The Second Vatican Council was a major event in the life of the Church and its multi faceted meaning needed strong, clear transmission and interpretation by the bishops to the clergy, religious, and lay faithful. In retrospect, it does not seem that such unified, lucid, authoritative instruction and direction was provided.[40] As a result, significant uncertainty and misunderstanding settled into Church life and culture, which led to various kinds of experimentation and innovation, some arguably good, some less so. Looking back, many observers today say that, at that crucial juncture, the American Church "dropped the ball" and as a result suffered harmful ambiguity, hesitation, and misdirection. Most of the changes instituted by Vatican II were very popular among most American Catholics. But it is not clear that ongoing effective catechesis of the young was among the results of the reforms.

Furthermore, after its original announcement in 1959, Vatican II gave liberal and progressive elements in the American Church hope that the Church would become a much more genuinely democratic, inclusive, egalitarian, modernized institution.[41] However, after the promulgation of the papal encyclical *Humanae Vitae* in 1968, and then especially once the pontificate of Pope John Paul II began in 1978, many of the hopes of progressives and liberals were dashed. The practical reforms instituted as a result of Vatican II proved to be substantial, but nothing like what most left-leaning Catholics anticipated and desired. Many in this generation of young, visionary, perhaps idealistic, strongly reformist, liberal and progressive Catholics eventually soured and in some cases became cynical and bitter.[42] Conservatives, for their part, contended with progressives about the changes afoot in the Church and certainly contributed to an increasingly polarized situation.[43] Whether justified or not, these conflicts introduced something of a critical, negative, and acrimonious element to Catholic culture and life in the American Church since the late 1960s.

A second big challenge to American Catholicism hit after Vatican II: many priests and men and women religious left their clerical roles and religious life by being laicized (if not leaving the Church altogether), and new vocations to the priesthood declined precipitously. Scholars disagree about the exact cause of this decline in vocations. For present purposes it is only necessary to recognize the facts. The number of priests and religious brothers and sisters in the American Church was never large, historically. But the early twentieth century saw impressive growth in the number of priests and religious brothers and sisters, to a high-water mark at mid-century.[44] Starting in the 1960s, however, that growth was dramatically reversed. Between 1966 and 1969 alone, 3,413 American priests left the priesthood and 4,322 women religious left religious life. Between 1965 and 1971, the American Catholic Church lost 10 percent of its priests. Furthermore, in just ten years between 1967 and 1977, the number of enrolled Catholic seminarians was cut in half. On a broader time scale, in 1964, 47,500 American Catholic men were preparing for the priesthood; by 1984, that number had dropped to around 12,000—a 75 *percent decline* in the number of seminarians. During that same time period, 241 Catholic seminaries closed their doors. In 1965, the Church had one ordained priest for every 800 Catholic laypeople; by 2002, there was only one priest for every 1,400 Catholics. Between 1945 and 1965, the number of vowed religious brothers grew from 7,003 to 13,152, but then it fell dramatically. By 1985, the number of religious brothers had declined by 22 percent from its 1965 high, and again by another 30 percent by 1998 (a total of 52 percent decline between 1965 and 1998).[45] Between 1966 and

1980, the population of women religious in the U.S. declined by 30 percent, the number of new recruits declined dramatically, and those women who remained in religious life were significantly older on average. Altogether, the loss of religious women between 1965 and 2002 was nearly 60 percent of the mid-century high point.[46] As a result of these losses and increases in the Catholic population, the number of American Catholic laypeople per Catholic priest, religious brother, and religious sister increased by 83, 174, and 163 percent, respectively, between 1965 and 1998.[47] Consequently, at a time when the Church was facing extraordinary new challenges in catechesis and faith formation, it was also suffering a dramatic reduction in the trained personnel necessary to conduct that work—as well as confusion and a crisis of confidence about what this decline in numbers meant.

In this era, moreover, the American Church lacked the material resources to implement and pay for badly needed initiatives and programs. For a variety of reasons, American Catholics are the least generous financial givers of all groups of American Christians and most groups of American religious believers (including non-Christians). Studies consistently show that the vast majority of American Catholics give only a paltry amount of money to the Church and other causes—even after figuring in support for Catholic schools.[48] For example, in 1960, American Catholics donated an average of 2.2 percent of their income, an amount well below the figure for most other American Christians and a number that has since declined.[49] Between 1963 and 1983, the average percent of income given by American Catholics in financial contributions declined by half, from 2 to 1 percent.[50] Twenty-eight percent of Catholics today give away no money at all, and 81 percent give less than 2 percent of their income in voluntary financial giving.[51] The relative stinginess of American Catholics as a group—despite a very generous minority of Catholic financial givers—means that dioceses, parishes, and other Catholic organizations often do not have the material resources to put in place trained staff in catechesis, faith formation, evangelization, Christian education, and youth and young adult ministry. If Catholics gave financially at rates anything like those of conservative Protestants or Mormons, for example, they could afford an impressive system of Christian education for the laity, especially for the theological and spiritual formation of children, teenagers, and emerging adults. But since the vast majority of American Catholics do not give money generously, the majority of their children and youth grow up in the Church often lacking adequate Christian education, formation, and direction that might lead to stronger Catholic faith and practice.

The two previously noted factors—the dramatic decline in priestly and religious vocations after Vatican II and American Catholics' meager financial giving—converged in the middle of the second half of the twentieth century to transform another historically crucial institution of the Catholic Church in the U.S.: Catholic primary and secondary schools.[52] For generations, these had been staffed by priests and religious sisters and brothers who were committed to the Church, mostly well-trained in Church teachings, and relatively inexpensive to employ. By the mid-1900s, the American Catholic parochial school system had developed into an impressive and unique institution—there was nothing like it in scale and character in the rest of the world, even the Catholic world. However, precisely when the changes described above were unfolding, most Catholic schools, like parishes, suffered a declining number of such dedicated and highly affordable Church teachers and administrators.[53] This was also precisely the moment that the younger Baby Boomers were in their school years. Lay teachers and administrators had to fill the gap, often doing impressive work, but still changing the character of Catholic schooling. In the 37 years following 1965, the number of priests, sisters, and brothers teaching in Catholic schools declined from 114,000 to only 9,000—a 92 percent drop. Laypeople, both Catholic and non-Catholic, make up more than 95 percent of all Catholic school teaching staff today.[54] Furthermore (in part due to the decline in Catholic family fertility, noted below), the number of Catholic school students dropped precipitously: for example, from 4.2 million diocesan and parochial elementary school students in 1960 to 2.3 million in 1980 (a 46 percent decline in twenty years).[55] As a result, between 1964 and 1984, 40 percent of American Catholic high schools and 27 percent of Catholic elementary schools closed their doors.[56] In sum, since 1965, "Catholic elementary and secondary education lost its traditional teaching staff, had to shift the major burden of funding from parishes to parents, closed almost 40 percent of its schools, and suffered more than a 50 percent decline in enrollment."[57]

Not only did lay teaching staff cost more to employ—which was (and is) a challenge, given the limited financial resources afforded the Church—in some cases they also proved less well-grounded in the Catholic faith and therefore less capable of passing on a robust Catholicism to their students.[58] Also, some Catholic schools, especially at the secondary level in suburbia, evolved into academically elite private academies that attracted tuition-paying parents with less investment in Catholicism per se than in these schools' academic superiority over area public schools, impressive sports programs, and college-admissions track records.[59] Usually this was more the result of pressures exerted by parents than the purposeful intentions of Catholic school administrators and teachers—but such changes sometimes did occur nonetheless. Many Catholic schools did and do carry on, sometimes valiantly, often serving poor and vulnerable urban neighborhoods.[60] But their capacity to educate in Christian faith the children of the one-quarter of the American population that is Catholic became increasingly difficult, just as the need was becoming more imperative and complex.

Important and consequential changes were also afoot during this time in the sphere of American Catholic higher education. Most Catholic colleges and universities had long been havens of Church culture and teaching for the children of the Catholic faithful, even if only a minority of them attended. These institutions wrestled in various ways in the early twentieth century with maintaining their distinctive Catholic cultures and pedagogical approaches.[61] And they were self-consciously different from Protestant and secular colleges and universities. Beginning in mid-century, however, leaders of many Catholic colleges and universities began to set their sights on further enhancing the academic quality of their institutions and becoming more accepted and respected within the broader field of American higher education.[62] This set into motion complex and often unintended processes of de facto academic acculturation, similar in timing, dynamic, and effect to the broader values and lifestyle acculturation of Catholic laypeople noted above. In part, Catholic students and their parents wanted a different college experience from what Catholic colleges had traditionally offered. With that and other pressures at work, many Catholic colleges and universities often unintentionally downplayed their Catholic identities and reoriented themselves to the assumptions, standards, and goals of secular higher education. Whatever positive consequences this change may have had on Catholic higher education—and surely there were some benefits—it cannot be denied that it further eroded the capacity of American Catholicism broadly to transmit to its best-educated young adults a clear, strong, distinctive version of the faith and practices of the Church.

With these transformations well underway, the year 1968 was an important turning point in the American Catholic Church. That was the year when on July 25 Pope Paul VI issued the papal encyclical *Humanae Vitae*, "On Human Life," which was a spiritual and theological reflection on human marriage and sexuality, in the context of which the longstanding Catholic teaching on artificial birth control was affirmed. To tell the story is itself to enter the storm of controversy that the encyclical ignited, which is not our intent here. For present purposes it is sufficient to say that, against the hopes and expectations of many, the encyclical condemned the use of artificial contraception as immoral and contrary to God's design for human sexuality, marriage, and life. The vast majority of American Catholics disagreed with that viewpoint, including many priests and even bishops. Many moderate Catholics in America were surprised and disappointed. Most liberals and progressives were stunned and appalled. Serious dissent arose in many quarters, further unsettling the Church.[63] Aside from the furor of public debate in reaction to *Humanae Vitae*, the event also had momentous consequences for Catholic laity. Rather than accepting the teachings of the encyclical as puzzling perhaps but authoritative nonetheless, a majority of American Catholics decided that the Church was wrong, that they as individuals had the right to make their own moral judgment on the matter, and that they would use birth control if they so chose.[64]

With that, a kind of epistemological Rubicon of authority had been crossed: for the first time, large numbers of American Catholics were, with seemingly clean consciences, in effect declaring their own personal authority to judge the validity of the teachings of the Church and decide whether (or not) to follow its moral directives. This choice had considerable psychological, symbolic, and cultural consequences for Catholic laity: adhering to Church teachings had now in practice become optional, and the agent authorized to adjudicate the options had become the individual believer, not the institutional Church.[65] Once that shift had been made, the so-called "cafeteria Catholic" was born—an epithet, incidentally, used by both conservatives and liberals in different ways against each other—and a whole range of beliefs and morals were put on the table for individual Catholics to choose for or against as they so wished. Thus, still in 1970, 70 percent of American Catholics reported believing that it was "certainly true" that Jesus Christ had given authority in the Church to Peter and his apostolic successors, the popes; and 68 percent believed the pope was infallible. Just four years later, however, those numbers had dropped to 42 and 32 percent, respectively, and a study of young Catholics in the 1980s found those numbers to be down to 20 percent.[66] By the 1980s, surveys revealed that two-thirds of American Catholics said that individuals, not the Church, should make their own decisions about the morality of contraceptives.[67]

To be clear, we neither blame *Humanae Vitae* as an ill-advised blunder, as some would have it, for provoking this momentous sea change among "the (otherwise) faithful," nor do we suggest that those who chose not to embrace the encyclical's teachings were justified in their actions. Our sociological point is more limited and descriptive: that *Humanae Vitae*, whether for legitimate reasons or not, provoked a storm of controversy and provided the crucial occasion when what was to become a majority of American Catholics made a kind of "declaration of independence" from the binding authority of papal teachings, deciding that they as individuals were authorized to make their own choices on such doctrinal and moral matters. And that had consequences for American Catholicism that reverberate down to the emerging adults we study in this book.

Socio Cultural Changes around American Catholicism

Nothing we have described so far in this chapter took place in a social and cultural vacuum that prevented outside influences from shaping American Catholics and their Church in the latter half of the twentieth century. The events and processes described above *also* transpired exactly when other, broader transformations of American culture and society were underway. Again, merely telling the story risks becoming mired down in conflict over different interpretations of its significance. But tell it we must, so we will do our best to recount it descriptively with as much balance as possible.

The two decades immediately following the Second World War were, as is well known, broadly characterized by a "return to normalcy" (or at least a temporary social construction of normalcy), notable forms of conventionality and conformity, a mini-revival in established religion, and a simultaneous focus on fighting the Cold War and enjoying the material prosperity produced by America's booming economy. As generalizations, those stereotypes of the era are largely true. But they also simplify and obscure, for other developments between 1945 and the mid-1960s planted the seeds of much more disruptive social and cultural changes that were soon to follow.[68]

Important among these was the black civil rights movement, which challenged racial segregation and discrimination, institutionalized new forms of grassroots organizing and protest, and propelled into new spheres of life the logic of liberal, individual egalitarianism.[69] For Catholics, the Farm Workers' Movement led by César Chávez and Dolores Huerta was significant in this way as well. A deepening American involvement in the anti-communist military conflict in Vietnam eventually led to a massive anti-war protest movement associated with and propelling a general anti-authoritarian popular posture. This period witnessed the heyday of liberal Democratic politics, culminating in President Lyndon Johnson's "Great Society" and "War Against Poverty," which set a tone in relation to which conservative and traditionalist voices sounded dated, and which inspired a generation of young people to civic and political activism. European existentialism and structuralism, which often had a bleak, anti-humanistic edge, exerted influence on American intellectual circles, including some religious institutions, during these years. This era also saw the rise of the "Beat Generation," a group of 1950s poets and writers—including Allen Ginsberg, William Burroughs, and Jack Kerouac—centered first in New York and later San Francisco, who emphasized themes of bohemian hedonism, nonconformity, creative spontaneity, experimentation with drugs, alternative spiritualities, and rebellious sexuality. The nonconformist Beats put an end to the last vestiges of the Protestant establishment's decaying power to censor publications and prepared the way through modeling and teaching for the next decade's youth and student movements, sexual revolution, drug experimentation, interest in "Eastern religions," political rebellion, rock-and-roll breakout (especially with the Beatles, named in part to associate with the Beats[70]), and the "flower child" and hippie movements. The Beat Generation contributed more broadly to the nascent cultural movement toward radical individualism in matters of morality and lifestyle, which established "New Rules" of self-fulfillment in the late 1960s and thereafter.[71] Planting more seeds of the sexual revolution and of the massive expansion and later tolerated public presence of pornography in American culture, the "lifestyle entrepreneur" Hugh Hefner launched *Playboy* magazine in 1953. *Playboy* grew into the massively profitable Playboy Enterprises and inspired the launch of copy-cat ventures, such as *Penthouse* and *Hustler* magazines in 1965 and 1974, respectively.

By the early 1960s, when Catholics had attained the same educational, occupational, and socioeconomic status as the average non-Catholic American,[72] the U.S. more broadly was itself on the cusp of a series of massive cultural revolutions, political upheavals, and social transformations. These are well known, so we only need to name, but not describe, them: the women's movement and "second-wave" feminism, the radicalization of the civil rights movement ("black power," etc.), the student and free-speech movements, the sexual revolution, the anti-Vietnam war movement, astrology and a "turning East" in popular interest in spirituality, widespread dissemination and use of the Pill and other new technologies of artificial contraception, the "divorce revolution," the normalization of moral diversity, the beginning of the gay rights and New Age movements, increased rates of unmarried cohabiting partners, Watergate and the subsequent suspicion of political authority, the mainstreaming of a more rebellious form of popular music, the growth and spread of the pornography industry, and a growing interest in individualistic pop psychology, "finding oneself," and "self-fulfillment."[73] Thus, just as American Catholics had finally "arrived" in the mainstream, ready to fully participate in and assimilate into conventional culture and society, America itself was undergoing a complicated set of profound changes, in which American Catholics also naturally participated and to a great degree accepted.

However readers personally evaluate these cultural and social transformations, it is clear that many, though not all, of them stood in tension with the Catholic Church's teachings, practices, and culture known until then. Even after the reforms of Vatican II, much of institutional Catholicism tended to emphasize authority, hierarchy, collective identity, the singularity of truth, self-renunciation, moral rectitude, redemptive suffering, accountability in penance, sexual chastity, and the value of celibacy. In a few cases, such as the fight for civil rights, anti-poverty organizing, and the anti-nuke movement, Catholicism could readily support the era's movements with internally coherent justifications. But in most instances, the movements and revolutions named above contradicted much of what the Catholic Church (indeed, what all but the most liberal strands of American religion) taught and stood for. The cultural outlooks, for example, behind "do your own thing," "tune in, turn on, and drop out," "whatever turns you on," "if it feels good, do it," "find yourself," and "I'm okay, you're okay" could not be reconciled with the inherited Catholic worldview and ethos.[74]

American Catholics of course did not fully capitulate to these movements, revolutions, and forces, which were often alien and threatening to faithful Catholicism. But neither, for the most part, did they strongly resist and withstand them in any countercultural way. American Catholics' upward educational and socioeconomic mobility, geographical dispersion in suburbia, and acceptance and acculturation into the American mainstream had largely dissolved the social-structural conditions that would have made that resistance possible. The "Tridentine fortress mentality" of pre–Vatican II American Catholicism had already been dismantled, for better or worse.[75] And the unintended destabilizing consequences of Vatican II and its aftermath in the Church, described above, further undercut the American Catholic faithful's capacity for unified response, cultural resistance, and countercultural practice. Moreover, when it came to political affiliation, most American Catholics in the 1960s and 1970s still leaned toward the Democratic Party. So as that party supported many of the liberal movements of the 1960s and 1970s, Catholics were firmly located in the organization in a way that made them especially susceptible to its liberalizing influences.[76] In various ways, therefore, American Catholics were transformed into the image of the new American culture and society that was taking shape around them.

Consider the impact of some of the changes listed above on American Catholic families, particularly as represented in rates of divorce, annulments, premarital sex, contraceptive use, ideal number of children, and religious intermarriage. Accurate historical data on divorce trends are hard to come by. But the available evidence suggests a significant increase in divorce among Catholics in the latter half of the twentieth century. According to General Social Survey data collected from 1972 to 1979, only 5.7 percent of Americans identifying as raised Catholic or currently Catholic who were born before 1900 had ever been divorced; 13.5 percent of those born between 1900 and 1909 reported ever being divorced; and 19.5 percent of those born between 1930 and 1939 (our emerging adults' grandparents' generation) reported ever getting divorced.[77] By the early 1970s, 16 percent of *current* American Catholics were divorced (a figure not including the growing number of those who divorced and left the Church,[78] who were included in the previously mentioned statistics). That number rose to between 20 and 27 percent in the mid-1980s, and again to somewhere between 33 and 37 percent a decade later. These are still lower rates than those of most other religious groups, but they nonetheless rose significantly over time and stood in tension with the Church's teachings about divorce.[79] Furthermore, while the Church issued no more than 300 to 500 marriage annulments annually prior to Vatican II and only 700 marriage annulments in 1967, by 1978 the Church approved 25,000 annulments.[80] Moreover, as to attitudes, in 1963, 52 percent of American Catholics said remarriage after divorce is wrong; by 1974, only 17 percent of Catholic said the same.[81] By 1979, a mere 11 percent of 18- to 29-year-old Catholics said that it was not okay for divorced people to remarry if they were in love.[82] In the mid-1980s, two-thirds of American Catholics said they wanted the Church to change its teaching to allow divorced Catholics to remarry in the Church.[83]

Attitudes about premarital sex and contraception changed dramatically in the same period. In 1963, 74 percent of American Catholics said sex before marriage was wrong; by 1974, that number dropped by half, to only 35 percent.[84] By 1978, only 23 percent of American Catholic adults said that sex before marriage is always wrong.[85] In 1955, about 30 percent of Catholic women used artificial contraceptives; by 1965, that number had risen to 51 percent, and again by 1970 to 68 percent. In the 1970s, more than 75 percent of married Catholic women in their twenties were using artificial contraceptives. During that same decade, survey data showed that nearly 90 percent of American Catholic women rejected the teachings of *Humanae Vitae* on birth control.[86] This growing Catholic use of artificial contraceptives eventually converged with the levels of use by non-Catholics, resulting in what scholars called "the end of 'Catholic' [high] fertility."[87] Between 1968 and 1985, the ideal number of children reported by American Catholics dropped from 50 percent of Catholics in 1968 saying four or more children were ideal to only nine percent of Catholics saying the same in 1985 (a number statistically identical to Protestant reports that year).[88] As to religious intermarriage, studies of large urban parishes, such as those of Boston and Detroit, show that in the late nineteenth century, well less than 10 percent of Catholic marriages were to non-Catholics. By the 1960s, that number had jumped to 34 percent; and, again, by the 1980s, to nearly 40 percent. Attitudinally, in 1958, three-quarters of American Catholics believed it was better for Catholics to marry other Catholics; by the 1970s that number had slipped to a bare majority, with a growing indifference to the question itself.[89]

In sum, during the very period that American Catholics became "structurally available" (through their entry into the American mainstream) and "organizationally vulnerable" (due to turbulence in the Church after Vatican II) to be highly influenced by surrounding socio cultural forces, American society itself underwent a series of profound revolutions and movements that were in many ways at odds with received Catholic teachings, morality, and culture. All of this, in fact, "unleash[ed] a traumatic identity crisis for American Catholics by the end of the twentieth century."[90] American Catholics as a whole did not strongly resist the influences of those surrounding revolutions, as they might have in former eras of their history. In various ways, many Catholics passively absorbed if not happily embraced them as enlightening and liberating. So while "in 1887, Catholics were struggling with the question of what it meant to be an American; comfortably American in 1965 [and after], they now struggled with a more fundamental question: what it meant to be Catholic."[91]

Taken together, these converging forces have been called a "perfect storm" that sank the more distinctively Catholic Church of pre–World War II history and left the post–Vatican II Church at least somewhat foundering at sea.[92] "Many Catholics embraced the liberal mainstream values of the postwar world with a fervor and devotion that were, if anything, far too uncritical and far too celebratory of American culture for the long-term health of their religious community. . . . This . . . uncritically but enthusiastically accepting [of] American cultural values succeeded sociologically in making American Catholics all but indistinguishable as a group from their fellow citizens in terms of ethical values, social mores, and cultural tastes."[93] That had big consequences for the character of American Catholicism ever since—outcomes that we think still influence the lives of emerging adult Catholics and ex-Catholics living in the first decade of the twenty-first century.

Returning to the Parents

Let us return to the matter of generational timing noted at the opening of this chapter. Perhaps the most relevant connection between the social and cultural changes we have described in this chapter and the emerging adults we examine below concerns the *parents* of those emerging adults. They were the first generation of Catholic youth who faced and grew up in the new American Catholic reality described in the previous pages. Born in the 1950s and early 1960s, they rode the breaking wave of Catholics' upward educational and economic mobility. They were the generational hinge of the residential swing from the segregated, urban, ethnic Catholicism of their own parents' generation to the mainstream, suburban, middle-class, fully "white" Catholicism into which they moved. Compared to previous generations, the parents of our emerging adults suffered relatively little hostility, discrimination, and ostracism for being Catholic. Their people had for the most part finally "arrived" and were enjoying the fruits of conventional American culture and society—including its booming economy and relative religious tolerance.

Many of these parents of the emerging adults we study below had early in life been exposed to the piety and practices of the stricter pre–Vatican II Catholicism of their own parents' and grandparents' generations. But as older children and teenagers they were submerged into the new, heady atmosphere of openness, experimentation, uncertainty, hesitation, disagreement, misunderstanding, and growing conflict and polarization that was set into motion unintentionally by the Second Vatican Council and its arguably less-than-ideal translation in the American Church. That, added to everything else noted above, had consequences.

First, these parents of our emerging adults would have been much less likely to go to church than their parents had at their age. In 1963, 71 percent of American Catholics reported attending Mass regularly; one decade later that number had dropped to 50 percent. Meanwhile, the rate of self-identified Catholics never attending church had doubled. Similarly, in 1963, 37 percent of Catholics reported going to Confession at least monthly; a decade later, just 17 percent did the same.[94] Even if the parents of our emerging adults still attended Mass regularly when they were young, the messages they heard in church would have emphasized God's embracing love over his holiness or punitive justice, individual conscience over compliance or obedience, the Church as "the People of God" over an institution-centered ecclesiology, ecumenical acceptance over parochial exclusivity, the importance of being in the world rather than separation from the world, and so on.[95] However one judges these messages, they certainly provide a different orientation to faith and life than older Catholic piety did. Moreover, the Catholic schools and colleges that the parents of today's emerging adults might have attended had likely been weakened in their Catholic identity and capacity to transmit Catholic faith and culture, however strong they might have grown in other ways. And just as the parents of our emerging adults were making choices about their own personal futures and life commitments, the institutions of the Catholic priesthood and religious orders were eroding in size and cultural respect and appeal.

What results did all of this have for the parents of the emerging adults we are learning about in this book? Speaking in generalizations is always dangerous, since different individuals and groups of American Catholics from this time period had different experiences. The results will also vary by social class. But to understand the larger matter at hand in this book, we must generalize, even while keeping in mind the many qualifications and complexities that our generalizations tend to overlook.

Generally speaking, we can say that—as a result of the many factors noted above—many of the parents of the emerging adults we examine in this book were not particularly well-educated in Catholic teachings and were poorly formed in Catholic faith and life—or at least they did not "take" to the education and formation they did receive.[96] This means that many proved ill-equipped to pass on the Catholic faith, particularly its doctrine, to their own children later. Most of the parents of our emerging adults came of age at a time when many Catholics were more focused on "making it" in America than on sustaining a distinctive Catholic faithfulness; when the Church itself was navigating a difficult transition of its own and struggling with some disorientation and organizational and cultural challenges; and when the American society and culture into which these Catholics were arriving and so ready to embrace was undergoing a series of dramatic transformations that often challenged if not repudiated the teachings and sensibilities of mainstream Catholicism. Again, there were definitely many forces of renewal in the Church at the time—movements like Search and TEC (Teens Encounter Christ), the Charismatic Renewal movement, new forms of campus ministry and youth groups, the Cursillo movement, and more.[97] The liturgical renewal movement of this era was also a significant force, often in ways that strengthened the Church. And many Catholics strived to serve their parishes and communities, even if they had not mastered Church doctrine. Nevertheless, the overall change in this era is clearly one of institutional weakening. As a result, when viewed from the perspective of the Church working to transmit its faith from one generation to the next, those who became the parents of the emerging adults we study below seem to represent something of a "lost generation," a link in the chain that was weakened and in many cases broken, a period in the "game" when the "ball" was too often dropped.[98]

Stated differently and with more emphasis on the bigger picture, the old system of Catholic faith transmission—which relied on concentrated Catholic residential neighborhoods, ethnic solidarity, strong Catholic schools, religious education classes designed to reinforce family and parish life, and "thickly" Catholic cultures, practices, and rituals—had drastically eroded by the time this generation (the parents of our emerging adults) came of age.[99] Yet no alternative approach to effective inter generational Catholic faith transmission had been devised and instituted to replace the old system—and indeed it is not clear that any such effective system has yet been put into place even today. A sense of change was in the air amid more than a little uncertainty, experimentation, conflict, and the loss of key Church personnel. In the course of subsequent events unfolding in the Catholic Church in America and worldwide, no sufficient "recovery" occurred from the breakdowns of this era to enable this generation to transmit its faith to the next. To be sure, Pope John Paul II (1978–2005) was noted for his uncanny ability to "connect" with young people, and the obvious successes of World Youth Day events were encouraging to many Catholics concerned about the future of the Church. But none of that directly addressed the systemic, institutional, parish-level challenges of and failures involved in passing on the Catholic faith to future generations of American believers.

Thus, when the youth who would decades later become the parents of our emerging adults passed through the years that were the most important for their instruction in and formation of lives of faithful Catholic belief and practice, the social, cultural, and institutional forces of the day created conditions that made it difficult to prepare them to someday pass on a strong Catholic faith and way of life to their own sons and daughters. Even parents who had been well-formed in their faith, as some certainly had been, had trouble passing it on to their children as the larger socio cultural and ecclesial context made that process a challenge. For those parents who had not been well-formed in the faith, the situation was even more difficult: the chances that their children would turn out to be strong Catholics were almost nil.

Sociological studies around the turn of the twenty-first century have shown that the single most important measurable factor determining the religious and spiritual lives of teenagers and young adults is the religious faith, commitments, and practices of their parents.[100] Whether they realize it or not, parents or parental figures today are the most important pastors that any youth will ever have. Day in and day out, parents define for many years what is real to, normal for, and expected of their children when it comes to religious belief, morality, and practice. Parents set the bar for religious faith and life for their children. Those youth may or may not reach that bar in their own lives. But very rarely do children ever exceed the standard of religious faith and practice set by their parents (especially when there are very powerful social forces at work around families, such as Catholics' mid–twentieth century upward mobility and acculturation described above). For this reason, previous research has con-cluded that adults looking for a "rule of thumb" to anticipate how their children will turn out religiously and spiritually (and otherwise) should rely upon this trustworthy dictum: "We will get what we are."[101] Generally speaking, what par-ents (and churches) will get out of their children in the future is what they them-selves are in the present—not what they wish they were, not an idealized vision that is rarely achieved, but what they themselves are on a regular basis. The best predictor of the character of the religious lives of offspring, in short, is the char-acter of the religious lives of those who brought them into the world and primar-ily socialized them into participation in it. That association is not determinis-tic—sometimes there are real mismatches between parents and children religiously—but it is probabilistically powerful and reliable: it will prove largely true in most cases. Therefore, we should expect that, in trying to understand and explain the religious and spiritual lives of Catholic emerging adults today, we can glean indispensable clues and insights from looking at their parents and the con-ditions in which they themselves grew up.

In making these observations we are in no way blaming or villainizing the parents of the emerging adults we are studying. They are the product of their own times (as we all are); they did not control the larger forces at work in soci-ety, even if they made individual decisions amid the opportunities and con-straints that surrounded them. In fact, the very purpose of setting these parents in the historical and social context described in this chapter is to show that the outcomes that happened are not mysterious, nor were they always purposely and consciously controlled by the individuals involved. We want to show that these outcomes, often unintended, are intelligible and explicable in light of that larger context and the events it precipitated. Of course, we are not suggesting that *all* of the features of emerging adult Catholic life today can be explained by their parents' faith and practice. The larger story of this chapter, in fact, is not about parents but about social and cultural transformations in the U.S. from economic prosperity, the expansion of higher education, and suburbanization to a growing tolerance for non-Protestant faiths, cultural revolutions, and so on. We do not intend to switch the basic analysis at the end here to focus exclusively on the role of parents. Many forces and factors all interact together to help explain the findings of this book. We must keep in mind, too, that most of the cultural and social forces that transformed the Catholic experiences of the parents of today's emerging adults continue to exert influences on youth in America—often with greater intensity than they did in the 1960s and 1970s.

Readers with stakes in certain visions of the Catholic Church's good may make various evaluations and judgments of the historical forces and their consequences noted above. In the end, readers can make informed normative and prescriptive sense of all of the findings of this book. In the meantime, our job as sociologists is to present the best possible sociological evidence and analysis of the matters in question, a task that does not entail assigning blame to or vindicating the actors involved. We seek instead to describe what happened at a crucial time in Church history in order to shed light on the real focus of this book: to understand and explain the religious and spiritual lives of Catholic and ex-Catholic 18- to 23-year-olds today. To continue moving in that direction, although still working within a preliminary historical framework, we turn next to a more quantitative analysis of changes among Catholic youth between the 1970s and the present.

Emerging Adult Catholics across Four Decades: 1970s to 2000s

This chapter provides additional historical context for our analysis of the Catholic emerging adults represented in our National Study of Youth and Religion sample, which this book examines. We do this by analyzing patterns of stability and change in demographic characteristics, religious behaviors and beliefs, attitudes toward social issues, and political orientation over the last four decades in the emerging adult Catholic population. As with our analysis in Chapter 3 of *Souls in Transition*, our approach here uses data from the General Social Survey (GSS), a top-quality and widely used survey of the American population over age 18, conducted annually or biennially since 1972.

With these data, we are able to quantify the demographic, religious, and social profile of emerging adult Catholics by decade, across four decades. By "emerging adult" in this chapter (unlike the rest of this book), we mean 18- to 25-year-olds. This approach holds age constant and allows us to examine changes and stability among different cohorts of Catholic emerging adults over time. Using this method, any differences we may find cannot be due to general life-course patterns (that is, social or developmental changes associated with aging) but must be due to birth cohort influences or the effects of the distinct cultural and institutional characteristics of the period in which the survey was conducted. By holding the influence of age constant, we are able to isolate generational and historical changes since the early 1970s. This analytical method provides us with a helpful overview of historical changes in the social and religious beliefs and behaviors of Catholic emerging adults.

We also include non-Catholic emerging adults as a comparison group in all of our analyses here. Most previous surveys of Catholic emerging adults lack this comparison group, so they cannot indicate the degree to which young Catholics are merely reflecting the dominant trends in social beliefs and behaviors or the extent to which young Catholics lie outside of the mainstream. The inclusion of this non-Catholic group in our analysis allows us to estimate whether Catholic

emerging adults are becoming more or less similar to their non-Catholic counterparts over time. We begin by assessing how Catholic emerging adults have
changed demographically in the last 35 years.

We should note that, in this chapter, we consider those emerging adults Catholic who identify themselves as such. While self-identification is certainly an
important marker of Catholicism, we recognize it is not the only one. In fact, the
question of who should be counted as Catholic ended up being far trickier than
we initially expected. Should we classify those who grew up in a Catholic household as Catholic, even if they no longer identify with the faith? Should we only
count emerging adults as Catholic if they are actively involved in their local
parish? We take up this issue in more detail in the Excursus, and use a more refined measure in subsequent analyses when allowed by the data. Unfortunately,
in the case of the GSS data we use in this chapter, we need to settle for a simple
indicator that is consistently measured over time. Self-identification, despite
some shortcomings, is what we have.

What we find in our analyses below can be summarized by three points. First,
with a few exceptions, *Catholic emerging adults across four decades display very
little change in their beliefs, attitudes, and practices.* Eighteen- to 25-year-old Catholics in the 2000s look very much like 18- to 25-year-olds in the 1970s on a variety
of measures. Whatever historical changes happened among Catholic emerging
adults on these measures, therefore, for the most part happened before the
1970s. That finding is consistent with our story in the previous chapter. It may,
however, deflate some commonly accepted accounts about changes among
Catholic youth in recent decades.

Second, *Catholic emerging adults across the past four decades look remarkably
similar to their non-Catholic contemporary peers.* We find very little that is distinctive in the beliefs, attitudes, and practices of Catholic emerging adults compared
to their non-Catholic peers.

Third, the one area that reveals a significant difference between Catholic and
non-Catholic emerging adults over time is in church attendance. *Catholic emerging adults exhibit a more dramatic decline in church attendance across these four decades than do their non-Catholic peers.* Since this difference is notable, we go into
greater depth analyzing what it means in later in this chapter. But first we focus
on demographic trends and comparisons, as a background to understanding religious, sexual, moral, political, and social beliefs and attitudes.

Demographic Profile of Catholic Emerging Adults over Time

We begin our analysis by focusing on demographic characteristics of Catholic
(and non-Catholic) emerging adults across four decades, starting in the 1970s.

Demographics

Ethnicity. Figure 2.1 examines changes in the basic demographic profile of Catholic emerging adults since the 1970s. We should be somewhat cautious in interpreting GSS changes in race and ethnicity over time, due to questionable measurement procedures in earlier decades.[1] With that caution in mind, we observe in Figure 2.1 a clear increase in the non-white population for both Catholics and non-Catholics over time. About 95 percent of Catholic emerging adults in the 1970s were white, but that figure declined to about two-thirds (67 percent) in the 2000s. The majority of those labeled "Other" by GSS administrators (29 percent in the 2000s) are likely of Hispanic ethnicity. Our own estimates based on NSYR data of the percentage of Catholics who are Hispanic suggest that the GSS's figure (29 percent) probably underestimates the size of this population (see Chapter 3).

Region of Residence. We also see a shift in Figure 2.1 in the region of residence of Catholic emerging adults over time. In the 1970s, emerging adult Catholics were overrepresented in the Northeast (particularly in New England) and underrepresented in the southern and western regions of the U.S. In the 2000s, 18- to 25-year-old Catholics are only slightly overrepresented in the Northeast, continue to be underrepresented in the South, and are most recently slightly *overrepresented* in the West.

Place of Birth. The changes in Catholic ethnicity and region of residence displayed in Figure 2.1 are likely both due to the increasing proportion of foreign-born and second-generation immigrants among American Catholics. In the 1970s, emerging adult Catholics were almost all native-born with native-born parents (97 percent). In the 2000s, less than two-thirds (65 percent) of emerging adult Catholics fall into this category, compared to 85 percent of non-Catholics in this age group. The influx of Catholic immigrants has thus altered the ethnic composition of young Catholics in recent decades and increased their representation in western regions of the U.S.

Marital Status. Figure 2.2 reveals a general downward trend in the proportion of emerging adults who are married, as a result of larger social trends that cause young people to delay marriage. But we observe little difference in this area between Catholic and non-Catholic emerging adults: smaller numbers of young people, both Catholic and non-Catholic, have been married as these decades have progressed, which increases their lifestyle options.

Educational Degree and Work Status. Similarly, although the proportion of emerging adults with post-secondary degrees has increased modestly over the last several decades, Catholic educational attainment is roughly similar to the educational attainment of non-Catholics. (Note that the large group of respondents whose highest degree is "high school" no doubt contains a substantial

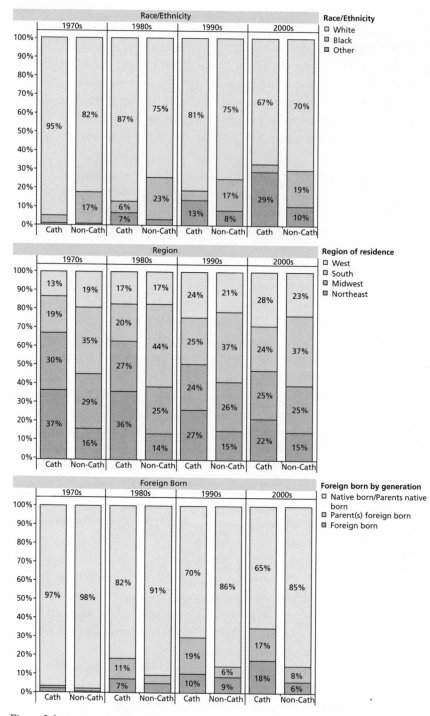

Figure 2.1 Source: GSS 1972–2008.

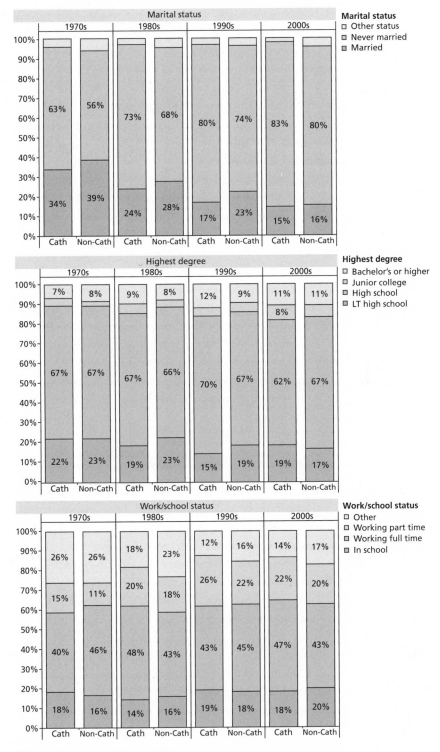

Figure 2.2 Source: GSS 1972–2008.

number of college and university students who would soon would move into the "bachelor's or higher" category.) With the exception of a slight uptick in the proportion of emerging adults working part-time, there are very few discernible trends in the occupational and schooling status of Catholic and non-Catholic 18- to 25-year-olds.

In sum, emerging adult Catholics in the last four decades have become less white with the large influx of Hispanic immigrants, most of whom are Catholic, to the U.S. Partly as a result, the distribution of Catholic emerging adults has shifted significantly during this time away from the Northeast, toward the West, and somewhat toward the South. Also as a result, a higher proportion of Catholic emerging adults today are foreign-born than in previous decades. Catholic emerging adults are less likely to be married today than they were in prior decades, due to the growing society-wide trend of delaying marriage. Educational attainment, an area in which former generations of Catholics achieved impressive gains before the 1970s, has increased only marginally among young Catholics in the last four decades. Not many changes are evident in the employment and education status among Catholic 18- to 25-year-olds from the 1970s to the 2000s.

Viewed in absolute terms, however, most Catholic emerging adults at the start of the twenty-first century were white and native-born. This population is spread fairly evenly across the country. The vast majority are not married and are either in school or working full-time. We have reason to believe that this generation of emerging adults will eventually match, if not somewhat exceed, the educational attainment of their parents.

Religious Practices and Beliefs

Recent research on young Catholics has painted a picture of generational decline in religious identity, participation, orthodoxy, and beliefs about institutional authority. There may, however, be methodological problems associated with some of these studies, at least when they focus on post-1960s Catholics. We argued in the previous chapter that generational changes were crucial at the middle of the twentieth century. But what do we find when we examine the religious practices and beliefs of Catholic emerging adults over the most recent four decades? The evidence shows that *Mass attendance has declined significantly*. Other measures of religious belief and practice, however, appear much more stable.

Mass Attendance. Figure 2.3 shows a significant decline in Mass attendance among emerging adult Catholics. In the 1970s, more than one-third of 18- to 25-year-old Catholics attended Mass at least weekly. By the 1990s and 2000s, only one-fifth were attending weekly or more often. Catholic emerging adults were also no more likely than non-Catholics (which includes those who do not identify with any religion) to go to church weekly; they are, however, more likely

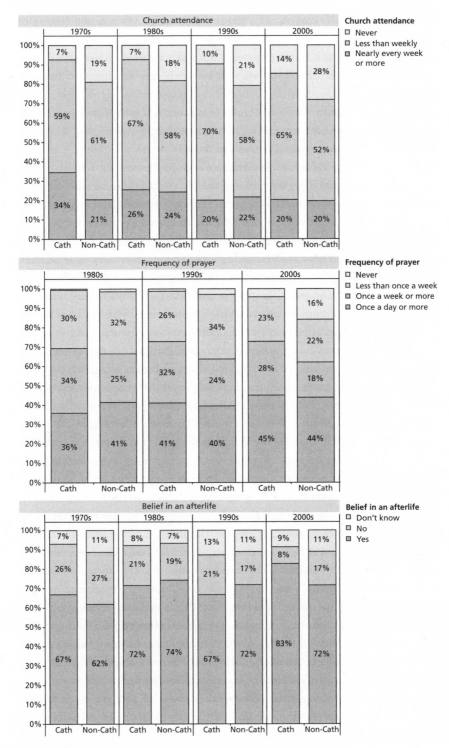

Figure 2.3 Source: GSS 1972–2008.

to attend occasionally (the middle category) than non-Catholics, who are more likely to never attend than Catholics (the top category). Stated simply, Catholic emerging adults have become somewhat less likely to attend Mass weekly over the last four decades; the large majority do not do so now and have not for many decades.

Prayer and Afterlife. The numbers in Figure 2.3 show that most emerging adults report praying at least weekly and believe in life after death. Not all indicators point to religious decline across the last few decades. Figure 2.3 actually shows a slight increase in the proportion of 18- to 25-year-old Catholics who report praying daily or more often since the 1980s (the first decade that the GSS asked about prayer)—although the proportion who report praying weekly or more has been fairly stable. We also note an increase in the proportion of Catholics who report believing in an afterlife, from 67 percent in the 1970s to 83 percent in the 2000s. Other research has demonstrated that this increase in belief in life after death is evident more broadly in the U.S. population and can be tied to birth cohort differences especially among Catholics (and Jews, though not Protestants), with more recent cohorts most likely to affirm a belief in life after death.[2]

Bible Beliefs. Other indicators confirm that there has been some degree of stability in young Catholics' religious beliefs (see Figure 2.4). Catholic emerging adults have always been less likely than their non-Catholic counterparts to take a literal approach to understanding the Bible, since the Church does not teach a literal understanding of Scripture (while some conservative Protestant traditions do). About one-fifth to one-fourth of the emerging adult Catholic population from the 1980s to the 2000s affirms that the Bible should be understood as the "literal Word of God." Nearly triple that proportion of young Catholics affirms that the Bible should be understood as the "inspired Word of God," with similar proportions maintained since the 1980s. (This question was not asked by GSS in the 1970s.) So although Catholic emerging adults are less likely than non-Catholics to take a literal approach to the Bible, they are more likely than non-Catholics to affirm the sacred character of the Bible (and less likely to choose the "ancient book of fables" option). We observe no real change in emerging adult Catholics' views of the Bible across these three decades.

Strength of Religious Affiliation. Since the 1970s, a majority of emerging adult American Catholics has not expressed a strong identification with their Catholic faith. In most decades, more than 60 percent of young Catholics classify their Catholic identity as "not very strong." The proportion of Catholic 18- to 25-year-olds who strongly identify with their Catholic affiliation has remained constant, at slightly more than one-quarter of the total. At the same time, the proportion of non-Catholics who identify strongly with their religious tradition has been *increasing*, from 32 percent in the 1970s to 43 percent in the 2000s. This increase may be partly due to the growing number of non-Catholic young people who

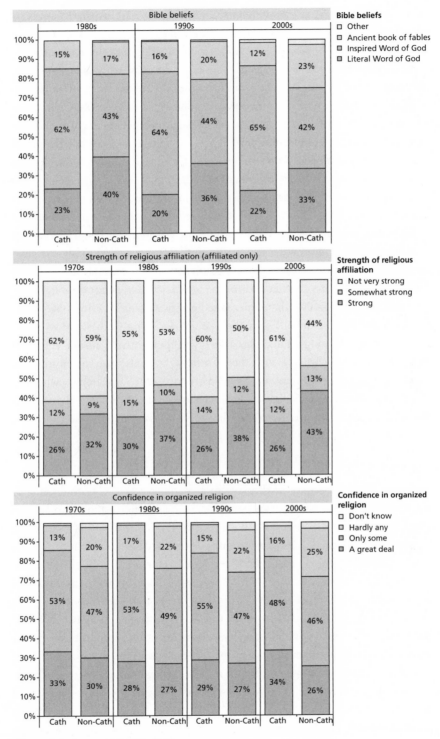

Figure 2.4 Source: GSS 1973–2008.

more recently identify as "non-religious" but who in the past may have nominally identified themselves as religious.[3] Comparatively, emerging adults who are nominally Catholic may be less likely to switch to a non-religious self-identification.

Confidence in Organized Religion. Emerging adult Catholics also show little change over the decades in their confidence in organized religion (organized religion in general, that is, not necessarily confidence in their own Church or denomination), although they tend to exhibit slightly higher levels of confidence than non-Catholics. About one-third express a great deal of confidence, about half only some confidence, and a minority hardly any confidence. No significant trends across the decades are evident here.

In sum, although there has been a decline in Catholic Mass attendance over the last four decades, five other indicators of religious belief and identity remain stable or increase slightly. Ideally, we would possess more and better indicators of religious faith and practice, especially some measures particularly designed for Catholics. But we are forced to work with the limited data that are available. The frequency of Mass attendance is of course a particularly important indicator because it is so integral to what it means to be a "practicing" Catholic. We therefore take up in more detail below the issue of declining Catholic Mass attendance among emerging adults. That roughly 60 percent of Catholic emerging adults identify only weakly with their Catholic faith also signifies a minimal degree of religious commitment. Even so, in contrast to researchers who find unmitigated decline in religious indicators across time, we believe the story of change across cohorts of emerging adult Catholics is more complex.[4]

Sexual Attitudes, Behaviors, and Media

Sex Before Marriage. Figure 2.5 displays the changing patterns of Catholic emerging adults' attitudes toward sex and sexuality. Beliefs about the morality of sexual intercourse before marriage have been mostly stable for non-Catholic young adults: about half think it is wrong to some degree and half think it is not wrong at all. Catholic emerging adults, however, have become more likely to find premarital sex morally acceptable, with 59 percent considering premarital sex "not wrong at all" in the most recent decade—an increase of 11 percentage points since the 1970s. That increase has not come from those who previously believed premarital sex is always or almost always wrong, but rather from the group who earlier said it is sometimes wrong. Even so, these attitudinal shifts are not massive. Most of the liberalization of beliefs on these issues among American Catholic emerging adults—as among non-Catholic emerging adults—happened before the 1970s.

Extramarital Sex. The opposite trend for attitudes toward extramarital sex, however, is clearly evident in Figure 2.5. Both emerging adult Catholics and

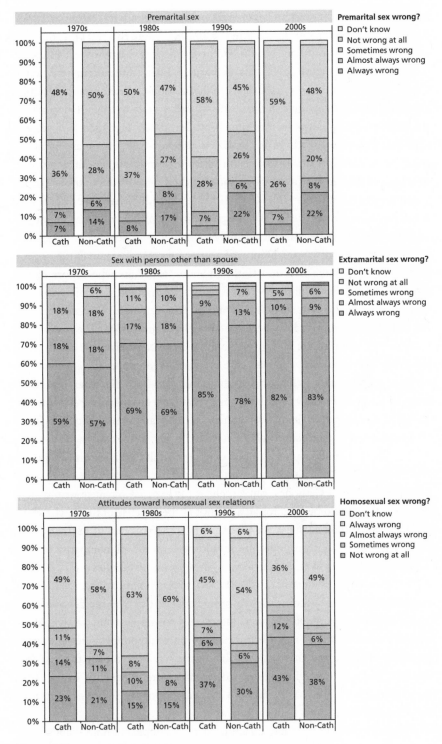

Figure 2.5 Source: GSS 1972–2008.

non-Catholics over time have become more likely to condemn extramarital sex, from less than 60 percent doing so in the 1970s to more than 80 percent in the 2000s. The vast majority of Catholics in the last decade disapprove of adultery.

Homosexuality. Figure 2.5 reveals increasingly liberal attitudes toward homosexual sexual relations among both Catholic and non-Catholic emerging adults. Despite a dip in acceptance in the 1980s—perhaps due to the initial spread of the HIV/AIDS epidemic at the time—by the 2000s, less than half of non-Catholic and only slightly more than one-third of Catholic emerging adults believed that homosexual sexual relations were "always wrong." This compares to a high of 69 percent for non-Catholics and 63 percent for Catholics in the 1980s for the same belief. Thus Catholic emerging adults have been somewhat more liberal on the morality of homosexuality than their non-Catholic peers and, like them, have become increasingly so.

Watching X-Rated Movies. Figure 2.6 shows a modest increase in the proportion of both Catholic and non-Catholic emerging adults who report having watched a sexually explicit, "X-rated" movie during the previous year—an increase of seven percentage points for non-Catholic and ten percentage points for Catholic emerging adults between the 1970s and 2000s. The majority of Catholic emerging adults report not having seen an X-rated movie in the previous year, but only barely is that the case in the most recent decade.

Pornography Laws. What do Catholic and non-Catholic emerging adults think of pornography laws and how might that have changed over the last four decades? A sizable majority of both young Catholics and non-Catholics believes that pornographic material should be legal but restricted to those who are legal adults. Eighty-one percent of Catholic emerging adults fell into this category in the 1990s and 2000s. This majority has increased over the decades, more so for Catholics than non-Catholics, but largely at the expense of those who believe pornography should be legal for all ages, not at the expense of those who think pornography should be illegal for all. In the 1970s, 10 percent of 18- to 25-year-old Catholics thought pornography should be legal for all, compared to only 2 percent in the 2000s (the equivalent figures for non-Catholics are 14 percent in the 1970s and 6 percent in the 2000s). So on this point of morality, Catholic emerging adults have become slightly more conservative over the decades.

Sex Education in Public Schools. Figure 2.6 shows that an overwhelming majority of Catholic and non-Catholic emerging adults supports sex education in public schools, and that majority has increased in size over the last four decades. Catholic emerging adults are slightly more supportive overall than non-Catholics. By the 2000s, fully 98 percent of young Catholics supported teaching sex education in public schools.[5]

In summary, Catholic emerging adults generally appear to hold slightly more liberal ideas about human sexuality than their non-Catholic counterparts, but

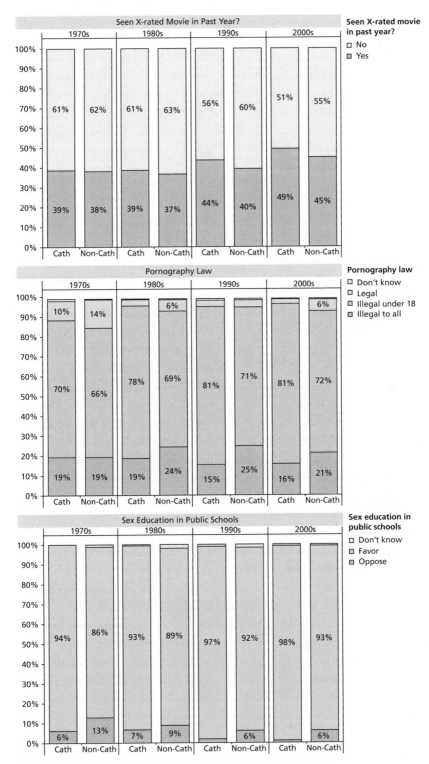

Figure 2.6 Source: GSS 1973–2008.

do not appear to have become dramatically more liberal regarding sexuality since the 1970s. In some instances, notably in attitudes about homosexual sexual relations, Catholics have become more accepting. But in other cases, such as extramarital sexual relations and liberalized pornography laws, Catholic emerging adults have adopted a more restrictive view of what is morally acceptable. In all of these instances, with perhaps the exception of premarital sexual relations, we find that Catholic emerging adults follow the general ebb and flow of public opinion for their age demographic over time during these decades.

Other Moral and Social Beliefs

Abortion. We turn our attention next to several moral and social beliefs that are associated with Catholic Church teachings. We include two different measures from the GSS on the morality of abortion. The first measures support for the current legal practice, which allows a woman to terminate a pregnancy for any reason. A majority of Catholic emerging adults, according to Figure 2.7, opposes this policy. There we observe a modest increase in support in the 1980s and 1990s, but then a decline in support for this liberal abortion policy in the most current decade (the 2000s). Approximately one-third of the emerging adult population now supports the right of women to choose to have an abortion for any reason, with little difference in support between Catholic emerging adults and their non-Catholic peers.

The second measure of support for abortion asks the respondents whether abortion is morally acceptable if the mother's health is endangered by the pregnancy. Strong Catholic and non-Catholic emerging adult majorities support allowing abortion under these circumstances. We see a slight decrease in support over time, with the most noticeable shift among non-Catholic 18- to 25-year-olds from the 1990s (89 percent support) to the 2000s (80 percent support). Catholic support ranges from 87 percent (in the 2000s) to 93 percent (in the 1970s). In summary, a majority of Catholic emerging adults opposes allowing abortion for any reason, although about one in three does support that view. However, the vast majority support the legality of abortion when an unborn child threatens the health of the mother, despite Church teachings against that policy.[6]

Teenage Birth Control. The GSS has included a survey item since the 1980s that measures support for providing access to birth control pills for 14- to 16-year-old females, regardless of whether their parents approve of their children using birth control. Once again, we see very little difference in attitudes toward this policy between Catholics and non-Catholics in the 18- to 25-year-old age group. Catholics are a bit less likely than others to disagree or strongly disagree with this policy, and overall two-thirds agree or strongly agree that teenagers should have access to birth control pills without parental approval.

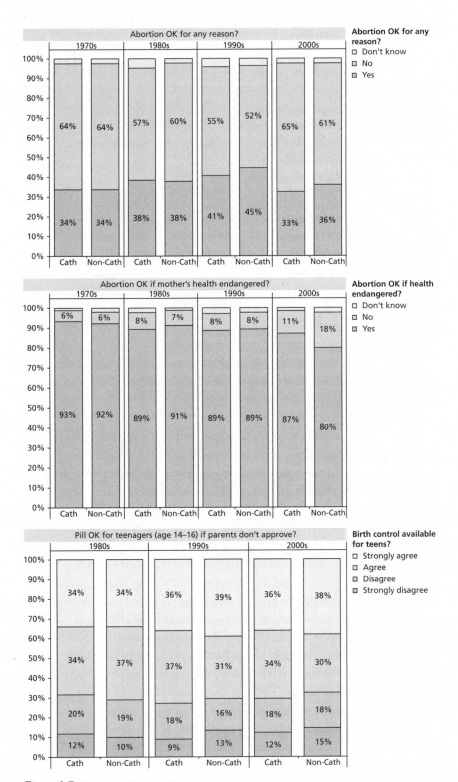

Figure 2.7 Source: GSS 1972–2008.

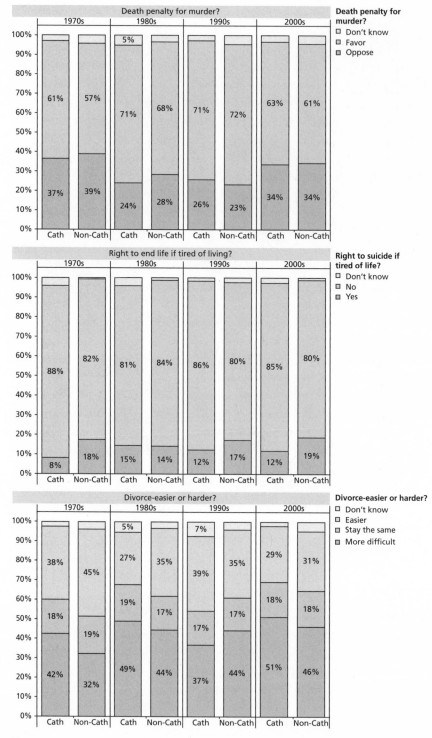

Figure 2.8 Source: GSS 1974–2008.

Those proportions are relatively stable over time, and the differences between Catholic and non-Catholic emerging adults are insubstantial.

The Death Penalty. The Catholic Church condemns the death penalty in almost all cases as morally unacceptable (see Figure 2.8). Nonetheless, support of the death penalty for murderers increased in the 1980s and 1990s among Catholic (and non-Catholic) emerging adults. In the 2000s, levels of support waned slightly, with a little more than 60 percent of both Catholic and non-Catholic emerging adults supporting capital punishment for convicted murderers. Again, there are no substantial differences between the two religious groups.

The Right to Suicide. Support for the right of people to commit suicide is modest, and slightly higher among non-Catholic than among Catholic young adults in most decades examined here, with sizable majorities of both groups opposing this right. Fully 80 percent of non-Catholic and 85 percent of Catholic 18- to 25-year-olds oppose the right to suicide in the most recent decade. No discernible trend emerges over time on this matter.

Divorce Laws. Emerging adults disagree over whether to make divorce easier or harder to obtain (or whether to keep current laws on the matter). In the 2000s, 51 percent of Catholic emerging adults supported making these laws more difficult while 46 percent of non-Catholics held the same view. Catholic emerging adults are in most decades (with the exception of the 1990s) more likely than their non-Catholic peers to support more restrictive divorce laws. There is also a very slight upward trend over time among both Catholics and non-Catholics toward support for making divorce more difficult, despite a dip in the 1990s.

To summarize, despite distinctive and strong Catholic Church teachings against abortion, birth control, capital punishment, suicide, and divorce, Catholic emerging adults hold views on these issues that are nearly indistinguishable from those of their non-Catholic counterparts during the past four decades. This is as true for 18- to 25-year-old Catholics in the 1970s as for Catholics of the same ages in the 2000s. At the same time, no major trend suggests that emerging adult Catholics have become any more likely to reject or ignore Catholic teachings across these decades.

Political Identification and Attitudes

Lastly, for comparative purposes, we examine the political identification and beliefs of Catholic emerging adults since the 1970s. Although Catholics have traditionally been a major bloc in the Democratic Party's national coalition in the U.S., in recent years there is evidence that this Catholic political party identification has been weakening. In the national presidential elections of 2004 and 2008, for example, a majority of non-Hispanic Catholic voters cast their ballot in favor of the Republican candidate (53 percent in both years).[7] Is this

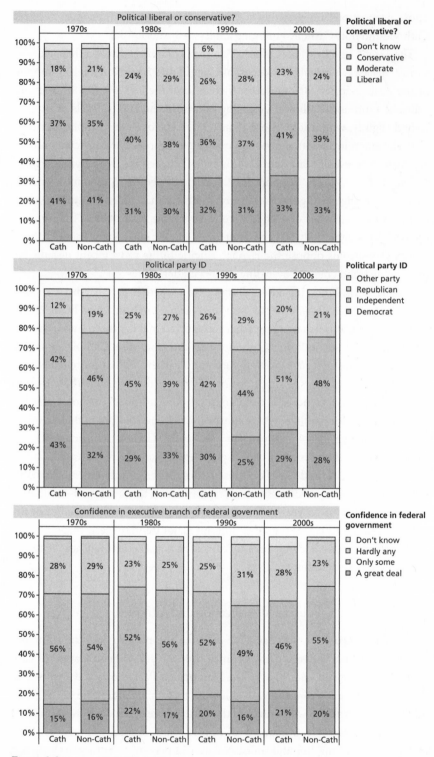

Figure 2.9 Source: GSS 1972–2008.

shifting of political identity also evident among Catholic emerging adults over the last several decades?

Political Ideology. In Figure 2.9 we focus on two indicators of political identity. The first asks survey participants if they are politically conservative, moderate, or liberal. The second measures political party identification. The proportion of Catholics and non-Catholics who describe themselves as conservative, moderate, or liberal within each decade is remarkably similar, with a decline in the proportion who identify as liberal and a small gain in the proportion who identify as conservative after the 1970s.

Political Party. What about political party affiliations? Catholic emerging adults in the 1970s are more likely to be Democrats, at 43 percent, than Republicans (12 percent). By the 1980s and 1990s, however, this distinctive party association was much less evident. Emerging adult Catholics are roughly as likely to be Democrats or Republicans as non-Catholics are during these decades, with the largest proportions saying that they are political Independents.

Confidence in Government. Figure 2.9 also reports on confidence in the executive branch of the federal government. The findings reveal that similar minorities of Catholic and non-Catholic emerging adults—hovering around 20 percent or slightly less—have high levels of confidence in the effectiveness of the executive branch of the federal government. The majority of both say they have "only some" confidence in the executive branch of the federal government. Furthermore, these differences have not changed substantially over the years. Again, we observe few differences between Catholic and non-Catholic emerging adults.

Government Support. Several indicators from the GSS measure beliefs about the proper role of the federal government in public life: support for government assistance for the poor, government-provided medical care for the sick, and government help for blacks. In each case, survey participants were asked to indicate whether they leaned toward favoring government action on the one hand, individual initiative on the other, or whether they fell somewhere in between these two positions. Their answers are displayed in Figure 2.10. Governmental action to remedy poverty drew significantly declining support among 18- to 25-year-old Catholics over four decades, dropping from 47 percent desiring increased assistance to the poor in the 1970s to only 27 percent in the 2000s (a 20 percentage point decrease overall). This decline is accompanied by an increase in the percentage who take the middle position (a 16 percentage point increase), while favor for individual initiative is mostly stable. Support for federal assistance for medical care for the sick and federal assistance for blacks has been mostly stable among emerging adult Catholics since the 1970s (with the former drawing support from 55 to 60 percent of Catholics, and the latter from around 20 percent). The "agree with both" middle position shows a small to moderate increase over time, with an 11 percentage point increase in the 2000s compared to earlier decades on both of these measures.

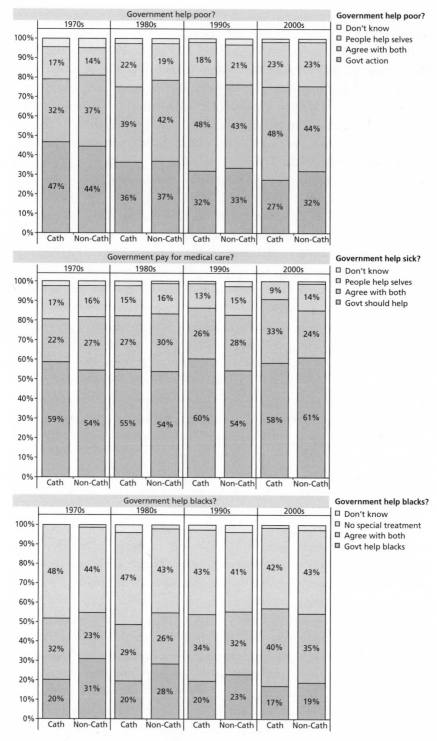

Figure 2.10 Source: GSS 1975–2008.

Non-Catholic emerging adults resemble their Catholics peers in their declining support for federal assistance for the poor and in their fairly stable support for increased federal assistance for medical care. However, non-Catholic 18- to 25-year-olds become less likely to favor assistance to blacks across these decades. The support of non-Catholic emerging adults for increased government assistance to blacks was higher than that of Catholics at first and then converged toward a similar position to Catholic emerging adults over time. In the 1970s, 31 percent of non-Catholic emerging adults supported this type of governmental intervention (versus 20 percent of Catholics), but by the 2000s, only 19 percent of them gave their support to increased government assistance to blacks (versus 17 percent of Catholics).

In sum, the political party identity of Catholics in this age group differed from that of non-Catholics in the 1970s in being more Democratic, but since that time it has shifted toward the Republican Party and Independent affiliation. Democrats, in other words, can no longer count on Catholic emerging adults to be any more loyal to their party than non-Catholics of the same age. Young Catholics' self-reported political liberalism and commitment to federal programs that assist the poor, the sick, and blacks have also been mostly indistinguishable from non-Catholics throughout the four decades that the GSS has been administered and asked these questions. Although the difference between Catholics and non-Catholics is not pronounced, Catholic emerging adults have slowly shifted toward the center position of favoring both government action and individual initiative over time.

Summary and Implications

We can draw several general conclusions from the preceding data. We may note exceptions to the patterns that we summarize here, but the following summary helps further contextualize this book's study of emerging adult Catholics in historical and life-course perspective.

The most striking (non-)trend evident in the GSS data is *stability* in beliefs and attitudes over time among both non-Catholic and Catholic emerging adults. Despite clear demographic shifts in ethnicity, region of residence, immigrant status, and marital status for Catholics, the broader cultural reservoir that young people draw upon to articulate their religious beliefs and attitudes toward public issues generally produces more similarity over time than differences. This stability is compatible with the sociological view that the cultural norms and values that shape humans' fundamental orientations to questions of identity and ethics are deeply embedded in social institutions and are therefore very slow to change.[8] That is not to say that no cultural influences affect Catholic emerging adults' religious and social beliefs. In our previous book, we argued that between 1972 and 2008, there developed a real cultural shift from modern, rationalistic, progressive cultural views which marginalized religious belief as irrational to a form of postmodern epistemological skepticism that, somewhat ironically, places religious knowledge and experience on a more equal footing with secular truth claims. Still, we want to argue here that this shift is only partial in nature, resulting from a gradual "trickle down" of cultural values from elite social institutions to more popular institutions, and that emerging adults draw upon both modernist and postmodernist justifications—seemingly more than on religious teachings—as they commit themselves to particular positions on various matters. At the same time, we recognize the limitations of general survey questions to capture these kinds of shifts.

This overall stability is important because it challenges the dominant "decline narrative" of some studies of Catholic young people, at least when referring to the time period since the early 1970s. Much, although certainly not all, of any decline in traditional beliefs and strength of Catholic identity that is evident in surveys of the Catholic population is likely due to the cultural expectations and institutional arrangements that are associated with certain phases of the American life course. The GSS data demonstrate that many indicators of religious commitment have remained virtually unchanged over the past four decades among this age group.[9] Whatever religious decline that may have happened must have taken place before the 1970s—an observation that fits very well with our analysis of generational change in the previous chapter. The crucial historical changes took place not between today's emerging adults and their parents' generation, but rather between today's emerging adults' parents' generation and the generation preceding them (the grandparents of today's emerging adults). In short, we believe that the 1960s were the most crucial years of change for American Catholics, not the 1970s or after. Our data in this chapter do not demonstrate that explicitly, since the GSS was not conducted before the early 1970s; however, our findings here are at least consistent with that view.

The GSS data above also underscore the *similarities* in beliefs and attitudes between Catholic and non-Catholic emerging adults since the early 1970s. When historical shifts in opinion and belief are evident in empirical data, it is usually *all* emerging adults who are affected, not only one subgroup. We find exactly this in changing attitudes toward homosexual and extramarital sexual activity, for example. We even find these patterns when it comes to social issues of distinctive Catholic concern, such as attitudes toward abortion, capital punishment, and governmental assistance to the poor. Our findings confirm that, at least for the last four decades, emerging adult Catholics tend to agree with public opinions and beliefs of their non-Catholic peers.

This leads us to two important conclusions related to the argument of the previous chapter. First, for at least two generations, most Catholics have been culturally assimilated into mainstream American culture. This means that—with the possible exception of the growing first- and second-generation Hispanic Catholic population—most of today's Catholic emerging adults have not grown up in households adhering to distinctive social and cultural practices related to their faith and ancestral home, as we believe was the case before the 1960s. While the labels "Polish Catholic" and "Irish Catholic" may still be used, they do not seem to be associated with meaningful distinctions in beliefs and attitudes on many relevant issues from the dominant American culture. This integration into mainstream American life is not something that the current emerging adult generation embraced in opposition to the outlook and practices of the previous generation, namely, their parents. Rather it is a position that they inherited from their parents.

Second, the similarities between Catholic and non-Catholic trends across most of the GSS measures examined suggest that when Catholics change their attitudes, beliefs, and behaviors over time, they are not departing from but drawing from shared American cultural streams. As will become evident from our interviews with Catholic emerging adults in Chapter 4 below, most Catholic youth do not draw upon their Catholic identity or the Church's official teachings as resources in order to arrive at a position on moral issues. For nearly four decades, 18- to 25-year-old Catholics have been quite similar to their non-Catholic counterparts in their attitudes on important social issues. As support for capital punishment increased and then declined among the non-Catholic majority, for example, it also increased and then declined among Catholics. As opposition to homosexual sexual relations declined among non-Catholics, it declined among Catholics as well. These similarities suggest that most Catholic emerging adults do not use their Catholic faith as a key resource for arriving at any counter-cultural religious, social, or ethical commitments.

The primary patterns evident in this historical analysis, then, are the stability of most views and practices of Catholic emerging adults over time and their similarity to their non-Catholic peers. There are some exceptions to these overall trends, however, which may illustrate what is changing among Catholic emerging adults. The most notable of these exceptions is the decline over time in emerging adult Catholics' Mass attendance in comparison to non-Catholics' church attendance. In order to contextualize this book's study of Catholic emerging adults, it is particularly vital to understand the social sources of this decline in Mass attendance.

The Decline in Emerging Adult Mass Attendance

Because regular Mass attendance is so significant in the Catholic tradition and because we have observed a marked decline in emerging adult attendance at Mass over time, we devote the rest of this chapter to exploring this matter more deeply. Before examining more data, however, we need to explain a conceptual matter concerning the difference between aging effects and birth cohort effects over time.

Understanding Aging and Birth Cohort Effects

It is crucial to understand the difference between aging effects and birth cohort effects. Nothing that follows will make sense without doing so. *Aging effects* are changes in social attitudes or behaviors that are typically associated with certain phases of the life course. Church attendance, for example, has historically tended to decline in late adolescence and emerging adulthood and then often rebounded in early adulthood, particularly at first marriage and the bearing of children. Not everyone follows this pattern, of course, but this has been a reliable age-associated trend in the U.S. population.

Birth cohort effects, on the other hand, are differences in social attitudes and behaviors that tend to be associated with groups of individuals who were born at roughly the same time. Popular notions of birth cohort effects are captured in generational breakdowns familiar to many Americans: the Depression Generation, the Greatest Generation, Baby Boomers, Generation X, the Millennials, and so on. The idea is that the distinctive historical and cultural characteristics of a particular time and place leave an imprint on individuals during the early years of life that continues to shape their social attitudes and behaviors as they grow older. Attitudes toward homosexuality, for example, follow a birth cohort pattern, with younger cohorts more liberal in their attitude than older cohorts and remaining so even as they age. Unlike social practices and views that change dramatically as people grow older, birth cohort effects tend to be relatively stable across the life course. In reality, most changes in social attitudes and behaviors exhibit a *combination* of influences associated with aging *and* birth cohort.

Why is it important to keep these concepts distinct? In a standard survey taken at one point in time, it is impossible to distinguish whether apparent differences between age groups are primarily due to aging effects or birth cohort effects. It is often tempting to attribute observed differences entirely to one or the other, despite the likelihood that both are at work. In prior research on Catholic emerging adults, observed differences have frequently been attributed to generational (i.e., birth cohort) differences.[10] Given the major changes in the Catholic Church over the last half century, the specific historical period within which young Catholics were raised in the Church undoubtedly influences their religious and social views. Still, we suggest by the end of this chapter that past research may have overstated many of these generational differences by attributing variance between age groups in cross-sectional survey data only to birth cohort effects and not to age-related life-course patterns.

Explaining Differential Trends in Church Service Attendance

Having established the distinction between aging and birth cohort effects, we turn now to examine more empirical evidence explaining the decline in regular Mass attendance among Catholic emerging adults over the last several decades. Figure 2.11 displays trends in attendance of religious services for Catholics and Protestants (of all ages) beginning in 1972. Immediately evident on the left side is the much higher proportion of self-identified Catholics attending church services nearly every week or more often in the early years of the GSS compared to Protestants. In the mid-1990s, however, the declining church participation of Catholics dipped below that of Protestants. In the 2008 GSS survey, the proportion of Catholics attending Mass regularly is approximately 10 percentage points lower than the proportion of Protestants attending church services regularly. Why has Protestant church attendance remained fairly constant over the last several decades, while Catholic Mass attendance has declined?

Parsing out aging effects from cohort effects is helpful for understanding the sources of this change and stability. Figure 2.12 plots the proportion of Catholics and Protestants attending church nearly every week or more often by age for all years of the GSS. We see there that both groups tend to increase their religious service attendance as they age (until age 80, after which church attendance becomes more difficult), but Catholics increase at a substantially steeper rate. How does this square with the different rates of religious participation over the past several decades? To find out, we plot the same variables in subsequent charts but

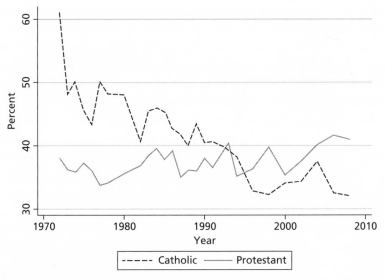

Figure 2.11 Percentage of Catholics and Protestants attending religious worship services "nearly every week" or more by year, 1972–2008. Source: GSS 1972–2008.

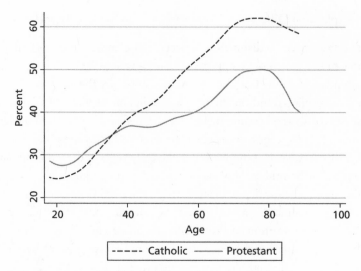

Figure 2.12 Percentage of Catholics and Protestants attending religious worship services "nearly every week" or more by age. Source: GSS 1972–2008.

separate subgroups of Catholics and Protestants by the decade in which they were born.

The results suggest that there are different sources of these aging trajectories. For Catholics, as evidenced in Figure 2.13, Mass attendance is relatively stable in adulthood within birth cohorts. In other words, self-identified Catholics do *not* seem to be steadily increasing their Mass attendance as they age. Recent birth cohorts of Catholics have lower levels of religious service attendance in adulthood than earlier birth cohorts. So we can cautiously conclude that the decline in Mass attendance over time has been primarily due to cohort replacement. That is, the Catholics who were born in early decades and attend Mass more regularly are slowly being replaced, through aging and death, by Catholics who were born in more recent decades and attend Mass less regularly. This is why we conclude that the steep increase in church attendance by age for Catholics in Figure 2.12 is *not* due to individuals attending Mass more frequently as they get older. Although we are not in the business of predicting the future, we doubt that today's emerging adult Catholics will substantially increase their Mass attendance as they age.

The replacement of older generations who attend church often with younger generations who attend less often does not explain the Protestant aging effect, however. As Figure 2.11 shows, Protestant church attendance has been relatively stable over time. Figure 2.14 plots a graph for Protestants that is analogous to Figure 2.13 for Catholics. There we see that Protestant church attendance, unlike Catholic Mass attendance, tends to steadily increase with age within birth cohorts. That is, individual Protestants are likely attending church more regularly

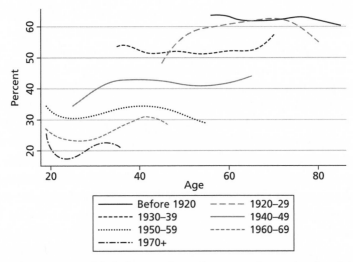

Figure 2.13 Percentage of Catholics attending religious worship services "nearly every week" or more by age and birth cohort. Source: GSS 1972–2008.

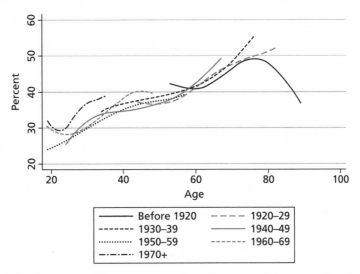

Figure 2.14 Percentage of Protestants attending religious worship services "nearly every week" or more by age and birth cohort. Source: GSS 1972–2008.

as they get older. So while religious participation changes across the life course of the average Protestant, the general life-course pattern remains roughly the same for Protestants born many decades apart. Unlike among Catholics, cohort replacement does not alter Protestants' level of religious service attendance, which has remained fairly steady across the last four decades.[11] We suspect, therefore, that many of today's emerging adult Protestants will attend church more frequently as they get older.

Important conclusions arise from these findings. First, it seems unlikely that declining rates of Catholic Mass attendance can be pinned solely on institutional changes stemming from the Second Vatican Council or the controversy over *Humanae Vitae*. If either of these factors had directly caused the decline, we would expect to observe one of the following consequences. We might expect to find a period effect, meaning a sudden decline in Mass attendance among *all* Catholics followed by a subsequent leveling out.[12] The data do not show such a trend. Alternatively, we might see a clear difference in religious participation between birth cohorts that came of age before these changes and those that came of age after. What we find instead, however, is a pattern of gradual decline in religious service attendance over subsequent birth cohorts. We do not think this means that the Second Vatican Council and the controversy over *Humanae Vitae* are somehow unimportant in understanding the historical trajectories of Catholic Mass attendance in the second half of the twentieth century. To the contrary, the internal institutional changes in the Catholic Church are part of a larger story that began before these discrete events and have consequences that continue to reverberate into the present. We are merely noting that theories suggesting that the decline in Mass attendance ended after the rocky decades of the 1960s and 1970s came to a close are not supported by the data.

We can draw another implication from our analysis: if falling rates of Catholic participation in Mass are primarily due to birth cohort replacement, as the evidence suggests—without the influence of some other dramatic force of change—we can expect further declines in Mass participation in the future as older cohorts of American Catholics pass away and are replaced by younger cohorts. This process will continue for some time into the future, even if recent birth cohorts have finally "bottomed out" and the religious participation of future emerging cohorts is not even lower. Still, we advise caution in making predictions about the future, particularly because the rapid increase in the proportion of first-generation Hispanic Catholics, who are different in a number of ways from native-born Catholics, may alter this picture.

Our analysis so far only partially explains the trends in Catholic religious participation since 1972. The reasons for the steady decline in religious participation between birth cohorts remain unclear. We have said that the decline is likely not attributable to specific historical changes in the Catholic Church, given the consistency we find in gradual changes across birth cohorts. Such a trend is more likely to develop from consistent life-course patterns in which Catholic Mass attendance is lower in adulthood than in childhood. In other words, if a Catholic is raised to attend Mass weekly, but by the time she is an adult and has children of her own she is only attending twice a month, then her children are almost certainly being raised to attend less frequently than she did in her childhood. If her children repeat a similar pattern, then their children will attend even less frequently. In this way, we would expect to find a gradual cohort decline in religious participation for Catholics.

We mentioned that previous sociological studies have established a general life-course pattern of declining religious participation in late adolescence and emerging adulthood, followed by a rebound accompanying marriage and having children.[13] If Catholics are not attending Mass at the same frequency in adulthood as in childhood, this could be due either to a steeper-than-average decline in Mass attendance during the transition to adulthood (Hypothesis 1), or to a shallower-than-average rebound in adulthood (Hypothesis 2). Either one (or some combination of both) would produce Catholic adults who attend Mass at lower levels and then raise their own children to attend at these or even lower levels.

We will investigate Hypothesis 1 first. In order to assess it, we compare Catholic and Protestant religious service participation from age 15 to 26 in the National Longitudinal Survey of Youth, 1997. These data were collected in 1997 from a sample of adolescents, ages 12 to 16. The same group of young people has received a follow-up survey every year. Since the year 2000, the survey has contained an item measuring religious service attendance. Figure 2.15 displays the results in this measure by age of the survey respondent.[14] There we see that, while both Catholic and Protestant youth attend religious services much less frequently as they enter adulthood and in roughly equal measure, the Catholics begin and end with lower proportions attending Mass. At age 15, the proportion of Protestants regularly attending church is approximately 12 percentage points higher than that of Catholics. At age 26 the gap is roughly the same, with approximately 11 percentage points more Protestants attending church services

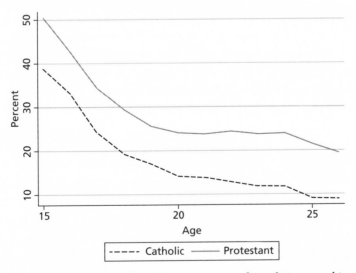

Figure 2.15 Percentage of Catholics and Protestants attending religious worship services "about once a week" or more by age, 15–26. Source: NLSY97 2000–2007.

weekly than Catholics. Thus, there does *not* appear to be evidence that the age-related decline in religious service attendance is substantially steeper for Catholics than Protestants.[15]

We next turn to test Hypothesis 2, the idea that Catholics may not "rebound" by returning to regular church attendance in early adulthood—after getting married or becoming parents—at the same rate as Protestants. To analyze this possibility we use the National Longitudinal Survey of Youth, 1979 (NLSY79). Unlike its counterpart from 1997, 18 years later, the NLSY from 1979 does not include measures of religious service attendance at every age. Measures of religious service attendance exist only in the 1979 survey and the 1982 and 2000 follow-ups.[16] Figure 2.16 presents religious service attendance for all ages available in the data.[17] It is clear, again, that Catholics and Protestants both become significantly less likely to attend church regularly between their mid-adolescence and early twenties. But higher proportions of Catholics attend Mass frequently all the way into their mid-twenties. Although the estimates are not as precise as those presented in Figure 2.15 (due to a lower number of respondents for each data point), the decline in attendance does not appear substantially steeper for Catholics than Protestants. However, between the ages of 25 and 35 (ages for which there is no religious service attendance data in the NLSY79), Protestants appear to return to higher levels of church attendance while Catholics do not.[18]

From these data we thus gain a clearer explanation of the decline in Catholic Mass attendance and the relative stability of Protestant church attendance observed in Figure 2.11. Both Catholics and Protestants attend church less regularly in adolescence and the early twenties. Protestants, however, often return to

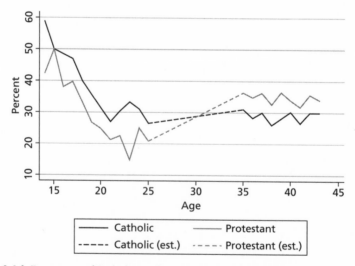

Figure 2.16 Percentage of Catholics and Protestants attending religious worship services by age. Source: NLSY79 1979, 1982, 2000.

regular church participation as they grow older, particularly when they marry and have children. But Catholics do not seem to return at anywhere near the rate of Protestants.[19] The result, on average, is that self-identified Catholics are raising their children to attend Mass less frequently than they themselves were raised in childhood and early adolescence. Conversely, Protestants, on average, are raising their children to attend church at roughly the same high rate as they did in their own childhood households. Thus, to summarize, we find in the data clear birth cohort effects underlying the decline in Catholic Mass attendance but only aging effects for Protestants.

While we believe that at least some of the "generational" effects found in previous research are attributable to patterns of attitudes and practices related to distinct phases in the life course (attitudes and practices that can be expected to change with age), Catholic Mass attendance appears to be a clear example of generational decline. For whatever reasons, the Catholic Church has struggled more than Protestants to pull emerging adults back into patterns of regular church attendance in adulthood. Why this may be the case is a subject to which we return in later chapters of this book.

Conclusion

We can conclude from these findings that today's Catholic emerging adults, although similar in most religious beliefs to Catholic emerging adults since the 1970s, are not exhibiting a particularly vibrant, robust faith and identity. One disadvantage of relying solely on survey data, and particularly on secondary survey data not designed to assess the population of interest, is that such surveys do not allow us to explore complex dynamics and subtle differences. The blunt instruments of survey data can map out the general landscape, but (to change the metaphor) they are unable to paint a fully realized portrait of the subject. In this way, the historical analysis presented in this and the previous chapter gives us a bird's eye view of Catholic emerging adults. Now, however, we need to move more fully into the worlds of Catholic emerging adults in all of their diversity.

3

A Statistical Portrait of Catholic Emerging Adults Today

We turn now to examine data from the National Study of Youth and Religion that describe 18- to 23-year-old Catholics in the U.S. today. This chapter explores NSYR survey data, while the next focuses on NSYR interviews with Catholic respondents. Our aim in these chapters is to map the internal diversity of U.S. Catholic emerging adults and highlight prominent themes.

We wish to move beyond the conclusions of previous research on young Catholics. The dominant methodological strategy of previous research, dividing the Catholic population by generation, has yielded some important findings about young Catholics as a whole. However, we think we can do more. Here we look at diversity *within* the population of emerging adult Catholics. By attending to social and religious cleavages within Catholicism we believe we are able to provide a more thorough account of some of the dynamics of emerging adult Catholic life. Previous research shows that younger Catholics in the U.S. are less involved in the Church, more likely to pick and choose their beliefs, more individualistic, and less distinctively Catholic than older Catholics. But we show here that this is not universally true of *all* types of emerging adult Catholics. Paying closer attention to different kinds of emerging adult Catholics provides clues to what factors contribute to successfully socializing Catholic youth into the faith, even if the majority might not be as faithful as the Church would like.

In this chapter we divide our sample of Catholics by certain religious and demographic variables in order to assess how subgroups conceive of and practice their faith differently.[1] Specifically, we break emerging adult Catholics into four types of groups: (1) by the Catholic types described at greater length in the Excursus below, (2) by ethnicity and immigrant generation, (3) by the Catholic self-identity of a parent of the respondent as traditional, moderate, or liberal, and (4) by religious homogamy of parents (i.e., whether both parents are Catholic or not). Each of these differences, we will see below, provides an important view on the variety of religious practices and beliefs within the Catholicism of emerging adults today. For each of these four groups, we examine different kinds of religious outcomes, including religious beliefs and practices during the teenage and emerging adult years.

For every table that appears in this chapter, we have also run more complex multivariate statistical models that remove the influence of some confounding factors. To avoid needlessly cluttering the chapter with statistical models, we have omitted these from the main text that follows; however, we do use them to report on statistically significant differences between the different Catholic groups. The tables below that measure distinct Catholic *practices* are taken from the first wave of the NSYR when respondents were adolescents. The corresponding statistical models we rely upon to find statistically significant differences control for parents' income and education, gender, race/ethnicity, age, and census region. The tables that report on emerging adults' religious *outcomes* come from the third wave of the NSYR when respondents were between 18 and 23 years old. The statistical models for these tables control for the factors just listed, and add measures of living at home, employment, school enrollment, personal earnings, and whether or not they receive financial help from parents. To be clear, the tables presented in this chapter do not adjust for these factors. Rather, we use the tables in conjunction with the multivariate models not shown to report on what level of confidence we can have that the differences between groupings of Catholics are real and not the result of other factors or chance alone.

We will begin with a sample defined by the expansive view of Catholics developed in the Excursus ahead, the "potential Catholics," including those labeled Completely, Mostly, Moderately, Nominally, and Family Catholics as teenagers. In what follows, however, there are instances where our sample has to be further restricted, and we are clear about that in the text and tables. Readers should remain aware that the population to which our statistical analyses validly apply may differ slightly from analysis to analysis.

Types of Catholics

We begin our analysis comparing categories developed in the Excursus below. Here we employ the first five (of seven total) categories there—Completely (N = 441), Mostly (N = 137), Moderately (N = 128), Nominally (N = 42), and Family Catholic (N = 243)—which can be viewed as a spectrum, moving from a full connection to Catholic faith and life to only a weak and indirect affiliation.

Completely and Mostly Catholics have multiple ties to Catholicism, reflecting all or lacking only one of the following characteristics during their teenage years: attending Mass, self-identify as Catholic, have Catholic parents, and reporting being raised Catholic. Their Catholicism embodies multiple, overlapping, reinforcing dimensions. We can therefore expect these young people's worlds to be most infused with the distinctive characteristics of the Catholic faith, more so than other Catholics.

At the other end of the spectrum, Nominal and Family Catholics have fewer indicators of Catholicism in their lives. Nominal Catholics self-identify as Catholic *or* attend Mass (but not both) but report no Catholic family connections. Family Catholics, by contrast, only report a family connection, but do not attend Mass or self-identify as Catholic. Their connections to Catholicism are fewer and more tenuous. (The last two Catholic types identified in the Excursus, Secondary and Previously Catholic, we leave out of our analysis in this chapter.)

Catholic Practices during Teenage Years. We begin by examining whether these different Catholic types are associated with differences in distinctively Catholic practices between the ages of 13 and 17. Results, which examine six different outcomes, are displayed in stacked bars with percents in Figure 3.1. (On these measures, we have removed the Nominally Catholic category because most of them were not asked these particular survey questions.[2]) The first outcome is whether respondents had been confirmed as a public affirmation of faith. Nearly half of both Completely Catholic and Moderately Catholic respondents reported that they have received confirmation (46 and 49 percent, respectively). Fewer Mostly Catholic respondents report the same (36 percent), and Family Catholics report the fewest adolescents who have received the sacrament of confirmation (31 percent).[3] After statistically controlling for possible confounding influences, we can be confident that the differences between the Completely and Mostly groups on the one hand, and the Family Catholic group on the other, are in fact real differences in the teenage Catholic population.

This same pattern across types of Catholics is evident for many other measures, with the exception of having sacred images or altars in the home. A full 92 percent of Completely Catholic respondents received First Communion, for example, while only 38 percent of Family Catholics have done the same. Similarly, 61 percent of Fully Catholic adolescents reported going to Confession in the past year, compared to only 11 percent of Family Catholics. The majority of Completely Catholic respondents (62 percent) reports praying the rosary or novenas, or offering special prayers to saints in the previous year, while only a small minority of Family Catholics has done the same (17 percent). The differences between Catholic types are less dramatic for questions about going on a religious pilgrimage, procession, or Way of the Cross and having sacred images or religious altars in the home. Twenty-five percent of Completely Catholic respondents report going on a religious pilgrimage, compared to 13 percent of Family Catholics. Fifty-five percent of Completely Catholic respondents report

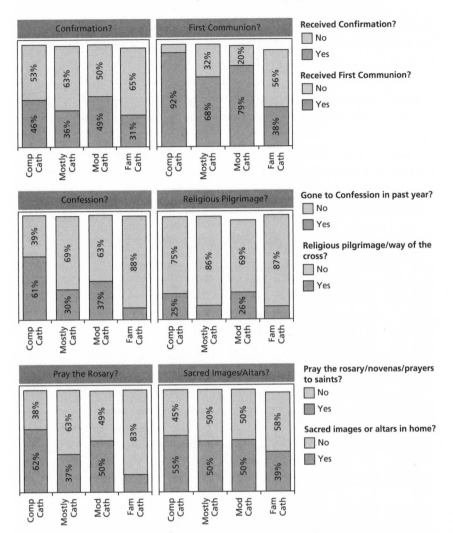

Figure 3.1 Catholic practices during teenage years by type of Catholic as teen.

having images or altars in their homes, compared to 39 percent of Family Catholics. In every single one of these instances, our multivariate models with control variables tell us that we can be at least 95 percent confident (and in most cases much more confident than this) that these differences between Catholic types really exist. In fact, on the measures of First Communion, going to Confession, and praying the rosary, we can be almost totally confident that Completely Catholic teenagers are different from every other group of Catholic teenagers.

In sum, we find evidence that Catholic youth reflecting multiple dimensions of Catholicism are more likely to engage in distinctively Catholic practices. This may not be surprising, but its importance can be easily lost. A distinctively

Catholic religious identity in the U.S. does not come from, say, a mere family affiliation with Catholicism. Youth must somehow come to see themselves as Catholic, to personally connect with the faith, whether by attending Mass or self-identifying as Catholic, in order to be more likely to live a more robustly faithful Catholic life. Family connections to Catholicism are not unimportant. Yet they do not appear sufficient in most cases to socialize young people into engaging in distinctively Catholic practices.

Faith Practices during Emerging Adulthood. What about practices of faith during emerging adulthood? Figure 3.2 (which now includes the Nominal Catholics) examines several measures of religious practice by 18- to 23-year-old Catholics. Remember that the types of Catholics we are comparing (Completely,

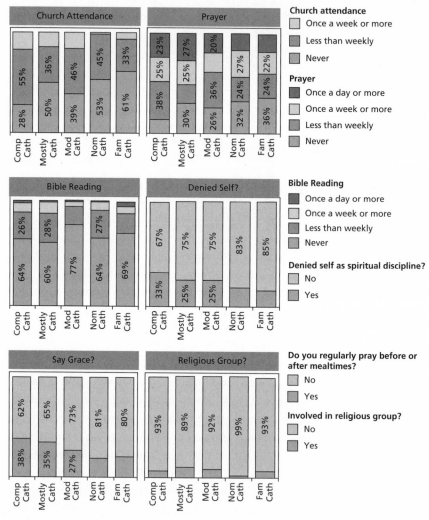

Figure 3.2 Religious practices during emerging adulthood by type of Catholic as teen.

Mostly, Moderately, etc.) refer to their religious situation during their teenage years, ages 13 to 17. We are thus focusing on emerging adults' outcomes as formed by their connections to Catholicism as teenagers.

We know that the most common measure of Catholic religious practice, Mass attendance, is relatively infrequently practiced among Catholic emerging adults.[4] Still, there is considerable variation in Mass attendance among emerging adult Catholics by Catholic type. The first three types—Completely, Mostly, and Moderately Catholic—show roughly the same levels of *weekly* Mass attendance (14 to 17 percent). But when it comes to *never* attending Mass, we find more variation, ranging from 28 to 50 percent. Completely Catholic emerging adults are least likely to skip Mass altogether. By contrast, the least-connected Catholics, the Nominal and Family Catholics, attend weekly Mass at much lower levels (1 and 6 percent, respectively) and have much higher rates of never attending Mass (53 to 61 percent). Additional models we ran tell us that Completely Catholic emerging adults are statistically different from all other Catholic groups in overall Mass attendance, with the exception of the Moderately Catholic group.

Next we examine two measures of private religious practices: personal prayer and Bible reading. Frequency of prayer varies significantly across different Catholic types. Nominal and Family Catholics are least likely to pray daily (17 percent), though the difference between them and the Mostly Catholics, who have the highest rate of daily prayer (27 percent), is not huge. The bigger difference, again, has to do with those who never pray. Completely Catholic emerging adults are quite unlikely to never pray. The other Catholic types are more likely to never pray, ranging from 26 percent to 36 percent. Our statistical models with control variables tell us that the differences between Completely Catholics on the one hand, and Family and Nominal Catholics on the other, are statistically significant (although we can only be 93 percent confident in the difference between Nominal and Completely Catholics, less than the conventional 95 percent or greater). Bible reading among emerging adult Catholics, on the other hand, occurs far less frequently than personal prayer. A majority of every Catholic group reports that they never read the Bible, and the differences between types are not large. Only between 6 and 13 percent of Catholic emerging adults read Scripture weekly or more often. We find no statistically significant differences between the Catholic groups on this measure.

We turn next to explore some less common measures of religious practice. Figure 3.2 shows the percentage of emerging adults who report fasting or denying themselves something as a spiritual practice in the previous year. This may include giving something up for Lent. We see a clear descending order in fasting or denying oneself for spiritual purposes across the Catholic types. One-third of the Completely Catholic emerging adults reports this, while only 15 percent of

Family Catholics report the same. Other types of Catholics fall somewhere in between those extremes. Our models that control for possible confounding factors confirm again that Family Catholics are different from both Completely Catholics and Mostly Catholics.

Saying a prayer before or after meals is a routine practice for nearly half of the American population.[5] While less than half of Catholic emerging adults regularly pray at meals, a sizable minority do so. Completely Catholic emerging adults are nearly twice as likely to report regularly saying grace as Nominal and Family Catholics (38 percent versus 19 or 20 percent, respectively). This pattern resembles the ones for fasting or self-denial. Our additional analysis confirms that the type of Catholic respondents were as teens makes a modest but statistically significant difference in how they practice the faith as an emerging adult.

The final measure of religious practice we examine here is participation in a religious group, such as a Bible study or prayer group, outside of regular worship services. We should note that most religious organizations host far fewer groups and activities for emerging adults than for children and teenagers.[6] So the supply of such opportunities is small. Also, American Catholics are less likely than Protestants to emphasize the importance of participating in religious groups and activities outside of Mass. We see in Figure 3.2 that very few Catholics of any type are participating in such groups or activities. Those in the Mostly Catholic group participate at the highest rate, which is still only 11 percent. The multivariate model with controls indicates that we can be reasonably confident that Nominally Catholic emerging adults (only 1 percent of whom participate in a religious group) differ from the first three types in their level of participation.

What do these numbers mean? First, the Catholic identity types of teenagers appear to exercise a continuing influence on their religious and spiritual practices into emerging adulthood. The categories we use here refer to facts about the lives of teenagers. Yet we discovered considerable differences in the religious practices of these various types five years later, during emerging adulthood. These differences are not the result of happenstance or events that transpire in emerging adulthood. Instead, most 18- to 23-year-old adults who practice their Catholic faith more actively spent their teenage years in social worlds more strongly defined by Catholicism. These patterns make it clear that the chance of a young person continuing to practice Catholicism into emerging adulthood depends to a large extent on his or her connections to Catholicism (through relationships, practices, and identity) during adolescence. However, this model does not apply to all possible religious practices. The adolescent years have a much greater influence on whether a young adult will attend Mass, pray at least sometimes, fast or practice self-denial, and pray at meals than on whether the same adult will read the Bible and participate in a religious group or activity outside of Mass.

Religious Beliefs during Emerging Adulthood. The next chart displays a few key measures of religious beliefs. The first part of Figure 3.3 reports respondents' beliefs about God, Jesus, and salvation. Completely Catholic emerging adults hold the most traditional Christian beliefs about God, with about two-thirds (68 percent) saying they believe God is a personal being who is involved in the lives of people. Comparatively, only a little more than one-third of Nominal Catholics hold this belief (36 percent). A full 54 percent of Nominally Catholic emerging adults believe in God, but think he is not personal. Our full statistical models confirm that Nominal Catholics and Family Catholics are indeed different from Completely Catholics on this measure. Catholic views about Jesus follow a similar pattern. Seventy-three percent of Completely Catholics affirm

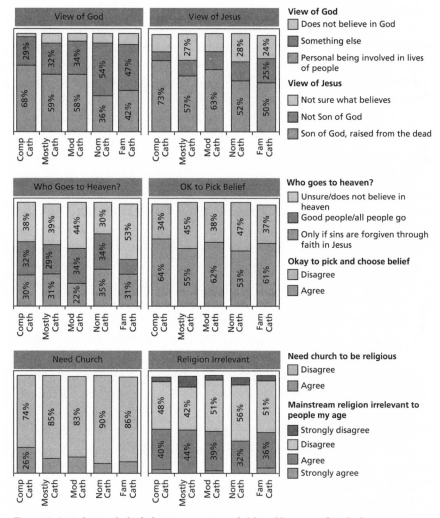

Figure 3.3 Religious beliefs during emerging adulthood by type of Catholic as teen.

the divinity of Jesus Christ and his resurrection from the dead. But only about half of Nominal and Family Catholic emerging adults (52 and 50 percent, respectively) affirm the same. These differences are not immense, but they are substantial and statistically significant in our further tests. Figure 3.3 also shows respondents' views on whether heaven exists and who goes there after death. The orthodox Catholic understanding of salvation is that only those whose sins have been forgiven through the merits of Jesus Christ go to heaven. Unlike the previous two measures of belief, on this question there is not a strong correlation between different Catholic types and an affirmation of this traditional Christian understanding of salvation. Weaker Catholics are generally more likely not to believe in heaven or not to feel sure about who goes to heaven, although the Nominal Catholics buck that trend. These differences, however, are not statistically significant.

Next we turn to Catholic emerging adults' beliefs about the relevance and authority of religious institutions. The differences between Catholic types for beliefs about God and Jesus Christ are less evident concerning beliefs about matters of individual conscience and the authority of the Church. A majority of all types of Catholic emerging adults believes it is acceptable to pick and choose religious beliefs without affirming the teachings of a religious faith as a whole. The Completely Catholic group is surprisingly the most likely to affirm this view (64 percent), while Nominal Catholics are the least likely (53 percent). But the differences are modest and display no clear pattern. Our additional analysis also reveals no statistically significant differences here.

Differences between Catholic types re-emerge in young adults' beliefs about whether Catholics need the Church to be truly religious, with 26 percent of Completely Catholic emerging adults affirming this, versus only 10 percent of Nominal Catholics doing the same. These differences were found to be statistically significant. Still, the overwhelming majority of all Catholic emerging adults believes that the Church represents only an optional component of a true Catholic life. Finally, Figure 3.3 shows Catholic young adults' views about how relevant they believe "mainstream" religion is to their age group, based on whether they agree with the statement, "Most mainstream religion is irrelevant to the needs and concerns of most people my age." Emerging adult Catholics are divided relatively evenly on this issue, with slightly more disagreeing than agreeing with the statement. Differences between Catholic types, however, are very minor and none are statistically significant.

In sum, the number of indicators of Catholicism during the teenage years— attending Mass, having Catholic parents, Catholic self-identity—shapes teens' Catholic practices (perhaps unsurprisingly), but also continues to influence faith and practice during emerging adulthood. A Catholic identity reinforced through multiple means during adolescence tends to result in more orthodox

Christian belief and practice during emerging adulthood. There are exceptions to this rule: there are not consistent differences between Catholic types when it comes to reading the Bible, belonging to a religious group outside of worship, and believing it is okay to pick and choose religious beliefs. On the whole, though, teenagers' connections to Catholicism seem to have a small to moderate continuing impact into emerging adulthood.

Hispanic versus White Catholics

In the middle of the twentieth century, various Catholic immigrant groups—Polish, Irish, Italian, French, and German—that previously had been seen as distinct groups becme united by a pan-ethnic "white," predominantly middle-class Catholic identity. The cultural mainstreaming of American Catholicism, described in Chapter 1, powerfully influences many emerging adult Catholics today. However, new ethnic realignments have occurred in recent decades that are changing the American Catholic landscape dramatically. The most significant of these is the "browning" of American Catholicism, particularly among younger Catholics, with the massive immigration of Latino Catholics from Mexico, Central America, and some Caribbean countries, such as Puerto Rico and the Dominican Republic.

Somewhere between 40 and 50 percent of emerging adult Catholics in the U.S. are of Hispanic descent, scholars now estimate.[7] However, the NSYR does not capture a full sample of Hispanic Catholics, in part because it is a panel study that began with U.S. adolescents. This means that immigrants who arrived in the U.S. between the adolescent and emerging adult years are not included in the NSYR, even though they are emerging adults now. U.S. Census estimates of 13- to 17-year-old Hispanics in 2003 lead us to conclude that about 35 percent of Catholic emerging adults who lived in the U.S. during adolescence are Hispanic. However, because of lower initial response rates among Hispanics and some sample attrition over time, Hispanics only represent about 25 percent of the emerging adult Catholics in the NYSR. We therefore carefully analyzed the impact that this had on our overall estimates of Catholic religious belief and social outcomes.[8] Our conclusion is that, despite the important differences between white and Hispanic Catholics that we identify below, *overall* estimates of religious practice, belief, and other life-course outcomes were not substantially biased as a result of the undercount of Hispanic emerging adults.

In this section, we break Catholics down into four different groups based on ethnicity and immigration status. The first group is composed of "white" Catholics and the remaining three are Hispanic Catholics. Other racial and ethnic types of Catholics—black, Asian, and so on—are too small in our sample to accurately analyze, and so are omitted from the figures we present. The sample of Hispanic Catholics we broke down by "generation since immigration." First-generation Hispanics are those who were not born in the U.S.[9] Second-generation Hispanics were born in the U.S., but their parents were born elsewhere. Third-generation Hispanics are those who had a grandparent or earlier ancestor immigrate to the U.S. Sociological studies of immigration often use these categories of generation because important social, cultural, political, and economic divisions commonly fall along these lines.[10] Here we will investigate whether such patterns are evident in our findings.

Catholic Practices during the Teenage Years. We first analyze distinctively Catholic practices of NSYR respondents as teenagers, 13 to 17 years old. Figure 3.4 shows differences in Catholic practices by ethnicity and immigrant generation. Among the Hispanic Catholics, there is a general, clear decline between immigrant generations in the proportion who report participating in these practices. In certain cases this decline is fairly substantial. For example, 97 percent of first-generation Hispanic Catholics report taking First Communion, while only 65 percent of third-generation Hispanics report the same. In several cases, the proportion of first-generation Hispanics who performed a given practice is roughly 65 to 90 percent larger (measured as percent change, not absolute percentage points) than the proportion of third-generation immigrants who did the same. Confirmation, Confession, and religious pilgrimage (or the Way of the Cross) all fit this category. In other cases, such as praying the rosary and having sacred images or altars in the home, the differences between generations appear more modest. Our full statistical models suggest that we should extend some caution in staking claims about differences between generations, however: most models do *not* find statistical differences between immigrant generations, with the clear exception of receiving First Communion. This simply means that our sample size is not large enough to confidently claim that the differences between immigrant generations exist in the general population. Still, the general pattern is similar across all of these measures, leading us to cautiously conclude that Hispanic teenagers not born in the U.S. are likely more distinctively or strongly Catholic than Hispanic Catholic adolescents who *were* born in the U.S. A larger sample of Hispanic Catholics would be necessary to verify this claim.

Judging by this trend, one might suppose that Hispanic Catholics become more like mainstream, white Catholic teenagers the longer they and their families reside in the U.S.[11] Still, our evidence shows a more complex picture than simple assimilation. While some measures fit this expectation, such as going on a religious pilgrimage or Way of the Cross or praying the rosary, other measures do not. For example, first-generation Hispanic Catholics and white Catholics are most similar (among all ethnicity- or immigration-related groups) in the

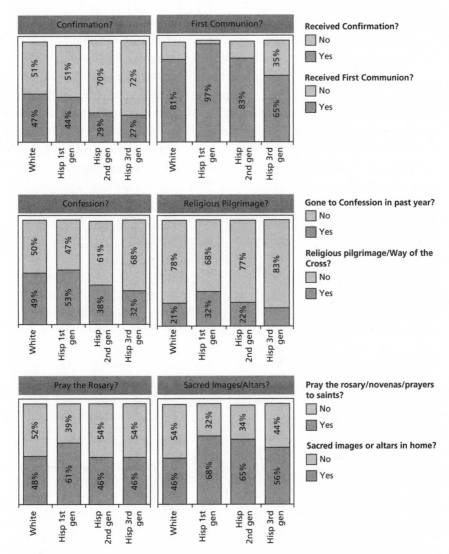

Figure 3.4 Catholic practices during teenage years by ethnicity and immigrant generation.

proportion who have received the sacrament of confirmation (44 percent and 47 percent) and who have gone to Confession in the past year (53 percent and 49 percent), which is not what one would expect if the assimilation process across generations brought Hispanics closer to white Catholics' practices. The percentage that has received First Communion is most similar for white Catholics and second-generation Hispanic Catholics, while Hispanic Catholics of all immigration generations are more likely to have sacred images or altars in the home than white Catholics. So a simple story of cultural assimilation and decline in the practice of the Catholic faith among Hispanic immigrants and their descendants is not the best interpretation of our data. We soon present an alternative account. But first we turn to religious practice and belief in emerging adulthood.

Other Faith Practices in Emerging Adulthood. Examining the Hispanic Catholic emerging adults in Figure 3.5, a similar pattern of declining religious practice by generation emerges for several, but not all, indicators. Measures of Mass attendance, personal prayer, and praying at meals follow this pattern (with statistically significant differences between these groups for Mass attendance and praying before meals). However, the popularity of practices that are emphasized less

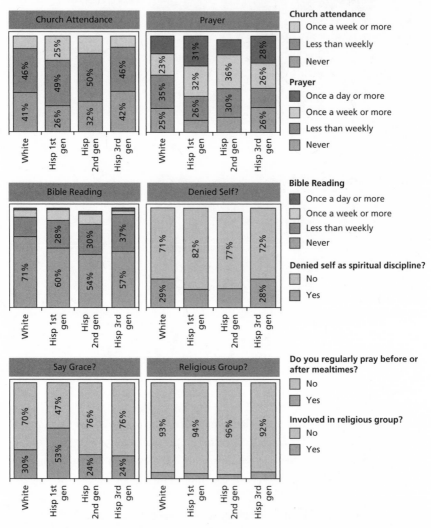

Figure 3.5 Religious practices during emerging adulthood by ethnicity and immigrant generation.

by many Catholics, such as personally reading the Bible and participating in religious activities outside of regular worship (such as prayer groups and Bible studies), varies little btween the Hispanic Catholic groups. This pattern parallels the findings in our earlier analysis of Catholic types. Lastly, the proportion of Catholics who report fasting or denying themselves as a spiritual discipline moves in the opposite direction among Hispanic emerging adults: first-generation Hispanic Catholics are the least likely to report this type of practice (19 percent), while third-generation Hispanic Catholics are the most likely (28 percent). These differences, though, are not statistically significant. Among all types of Catholics here, third-generation Hispanics and white Catholics appear most similar on the measures of religious practice examined. The notable exception to this is reading the Bible, as all Hispanic Catholic emerging adults report doing this more frequently than white Catholics. Those differences are not that substantial or statistically significant, however—71 percent of white Catholics report never reading the Bible, while 54 to 60 percent of Hispanic Catholics report the same.

Religious Beliefs in Emerging Adulthood. First-generation Hispanic Catholics are most likely to affirm official Catholic teachings about God and Jesus, while white Catholics and third-generation Hispanic Catholics are the least likely to hold orthodox views, according to Figure 3.6. Note, however, that the differences among Hispanic Catholics are only slight with respect to views of God, and we cannot be confident that groups are truly different from one another after statistically controlling for other factors. We can be modestly confident (about 90%) that there are differences between first- and third-generation Hispanic Catholics in orthodox beliefs about Jesus Christ. Turning to the issue of salvation, there do not appear to be substantial differences among ethnic groups concerning orthodox Catholic beliefs. But there are some other notable differences. First-generation Hispanic Catholics are the least likely to not have an opinion on salvation or to disbelieve that heaven exists. Comparatively, nearly half of white emerging adult Catholics are either unsure of what they believe about salvation or do not believe in heaven. Even this difference, however, does not reach statistical significance in multivariate models because of the small size of the first-generation Hispanic group. We advise readers to take these differences as suggestive of patterns that are likely present among emerging adult Catholics, but ones that need further testing with larger samples to confirm.

Beliefs about individual conscience and Church authority also show some variation by ethnicity and immigrant generation. First-generation Hispanic Catholics are the least likely of all Catholics to believe that it is okay to pick and choose beliefs (46 percent), and the most likely to believe that the Church is necessary to be truly religious (45 percent). They thus appear to be the least individualistic about their faith. By contrast, 65 percent of white Catholics believe

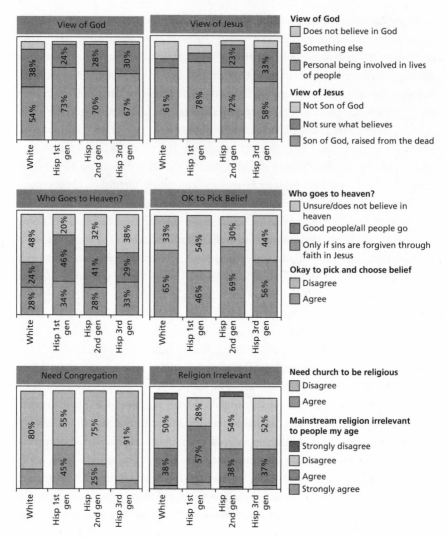

Figure 3.6 Religious beliefs during emerging adulthood by ethnicity and immigrant generation.

picking and choosing beliefs is okay, and only 20 percent say that the Church is necessary for authentic faith. It is a somewhat surprising finding, then, that first-generation immigrant Catholic emerging adults are most likely to agree that mainstream religion is irrelevant for people their age (64 percent agree or strongly agree). Only slightly more than 40 percent of the respondents in other Catholic categories agree or strongly agree. The difference between the first-generation Hispanics and all other groups is statistically significant, even controlling for a host of potentially confounding factors. It seems to us that there are two possible explanations for this. It could be that the word "mainstream" is being interpreted culturally and has a negative connotation for many Hispanic immigrants who sense that they are not in the cultural mainstream. It could also be that respondents are not saying whether religion is relevant in a normative sense. Rather, respondents may merely be agreeing that in their experiences with people their own age, mainstream religion does not seem that relevant, even if they personally believe it should be. It seems to us that the most religious respondents would also be the most likely to make this observation.

Hispanics are a rapidly growing segment of the Catholic Church, and will soon represent the majority of American Catholics. Yet according to our findings, Hispanic emerging adults are not all the same in terms of their religious practices and beliefs. Important differences exist between immigrant generations, although due to the small size of some of these groups in our sample we do not want to overstate our case. First-generation immigrant Hispanic Catholic emerging adults tend to be more traditional and less individualistic than later generations, according to our data. This is consistent with research suggesting that immigrants frequently rely on religious communities for aid in negotiating the transition from home country to host country.[12] Becoming involved in the parish community is often a good way to navigate new social, economic, and political environments. Religious communities also preserve and reinforce ethnic identities for first-generation immigrants.

Second-generation immigrants, by contrast, may feel the need to define themselves against their parents' generation. In our data, their beliefs tend to be less traditional and their practices are less frequent on most measures. Still, we should not read too much out of these findings. The differences in life experience between the first- and second-generation Hispanic Catholic emerging adults may not be large. Because we are measuring generations here from the first wave of survey data, when the respondents were teenagers, most were not arriving in the U.S. on their own. They were coming with family members, often parents. If they arrived at a young age, then their experiences may differ much from those of Hispanics who were born in the U.S. to foreign-born parents. Because of this, those who immigrate to the U.S. as children are sometimes referred to as "the 1.5 generation." Their typical experiences fall somewhere between the experiences of those born in the U.S. and those immigrating as adults.

Finally, the third-generation (and later) Hispanic Catholics are, for the most part, less religious than the first and second generations. However, this does not mean that they are identical to white Catholics. They are in fact considerably less likely to have been confirmed, to have received First Communion, and to have attended Confession in the previous year. We are hesitant to make too much of these distinctions, although it does appear that a form of nominal Catholicism is more common among third-generation (or greater) Hispanics than among white Catholics. This may be because Catholicism becomes intertwined with the ethnic identity of many Hispanics. If so, white Catholics may feel more free to disaffiliate from the faith entirely, while Hispanics may feel the need to retain their Catholic identity for cultural reasons, even if they do not practice their faith.

Catholicism by Parental Types

We now move to assessing the type of Catholic home in which our survey respondents were raised. Past research using the NSYR has found that parents exert a substantial influence over the religious lives of their children, for better or worse.[13] Even when American adolescents and emerging adults are not conscious of these influences, the evidence clearly demonstrates that the religious practices and beliefs of parents matter greatly for the religious lives of their children. We suspect the same pertains for Catholicism. We explore this question in two ways. First, using data from the first wave of the NYSR, we examine whether the self-identification of the survey-responding parent as a traditional, moderate, or liberal Catholic shapes the faith practices and beliefs of the child.[14] We then turn to religious homogamy—that is, whether both parents share the Catholic faith or hold different faiths—and the family structure of the household.[15] Here we discover whether it matters if the spouse or partner of the parent respondent is also Catholic, if the spouse or partner is not religious at all, and if there is no spouse or partner in the household at all.

Catholic Practices during Adolescence. Figure 3.7 displays the findings related to the self-identity of Catholic parents. These measures show clearly that Catholic teenagers whose parents call themselves traditional Catholics are the most likely to report participating in the Catholic religious practices shown here (with the exception of receiving First Communion). The teenagers least likely to participate, in all six practices measured, are those whose parents report being liberal Catholics. These differences are consistent as well as statistically significant in multivariate regression models, but still often quite modest. Teenagers with conservative and moderate Catholic parents are equally likely to report receiving confirmation (46 percent), and those with liberal parents are only slightly less likely to report the same (39 percent). The greatest absolute difference between groups is about going to Confession in the previous year—56 percent of teenagers with conservative Catholic parents report having done so, while only 38 percent of those with liberal Catholic parents report the same. So while the general pattern is clear, and we can have statistical confidence in these results, the overall differences are not very substantial.

Whether teens' parents are both Catholic exerts a similar influence on their religious practices, as Figure 3.8 shows. With the exception of having sacred

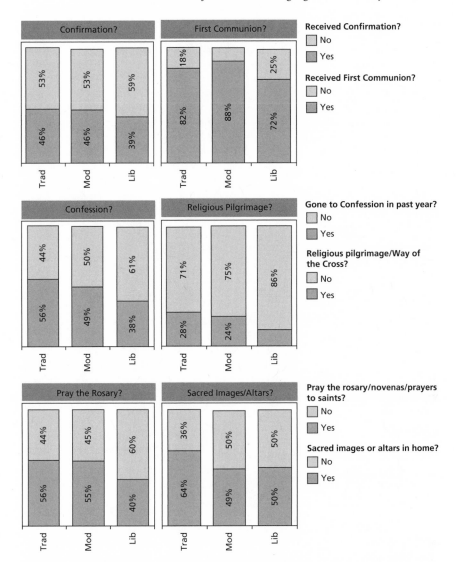

Figure 3.7 Catholic practices during teenage years by Catholic self-identity of parent.

images or altars in the home, adolescents in homes with two Catholic parents are more likely to report participating in the Catholic practices shown, even after accounting statistically for possible confounding factors. However, many of the differences are not great. The only substantial differences between teenagers with both Catholic parents versus one Catholic parent (plus a second parent of another faith) is the percentage who receive First Communion (89 percent versus 73 percent, respectively) and who report going on a religious pilgrimage, procession, or Way of the Cross (23 percent versus 12 percent, respectively). Catholic teenagers who have one Catholic parent and one non-religious parent

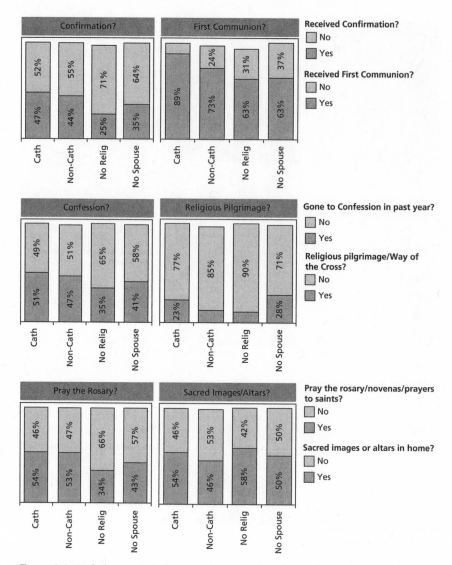

Figure 3.8 Catholic practices during teenage years by religious homogamy or difference between parents.

participate in these practices at noticeably lower rates. This group is the most different from the teenagers who live in households with two Catholic parents (25 versus 47 percent report receiving confirmation, 63 versus 89 percent report receiving First Communion, and 34 versus 54 percent report praying the rosary). The numbers for teenagers who come from single-parent Catholic homes mostly fall somewhere between those from homogamous Catholic households and those with one Catholic and one non-religious parent. The exception to this pattern is participation in a religious pilgrimage, procession, or Way of the Cross.

Twenty-eight percent of teenagers from a single-parent Catholic household have done this practice, the highest of all of the groups measured.

Other Faith Practices during Emerging Adulthood. Do these parental influences continue into emerging adulthood, when many children no longer live with their parents? Yes. Figure 3.9 displays the frequency of religious practices measured in the third wave of the NSYR by parents' religious self-identification in the first-wave survey, when our youth respondents were 13 to 17 years old. The most striking finding is the difference in Mass attendance. While 27 and 29 percent of

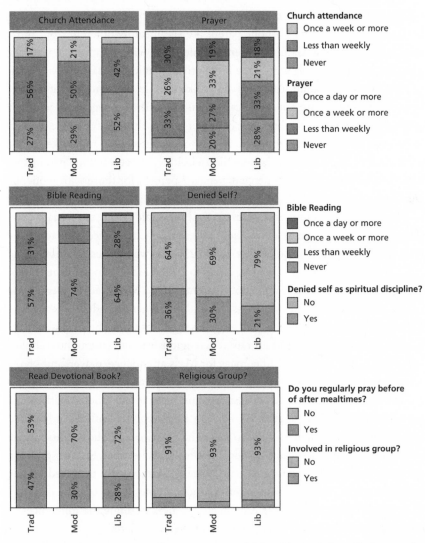

Figure 3.9 Religious practices during emerging adulthood by Catholic self-identity of parents.

emerging adults do not attend Mass at all among those whose survey-responding parent is traditional or moderate, respectively, fully 52 percent do not attend Mass at all who as a teenager had a liberal Catholic parent. Only 6 percent of emerging adult Catholics raised with at least one liberal Catholic parent attend Mass weekly. By comparison, about one in five emerging adult Catholics from traditional or moderate Catholic households do the same (17 and 21 percent, respectively). Patterns are similar, although less stark, across other variables shown in Figure 3.9. Frequent personal prayer, fasting or self-denial, and praying at meals are performed least by emerging adults who as teenagers had at least one liberal Catholic parent, and most by those with at least one traditional Catholic parent. In all of these measures, our full statistical models tell us that emerging adults who had a liberal Catholic parent are significantly different from those who had a traditional Catholic parent. While those with a traditional Catholic parent are the most likely to read the Bible privately at least occasionally (43 percent), all emerging adult Catholics are unlikely to do this, and the differences between the groups are not statistically significant. The same goes for joining a religious group such as a Bible study or prayer group. These activities are unlikely to be performed by all emerging adult Catholics, but slightly more likely to be performed by those from a Catholic household where at least one parent self-identified as conservative (9 percent, versus 7 percent for those with moderate and liberal Catholic parents).

Differences in religious homogamy of the household during the teenage years also reveal similar patterns across these religious practices, according to Figure 3.10. Emerging adult Catholics, ages 18 to 23, who were raised in a household with two Catholic parents are more likely to attend Mass than the other types: 16 percent of those with two Catholic parents attend Mass weekly as emerging adults, versus only 4 percent or less for Catholic emerging adults with a non-Catholic second parent. Most other religious practices shown here are also more frequent among emerging adults raised in religiously homogamous households, with statistically significant differences for Mass attendance, prayer, and saying grace before meals. Once again, personal Bible reading and attending religious groups and activities outside of Mass are infrequent for all groups. At the same time, on most measures, growing up in a single-parent Catholic household seems to have an influence similar to that of having two Catholic parents (and in no case are there statistically significant differences between the two groups). Bible reading and personal prayer are actually more widely practiced among emerging adults raised in single-parent Catholic homes.

Religious Beliefs in Emerging Adulthood. We next examine the differences in religious beliefs between emerging adults raised in different types of Catholic households. The results are shown in Figure 3.11. Emerging adults raised with at least one traditional Catholic parent are more likely to hold orthodox Catholic

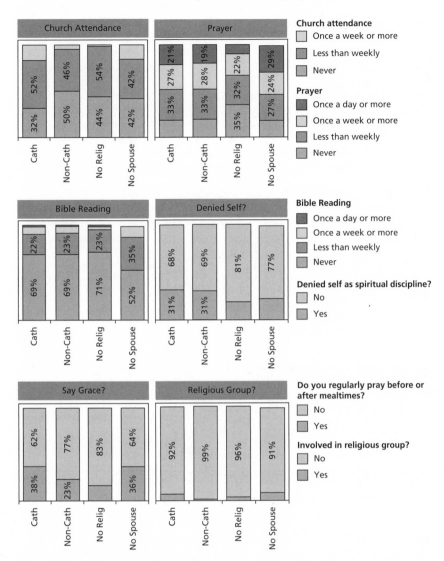

Figure 3.10 Religious practices during emerging adulthood by religious homogamy or difference between parents.

views of God and Jesus Christ. Comparatively, those raised with at least one liberal Catholic parent are roughly evenly split between believing in a personal God and believing something else about God (including that he does not exist), while 70 percent of emerging adults from traditional Catholic homes believe in a personal God versus 30 percent believing something else about God. Nearly four out of five (79 percent) in this traditional-parent group believe in the divinity and resurrection of Jesus, while only 56 percent from liberal Catholic households believe the same as emerging adults. Uncertainty is much higher in this

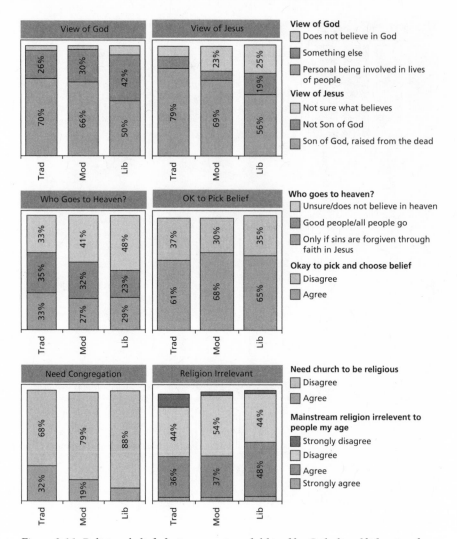

Figure 3.11 Religious beliefs during emerging adulthood by Catholic self-identity of parents.

latter group, with a full quarter not sure what they believe. Both beliefs about God and beliefs about Jesus are significantly different between liberal and traditional categories in our full models. The other measure that shows the same strong correlation with type of parental Catholicism is whether the respondent believes a church congregation or parish is necessary to be truly religious. While most emerging adult Catholics do not believe a congregation is necessary, nearly one-third of those with a traditional Catholic parent in adolescence do believe this. Only 19 percent of those with a moderate Catholic parent affirm the same, and a mere 12 percent from liberal Catholic households. These differences hold up even after controlling for other possible confounding factors.

Other religious beliefs of young adults vary depending on the Catholic identity of the parent respondent at the time they were teenagers, but in more complex ways. The percentage that adheres to orthodox Catholic beliefs about salvation, that people go to heaven whose sins are forgiven through Jesus Christ, are roughly the same across all three groups; however, those from liberal Catholic households report more uncertainty about and disbelief in heaven (48 percent, versus 33 percent of emerging adults from traditional Catholic households). These differences are statistically significant. Also, more emerging adult respondents from liberal Catholic households report agreement with the statement that mainstream religion is irrelevant for people their age, while a greater proportion of those with a traditional Catholic parent (12 percent) strongly disagree with that statement (compared to 3 percent of those with a moderate or liberal Catholic parent). Once again, these results are statistically significant. Lastly, a similar majority of Catholics from all three groups (61 to 68 percent) agree that it is okay to pick and choose religious beliefs without having to accept Catholic teachings as a whole. No statistical differences are evident after controls are introduced.

Finally, once again, the results are similar when we examine Figure 3.12, where groups of Catholic emerging adults are defined by the religious homogamy of the household in which they were raised during the teenage years. On the same three measures—beliefs about God, Jesus, and the importance of church congregations—those emerging adults who had two Catholic parents are somewhat more likely to hold more traditional, less individualistic beliefs, when compared to those who as teenagers only had one Catholic parent. In all of these cases, these differences reach statistical significance. On the other measures (who goes to heaven, picking and choosing beliefs, and the relevance of religion to emerging adults), the results are not as clear. Still, again, emerging adults who as teenagers had one Catholic parent and one non-religious parent are the least likely to hold traditional and non-individualistic religious beliefs, as measured here. Also, too, as was evident in many of the measures of religious practice, those who lived as teenagers in a single-parent Catholic home tend to fall in their beliefs somewhere between those who grew up with two Catholic parents and those living in a two-parent home split between one Catholic and one non-religious parent. None of these differences are huge, however.

In summary, the type of Catholic household in which emerging adults were raised as teenagers continues to make clear, although often modest, differences in their religious practices and beliefs. On numerous important outcomes, emerging adults with parents who described themselves as traditional Catholics stand out from other types of Catholic emerging adults. On other outcomes, those with a self-described liberal Catholic parent stood out as different. But the general pattern is clear: *Catholic teens from (what we can infer to be) more*

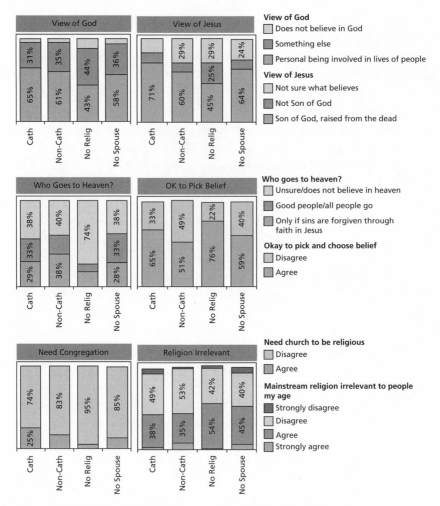

Figure 3.12 Religious beliefs during emerging adulthood by religious homogamy or difference between parents.

traditional Catholic households end up practicing their faith somewhat more regularly and holding somewhat more traditional or orthodox beliefs 5 years later, as 18- to 23-year-olds. Likewise, *American emerging adults who as teenagers had two Catholic parents appear to be somewhat more committed and orthodox in their faith as 18- to 23-year-olds.* The differences are not immense, but they are significant— enough to matter to many parents and Church leaders, at least. Inversely, those who are furthest from orthodox Catholicism, particularly on matters of religious belief, are emerging adults who as teenagers had one parent who was Catholic and one who was not religious. In short, *the Catholic faith seems more likely to stick with youth when their parents are more traditional Catholics, not liberal, and when both parents, not only one, are Catholic.*

The "Kitchen Sink" Analysis

The categories we used to compare different types of Catholic youth overlap in multiple ways. One emerging adult may be a first-generation Hispanic immigrant who is Completely Catholic, with two Catholic parents who are liberal. Another may be a white Nominal Catholic, with one traditional Catholic parent and one non-religious parent. Which of these factors matter most for the outcomes measured in this chapter? Are some consistently important while others fall by the wayside as young people navigate the complexities of adult life? To evaluate the impacts of various factors, we ran statistical models that use all of the primary characteristics we have explored, along with a set of additional control variables, to predict religious outcomes. This type of multivariate analysis tells us whether, for example, being a first-generation Hispanic Catholic is important in its own right, or whether it's really some other factor that more directly explains the differences between first-generation Hispanics and other Hispanics.[16] In other words, what variables "survive" when we toss everything in?

We can approach this question in two different ways. On the one hand we can look at this in terms of the outcomes. Which class of factors—Catholic type, ethnicity/immigration status, parent Catholic identity, or religious homogamy—best accounts for the variability of religious outcomes among young Catholics? To measure this, we used a test statistic that approximates the percentage of the outcome explained. In every case we compared the difference in this statistic between the model with every factor included to a model where one factor is removed (e.g., a model with all of the variables except parent Catholic identity). The larger the difference in variance, the more unique explanatory power that factor has. Here is what we found with this approach[17]:

For the set of distinctly Catholic outcomes (receiving confirmation or first communion, praying the rosary, going to Confession, going on a religious pilgrimage, and having sacred images or altars in the home), the measure of Catholic type we developed is the clear winner. In four of the six Catholic outcomes, the variables that make up Catholic type have the most direct influence of any factor. This certainly makes some sense. Since Catholic type is the most direct measure of the degree of Catholic identity, that it best predicts uniquely Catholic practices stands to reason. The set of variables that measured Hispanic ethnicity/generation contributed the least to explaining the variance in these particular outcomes. The measures of Catholic type also took the top place for three of the six measures of religious practices that were not Catholic-specific. Parent identification as a traditional, moderate, or liberal Catholic explained the most variance for two outcomes, and religious homogamy for the remaining one. Once again, Hispanic ethnicity/generation had the least unique explanatory power. Finally, for the six religious beliefs that we analyzed in this chapter, no factor emerged as the most influential. Catholic type came out on top for two, parent self-identification for two, and religious homogamy and Hispanic ethnicity/ generation each for one. Overall, the Catholic type variable appears to account for the most unique variance in our outcomes and the Hispanic ethnicity/ generation variable the least. The other two measures of parent and household Catholicism are somewhere in between.

But this is not the only way to analyze which factors matter. We can also account for influence in terms of the effect size[18] of each variable instead of the overall variance explained. Being a first-generation Hispanic Catholic, for example, may be an important predictor of religious difference, but the group of first-generation Hispanic Catholics is so small in the NSYR that it may explain little overall variance in outcomes for the entire Catholic emerging adult population. When we look across our "kitchen sink" models we find several individual variables that consistently have larger effects, even after controlling for all the other variables. In four of the six Catholic-specific outcomes, we find that the difference between Family Catholics and Completely Catholics has the largest effect. (In a model like this, the impact of each category is assessed by comparing it to some reference category—in this case Completely Catholics.) This variable scores a close second in effect size for a fifth outcome as well. Once again, this makes sense, considering that the outcomes we are assessing are Catholic-specific and our Catholic type measure is designed to measure Catholic identity. Catholic type matters less when it comes to other religious practices in emerging adulthood (it only topped the list of factors for one of the six practice outcomes). For these other religious practices, the measures of Catholicism in the household as a teenager seemed to have the largest effect size. The difference between having a liberal and traditional Catholic parent predicted the largest differences on two of the practices, while the difference between having two Catholic parents versus only one mattered the most for an additional two measures. These same two factors, religious homogamy in the household and the Catholic self-identity of the parent respondent, had the biggest overall effect size for the six religious belief outcomes as well. For three of the six outcomes, the difference between a liberal and traditional Catholic identity of the parent had the largest effect size, and in two of the remaining three outcomes the difference between having two parents who were Catholic versus one Catholic and one non-religious parent had the largest effect size.

In sum, there is no single factor which is consistently the most important or that controls all relevant outcomes. However, there are two general patterns worth noting: (1) Catholic type consistently matters the most when measuring specifically Catholic religious practices, and (2) Hispanic status and generation have less explanatory power than the other factors we have explored in this chapter.

Conclusion

In this chapter we set out to explore the diversity within U.S. Catholic emerging adults. Instead of treating young Catholics as a single bloc (which has been the primary strategy elsewhere), we tried to show how a number of divisions internal to Catholic emerging adults matter for their religious lives. We looked at four such divisions. We compared those who had multiple overlapping Catholic indicators in the NSYR to those who only had a few or one; we compared white Catholics to first-, second-, and third-generation (or more) Hispanic Catholics; we compared emerging adults who had grown up with a parent who identified as either a traditional, moderate, or liberal Catholic; and we compared whether both parents identified as Catholic or only one. On most measures of religious practices and beliefs, we see meaningful variance between these internal divisions (though one consistent exception is belonging to a religious small group outside of attending Mass). The differences are sometimes quite sizable (e.g., for the importance placed on belonging to the institutional Church for being religious), but most of the time they are small to moderate. The basic patterns are generally consistent across belief and practice, although there were some exceptions. Catholics who have multiple, overlapping indicators of being Catholic practice their faith more actively and have more traditional beliefs than other Catholics. The same goes for Catholics raised in homes where both parents are Catholics and those with a parent who characterizes their Catholic faith as traditional (as opposed to moderate or liberal). The differences between white Catholics and Hispanic Catholics were a bit more complex. In many instances, first-generation Hispanic Catholics (those who were born outside the U.S.) are more traditional in their practice and belief. But this is not true for all the outcomes we examined. In some instances, white Catholics and first-generation Hispanic Catholics were similar, and third-generation Hispanic Catholics (those whose grandparents or earlier ancestors were foreign-born) were less religious than both. Still, in most instances, within the Hispanic Catholic population, we saw a move from more practices and traditional beliefs to fewer practices and traditional beliefs as the emerging adults are generationally removed from immigration.

These inconsistencies may be one reason why Hispanic status and generation, when compared to white Catholics, do not appear to have a strong direct influence on many of these outcomes after accounting for other factors. The

other three domains consistently seem to be more powerful independent predictors, and Catholic type (our measurement of how many Catholic markers the
respondents possess) seems to be the most important when predicting
Catholic-specific practices. Still, this does not mean Hispanic status and immigrant generation are unimportant in the religious lives of emerging adult Catholics. These identities may work indirectly, through other factors, to influence
belief and practice.

4

Emerging Adult Catholics, Their Faith, and the Church in Their Own Words

This chapter presents the results of our analyses of interview data from the third wave of in-person interviews we conducted with 41 emerging adults who had as teenagers identified themselves as Catholic or who were raised in Catholic families. Our purpose here is to examine what happens to the Catholic faith and practice of those youth as they journey into the early years of emerging adulthood. Here is what we found in general terms. Of the 41 young people who counted as Catholic in our first interviews, fully 29 had by our third interview five years later either left Catholicism altogether, become estranged from the Church even though they still consider themselves Catholic, or simply become religiously inactive even though they are not particularly alienated from the Church. The other 12 Catholic emerging adults we interviewed remain active within the Catholic Church to one degree or another.

After briefly describing our interview data, this chapter presents an analytical typology of different kinds of emerging adult Catholics (and ex-Catholics). To illustrate these categories, we then tell the stories of seven specific emerging adults, each one representing one of the six categories in our typology. We close by highlighting a number of significant themes that emerged from our interviews with Catholic emerging adults.

Before moving ahead to our findings, a word about the nature of our interview data is warranted. The third wave of 230 total interviews with emerging adults we conducted in 2008 included 41 people who had counted as Catholic in their first-wave survey data. This means that when these young adults were teenagers, between the ages of 13 and 17, five years earlier, they were categorized as Catholic, either because they themselves identified as Catholic or because their parents made clear in their survey answers that theirs was a Catholic family.[1] Our interview respondents were sampled to provide diversity across types of religions, ages, socioeconomic backgrounds, races, ethnicities, regions of residence, neighborhood types, and other demographic factors. This means that our interview data are not nationally representative; each interview respondent did not have the same probability of being selected to conduct an interview as every other youth in the U.S. Our survey data, reported on in other chapters of this book, are nationally representative. But our interview data are only quasi-representative of emerging adults.[2] Readers should bear this in mind as they interpret our analyses of the findings below.

Six Types of (Ex-)Catholic Emerging Adults

In the following pages, we tell stories of seven different emerging adult Catholics who illustrate six distinct places they have come to stand in relation to their faith and Church. Table 4.1 summarizes the six different positions that emerging adults who as teenagers were Catholic represent.[3] The stories below do not reveal all the paths that young Catholics could possibly take to end up in these different religious positions. But we think they are helpful for understanding some of the main ways that teenage Catholics' religious lives evolve and the positions in which they can end up as emerging adults. After describing these cases, we will talk more generally about what larger themes they seem to reflect. We will then draw conclusions from our larger sample of interviews about what may contribute to emerging adults remaining Catholic or falling away from the Church. We remind readers that the following cases reflect stories told from the *early* half of emerging adulthood—not the full range, which is normally thought of as running from ages 18 to 29. Things may of course change as these emerging adults reach their latter twenties. But this is where they stand at the ages of 18 to 23.

Apostates. Seven of our 41 emerging adult Catholic interviewees have given up their Catholic identity and any religious identity at all. "Apostates" currently hold no personal religious identity. They are critical of the Catholic Church and no longer want to maintain even a nominal Catholic identity. Apostates are emerging adults who intentionally distance themselves from the Church. For them, faith and religion have stopped providing any appeal, plausibility, or relevance. Some of these apostates have been uninterested in Catholicism specifically and religion generally for a long time, despite being raised Catholic. "Jae" and "Steve," two case studies we provide below, offer good examples of this type of formerly Catholic but currently unreligious emerging adult.

At the time of our third wave of interviews, Jae, a tall Korean American from the mid-Atlantic region, was 21 years old, finished with college, and trying to find some direction for his life. He was to begin law school soon, but not at the school that he really wanted to attend. He told us he realizes now that he probably should have studied more and partied less with his fraternity in college. Jae, by his own admission, comes from a privileged background, the son of

Table 4.1 **Emerging Adult (Sometimes Ex-)Catholic Types, Ages 18–23 (Number in Interviews Out of 41)**

Apostates (7)	Have abandoned their Catholic identity without adopting different religious commitments. Are critical of the Catholic Church and do not want to maintain even a nominal Catholic identity.
Switchers (5)	Have given up their Catholic identity and replaced it with a new religious identity (all in our sample have become evangelicals).
Estranged (11)	Hold on to a Catholic identity but are critical of Catholicism and make efforts to distance themselves from the Church. They seem unlikely to return to the Church in the future.
Nominal (6) (Dormant subgroup)	Maintain a Catholic social identity but are not practicing. Make no attempt to distance themselves from Catholicism or to adopt a different faith. (The dormant subgroup refers to the nominal Catholics who were active when they were younger and seem likely to return to the Church if and when they have children.)
Engaged (12)	Attend Mass regularly and find faith to be important and meaningful, even if they cannot articulate its doctrine or what makes it distinct or important, and even if they do not believe all that the Church teaches. Also includes Catholics who attend Mass irregularly but embrace a Catholic identity, actively practice Catholicism in their daily personal lives, and understand the doctrines of the Church.
Devout (0)	Practice faith consistently (e.g., regular Mass attendance), are able to articulate Church doctrine and differentiate Catholicism from other religions, believe most of the Church's teachings, and expect to continue to live as Catholics in the future.

Source: NSYR 2008.

hard-working immigrants who provide him whatever he needs. He admits that he's been selfish most of his life and has taken for granted the fruits of his parents' labors. Jae wears a diamond earring and carries a Blackberry that he repeatedly checks over the course of the interview. He seems sad or depressed, especially when discussing the challenges of full adulthood. His body language implies discomfort as he thinks about some of life's big questions. It seems that despite or maybe because of Jae's privileged past, the challenges of post-college adulthood have hit him hard. He describes the difficulties of transitioning out of college at some length:

> I have to change things. For one, I've been a pretty irresponsible person. I'll get parking tickets. I didn't always achieve as well as I wanted to. I didn't always reach my potential in college. I always had a mentality to do what I had to do to get by, and then the rest of my concentration was towards having fun. I have just [recently, however,] started looking at my life more the opposite, as concentrating [first] on succeeding, and then whatever energy or time I have left over I can look towards pleasing myself. It's just the weight of responsibility that is kind of shifting. Now, it's just little things, like, waking up early, I have to take this earring out of my ear, I'm not gonna be able to wear my hat backward, I have to iron my clothes when I leave the house. It's money, I'm gonna have to think about every spending decision I make, as opposed to, say, I would use premium gas, but now I have to use regular because 20 cents add up. I guess it's just making more wise decisions, thinking more long-term. I think that the biggest problem with myself right now is that I am too laidback, relaxed. My parents have always made life so comfortable for me that, you understand what I'm saying, right?

Jae's troubles might sound petty to real adults, but for him these are serious growing pains, real struggles he is facing in his life—about money, success, and his future. Religion, notice, is not part of his concerns at all.

Jae's parents are both devout Catholic believers. According to Jae, they have strong morals and values and care about things like honesty and fair play. He describes his dad as a "man of ethics." He says that his parents are all about giving, while "I'm all about taking and giving less." When asked whether he sees himself as similar to his parents in terms of religious beliefs and practices, Jae reports that he only attends Mass on holidays, "here and there," although his parents and younger brother and sister attend regularly. He says he attended Mass up until the ninth grade, when he started rowing on crew. After two years of sports involvement, "I just, you know, gave up on church," Jae told us. He says that his parents respect his right to decide about his religious faith for himself. When later in our interview we asked Jae about his religion, he replies, "I don't have one."

Jae tells us why he fell away from the Church at an earlier age. "I don't like being told what to do," he explains. "I have always had a thing against authority, and I got this impression that, it's like too much like a cult, there's too much pressure." We asked him to explain further.

First, I started to question why the Catholic religion was the one religion I should believe. Why not Buddhism? Why not Judaism? Why not
whatever religion is out there? And I feel like it has to be scientifically
proven, I can't work off beliefs. Because you don't know who wrote that,
you don't know if that was just some [myth]. It's just too far back, there's
not enough scientific evidence to convince me that the Catholic religion is the one religion to believe in. [But] that is the one religion that I
would follow if I *had* to choose one, because of my family. Second, the
church that I went to was a Korean church, and it never really touched
me. It never really made me feel like a better person because I went to
church or it never really benefited me. Maybe it was because I was at
such a young age, I was still immature and childish.

Jae did not strike us as an atheist as much as a pragmatic agnostic. Part of the
pragmatic aspect is this: it comes out in his interview that one reason he resists
joining a Catholic community is that he knows it will challenge his partying lifestyle. He does not want to feel bad about himself. It is not that he is convinced
that there is no God. He is just trying to balance an active party life with achieving a financially successful future. So Jae worries that:

If I went back to church, I would have to change so much about myself.
I just don't want to get into that now. I feel like there's a lot of effort in
following a religion, and with all that's going on in my life right now,
I don't want to get into that. Another thing is, I feel like you can't just
go to any church once you join, like, a certain church. You have to get
to know all the people and it's like a little community. I don't want to
get into a church community, you know, that's not my style. There are
several reasons—it's just easier not to follow a religion, is what it comes
down to. It's easier for me and I don't see any reason why I should follow
a religion at this point in my life.

At the very least, Jae seems to have some notion of the commitment involved in
rightly practicing the faith in which he was raised.

Some readers may view Jae as a bit of a loser. But not all Catholic apostates
sound like him. A second apostate case, "Steve," is more successful, well adjusted,
and better directed. Steve is from the Midwest, where he also currently attends
college. Our interview notes describe him as tall and skinny, but in shape,
healthy, and handsome. At the time of our first two interviews with Steve, he was
an engaged Catholic. When we conducted our third survey with him, he was an
involved evangelical Protestant (so at that time he would have counted as a
"switcher"). Here is how he summarizes his religious history:

> I grew up Catholic. But I would say I was like really religious for this year
> and a half that I was an evangelical Christian. I grew up Catholic, but
> that [evangelical phase] was when I was really serious about it. When I
> was growing up, I was, yeah, crap I gotta go to church on Sunday. And
> then [during the evangelical phase] it was like, I wanted to go to church
> and stuff like that. So I would say Christian for the most part.

But by the time we conducted his third in-person interview, only a few months
after his last survey, Steve identified himself as an agnostic. He said he is no
longer either Catholic or evangelical. At the very most, he said, he's a "secular
Christian."

Steve is a confident emerging adult, decisive in his answers and clearly focused throughout the interview. He is intelligent, ambitious, and highly focused
on his goal of becoming a surgeon. His family seems to be stable, loving, and
supportive. At the time of our third interview, Steve was about to begin his sophomore year at a university in a state neighboring his home. He has a full-tuition
scholarship, the earning of which he named as a big accomplishment of previous
years. Steve was double majoring in biology and chemistry, with a minor in
psychology. He was also working 40 hours a week at a local hospital over the
summer, in order to gain experience and see "what a hospital is like." Steve strikes
us as a compassionate young man. When asked what he would do with it if he
unexpectedly inherited $100,000, for example, he said he would pay for his
school costs and his siblings' college tuition, and give some money away, "to do
some type of social justice with it, because why would I deserve to get that
money any more than anyone else?"[4]

Steve describes his family ties as much closer than he thinks is normal for
"other kids my age." He elaborated: "I really feel like I can talk to my parents
about anything, and that we can have really deep conversations. My friends,
the way I see them treat their parents, just very different. They seem to be less
inclined to tell them anything—they've kinda seceded from them, living with
them more than having a relationship with them." What are the kinds of
things Steve talks with his parents about? "Literally everything, religion, politics, or just things going on in my life, too. I can really be open with them
about anything." Aside from having an open conversational life with his parents, Steve sees himself as similar to them in his outlook on life, despite
having not too long before encountered some major differences with them
because of his evangelical faith. In terms of similarity to his parents' religion,
Steve reports:

> I haven't been to church with my parents in months. When I was grow-
> ing up we went to church every Sunday and celebrated Christmas and
> Easter. They took me to Sunday school, that's pretty much the extent of

our religious leanings. But now, it's not so much organized religion. It's more that I debate and talk with my parents about it. That's more the extent of our religious [connection].

What are some of the religious topics about which he talks with his parents?

About the existence of God, whether or not God exists. We get into a lot of philosophical arguments, with my dad. My mom, she kinda plays more to the emotional side of religion, like how her close friends who are really religious, she feels like their life is more complete for some reason. I can see that easily, because they don't really seem to worry about things the way I see it. I talk to my mom about the role of religion in people's lives, and she likes to ask me questions, since I'm really into philosophy and religion, about arguments about this and that or why people say God exists and whatnot. So I talk about that more with her, explain it to her and not argue, like I do with my dad, because he was a philosophy major. I argue with my dad and talk with my mom for the most part.

We asked Steve how and why his religious faith has changed.

Well, the last two years I considered myself a conservative Christian, and I would say now I kinda got sucked into it, like the emotional part of it. Being part of the group like that, but even when I was hanging out with this group of really Christian kids, going to church every Sunday, studying the Bible on my own, I still questioned everything. It's just my nature, it's who I am. I'm just a person who questions everything, so I still disagree with them on a lot of things. I would say I was a wholehearted believer, but I think that's fallen apart since last fall. Even then I was beginning to fall apart about this faith that I thought I had, which I don't really think is that real at all. I think, with what I've learned at school and just reading things on my own and just talking about things with people, I'm not really sure if I believe this.

Despite his conservative Christian phase, Steve thinks his parents are now "very happy" with how he is religiously. It turns out that they are all very much alike. His father, he reports, is "like me, he questions everything and he's more of a skeptic than someone who just believes things with blind faith." His mother, he says, is happy with "whatever makes me happy," even though "she wishes I still had that faith, because she's convinced that having blind faith or just really strong faith in general makes life easier." Ultimately, Steve reports, religion doesn't affect his family's relationships beyond being grounds for debate.[5]

Steve sees himself as a deep thinker, a person who likes to ponder "really complex things." He considers himself, as mentioned above, a "secular Christian"— by which he seems to mean acting ethically like a Christian even though he does not believe Christian truth claims. This idea came up when we asked him how he makes decisions about right and wrong.

> I would say I still draw a lot on my experience with this religious group of friends, and I would still consider myself more of a secular Christian. And at least in terms of social justice, following Christian teachings, like putting others before yourself, I think that's still something that's pretty important to me, even if I might not believe the religious part of it, I still believe in the secular part of doing good and leaving the world a better place than you found it.[6]

Steve isn't sure about his purpose in life, but he has a general idea that he'd like to "help other people."

> If you would have asked me this a year ago, I would be able to answer it really easily. But it's a lot more difficult now. If you're asking me in terms of, like, a meaning of life, heck I don't know. But I still feel like it's really important to me and it gives my life meaning to help other people, and I feel like I'm going to be able to do that through medicine, so that's how I feel about the direction in my life. I'm going to work really hard in school so I can go to med school and be successful in a career that I'm pretty sure that I'm going to love and it's going to be socially responsible. So I don't know really where I get this sense of like [interest in helping others], but I feel it does give me some sense of direction.

At the same time, Steve also feels "somewhat disoriented," in that he does not know exactly "what it all means, where it all comes from, but at least I feel like I have some sense of purpose." Pressing Steve specifically about religious faith, he declares that he is an agnostic "right now." So does he retain any Catholic identity, any sense of being Catholic? "No, not really." He says that even his once-engaged Catholic family has become less so. "I don't know, I don't think much of my family does really, you know, like my mom grew up Catholic, but I don't really see her being that close to it anymore either. I don't think they go to church that often anymore. I think my whole family has kinda drifted away." Steve reports that he has come to realize that he can't accept the arguments made by a lot of Christian apologetics. Like which?, we ask.

> Like for example, they would say look at this detail in the Bible, it's historically accurate and therefore the rest of the Bible is right. I look at that and, if you want to believe that, well, sure it's a convincing argument. But it's really a logical fallacy because it can apply to any other

historical document. You could say, you know, look at this document about Alexander the Great who said he was a god incarnate, and it says he existed and that's historically accurate. So it's kinda like they only take it one way, because the Koran is also historically accurate but we disregard all of that. So it's a really one-sided thing I was looking at, and the way I look at it now, well, it's just logical fallacies, and they're easy to believe and play to your emotions and it's something you really want to believe even if it's very hard to make it all work.

We probed about ways that he thinks he might have changed religiously or spiritually since he was 13 years old. "Well I know a lot more about it now and what being religious means. When I was 13, I just went to church, that's just what I did. I didn't understand anything and, like Catholic theology, I didn't understand any Catholic theology, anything historical. I believed in God then, but I didn't know what that meant." And what since then has changed?

As I got older, I got more into the history and theology and philosophy behind the existence of God and things like that. I looked a lot into the history and a lot of things that weren't so complicated [when I was younger]. Which is a big problem I have now [having learned more about complications]. I really feel like it [evangelicalism] did play with my emotions, like, wow, I really like this, this is giving me hope. But that's what it does, it's geared to positive things instead of bad things, which is probably what most religions do. It's people hoping to go to heaven and an attempt at salvation, it made me feel comforted when I was reading that. And just like, okay we're gonna learn some of more and get the gist of this. And then the real [problematic] part kinda eventually [hit], your emotions can't be the standard or way of thinking something, you know? You can't force yourself to believe something that you really don't.

At this point, Steve is "not sure" if God exists, but is open to a "deist god, god who created the universe and walked away. Like, I would say if I were spiritual at all, I would be a deist." He does say that he probably will visit a church at some point: "I'm sure I will attend church at least once." For what purpose?, we ask. "I dunno, I really don't know." Ultimately, Steve simply wants to live well and be proud of the life he lives. Summarizing an outlook common to many emerging adults, he says, "There's nothing in particular that I really want to do, I just want to be happy."

In sum, then, Steve's intelligence and curiosity seem to have driven him to explore and deepen his understanding of religious faith. He did not find much in the Catholicism of his upbringing to satisfy him. His parents did not seem to have set an example of strong, intellectually grounded, faithful Catholics. That made him susceptible to the pull of evangelical Christianity, which he found attractive because of the depth of involvement it entailed, the tight peer group it involved, and the (seemingly at first) solid intellectual answers it offered. Steve had become a switcher. But then, because he could not ultimately accept the logic of the evangelical arguments provided to answer his questions, he felt he had to drop his religious belief entirely. His current ties to Catholicism are tenuous, at best.

It is difficult to predict what the future holds for Jae, Steve, and the other apostates like them when it comes to Catholic faith. But at present, it does not appear that the Church, faith, or Christian practices will play a significant part in their personal futures.

Switchers. Some of those we interviewed who were Catholic as teenagers had by our third interviews remained religious but no longer saw themselves as Catholic. Five of the 41 formerly Catholic youth whom we interviewed had become what we call "switchers." These emerging adults have given up their Catholic identity and replaced it with another religious identity. All five switchers in our interview sample had become evangelical Christians (though certainly some switchers in the larger population not represented in our sample have joined other faith traditions). These emerging adults did not leave the Catholic Church because they were against religion per se. In some cases they left because they did not think the Catholic Church did a good enough job meeting their religious needs or wants. In other cases, the social influence of other people with whom these emerging adults had important relationships led them into a different religious tradition. One example of a formerly Catholic switcher we call "Mindy."

When we met up with Mindy for her third interview in our study, she described herself as a Christian. "I'm not a certain denomination, just Christian," she said. At the time, her parents were also attending a non-denominational Protestant church. But they had not always done this. In fact, Mindy was the first in her family to take steps away from the Catholic Church. Her parents later followed. When we first met Mindy as a teenager, she was a pretty 17-year-old white girl living in the Midwest. She was tall and thin, was dressed in trendy clothes and jewelry, and wore lots of makeup. At the time, she lived with her mom, dad, and younger brother. She had grown up in the Catholic Church, attending Mass often. But already during her first interview, Mindy told us that her family had stopped attending Mass as much as they used to, just because they had gotten busier in life.

In retrospect, it was evident even at age 17 that Mindy was showing signs of leaving the Catholic Church. At the time of her first interview, she had been attending a non-denominational church with a friend, in addition to occasionally attending Mass with her family. She felt that the non-denominational church represented views closer to what she personally believed. She liked the adults at that church and enjoyed the company of many teenage friends there as well. Mindy had already at age 17 stopped calling herself Catholic. She was happy with her new-found non-denominational church. Mindy's parents were okay with her decision to attend a non-Catholic church. She told us that they even attended with her at times. She said that her parents liked her new church, but that they were not completely sold on it, since they had been Catholics their whole lives and preferred its familiarity. By our third interview, however, Mindy's parents had come around. By that time, they had moved out of the state, but (according to Mindy) before they left they had been attending her non-denominational Protestant church regularly.

When we met up with Mindy again in our third interview, she was 22 years old and living in the Midwest while attending college. She is still a trendy dresser, pretty, and wearing a lot of makeup (our field notes describe her as "very mascara-ed"). Mindy looked to us like a stereotypical "sorority girl." As we said, she had come to consider herself a non-denominational Christian. Catholicism is a thing of her past. She continues to see herself as very similar to her parents in terms of religious beliefs. She says "I'm not 100 percent similar, but I think in general we have a lot of the same values. There are certain things that we definitely differ on, but the majority, 75 percent of it we agree on." They celebrate religious holidays together, for example, and attend church together when Mindy is visiting them.

Recently, Mindy took a year off school to work in Europe as a nanny. She describes it as one of the more important experiences she's had recently:

> That was pretty big, just like the whole year off because I really didn't know, I was changing my major and my aunt was like, "Take a year off." I became a nanny for a year in Europe, for people my aunt knew, people involved in professional sports, so I got to do some pretty cool things, go on some pretty cool vacations, and I learned a lot about how I would want to raise my family. I learned a lot from the experience definitely. I was like the kids' mom, basically. The mom didn't really do anything. It was definitely eye-opening for sure. That's probably the most significant thing that's happened to me in the past couple of years.

Mindy tells us that her friends and family would describe her as "a little scatter-brained," "outgoing," and "caring." She is most proud of her ability to get along with people and to adapt to different situations and people. She wishes she could change her tendency to procrastinate and make rash decisions without thinking about consequences. She tells us that she is satisfied overall with where her life is going. Mindy has a boyfriend. She and her friends "have a lot of the same interests. We like the same music. We have a lot of the same opinions about issues and we like to do the same things." But they differ on some political issues, so she and her friends just don't talk about them. When asked what types of people she avoids, she told us she doesn't like judgmental or negative people and that "I'm not a big fan of drunken frat boys, that whole scene. Other than that, I'm pretty open to people in general I think." Mindy says she cares about people. She believes that people have a moral responsibility to help others:

> I believe in volunteering, if you have the time to volunteer, because no matter what there's somebody who has more than somebody else usually at some point. Even if you don't have a lot, you can always find a way to give a little bit. It doesn't have to be money, it can be time or something like that. I think that we have an obligation to help other people if you have means to, because I feel like the world wouldn't work if people didn't help each other out somewhat. I'm not saying everybody helps everybody else, but I think that's just part of how the world runs. We need that.

Mindy is disaffiliated from the Catholic Church, yet church remains very important to her. Mindy is one of the rare emerging adults, Catholic or otherwise, who mentions (even before we specifically asked about church) youth group and her church community as places where she thinks she most belongs. When asked what makes her feel a sense of belonging at church, she told us, "I feel like I learn a lot from it and everybody's there for the same reason, to learn and become a better person, to learn how you could improve your and other people's lives." Mindy attends religious services at a church that has three different local branches. She tells us she goes as often as she can, which ends up being "maybe twice a month." She attends the specific church she does "because I really like the way that they teach things. I really like the way that it's set up. I feel like everybody there or most people there feel the same way I do about stuff." She attended a similar church with her family before they moved out of state, but now she attends a different church near her college.

Mindy prays "probably once a day. I don't know, maybe more, maybe less. Generally once," about "issues, like world issues somewhat sometimes. Sometimes to give me directions, sometimes to help somebody that I know needs help or to give thanks for things that I have. Stuff like that." She also "sometimes" reads the Bible. She used to read it more often, and that gave her "more insight into answering questions I had about my religion. Some things I feel like it's hard to accept in certain aspects of my religion, but reading the Bible definitely explained stuff to me, I guess you could say. It made it easier for me to express certain things." Mindy believes God is "the creator of everything" and that "he creates the good things and gives us the opportunity to do good or bad, make choices." Jesus is "the son of God, and I think that I probably don't separate them as much as I should really. I think to me Jesus is what you read about in the Bible and he became one with God again after he ascended to heaven and stuff." Mindy believes in heaven and hell and thinks one gets to heaven by being a good person but also by "accepting God into your life." (In both her Christology and beliefs about salvation she thus holds beliefs that are semi-heterodox among both Catholics and traditional Protestants.[7])

Mindy thinks her faith has a "pretty big influence" on her life. She says that it helps her "determine my path, my goals, direction, and helps me choose my opinions on certain issues and stuff." She doesn't talk much about the Catholic Church or being formerly Catholic. By the time of our third interview, Mindy has been "just Christian" for long enough that Catholicism simply does not come up much. She does talk about being in a "religious group" when she was in high school, but she "didn't really like it" and "didn't really pay attention." She told us that what she learned from that experience was "that a lot of people in religion force it and really act the way that they think they should act because of that, and don't actually act the way it moves them, you know what I mean? That type of thing, they just pretend, like go through the motions." Mindy also tells us she's a lot stronger in her faith than she was at age 13. Here is one of the few times that she really talks about changing religions:

> I think I'm a lot stronger in my faith. Before I was just going along with what my parents thought. Then, [I went through a time when] I had a lot of questions and I definitely didn't go along with [what] my parents thought for a while, and I questioned everything that I needed to think about, and realized that because my parents think one thing doesn't mean I have to think it too. So I kind of formed my own opinions and I'm a lot stronger than I was. Before I would say it was because of my family that I was Christian, and now I'm Christian because of my own choice.

Mindy discusses the Catholic Church most directly when we ask her about her views on "institutional religion," about which she says:

> I guess I am a little put off by certain aspects of it. I grew up Catholic, so I'm a little put off by the organizations of that much of it [i.e., the Catholic part of American religion]. I also am Christian, though, so that's organized religion. The church I go to is less organized than the Catholic

Church I went to. But, then again, I've been to Catholic churches that aren't as organized and conservative as mine was. I don't know. It just depends on the religion and church.

Exactly why Mindy switched churches is a bit of a mystery. Most likely, it seems that her early experience in her family's particular Catholic parish, which she viewed as too conservative, opened her up to a friend's invitation to attend a non-denominational church, which she found accepting of her and offering a nice community of people her age. Mindy then brought her parents along to this new church and approach to Christianity. By our third interview, Catholicism had become something of the distant past for her entire family.

Mindy says she thinks she will still be attending church when she is 30 years old and hopes to be stronger in her religious faith and beliefs. Overall, she expects that she'll be pretty similar to the way she is now. When we ask her what she wants out of life, she says, "Ultimately, I want to raise a good family and kids who do things to help improve the world, and I want others to know that I actually made a difference in some people's lives." She adds that she wants to travel, grow stronger in her religion, and "hopefully run some nonprofit organization at some point in my life and live close to my parents." Mindy has not strayed from Christian faith. She sees it as an important, guiding force in her life. However, it appears that her faith will remain a version of non-denominational Protestantism, not the Catholic Church.

Again, much about why Mindy and her family switched churches and ultimately religious traditions is a mystery. It seems to have been caught up in the social relationships that Mindy had as a teenager and into emerging adulthood, and her dissatisfaction with her home parish. Her connection with non-denominational Christians who provided her with a peer group opened the way for her to stay rooted in faith yet escape what she saw as the too conservative mindset of her parish. Switchers take a wide range of personal journeys to end up in a different religious group from the one in which they began. However, it does seem that personal connections to others outside of the Catholic faith and a dissatisfaction with the Catholic Church in general or a home parish in particular are factors that contribute to a lot of switching.

Estranged. Eleven of the 41 emerging adults we interviewed hold on to a nominal Catholic identity but make intentional efforts to distance themselves from religion in general, which for them in practice means the Catholic Church. These "estranged" emerging adults hold quite critical attitudes towards religion, and as a result separate themselves more completely from the Church than do their nominal peers. They have not completely given up their Catholic identities. But their disagreements with religion make deep involvement in the future seem unlikely. "Rob" is one of these emerging adults.

When we met up with Rob at age 19, he was still living in the same mid-Atlantic state where we had interviewed him twice before. Rob is white, with a slight build, small stature, and longish brown hair, and he is dressed in a heavy metal band's tee-shirt. His interviewer's field notes describe him as "easily the least talkative respondent. He doesn't have a lot to say, but enough to keep it interesting." At the time of his third interview, Rob had just finished his first year of college and told us that he likes being an emerging adult. "I think it's fun," he said. "I mean, I like taking on more responsibilities." He recently applied for a dorm R.A. position at his college, not only because it pays for his room and board but because "I like the responsibility." When we asked Rob what was new in his life, he mentioned that he was about to become an uncle again to his sister's second child. This will be his third niece or nephew, born to one of his three sisters. Rob also has an older brother. Overall, he seems fond of his growing extended family.

Rob has lately been working at a fast-food restaurant full time over the summer, and living at home. He tells us that that arrangement is "all right. My mom drives me nuts, like usual. She's always like, 'clean your room.'" But, luckily for him, he's not home enough for the close quarters to cause real conflict. "I'm working a full-time job and I'm not home that often. Between a fulltime job and a girlfriend, I'm not home that often." Rob is fairly financially independent, compared to most of the other 19-year-olds we interviewed. He receives money from his parents "every once in a while, I mean like 20 dollars here and there, and they'll pay for stuff, but, I mean, I have my mom write it all down so I can fully reimburse her when I can." While his parents may not provide Rob with unlimited financial resources, he feels very close to them, especially after his dad recently had a health scare:

> I feel really close to them. I mean, I try to, like, do things with my dad and mom to, like, make us stronger. My dad, like I think he, I think it was a heart attack, it might have just been he had closed arteries, which is probably just as scary, I mean he could have died. So I'm trying to hang out with him more.

Rob strikes us as a dedicated, hard-working college student who cares deeply about his family and girlfriend.

At the time of his third interview, Rob had hope that God exists, but he didn't know whether or not God is real. He told us, as he had in interviews past, that his family hasn't attended Mass since his mom's mother died, when he was around 10 years old. His mom had been the one who put in the effort to keep his family going to Mass, since his dad comes from a Jehovah's Witness background. But since the death of her mother, Rob reports that she doesn't care much about religion anymore. He said this isn't a problem for his parents, however, since they are similar in their beliefs:

> Ever since my grandma died on my mom's side, my mom hasn't even really cared much about religion. I mean, I don't want to say she doesn't care, but we haven't gone to church since she died, which was like the late 1990s. And my dad, I mean, we've always celebrated Christmas, so it's obviously not a problem with him.

Still, Rob says that his whole family believes in God and that they attend Mass on holidays. And while he says he is "not really" religious, he replied to our question "if someone asked what religion are you, what would you say?" by answering "I would tell them Catholic." When we asked him what it means to him to be Catholic, he answered, "I mean that I believe in God and basically I celebrate Christmas," and then laughed. Rob was baptized and confirmed as a Catholic, but his family's distance from the Church early in his life has left him a very meager Catholicism.

When Rob was interviewed earlier in our study, at age 16, our interview notes described him as the "teenage version of Pascal's wager" (though perhaps not properly understood). For Rob, it seemed safer to believe in God, just in case, than to give up faith entirely, though he did not put much effort in. The 16-year-old Rob saw church as a good experience when they attended, but that was a long time ago. At that point in his life, Rob was optimistic in expecting that he would attend Mass more when he was 25 years old. However, when we interviewed him again at 19, he no longer saw himself attending church in the future. Rob is now much more negative towards the Church and religion in general. When asked what keeps him from becoming more involved, he explains: "I don't want to call religion a joke, but more and more it just kind of seems like it. Like at McDonald's every once in a while this old guy will give me like a mini-Bible and I read it and it just seems like it's preaching at me, and I just don't want to be preached at." When we asked him to explain further, he continued:

> I don't know, it tells me what to do basically, like you gotta buy this book, this version of the book, and pray this, and like I think it said pray this every night and it said I am a hell-bound sinner and I was just like, duh. It just made me laugh and, I don't know, it makes it seem like religion is more a joke. Like they wanted you to pray that every night? Like, you don't know me.

Rob says he doesn't see himself returning to the Church when he has children. Considering his very thin religious education and minimal experience in the Church, that seems quite likely.

Not all estranged emerging adults start from such a thin religious foundation as Rob, but we think his case is illustrative. At times, Rob seems to have no problems with the Church. At other times, he rants against the domineering power of religion and its irrationality, as he sees it. Rob, it seems to us, shows that the lack of a sound religious education can lead to gross misunderstandings of the Catholic faith and thus to an inability to engage with, and even an aversion to engaging with, religion at present and likely into the future.

Nominals (and Dormants). The next type of emerging adult Catholics, to which we turn, we call "nominals." Six of the 41 young adult Catholics we interviewed maintain a personal Catholic social identity but are not practicing the Catholic faith. Unlike the estranged, however, these nominal emerging adults generally make no attempt to actively distance themselves from Catholicism. This group seems likely to continue to be nominally Catholic or perhaps to return to the Church when it is time for their children to be baptized and confirmed. But few nominals seem on a trajectory to become significantly more involved in the Catholic Church now or in the future. (Within this nominal type, we also identified a "dormant" subgroup which refers to those who were more religiously active when they were younger but who are not now practicing faith. The dormant seem more likely to return to a more engaged level of practice when they marry and have children—although, as emerging adulthood as a life phase is increasingly extended, the likelihood of dormant Catholics returning to the Church probably diminishes.) The story of "Cassandra" illustrates what a nominal often looks like.

Cassandra is a white female from New England who belongs to a fairly observant Catholic family. At the time of our third interview, she was 23 years old. Cassandra is overweight, stands about five feet, six inches tall, and has long brown hair. When we met up with her, she was dressed in jeans and a tee-shirt and covered in dirt from her work on a farm. Our interview notes describe her as "pretty scattered" and wondered whether she might have been high on marijuana (she did tell us that she smokes pot and that she could not focus on our questions or elaborate her answers). Cassandra reported that she had just graduated college at the state university not too far from where she is living. She was working at a farm for the summer and living with one of her friends and her friend's children. She prefers this arrangement to living at home, because she hasn't lived at home since she left for college and, she reports, "I'm sick of my parents."

Cassandra describes herself as "pretty laidback, easy-going," and "hard-working." She is proud of herself for getting a college degree and "I guess doing fairly well so far in my life." She says she has "good friends" and "good health" going for her. Cassandra wishes she was "naturally super smart" and that she could communicate her feelings better, instead of just getting angry and leaving arguments in frustration. For the most part, she reports that she's happy with where her life is going—though from our perspective it is not exactly clear where her life *is* going or what her goals are. She says she's happiest meeting new people and working with horses and children. And she is most depressed when she thinks about "not knowing what I want to do when I grow up, not knowing how I'm going to pay for what I want to do when I grow up, concerns about family, family's health and well-being." So despite Cassandra's assertion that she's happy with life, clearly she has some anxiety about the future and how she is going to get there.

Cassandra grew up Catholic, but stopped attending Mass after high school. Five years earlier, in our first interview, she had described her family's religion as a somewhat unifying force, since they went to Mass and attended Christian music concerts together. At that earlier period, Cassandra already had some disagreements with her parents and the Church on topics such as sex outside of marriage and cohabitation. At the time of our third interview, Cassandra considers herself Catholic, but doesn't practice the faith. She says she prays "a little bit" about "friends and family, that, uh, they're healthy and happy, and, um, my like direction in life, I guess just certain things in the world in general." She doesn't know if she ever gets an answer to her prayers, but "I guess I'm happy that I do it anyway." Cassandra doesn't read the Bible, although she did in her early high school years. She believes in God, who is "just like a comfort," and Jesus "like the son of God that he sent here to save us from all our sins." But she also believes in karma and in "just being a good person." Cassandra believes in heaven and hell, explaining how or why people end up in one or the other in this way: "I guess what people like my parents and strict people would say would be like, you know, follow all the rules and stuff and read the Bible and be baptized and everything like that. But I think it's probably more like how you lead your life and how good you are to people, um, I don't know, if you try and do the right thing and you, I don't know." For Cassandra, the "rules and regulations" of Catholicism seem unimportant for actually being Catholic. And while she says religion is in the back of her mind, she does not think it shapes her life much.

Cassandra attends Mass occasionally when she goes home for the holidays at Christmas and Easter. She tells us that for the most part she agrees with her parents about religion but she is just "less strict." Mass attendance is not really important to her, while her family continues to attend regularly. Asked to describe herself to us in terms of religion, Cassandra tells us she believes in God, "certain things in nature," and karma. When we ask if there is a particular religion by which she defines herself, she replies, "I mean, I'd say I'm a Catholic. That's what I was brought up as." When we asked her what she thinks of the Catholic Church, she replied:

> I don't necessarily agree with all of it. I think a lot of it is just tradition, and the world, like people have changed so much, but the religion

hasn't kept up with it, that it's just kind of not super-practical. I think
the teachings and the beliefs are something that can, should be toned
down because it's ridic— It's kind of like impossible to live by and truly
be happy and yourself.

At the same time, Cassandra is glad that she was baptized and got her First
Communion in the Church. She says she'll get married in the Church as well.
However, later in the same interview, when we ask if she'll attend Mass when
she's 30 years old, she says, "probably not." The line between "nominal" and
"estranged" is admittedly thin at times. However, we think that nominals like
Cassandra stand a better chance of actually returning to the Church, or at least of
holding on to a nominal Catholic identity, than estranged Catholics, because,
while they disagree with the Church on some points, they are not generally
hostile towards the faith, but rather see it as a positive source of family identity
and togetherness.

Another nominal emerging adult, "David," we think demonstrates the potential to return. When we asked David what he thought he would be like religiously
at age 30, he told us "I would still be Catholic. When I'm 30 years old, if I have
kids, I'd probably be back to church." We asked: do you think your religious
views and beliefs might change? "I don't think so. I think my views are pretty
steady at this point." And your attendance? Would that change? "Uh, I guess that
if I have kids, I'd probably be back to church." So, we probed, why would that be
important? "Just to make sure that they get their morals. Make sure everything's
right with them." As David shows, at least some nominal emerging adults have
the intention of returning to the Church after a period of dormancy. However, as
these emerging adults probably extend their settlings down far into their futures,
we can't be sure that they will fulfill their intentions to return to the Church.

Engaged. Twelve of the 41 Catholic emerging adults we interviewed fit into a
category that we call "engaged." These self-identifying Catholics are one of two
types. The first regularly attends Mass and finds their faith important and meaningful in their lives, even if they cannot articulate its doctrine well or say what
makes it distinct. The second type are Catholics who do not attend Mass regularly but who are actively Catholic in their day-to-day lives, understand the doctrine of the Church, and find it personally meaningful to be Catholic. These
emerging adults do not pass the bar we set for the most actively engaged Catholics (the devout), described below, in that they experience some doubts about
Church doctrine and are sometimes half-hearted in practice. But they are definitely involved in the Church and will likely continue to be so into the future.
"Maria" is an example of an engaged emerging adult Catholic.

Maria is a Mexican-American living on the West Coast. She was raised by her
mother but has some contact with her father. Both of her parents are originally

from Mexico while she was born in the U.S. Maria was 19 years old at the time of our third interview. She is quite short in stature and stylish, but also somewhat tomboyish in appearance. Our interview notes describe her as talking incessantly. Hers was one of our longer interviews because of the great amount she had to say.

When we met up with Maria for our third interview, she had just been accepted into a program at a local community college, although she had already been earning college credit in some of her high school classes. She was looking forward to college classes in the fall, after having worked in childcare over the summer. Maria is clean-cut, avoiding people who do drugs and drink excessively. At the time, Maria had a boyfriend of more than a year. They were sexually abstinent and she intended for their relationship to remain that way. She said she doesn't have to personally figure out right and wrong, because she believes what her religion says and pays attention to the good she can glean from her larger cultural environment.

Maria said one of the biggest events in her life over the last couple years was the death of her maternal grandmother, with whom she had been living. Her death has been hard on both Maria and her mother. Maria has one older sister who no longer lives at home. Since her sister left, she reports, she and her mother have been fighting more. Maria insists that she loves her mother, and doesn't want to leave home, but says they both have bad tempers. She describes her mother as strict and discouraging of emotional displays, which she links to her upbringing in Mexico. When we ask Maria what she and her mother fight about, she said that religion is one of the issues:

> Lately we've been fighting over certain views. These past couple of years she wanted me to do my Confession, but I haven't done it in a couple of years. I am Catholic and Christian, I still have this moral belief in myself that I don't want to do Confession until I'm ready to start changing. Because I've seen a lot [of] people Confessing and . . . soon, like a week later after going out of the Confession box, they are doing it all over again, and say that they tried, and I don't see doing a week's work and then slowly giving up by the end of the week as trying very much. So I don't like going unless I feel that I'm ready to make changes. I change myself occasionally, like going to church and I used to go to Bible studies and stuff. So reading and talking to friends and thinking philosophically, I've learned and I think of what I'm ready to accept and what I'm ready to change and I start changing slowly. But we fight about that a lot because [my mom] wants me to confess and I tell her that I don't feel comfortable enough to go to church and confess to a priest about something that I'm not yet ready to commit to changing yet.

Both of Maria's parents are devout Catholics, in her opinion. And despite her disagreements with her mother, when we interviewed Maria both the first and third times, her religion seemed to echo her mother's. While Maria is quite happy with the Catholic Church most of the time, she doesn't see attendance at Mass in the same light as her mother. She says:

> We go to church together and she tries to take me all the time. [Laughs.] And sometimes, all the times I don't go, I don't try to make excuses. The reason I don't go, it's because I don't feel to go [sic] and she always says that no matter if you feel or don't feel, it's still you should go no matter what. And being stubborn as I am, if I don't want to go, I really don't feel to go, if I don't feel spiritually into it, I feel that I'd be going there for no reason and I'll just sit there and not feel anything, which is I think worse and more disrespectful than not to go there.

Why is that?

> Because I feel if I go there and I'm not into it, I'm not listening, I'm not doing anything, I feel like I'm disrespecting him [God] in front of his face, and I'd rather him know that I'd rather be home trying to better myself at my home level where I feel safe and where I feel somewhere in the level of I'm not disrespecting him to the extent that I would be if I went and not paid attention.

For Maria, and seemingly also for her mother, being Mexican and being Catholic seem to blur together. When we asked Maria what it means to be Catholic, she says it's having a First Communion and a *quinceañera*. Along with her mother, Maria practices Santeria (a syncretistic spirit religion originating in West Africa and the Caribbean), which she insists is a Catholic practice:

> Santeria is Catholic as well, except it's more involved in the ritual, the Mexican ritual culture which is like remedies of help, like you will clean your soul or your bad things with an egg, a purified egg or holy water. So basically it's the same as Catholic except it's more delved into the Mexican culture of what makes you feel better, who to pray to when you need help, who to ask for help, what remedies, what tea to make you feel better, all those things.

While clearly identifying as Catholic, Maria says that she feels that all religions are basically the same, even Buddhism. Catholicism is important to her, she tells us, because it is a social identity, and this part of her religious identity might be stronger than the spiritual aspects at this point in her life. Maria says belonging to a faith tradition is important because it gives you a place to belong, a definition of self, and community:

> If you tell people, "I'm not Catholic, I'm not anything," that's who you are [not anything]. If you're Catholic, you have some beliefs that relate to other Catholics. That's who you are. You relate to certain people . . . and I think that's what basically it is.

Essentially, for Maria, being Catholic is simply identifying with Catholicism and trying to do *some* of the Church's rituals. As for herself, Maria definitely identifies as Catholic, is thoughtful about her religion, and actively practices much of it. Despite holding some unorthodox views (for example, "I am my own temple, and I am my own religion"), she says she attends Mass almost weekly with her mother and prays regularly. Maria also reports that when she has children, she wants them to be raised Catholic as well.

Being an engaged Catholic does not mean being entirely orthodox or fully catechized. Yet engaged emerging adult Catholics enjoy their faith and are more or less engaged with and in the Church. They view their Catholic identity as important, as something they'd like to pass on to their own children someday. Some of them, including Maria, also express that they may someday become more devout in their practice.

Maria and engaged emerging adults like her have held on to their faith and practice. We see in the case of Maria the influence of her relationship with her mother. While at times this relationship is antagonistic, as Maria does not always agree with her mother's opinions on religion, it is also formative and important for shaping her ideas about religion and practice. Catholicism is very much a part of Maria's identity in a way that goes beyond a nominal Catholicism. Catholicism shapes her engagement with the world in clear ways; it is not simply a label but a mindset. This orientation toward faith and the world is what marks these emerging adults as engaged.

Devout. We created the theoretical category of "devout" emerging adult Catholics to fill out the complete logic of our typology. However, we did not actually interview any emerging adult Catholics who fit this category. Of the 41 Catholic emerging adults we interviewed, none regularly attend Mass, espouse well-expressed Catholic doctrines, and evidence the importance of their faith in their daily lives. For some Catholics, this may be setting the bar pretty high, but we think it worth creating this category, since at least some interpretations of what the Church hopes for from its members resemble this devout type. There are definitely some devout emerging adult Catholics in the U.S. (we know many at Notre Dame, for instance). But none of them showed up in our study's sample of 41 interviewed Catholic emerging adults. We did find, as noted above, many engaged emerging adults, who are often very serious about their faith, love the Catholic Church, and view Catholicism as providing an important personal identity. However, there was always something about these engaged cases that prevents us from categorizing them as devout. It might be sporadic attendance at Mass or major doctrinal differences with the Church. So none had the entire religious "package" that qualified them as devout. To illustrate this point, we share the story of "Tommy," an engaged Catholic who we think comes closer than most interviewees to being devout, even if he does not fit the bill entirely.

At the time of our third interview with him, Tommy was a 21-year-old white male living in the Mid-Atlantic region, where he grew up. Over the summer that his interview took place, he was working in the surgical wing of a hospital, while studying for the MCATs between his junior and senior years of college. Tommy is tall and handsome, looking mature beyond his years; especially when wearing his hospital scrubs he could pass for being in his early 30s. Tommy is also confident and focused. He comes from a solid, stable family situation and he's very career-oriented. He describes his life as very stressful, as he studies and applies to medical schools. At the time we interviewed him, he was working eight- to ten-hour days at the hospital and was obviously very committed to the career path he had chosen.

Tommy is Catholic "born and raised" and goes to the same church as his mother and father every Sunday while he is home. His other siblings choose not to attend. Even when Tommy is at school during the year, he attends Mass weekly. He tells us he prefers his church at school to his parents' at home. Tommy's family openly engages in debate about faith and religion. He describes his parents as more old-fashioned in their beliefs, but says they all mostly agree. When asked to describe his religious identity later in the interview, Tommy simply stated "Catholic. I would say I'm, you know, moderately religious, I guess, on a scale." But despite his self-assessment as "moderately religious," Tommy can talk more articulately about his Catholic faith than most of the other engaged Catholics we interviewed. When asked what it means to be Catholic, for instance, Tommy tells us:

> Well, I mean you're baptized in the Catholic Church and then you're confirmed in the Catholic Church and you're supposed to be an adult member. They always say the difference between a practicing Catholic and a non-practicing Catholic is church. I mean, so I consider myself a practicing Catholic when I go to Mass.

Tommy also believes completely in the traditional doctrine of transubstantiation— the belief that bread and wine become the body and blood of Jesus Christ during the Mass—and stands firm on this position, even when we probe him about it.

He could explain why he preferred Pope John Paul II to Pope Benedict XVI, and says he hopes that Pope Benedict will travel more to the people the way Pope John Paul II did. About being Catholic he reports, "I've always enjoyed it. Ah, the tradition, lots of tradition, lots of history and things like that."

Yet Tommy does have differences with the Church. He disagrees, for example, with requiring priests to remain celibate. He doesn't "necessarily agree" with the Church's position on abortion:

> You know our Catholic view on that. I used to think that taking, ah, the unborn child or whatever was wrong, and personally I don't think I would ever do that. But I don't think we as individuals have rights to tell someone else whether they should do it or not.

Tommy also disagrees with the Church's teachings on sex before marriage and homosexuality. He himself is sexually active and finds the Church's position to be "narrow-minded" and even "just ridiculous." Similarly, when it comes to homosexuality, Tommy thinks the Church should be more open-minded and accepting. At the same time, he thinks the Church generally gets a bad rap that it doesn't deserve. He thinks the sex scandals and the Church's sometimes inglorious history have just been "blown up."

Despite his disagreements with the Church on some points, Tommy is genuinely happy to be Catholic. He expresses to us what he finds particularly important:

> I like the Catholic Church because you can go anywhere in the world on Sunday and it's the exact same thing. You know it's structured in that way, what the readings are going to be. The only thing different would be the language or the overall homily by the priest.

When Tommy envisions himself at 30 years old, he expects to still be Catholic and attending Mass regularly.

Tommy's positive experience of the Catholic faith notwithstanding, he does not meet our typology's description of devout. He attends Mass regularly, loves his Church, and thinks seriously about Church doctrine. However, he disagrees with the Church on abortion, premarital sex, priestly celibacy, and homosexuality. And that, as we have defined it, keeps him in the category of engaged.

Some Observed Themes

Describing these cases of real emerging adult Catholics (and former Catholics) should help readers to visualize some of the details, particularities, and religious trajectories of their lives. But stories are not enough. It is also necessary to step back and think more analytically about the big picture that these and other cases together provide for us.

A General Lack of Hostility. First, we found little evidence among the emerging adults we interviewed of genuine anger at the Catholic Church as an institution or of suspicious, accusing attitudes toward priests or religious. Most of these emerging adults, even the estranged and apostates, are generally not outraged or bitter with the Church. A few are "mildly disgusted" with what they see as a patriarchal stance of the Church on women in leadership or with the Church's views on homosexuality. But few were much bothered by even these beliefs and practices, perhaps because they did not feel personally constrained by them. In fact, many Catholic emerging adults, even the estranged, held their own parish priests in high regard, even though already by our first interviews most were well aware of the priest abuse scandals.

When we asked "David" whether he likes being Catholic, for example, he told us: "Seems alright to me. I don't have any major qualms with it." When we further probed to see what he thought of some people's anger towards the Church, he said: "I mean, I think every institution obviously has its flaws, but you look at any church, any religion, there's some flaws there, so." The Church's defects don't particularly bother him, since all organizations have shortcomings. "Cassandra" provided a similar sentiment, as noted above. When we asked her about any disagreements she has with the Church, she described it as "too rigid," but went on to tell us that, "I'm glad I'm baptized and I'm glad I got my First Communion, I'll get married in the Church."

Even "Claudio," an atheist emerging adult who has distanced himself from Catholicism because of his homosexuality, is not hostile towards the Church. He told us:

> Actually, I think ever since I kinda stopped going to church when I was in high school, and it was for no other reason than I just felt I was too busy and it was a waste of time. I think I actually go to church more now than I [did] before, just because now I realize it more, I think of it more as a cultural thing and if I get pleasure from it then I'll do it. As opposed to before, I used to think that the Church was against me, so it was kinda my obligation not to go because I didn't agree with anything that they said. But you know, a lot of Catholic churches here are really liberal, one of my priests he was talking about, he had a sermon and he mentioned homosexuality and he said that there are repressed people and people shouldn't be prejudiced against them. And that was pretty amazing. So I don't have anything against Catholicism in that sense.

Overall, then, although apostates and the estranged tend to display more antipathy towards the Church than nominal and engaged Catholics, few emerging adults express a lot of hostility towards the Church, even when they do disagree with it.

The Lapsed Majority. We cannot of course be certain where any particular emerging adult will end in their religious journey through life. But perhaps an obvious point we want to make concerns the large number of lapsed Catholics among the emerging adults we interviewed. Among the 41 cases of sampled youth who began our study as Catholic or belonging to obviously Catholic families, we found by our third interviews five years later only 12 who could be considered engaged and none we could categorize as devout. We must remind readers that our interview sample is not strictly representative of all Catholic youth in the U.S. Even so, after setting the standard relatively high for who would be counted as "Catholic" in our first wave of data collection, we found that relatively few of these Catholic youth were engaged in any meaningful way with the Catholic religious tradition by our third wave of interviews. About 61 percent of our interview sample proved to be nominals, estranged, or apostates. And another 12 percent had joined evangelical churches—with perhaps another one or two others (2 to 5 percent) showing signs of heading in that same direction. That, combined with the statistical analysis of survey data in our other chapters, speaks volumes.

Our lapsed Catholics started from different points and took different paths to their current level of engagement with the Church. Some come from seriously Catholic families and have fallen away. Others never had a strong grounding in the Church in the first place. The stories of Jae, Steve, Rob, and Cassandra were illustrative on this point. "Claudio," who was mentioned above, provides another example of how this lapse can occur. Claudio is a Filipino living in the upper Midwest. He's a serious young man who is studying biology at the state university, and he comes from a family of committed Catholics. His parents attend Mass regularly. However, when we met with Claudio for our third interview, we found him to be an articulate and committed atheist. He is also gay. Despite his atheism, Claudio is still positive about the Church, finding pleasure in its music and rituals. He told us "At Christmas we usually attend Sunday night mass and I enjoy that. I enjoy medieval Catholic paintings. I hope to read the Bible cover to cover someday just to know for sure what's in there. Let's see, what else? I like the hymns, I like the hymns at church." He attends Mass more regularly now than he has in the past. We think that a large part of Claudio's alienation from the Church has stemmed from his struggle to find a place for himself within the Church as a homosexual male ("I used to think that the Church was against me, so it was kinda my obligation not to go because I didn't agree with anything that they said").

Despite his discomfort with the Church, Claudio sees Catholicism as part of his Filipino ethnic identity. He knows Catholic theology better than many of the engaged Catholics we encountered. However, he wishes the Church was more conversant on matters of science and he is skeptical of the idea of "blind" belief. When we asked Claudio what gives him a Catholic identity, he told us "just family really, just tradition, it has nothing to do really with what I actually believe in, I consider myself culturally Filipino, but it's not something that I think about constantly or even something that I take comfort in, I don't think it's important." As an atheist who still at times enjoys the rituals of the Church, Claudio presents another example of the varied and complicated paths that emerging adults can take away from the Church.

Despite our emphasis here on the preponderance of lapsed Catholics in our sample, we want to emphasize that there are among our engaged Catholics some emerging adults who, if not perfect in faith and practice, still reflect fondly upon the Church. "Emily" represents one such case. When we asked Emily if there were any things she saw as essential or central to being Catholic, she told us, "What I like about Catholicism that other religions don't have, like I've been to other masses, maybe when I'm staying with friends or whatever. I like that we have Communion. I like the idea of the wine, the blood of Christ and the body of Christ, I like that, so that's one thing we have that a lot of religions don't have that I think is—is special." We pressed further, "So transubstantiation?"

> Yeah. I think that's important that, you think you're, you know, that you're trying to have your sins forgiven on a weekly basis or however often you may go, or say that you're sorry for what you've done. But I think the idea of it and the practice of it, of Communion is important, and that's probably one of the things that I missed over others. I like that we have organized prayer. But I have also been to other churches, Baptist churches and Methodist churches, where they don't and it's also a very nice Mass [sic]. Like it's good to kinda just go with the flow and not just have everything kinda set out for you like we [Catholics] do.

However, despite the "Emilys" out there who still engage actively with the Catholic Church, there are many more "Jaes," "Robs," "Cassandras," and "Claudios" to go around.

Taking a Break. Most of the usual caveats regarding religion in the American life course probably apply here, however: many of the emerging adults we interviewed half-expect to become religiously active again when they get married and have children. Our term "dormant" particularly applies to these types. However, it can be difficult to distinguish mere dormancy from an entirely nominal identity. Dormant emerging adult Catholics would only be definitively revealed as having been dormant should they return to the Church upon starting a family, so it is too soon for anyone to tell whether or not any of the cases we think are dormant are actually permanently nominal.

"Lucy" and "David" (the latter of whom we mentioned in the nominal section earlier) both provide examples of what we think dormant emerging adults look like. During Lucy's first interview at the age of 16, we found her to be a happy-go-lucky, generally good kid living in the Southwest. She had attended Catholic school for most of her life and still enjoyed going to a youth group once a week despite the fact that most of her peers had stopped going. At our second-wave interview two years later, Lucy was no longer involved in church activities on a regular basis. At our third interview, she tells us you don't really need to attend to be a good Catholic, and she rarely does. When we ask Lucy what it means to her to be a Catholic, she says, "Well, I don't necessarily follow every single guideline. I don't go to church every single day, I don't have time for that. I don't follow everything the priest says. I think the most important thing is believing in God and morals." When we ask if she likes being Catholic, she responds, "I mean, it's kind of, not necessarily who I am. It's more how I grew up. I think that it's important, yeah, less. It's how I grew up and that's just what it is." We inquire if she has changed at all in the past couple years religiously or spiritually. "No, I don't think so. The only thing I've changed is that I don't go to church as often. It's just kind of hard with all the other things I have going on." We ask her where she sees herself heading in terms of her religious participation. "I mean, I'm not gonna become a priest or a nun or anything like that." We fully agree she is not headed for a devout life, yet because of her early involvement with the Church and her continued nominal engagement with it, we suspect she might return when she has a family of her own to raise.

"David's" potential for being a dormant Catholic, rather than a lifelong nominal Catholic, is much clearer. David is a 21-year-old white male living in the Midwest when we meet up with him for his third interview. His family as a whole seems to attend Mass less frequently than in the past. He tells us that he was "raised Catholic and got all the moral systems and that, from that" but that "nobody in my family goes to church much now." The reason? "We went until . . . my sister got through the education system, that kinda stuff, Catholic Church." So, we ask, she went to a Catholic school? "Uh, she went to, well we had this program called CCD. It's Catholic education. You learn a lot about traditions, that kinda stuff. Then they take you through all sacraments." We question further, so your parents wanted you guys to go through that? "Pretty much. Make sure we had our values in line, that kinda stuff." But now that you have that, you don't really need to go to church?, we asked. "Right."

Now that David has his "values in line," he doesn't "really find church necessary. Just gotta, it's there to reinforce your faith." So, we ask, do you think you'll participate more as you get older? "Uh, I would say so. It's mostly just . . . it's at this point I don't see any purpose for it." As we noted earlier, near the end of the interview, we asked David what he thinks he'll be like religiously when he's 30 years old. Living up to what we think a dormant Catholic would say, he tells us "I would still be Catholic. When I'm 30 years old, if I have kids, I'd probably be back to church." We asked him why that would be important. "Just to make sure that they get their morals. Make sure everything's right with them." The challenge for the Church here is that there are almost ten years between David's current age (21) and the age at which he sees himself potentially back in the Church. As young adults increasingly delay marriage and child-bearing, we wonder how many of those who have the intention of returning to the Church later in life will actually do so.

We think a "crowding-out effect" may be at work among many of these emerging adults "taking a break." Many try to balance the demands of hard work toward a successful career (in an unforgiving economy at the time of our study) with an active social (that is, partying) lifestyle, which leaves them little time on weekends to attend Mass and participate in other religious observances. Some youth seem to *expect* to be religiously inactive during their pre-marriage, emerging adult years. Having completed the major sacraments of initiation and religious transitions (baptism, CCD, confirmation, etc.), many Catholic youth head into a period of what almost seems like a normative religious dormancy, which they believe does not make them irreligious or not Catholic. "Taking a break from religion" is, in the view of many, a normal part of emerging adult life. Now that they have jumped through all the major "hoops" of Catholic faith, they can settle back and put off further religious practices until marriage and having children bring it to the fore of their lives again. Many emerging adults told stories about their parents following very similar patterns: they guided their children's initiation into the faith, only to then return to religious dormancy themselves after all of their children had successfully received confirmation. The life and practices of the Catholic Church are thus commonly viewed as matters one can step into and out of as one chooses, with little harm done to one's Christian faith.

Premarital Sex versus Church Teachings. The Church's prohibition of premarital sex came up over and over in our interviews with emerging adults. Several of the more religious respondents feel guilty about having had sex before marriage. Many guys, for example, agree intellectually with the Catholic Church's teaching on sex—and so do their girlfriends—but have trouble living up to this position in their own lives. One, for instance, told us that saving sex for marriage is "a good idea, but not very realistic." For others, the teaching is a source of contention and frustration with the Church. Not many emerging adult Catholics were highly critical of the Church's teaching on abortion. But the rule about premarital sex chafed at many we interviewed. Cassandra, for example, whose story we examined earlier, commented that the Church needs to "tone down" its moral requirements to make it relevant for contemporary times since, "It's kind of like impossible to live by and truly be happy and yourself." Emily, the engaged Catholic we quoted earlier, told us:

> I see the positive of it because they don't believe in contraception because it's obviously preventing God's work, but again with religion, it should be changing with society. I don't think it's wrong for somebody to sleep with somebody. I think you should be ready emotionally for anything that may come up. You know, if you were to get pregnant you should make sure that you are gonna be able to handle that. Either make sure that you're giving the baby up for adoption, or that you're able to provide it a good home, and also make sure that if you're going to [have sex], that you need to make sure that you're safe because there's just disgusting diseases out there.

Like many other emerging adults, Emily doesn't think the Church is quite "with the times" on this issue.

Many emerging adults pursue (what they think might be) happiness through experimentation—by "trying out" and "trying on" different identities, careers, relationships, and intoxicating substances. Both the traditions of the Catholic faith generally and its prohibitions against unmarried sex, heavy drinking, and illegal drugs specifically are completely at odds with what it means in this culture to "come of age" as a mature or fulfilled emerging adult, as our interviewees see it. A basic incongruence exists between the central assumptions and values of emerging adult culture and those of the Catholic Church. Many of the teenagers we interviewed in our first wave of data collection agreed with the Church's teaching against sex outside of marriage; but five years later, by wave three, when they had entered emerging adulthood, almost none still held this view and only one or two of those we interviewed actually followed it for religious reasons.

Of course, it is likely that when these youth marry (assuming most will do so) they will find upholding the Church's teaching on sex easier to live with (at least when it comes to adultery, although they will probably ignore the Church's teaching against artificial contraception). If so, the emotional distance they now feel from their faith or with the Church as an institution will likely be reduced. At the same time, the significant increase in the number of years lived between high school graduation and marriage will provide more time for these emerging adults to drift in their identities and commitments away from the Church. That will also increase the chances that they marry outside of the Catholic faith, if for no other reason than that their social networks are likely to become more pluralistic the longer they live away from home and the Church. To be clear, our point here is strictly analytical. We are not proposing any recommendations to change Church teachings—as our role as sociologists in no way positions us for that—but are rather describing what seems to be a major stumbling block for many Catholic emerging adults who otherwise might wish to be more closely tied to the Church.[8]

The Importance of Place and Social Networks. We noticed in analyzing our interview data that geography sometimes makes it more difficult for emerging adults to remain Catholic. We observed that in the South, older teenagers and emerging adults tend to have social networks that include evangelical friends, family members, and co-workers. Conversations with these non-Catholic relations sometimes became the basis of critical comments about Catholic doctrine among switchers or potential switchers.

"Carlos," for instance, is an emerging adult who now defines himself as a non-denominational Christian instead of a Catholic. His father is an evangelical Protestant, which is a big part of his story. However, we also think that Carlos might in part be responding to the social context of the Southern state in which he lives and the large number of evangelical Christians who live there. We see evidence of this when Carlos describes his reasons for becoming more religious after the age of 13:

> Honestly, because of friends I was around. They were Christians. In high school I started hanging around with people where they were fairly religious, and I was dating a girl who was very religious. It was fun, it was awesome, I learned a lot, and it was cool to have a good Christian relationship.

In addition to the immediate context of a state or high school, we saw that at times the U.S. itself functioned as a less-than-hospitable environment for being Catholic. "Andres," for example, who grew up in a very traditional Colombian immigrant family, commented on how much easier it is to go to Mass and be religiously observant in Colombia (where he'd spent a year after graduating high school) than in his new home in the U.S. At one point, Andres said that he thought religion was becoming less important in his life. When we asked him why, he told us "I think the way of life over here [in the U.S.], you know? Like my church [here], I wouldn't be surprised if the people are even working on Sunday mornings because work, time, other stuff, you know?" So the way of life in the U.S. interferes with the ability to do everything one's expected to do? "Yep. Because I know in Colombia, it's [religion's] a lot more important." People are a lot more involved? "Yeah, a lot more involved [with the Church], a lot more. That's what I'm saying, like in Colombia they'll stress religion a lot more than here, you know, go to church, if you don't do that, it's bad, you know? Over here, because of the way of life, the way it is, you know people are kind of drawn away from religion a little bit more, they want society, more [of that] life here." And, we asked, do you like that about Colombia or not? "Yeah, I mean I think it's a good way of uniting people, you know, everybody has something more in common." Thus, Andres finds that the American way of life competes directly with his religious faith.

Finally, the places emerging adults work and the friends with whom they come into contact can also have a big impact on their perceptions of their own religion and connections to the Church. "Raul," currently an engaged Catholic who shows potential for becoming a switcher in the future, discussed the importance of his connection to evangelical Christians at his workplace, a car dealership:

> There's this one dude at work, he's joyful every day, just happy every day. He's always talking to everybody and he's a good dude and he made me want to develop a better relationship with God also because I want to be happy. I want to be joyous. I want to look at the better things in life and the good things in life, instead of just always looking at the bad, because that's how I used to be. I used to be pessimistic all the time, but now it's like, just from looking at him I've learned a lot. I've gotten closer.

Raul still considers himself Catholic because he prays to Mary. But he has recently started attending a Bible study with his friends from work, and he talks quite a bit about finding Jesus and having a "more personal relationship with him." Having social networks that provide ties to non-Catholics make alternative trajectories of faith—conversion to another religion or simply falling away from Catholicism—more likely. Living in an area where there are not many other Catholics can in some cases intensify a Catholic's faith, but it also makes remaining Catholic fairly difficult for some emerging adults.

Lack of Compelling Church Programs for Emerging Adults. Although some of the emerging adults we interviewed had been involved in parish youth groups as teenagers, none were involved in any Church-related post—high school groups for young adults in our third wave of data collection, not even Newman centers in college. This is particularly significant given evangelical Christians' outreach to young adults. "Raul" and others we interviewed had been invited by evangelical peers to attend Bible studies. And "William" told us that he had attended a Pentecostal prayer breakfast, where he had had a religious experience. But we saw little evidence in our interviews that Catholic parishes actively seek to connect and minister to unmarried young adults.

This lack of Church-based emerging adult community is even more challenging for young Catholics in light of the Church's teachings against sex outside of marriage. We find some evidence that some Catholic emerging adults would like to follow Church teaching on sex, but they find it difficult—if not impossible, in their minds—in part because they know of no way to have an active social life and to date that does not involve having sex. There are precious few "pools" of Catholic emerging adults openly committed to the Church's norms in which they could attempt to live out these teachings together. As a result they feel isolated and unsupported. Some Catholic emerging adults try to obey Church teachings and fail, and conclude that those teachings are outdated and unrealistic. Many then go into a period of religious dormancy or get fed up and leave as what we have called apostates.

Little Apparent Effect of Catholic Education. We found that Catholic schooling, even attendance at Catholic colleges, rarely played an important role in shaping the religious outcomes of the Catholic emerging adults we interviewed. This may result in part from the fact that sometimes parents' reasons for choosing a Catholic school for their children and young people's reasons for choosing a Catholic college can have little to do with religious concerns.

"Eric's" parents sent him to a Catholic school, for example, for the "structure" it offered him, although he still ended up being caught dealing drugs. When we asked Eric if he thought of himself as a Catholic, Catholic school was the one thing he mentioned. He told us "I would just say that I went to Catholic schools for a long time, most of it out of habit. And it's also sort of a cultural thing more than a religion for me. I mean, I just think everyone should make up their own mind on what they think about that, but it's nice to have that structure and as messed up as it is, you know." Despite his evaluation of the Church, he tells us "I'm still gonna have my kid baptized and I'm still gonna take him to church until they start asking me questions about 'why are we doing this? This is stupid, I don't understand, do you believe in this?' Then I'll be like 'alright, you know, this is what I think, you make up your mind [about] what do you think.'" Why is he going to do that?, we asked. "Because that's, I mean, that's what I did for myself, because I had some, going to Catholic grammar school and stuff, you just got somebody trying to shove this idea down your throat and I'm not the kind of person that's just like oh yeah, tell me, tell me what's right." Eric's experience with Catholic school seems to have provided some sort of effect: he's willing to put his own children in a Catholic school until they have their own questions— at which point he's willing to admit he thinks the whole thing is a sham. This is surely not the kind of result Catholic education aims to achieve.

Other youth were sent to Catholic schools because of their superior educational quality, compared with local public schools. This is not to say that Catholic schools have no religious impact on their students. At least two respondents spoke highly of their religion classes and teachers at Catholic school, but even they were not religiously engaged as emerging adults.

We draw virtually the same conclusion regarding emerging adults attending Catholic colleges. Only two of the six who attended Catholic colleges appear even remotely engaged in the Catholic Church at the time of our third interviews, and one of these attended college for only one semester. "Brett" attended a Catholic college, which appeared to have a positive religious effect in his life. For most, however, it is hard to see if the Catholic college experience has made any impact on their lives of faith. "Jessica's" mother hoped that attending a Catholic college would strengthen her daughter's faith, but nothing of the sort took place. Even though most of Jessica's friends were Catholic—some even from very conservative families—by the second semester of her first year, none were attending Masses held in the college chapel. (Again, the findings from the interview sample we are analyzing here are certainly suggestive of larger trends, but the sample itself is not nationally representative, and so these findings cannot be taken as strictly representative of the emerging adult Catholic population.)

The Importance of Fathers. Our interview data strongly suggest that the religious faith and practices of fathers play a particularly important role in determining the religious trajectories of their sons and daughters. There are exceptions in our data. But they are exceptions to a clear rule. Not a single estranged emerging adult, for example, had a father who was an engaged Catholic. Although some of the estranged emerging adults' fathers were nominal Catholics, most of these 11 fathers were either non-religious or religious "others" (typically non-observant Jews or readers of books on Buddhism, or both). The father of "Rob," the estranged emerging adult we highlighted earlier in this chapter, serves as one example. While Rob's mother was the backbone of the family's Catholic faith until her own mother's death, Rob's father was raised as a Jehovah's Witness and later became mostly non-religious, even if still willing to accompany his wife to Mass. The father of "Steve," also observed above, is not a model of a committed Catholic parent for his son. He seems more interested in debating the philosophy of religion than in fostering a strong faith in Steve. In part as a consequence, Steve is a Catholic apostate.

"Jim" is an estranged Catholic with a mother who, he says, is "straight into Catholicism" and a father who is "very unreligious." Jim describes his father this way:

> He was born Catholic and so was I, my mom was too. But he has taken the role of, he reads a lot of Buddhist books, I would say he's more into the religion of Buddhism than anything. The little Buddha Maitreya statues and things like that in his house and seeing those as a little kid is kinda like, you know, as a little kid those things go "Ooh, little fat man that's made out of wood, that's so cool." As I grew older, I kinda grew towards that custom in a certain way. Thinking like maybe those people are right in their ways of thinking and not only limiting myself

to thinking about Christianity. Thinking about Buddhism, the Jewish religion, many types of other religions and things like that. I'm thinking of, different religions, you know. Thinking that maybe Catholicism isn't the only one out there. And opening my mind more as I grow up.

This case illustrates what the broader evidence confirms: that having one parent question the faith of the other usually undercuts the transmission of that faith to the child.

"Renee," another estranged Catholic emerging adult we interviewed, provides yet a further example. Renee adores her father. Although she became highly involved at her parish and Catholic school early in her teenage years, even attending a church youth group for a while, by age 18 (at our first interview) she had begun to have questions that obviously mirrored those of her father, whom she said takes a laissez-faire attitude toward the Catholic faith. By our second interview, Renee called herself "unreligious" and was deeply involved in the party scene and devoted to developing her career. Even so, she expressed only praise for her parish and the religion courses she took at her Catholic school. Her distance from the Church grew in spite of her attending a Catholic college. By our third interview, Renee tells us that, while she is similar to her mom in that she tries to be a "good and virtuous person," she is more similar to her dad and stepmother:

> My mom is religious, where she sees going to church every week as pretty much the only way you should do it, and I don't go to church every week. And my dad and my stepmom[9] don't go to church or anything. I am a spiritual person and I pray and do all those things, but I do them at home and I don't really go to Mass.

Like other estranged youth, despite her highly religious upbringing, Renee is clearly given permission, if not outright modeling and inspiration, from her father to disengage religiously—to explore, dabble, do her own thing.

As a related point, faith is viewed by some, especially male, emerging adults as feminine and thus to be kept at a distance. In an exchange about whether he ever discusses religion with friends, for example, "Jim" says succinctly what some of the emerging adults we interviewed imply, namely, that Catholic faith is properly a matter of the private sphere of life, which, to him, makes it a "female" matter: "Nope, pretty much a private matter." It is?, we asked. "You know," he replied, "it's kind of feminine to talk about that kind of stuff, so you just kind of keep it a secret, much to yourself." In other words, people, especially young men, should not talk about religious matters among friends, whether they share the same faith or practice different traditions, because religion is private and therefore feminine, and so a side of life not to be shared with others. This association seems connected with the tendency for mothers and grandmothers to be keepers of the religious tradition in many Catholic homes. There are exceptions, of course. But amidst such exceptions, it appears that emerging adult Catholic guys who practice their faith freely and openly do so in part because for various reasons they feel less constrained by the dictates of mainstream masculine gender norms. For example, in addition to being a religiously engaged Catholic, "Luis" was a "stay-at-home big brother" at the time of our third interview. Constructing resistance to the dominance of masculine gender norms and practicing Catholic religion go together for him. Meanwhile, the estranged "Renee," discussed just above, follows her father's more "masculine" approach to religion, by remaining skeptical, branching out, taking risks, doubting, trying new things, acting independently, not letting others shape her religious beliefs or lack thereof. Several fathers of those we interviewed seem to enjoy reading about or dabbling in Buddhism, as we have mentioned. It's almost as though experimenting with Buddhism serves as a badge of intellectual independence. Since many of the emerging adults we interviewed see their Catholicism as largely "inherited," they wonder if, by refusing to entertain other faiths, they are merely following blindly in the paths of ascribed tradition. In contrast, by making religious conversion a "personal choice" and characterizing faith as a "battle," evangelicals may provide men with a means of being religious in an independent way that doesn't feel (what to them seems troublingly) feminine.

Yet it is not the case that having grown up with an active and committed Catholic father guarantees an emerging adult's strong religious commitment. In fact, three of the five apostates we interviewed had Catholic fathers who were engaged or devout. But in contrast to the emerging adults who are estranged, these youth take religious claims seriously—seriously enough to reject them outright. They are not merely dabblers or bored with religion. They are apostates. In other cases, the fathers' religious practices seem to matter less; but those cases are few and require a very close bond between mother and son or daughter. Even in such cases where mother and child have a very close relational bond, just seeing dad not attend Mass and hearing him express religious doubts are enough to make many young Catholics begin to question their mother's beliefs early in life.

We might summarize our point about parents by saying the following. The faith of mothers is important in the formation of the faith lives of their children. Committed Catholic fathers are not a *sufficient* condition for producing children who will be committed Catholics down the road. However, in most cases, having a committed Catholic father seems to be a *necessary* condition. Having a doubting and uncommitted Catholic father appears in many cases to be a sufficient condition for a Catholic child to be an uncommitted and even an alienated

Catholic as an adult. In short, the faith of Catholic fathers is powerfully determinative of the future faith of their children.

Conclusion

The story of emerging adult Catholics told here is not particularly positive, at least viewed from the perspective of the Catholic Church. Of the 41 Catholic teenagers with whom we began, only 12 became active Catholic emerging adults. By our third interview, 29 are religiously inactive, estranged from the Church, or entirely non-Catholic. At the same time, this is not a completely "lost generation" for the Church. Despite the preponderance in our sample of (ex-)Catholics who are not practicing their faith as the Church teaches it should be, a significant minority of emerging adults in our sample are engaged Catholics and are planning lives in which they will pass their Catholic faith on to their children. In the second half of this chapter, we identified a variety of factors that seem—based on our interview data—to explain some of the differences (or similarities) in Catholic emerging adults' varying commitment to and engagement in the Church.

Who Actually *Is* a Catholic?

Who, when it comes to social science analysis of emerging adults, actually *is* a Catholic? The answer may seem simple: people who say they are Catholic. But answering this surprisingly complicated question is actually not so easy. If young people self-identify as Catholic, should social science treat them and only them as such? When we step back and consider *how* we know or come to believe that certain young people are Catholic, we will realize that the classification process in social science is actually more difficult. What criteria do or should we use to categorize people as Catholic?

Some observers believe that for people to be described as religious, much less as belonging to a particular religion, they must be actively *involved in* or *associated with* that religion. For them, calling someone Catholic who does not attend a Catholic church or identify as a Catholic would be problematic. Others, however, contend that growing up in a Catholic household definitively shapes one's life as Catholic, regardless of one's subsequent association with Catholic identity and practices. Yet others argue that none of these markers in isolation is enough to make someone Catholic. According to this more stringent standard, people need to identify as Catholic, attend Mass regularly, and engage in other Catholic practices in order to be regarded as truly Catholic.

So which American young people *are* Catholic? Our own theoretical reflection and empirical analyses tell us that this question does not have a straightforward answer. American youth today often experience unusual life situations that complicate the way they understand and express their religious affiliation(s) and identity(ies). We think that social scientists need to reconsider how to determine who gets classified as Catholic in order to ensure the validity and reliability of our analyses. In this chapter, we approach the matter by taking a multifaceted, combinational approach. We believe it highlights the various ways that emerging adults experience being Catholic and the various influences Catholicism has on their lives.

Initial Considerations

Our goal is to make sure that the correct youth count as Catholic (and not Catholic) when we study how religious affiliation or identity affects different religious and other life outcomes. We want to avoid having the "wrong" youth count "for" and "against" Catholicism on those outcomes. For example, suppose that we are interested in how "being Catholic" as an emerging adult is associated with differences in the importance of religious faith, Mass attendance, or engaging in risky behaviors. We must combine all who are Catholic and *only* those who are Catholic in the "Catholic" group, so that we can examine these outcomes in their emerging adult years as compared with those of non-Catholics. If the "Catholic" group fails to include some youth who actually are Catholic, then we are not making a valid comparison. The same is true if we include some youth in our Catholic category who are not actually Catholic. So the validity of any analysis of "Catholics" depends on grouping all of those who are Catholic as "in" and excluding all of those who are not Catholic as "out." Only then can any true "Catholic effect" be detected and analyzed.

Consider some of the basic problems that can arise in this process. Perhaps the criteria by which we decide who belongs in the Catholic category are associated with other measures that we are interested in understanding and explaining in terms of Catholicism. In this case, the very methodological act of categorizing Catholics *helps to determine the findings* about Catholicism, and the categorizing itself (rather than *being* Catholic) produces the results found. Suppose, for example, that we want to know how frequently Catholic youth attend Mass once they become 23 years old. Suppose further that we only count as "Catholic" the 23-year-olds who report on a survey that they are Catholic. What then? Many who were Catholic as children but have since abandoned and stopped practicing their faith may no longer call themselves Catholic on surveys. As a result, they will be dropped from the analysis, which will cause us to overestimate the number of Catholic youth who attend Mass as 23-year-olds. Those findings are invalid because they were driven in part not by the facts of the real world but by the way researchers categorize Catholics. To understand Catholics today as social scientists, therefore, we must pay close attention to the methodological challenges involved in categorizing "Catholics."

Academic researchers have generally overlooked this issue.[1] The majority of studies using nationally representative data rely on measures of self-identification as Catholic or attendance at Mass.[2] Other studies that have sought to use a more multifaceted approach to examine Catholics have relied upon data from samples of self-identified Catholics or Catholic parishioners.[3] These studies base their conclusions on data derived from the start by criteria that are too narrow. We argue that studies must take a broader view when determining which subset of all respondents should be categorized as Catholic, and we offer a more refined set of filters through which to do so.

Much of this book explores the practices and behaviors of Catholic emerging adults, ranging from Mass attendance to illicit substance use. We also examine whether they do these things at higher or lower levels than their peers affiliated with other religious groups. This book also addresses *why* and *when* Catholic youth engage in these practices and behaviors, and why they sometimes drift away from their religious faith as they transition into emerging adulthood. But, again, before trying to answer any of these questions it is crucial that we first establish who counts as Catholic and who does not.

First we will compare and contrast the measured characteristics that could potentially be used for this purpose. We argue on theoretical grounds that any single measure produces a flawed sample of Catholic youth, some being too inclusive and some too exclusive. To make our case empirically, we illustrate with a nationally representative sample of youth how each single characteristic, used in isolation, produces different categorizations of youth as Catholic. We then argue for a combinational approach to identifying a valid Catholic sample. Knowing that being Catholic is a multifaceted reality, expressed through a diversity of traits and experiences, we believe that the most effective method for determining which emerging adults should be counted as Catholics must employ multiple indicators. Finally, we demonstrate how this combinational approach allows for a more nuanced and discriminating categorization of Catholic youth and, we think, better empirical findings.

Considering Criteria for Classifying Emerging Adults as "Catholic"

What are the strengths and weaknesses of the factors mentioned above as sociological tools for categorizing the "correct" people as Catholic?

Attending Catholic Mass. People's place of worship is a common metric for classifying religious affiliation and seems, in many respects, to be a clear and direct measure: ask respondents where they attend religious services, find out the religious tradition of that place of worship, and label the respondents accordingly. Current trends in religious practice in the U.S., however, coupled with some unique aspects of young people's lives, make relying solely on people's place of worship to determine their religious affiliation problematic. Religious attendance can be a relatively weak indicator of people's actual religious affiliation. Catholics' rate of weekly service attendance has been slowly declining, while more occasional and sporadic attendance has become the norm. Many Catholics have stopped making Mass a part of their weekly routines, without completely abandoning church attendance altogether.[4] Some still seem interested in attending religious services enough to maintain a nominal connection to their faith, but not so frequently that it reflects a central aspect of their identity.

Are "Christmas-and-Easter Catholics" just as Catholic as those who attend Mass weekly? If this distinction matters, using place of attendance as the only marker of religious affiliation may classify as Catholic many people who for all intents and purposes are not Catholic. Attending Mass once every other year may not be enough to be counted as a true Catholic, and yet such people most likely would name a Catholic parish on an attendance question and consequently be defined as Catholic.

Qualifying the place of worship question with some indicator of the frequency of attendance would seem to be an ideal solution to the problem of over-inclusion. While this strategy may help social scientists eliminate truly nominal Catholics, it introduces some arbitrariness to the classification of who is Catholic, which may in turn create the opposite problem of excluding people who *should* be considered Catholic. Whoever makes the classification is forced to decide what level of Mass attendance is high enough to count. If someone attends a Catholic church several times a year, is that person Catholic? What about once a month? Once a week? There may be some who, for a variety of reasons, fall below these thresholds but who many would say should nevertheless be classified as Catholic based on other factors, such as a Catholic upbringing.

These problems impinge on attempts to classify young people as Catholic. Traditional religious rites and practices have become less central to what most youth across all religious denominations consider to be the defining elements of being "religious."[5] Many see religious service attendance as a nice thing to do if you happen to have the time, but not as a necessary marker of being a person of genuine faith. Where people attend religious services, therefore, may not be an adequate indicator of religious affiliation.

Even among youth who attend religious services frequently, place of worship may be a flawed way to determine religious affiliation. One concern with the standard "church attendance" survey question is the assumption that respondents only attend one place of worship. But it is not uncommon for American teens to attend multiple, sometimes quite dissimilar, services or youth group meetings of different religious traditions. Some observers have labeled them "religious consumers" or "spiritual seekers" in order to describe this pattern.[6] Accordingly, young people are said to reject traditional, fixed notions of religious affiliation in favor of picking and choosing from a variety of religious traditions, borrowing from whatever religion fits their felt needs or social associations— which may lead them to attend several types of religious services.

Youth today also occupy a less stable structural situation than most adults. Often, they do not decide where they attend religious services. Parents may compel their children to attend worship services with them. At the same time, those youth also may independently seek out a secondary religious service to attend, perhaps with friends or romantic interests. Additionally, increasing rates of divorce since the 1970s, including among Catholics, have produced many more two-household families in the U.S., with many children of divorced parents splitting their time between mom and dad. Adolescents may attend worship services while staying with both parents, and if the parents attend different types of churches, their children may have equally high attendance at two separate denominations or types of churches. Finally, youth today are more mobile in their social groups, changing friends and romantic partners relatively frequently.[7] Moving between peer groups over time may draw youth to attend several different types of religious congregations during the course of a year.

In sum, although religious service attendance is often an important marker of religious affiliation, especially for adults, due to the reasons above it cannot count as the sole determinant of teenagers' and emerging adults' classification as Catholic.

Religious Self-Identification. What about just asking people what their religion is? Religious self-identification is another common measure that social scientists use to classify people religiously. But as straightforward as it may seem, using religious self-identification alone is also not without shortcomings.

The question "What religion do you consider yourself?," which scholars often use to assess religious self-identification, fails to capture any indication of strength of identification or commitment. Merely saying that one is Catholic or anything else is easy. Given the social pressure in much of the U.S. to be at least somewhat religious, some respondents may offer researchers a religious affiliation, even when little else in their lives reflects that identity. Does calling oneself Catholic while hardly or never acting like one make one in fact Catholic? If the answer may be no, then relying only on a religious self-identification question will not result in accurate categorization.

In addition, the self-identification measure is complicated by two issues specific to youth and Catholicism. In-depth interviews with teenagers and emerging adults by Smith and colleagues revealed a strong individualism coupled with philosophical relativism among most youth today.[8] Most young people seem to believe that the ultimate goal in life is to be happy and to be a "good person," and that the means to such happiness must be decided by individuals for themselves. No one can tell anyone else that what they are doing is morally or intellectually right or wrong, because there is, they assume, no objective right or wrong.

This outlook contributes to American youth's unwillingness to subscribe to institutional labels. Identifying as Catholic limits young Catholics' individuality, some may think, because it would explicitly affiliate them with a group that has definitive guidelines and rules for leading a good life. Other scholars suggest that youth are more likely to see themselves as an "army of one" and sometimes a "church of one."[9] Furthermore, boxing themselves into a particular church might make it harder, in their minds, to maintain a relativist viewpoint and a tolerant acceptance of all alternative groups and beliefs. Identifying as Catholic means distinguishing between Catholics and non-Catholics, which forces some judgment of that relationship (i.e., is it better to be Catholic or not?). Individualism and relativism exert pressure on youth against identifying with a specific religious group, such as the Catholic Church, even if by objective measures they clearly are Catholic.

This dynamic does not seem, however, to decrease the likelihood that youth will identify as religious generally. Rather, it seems to have increased the proportion claiming to be "Christian" or "just Christian." Doing that allows teens to stay within the wide cultural mainstream without relinquishing their individuality or committing to any particular truth.[10] Being "just Christian" permits young people to define exactly what that means for themselves and to distance themselves from the particularities of any specific religious tradition. This aids the avoidance of normative evaluations or judgments of others. Using "just Christian" as a religious label may thus be a cognitive move that allows for a more expansive view of the self, but is not linked to actual changes in religious behaviors and beliefs—that is, youth may still look and act like they belong to specific religious denominations. When this is so, using only self-identification as a tool for classifying religious affiliation can be misleading.

Some teens also explicitly claim to identify with multiple religions. Claiming multiple church or denominational affiliations does not seem to confine teens as much as claiming a single, primary religious identity. This may reflect young people's interest in borrowing from multiple religious traditions (although evidence suggests that such borrowing is uncommon), and their fluid social locations. Just as they might attend multiple churches with divorced parents, friends, or romantic partners, they may also publicly identify with each of these churches or religious groups. Adding to this increased multiplicity in religious affiliation are the effects of a decrease in cultural restrictions on interdenomination marriages. It is much more common for youth today to have parents who are two different religions—for example, a father who is Jewish and a mother who is Catholic—than in the past. In such situations it would not be surprising for youth to claim identification with each or neither. But for the purposes of social science, should such a youth be counted as Catholic or not?

An associated problem is how to treat youth who claim Catholicism as their second religious identity. When young people claim "just Christian" first and Catholic second, for instance, it might seem appropriate to classify them as

Catholic. But should these two types of religious self-identification be treated as identical? It is even more difficult to know how to categorize youth who split-identify with a specific denomination, such as Methodist or Episcopalian, as well as Catholic. If *any* identification with Catholicism is all that matters for classification purposes, then clearly such youth should be classified as Catholic. But in this situation, the earlier concern about people simply saying they are Catholic is heightened, because youth may be listing all religious groups with which they have *any* connection rather than the one or ones that centrally define their identities.

These kinds of messy issues turn what may seem at first to be a clear marker of being Catholic into a potentially unreliable measure. Like relying only on place of worship, relying on religious self-identification alone may lead to inaccurate classifications and flawed analyses.

Parental Church Attendance and Religious Identification. The possible indicators of youth being Catholic examined so far have been characteristics of the individual. For many people, however, religion is not just an individual matter. Family and community must be included when considering the formation or definition of one's own religion. The role of family is particularly important in shaping the religious identities of teenagers and emerging adults.

It is helpful to consider why moving the basis for defining who is Catholic outside the individual person might matter. Much research has shown that different aspects of religion can influence people's behaviors differently. Studies have also shown significant differences between religious groups in adolescent outcomes.[11] These studies are typically based on certain theoretical assumptions. Differences in behavior are sometimes hypothesized to stem from differences in the values, morals, and beliefs of each group, which are transmitted to young people and used by them to make decisions. Other scholars are more skeptical of this *direct* value-based mechanism, and instead point to the importance of other causal processes.[12] One alternative theory suggests that adolescents who belong to a certain religious group develop important social ties to peers and adults in the group. These social ties would be put at risk if adolescents participated in behaviors that violate the values and beliefs of that particular group. Therefore, religious adolescents guide their actions according to those behaviors that will best sustain these valued relationships and avoid behaviors that risk breaking them.

These and other causal mechanisms will be explored in more depth in other chapters of this book. Important for present purposes is the idea that neither causal explanation relies directly upon youth claiming a particular affiliation. Rather, young people must either be taught the key beliefs and values of a religious group, which they accept and internalize, or they must develop valued relationships with people from that religious group who are committed to those beliefs and values. Even if a teen or emerging adult does not claim to be Catholic, attend a Catholic church, or participate in any Catholic spiritual practices, just having Catholic parents or other significant relationships might instill in him or her Catholic values, beliefs, and morals that can influence his or her actions. Or youth may believe that their valued relationship with their parents or others could be jeopardized if they acted against those values, beliefs, and morals. If we want to know how "being Catholic" influences behaviors, then the religious affiliation of important others, such as parents, may be a valid marker of which adolescents should be counted as Catholic for social science analysis.

Should youth who have no personal direct Catholic markers (e.g., self-identification, Mass attendance) but whose parents are Catholic be counted as Catholic or not? If so, the starting point would be parents' religious affiliation and church attendance. Yet that brings with it the general problems (discussed above) associated with using attendance at worship services, self-identification, and behaviors for classifying people's religion. Although adults may not suffer from some of the aforementioned adolescent-specific issues, such as structural instability, relying on parents' religion to classify their children has its own problems. The first of these is determining how strong the Catholicism of parents must be to justify classifying their child as Catholic. If their child does not attend Mass at all, would Mass attendance only a few times a year by parents be enough to lead us to classify their child as Catholic too? Or do parents need to be more definitively Catholic for us to feel confident counting their child as Catholic? If so, how much more definitively?

We believe we should base our determination of parents' faith on the theoretical causal mechanisms that seem to make religious affiliation or identity important in the lives of their children. This means that the standard will vary depending on the topic under study. If we are interested in finding out whether teens who have been exposed to any sort of Catholic beliefs are more or less likely to engage in some particular behavior, then using a lower standard may make sense. Even if a parent is only attending Catholic Mass several times a year, their children most likely would be aware of the general views and values of the Catholic Church. On the other hand, if we believe that being Catholic is only influential when a young person has developed meaningful Catholic social ties, then the level of religiousness of the parents may need to be set higher.[13] For example, in order for youth to believe that their relationships with their parents would be threatened by engaging in behaviors discouraged or condemned by the Catholic Church, being Catholic would probably need to be an important aspect of the parents' identity.

Using parental religious classification to categorize children's affiliation becomes even more difficult with the increasing diversity of religious identities and affiliations within American families and with the proliferation of blended and non-nuclear family structures. Traditional, two-parent biological families are frequently easier to classify, as the parents in those families often share similar religious identifications and levels of religious participation. But although many spouses maintain similar levels of religious practice and identify with the same religious group, the increasing rate of inter-religious marriages has expanded the number of U.S. children growing up in dual-religion households.[14] And even when parents share the same identification, one may be more highly religious than the other. Mothers attend religious services at higher rates than fathers and are more likely to be involved in congregational activities.[15] All of these considerations become more complicated when a teen's parents are separated or divorced.

When classifying the religious strength of parents, analysts must decide whether to use the religiously "stronger" of the two parents or whether some average of the two is more appropriate. The question is whether having one very strongly religious parent and one minimally religious parent is the same in influence as having two very strongly religious parents, two average-strength religious parents, or even two minimally religious parents. Some argue that having one parent who is not very committed to religious faith and practice signals to children that religion is optional, thereby limiting the influence of the more committed parent. Others argue that a religious "division of labor" takes place, such that children may see religion as the rightful domain of one committed parent, and thereby still receive the same religious influence as in a jointly committed household. Complicating the matter further, if the latter theory is true, then religious influence may also depend on whether the more strongly religious parent is the mother or the father and, in combination, whether the youth in question is a boy or a girl. When divorced parents remarry, the situation gets even more complex, as youth may actually have not two but four parents (including step-parents). In such cases, how high must the bar of parental religiousness be set for their religion to influence how we categorize the religion of their children? And which parents, if any, should be weighted more than the others?

The question of assessing possible parental religious influence on children for purposes of religious classification likewise becomes complicated when both parents are highly committed religious believers but to different religious groups. Can or will children internalize both sets of beliefs, values, and morals equally? Can a child become, for example, both a strong Catholic and a strong Methodist or Jew concurrently? Or do different beliefs tend to negate the influence of both? There is some evidence to validate the latter view. Still, if our theory of causal mechanisms necessitates knowing which youth are exposed to Catholic beliefs and values, then their having a highly committed Catholic father may legitimately lead to the inclusion of that child as "Catholic," even if the mother is, say, a strong Baptist.

All of these questions and complexities highlight the need for further attention and rigor when defining exactly who should be included as a Catholic for social science analysis.

Having Been Raised Catholic. This criterion is slightly different from the previous markers because it does not necessarily reflect either the youth's or the parent's current religious situation. Remember that our goal is to identify for analysis all and only those youth who are "Catholic"—perhaps meaning those who have been exposed to Catholic beliefs and values—in order to examine their religious and life trajectories across the transition from the teenage years into emerging adulthood. With that in mind we might consider being raised Catholic as a valid marker for being included in the Catholic category for analysis, even when respondents and their parents show no signs of being Catholic at the time of the study.

This approach may raise the critique that retrospective reports should not be used to determine current religious affiliations. But a basic thought experiment undermines the thrust of this criticism. Imagine we are trying to determine whether a 19-year-old girl should be classified as Catholic. When asked about her attendance at services, religious identification, participation in Catholic practices, and parents' religiousness, she does not report any connection to the Catholic Church, but instead claims to be "not religious." Further questioning, however, reveals that, until she moved out of her parents' home, only three months previously, this emerging adult attended Mass at a Catholic church frequently and identified as a Catholic. If we are interested in how "being Catholic" influences particular behaviors in emerging adulthood, most people would agree that this emerging adult should be included in our Catholic category. But what if this hypothetical youth reported attending a Catholic church and identifying as Catholic only up until age 16? Or age 14? Or age 12? Where should we draw the line in having been raised Catholic or not Catholic?

These questions become even more complicated when a respondent has "switched" and so currently affiliates with a different religious group, such as a Presbyterian or an independent Bible church. In such situations, emerging adults may have had extensive exposure to Catholic beliefs and values in the past, but the impact may be minimized due to their commitment to a new set of different, potentially conflicting, religious beliefs and values. In other cases, the Catholic upbringing may still exert strong influences. So if one is interested in studying any survey respondent who has ever been exposed to Catholic beliefs or values, whether respondents were raised Catholic can be a useful marker. But in situations where current beliefs and identities are of central concern, this criterion should be treated with caution in determining who is Catholic.

Summary. The discussion so far raises more questions than it answers. We have tried to illustrate the difficulties involved in what seems at first to be a straightforward question that needs to be answered to begin any study of Catholic youth. These problems may call into question previous estimates of the number of Catholic young people in the U.S. and the effect of their being Catholic on behaviors or attitudes of interest. Failing to classify carefully and accurately who is Catholic will distort any assessment of the effect of being Catholic, and what at first may seem to be a technical methodological concern can have major empirical and theoretical consequences.

Relying on any single survey measure to determine who is or is not "Catholic" is fraught with problems. Unfortunately, most previous studies have not had access to the full range of measured characteristics and behaviors we have discussed above, making accurate assessment of young Catholics difficult. The remainder of this chapter uses NSYR data to illustrate how including a larger range of religion-related characteristics can produce a more nuanced means of determining who belongs in the Catholic category for this kind of analysis. This careful classification process provides a solid foundation for us in subsequent chapters to produce clearer and more accurate analyses of what being Catholic means for youth as they become emerging adults.

Assessing Teenage-Years Criteria

As a first step toward identifying the teenagers who should be classified as Catholic, we examine how many of the first-wave NSYR respondents exhibited each of the characteristics discussed above. The respondents were between 13 and 17 years old at the time of that initial survey in 2002 and 2003. That first wave of data collection also included a survey with one of each teenager's parents.

Figure E.1 displays the percentage of the overall sample (including non-Catholic teens) that reported each of the traits that might be used to define someone as Catholic. The most prevalent characteristic, at almost 25 percent of the sample, is the teenager's parent attending Mass. About 20 percent of surveyed youth attend Mass, self-identify as Catholic, report being raised Catholic, or have a reported parent spouse/partner who is Catholic. The remaining characteristics all represent less than 5 percent of the overall sample, but do help identify additional potential Catholics. For example, almost 3 percent of youth attend Mass in addition to primarily attending another, non-Catholic church. That is a low percentage, but it represents 90 additional teens in a sample of 3,290.

Using the characteristics in Figure E.1, we can create a sub-sample of survey respondents who show any sign of being Catholic. Of the original 3,290 survey respondents, 1,127 reported at least one of the eight Catholic behaviors and

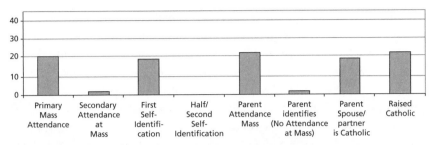

Figure E.1 Percent of Wave 1 teenage respondents reporting different Catholic identifiers (N = 3,290). Source: NSYR Wave 1. Notes: Categories are not mutually exclusive, meaning one respondent can belong to multiple categories. Secondary attendance defined as reporting a Catholic church as the second place of attendance and attending there many times a year. Weighted percentages are shown.

identities shown in Figure E.1 Let us call this sub-sample "potential Catholics." We are not suggesting that all 1,127 of these teenagers should ultimately be classified as Catholic—merely that this sample provides the broadest possible starting point from which to examine youth who have some connection, whether direct or indirect, to the Catholic Church.

Figure E.2 is identical to Figure E.1, except that here the number of "potential Catholics" (i.e., 1,127) is used to calculate the percentages. Although showing the same general pattern, Figure E.2 more vividly illustrates how prevalent each characteristic is amongst those youth who might potentially be considered Catholic. Again, parent attendance at Mass followed by being raised Catholic, teen attendance at Mass, and teen self-identification are the most common characteristics among the potential Catholics.

What is interesting to note from Figure E.2, however, is that no single characteristic applies to all, or even the vast majority of, potential Catholics. The highest

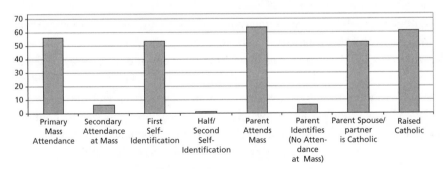

Figure E.2 Percent of Wave 1 potential Catholic respondents reporting different Catholic identifiers (N = 1,127). Source: NSYR Wave one. Notes: Categories are not mutually exclusive, meaning one respondent can belong to multiple categories. Secondary attendance defined as reporting a Catholic church as the second place of attendance and attending there many times a year. Weighted percentages are shown.

percentage any one characteristic achieves is parent attendance at Mass, which includes only 65 percent of all potential Catholics. Some of the less frequently cited characteristics also account for higher proportions of potential Catholics than one might expect. Almost 8 percent of this group attends Catholic Mass as a second worship service, for instance, and 7 percent have a parent who does not attend Mass but self-identifies as Catholic. This lack of one dominant characteristic defining potential Catholic youth confirms our argument that determining who is "Catholic" is not a straightforward matter and that relying on a single indicator to do so can be problematic.

We have so far considered each Catholic characteristic in isolation of the others. Skeptics may argue that this exaggerates the need for including multiple characteristics. In order to more clearly show how many "new" cases are captured by each characteristic, Table E.1 displays the number of youth who satisfy each criterion *but not* the ones listed above it. There we see, for example, that 119 teenagers self-identify as Catholic but do not attend Mass, while another 128 teenagers have a parent who attends Mass but do not attend Mass or identify as Catholic themselves. The exact numbers depend upon the particular ordering of the factors examined, of course, because a youth is no longer "eligible" once he or she has been classified as Catholic by a preceding characteristic. The ordering for this table was chosen based on the most commonly used categorization criteria in previous research, and the cumulative frequency and percentage columns are included to provide more information.[16] The cumulative frequency shows how many youth are classified as Catholic based on *any* of the criteria up to that point. For example, 876 youth attend Mass, self-identify as Catholic, *or* have a parent who attends Mass. While the individual frequencies would change if we altered the ordering of these three factors, the cumulative frequency of 876 would remain the same.

What does Table E.1 tell us? First, it shows that relying only upon the typical measures of attendance at Mass (as one's primary church attendance) and self-identification fails to include a significant portion of potential Catholic youth. Only 748 (66 percent) of the potential Catholics in the NSYR either attend Mass or self-identify as Catholic. That means that 379 (34 percent or one-third of) potential Catholics are missed when using only these two criteria. Thus, by not considering the other indicators, and so perhaps not accurately defining who should be included in the Catholic category, we might immediately bias any claims about the relationship between being Catholic and important religious and non-religious behaviors and life outcomes, simply because of our flawed categorization methods.

Second, turning to the less commonly used factors, parents offer a major means of identifying Catholic youth. An additional 259 cases (23 percent of our potential Catholics) can be classified based only on a parent's Mass attendance or on that parent or their spouse identifying as Catholic.[17] Note that these 259 teenagers did not report a personal attachment to or identity with the Catholic

Table E.1 **Number of Respondents Captured by Each New Criteria (N = 1,127)**

Criteria	Frequency	Cumulative Frequency	Cumulative Percentage
Primary Mass Attendance	629	629	56
First Self-Identification	119	748	66
Parent Attends Mass	128	876	78
Parent Spouse/Partner Is Catholic	99	975	87
Parent Self-Identifies (No Attendance at Mass)	32	1,007	89
Secondary Attendance at Mass	57	1,064	94
Half/Second Catholic Self-Identification	9	1,073	95
Raised Catholic	54	1,127	100
Total	1,127	1,127	100

Note: Unweighted counts are shown.

Source: NSYR Wave 1.

Church. But if we are interested in their exposure to Catholic values and beliefs, then it would be crucial to include these 259 teens in the Catholic category. Neglecting to use parents' religiousness as a classification factor in this case would result in a sizable underestimation of who should be considered Catholic, which could then bias the study's findings.

This particular group of teenagers is especially important to social scientists who study religious disaffiliation (and to people concerned about the future of the Catholic Church). These are youth approaching the emerging adult years with seemingly no direct affiliation with Catholicism, even though they appear to have Catholic parents. Understanding why these teenagers have not developed or maintained a personal connection with the Catholic Church, despite their apparent upbringing, could provide important insights about how people leave or drift from religious groups as they grow up. (Thus they also have significant implications for youth pastors and catechists who want to maintain young people's commitment to the Church and its faith.) Again, if we only rely upon the typical sociological indicators (attendance at Mass or self-identification as Catholic) to determine who are the Catholic youth we should analyze, we will entirely miss this important subgroup of arguably Catholic youth.

Finally, Table E.1 shows mixed findings about the necessity of including "secondary" characteristics for categorizing young Catholics. As discussed above, teens' fluid life situations can create multiple religious affiliations, making places and types of second attendance and identification potentially important characteristics of their religiousness. The results for youth who attend Catholic Mass as their second place of worship and who report being raised Catholic demonstrate the usefulness of these secondary characteristics for classifying youth. A total of 57 teenagers (5 percent of our "potential Catholics") report attending Mass as a second place of church attendance, even though they do not self-identify as Catholic or have Catholic parents. These youth are most likely attending Mass with friends, romantic partners, or non-resident parents, such as step-parents or extended family members. Whether they are seeking out Catholic Mass as an additional source of religion or are participating as a result of situational constraints (i.e., splitting time between two homes), these young people are still presumably being exposed to the teachings and practices of the Catholic Church, and therefore may arguably need to be included in a classification of Catholic youth, depending on the exact analysis.

Similarly, 54 youth (5 percent) have no current connection to the Catholic Church (through Mass attendance, self-identification, or Catholic parents) but report having been raised Catholic. Unfortunately, it is not possible with these data to know exactly what being "raised" Catholic means to these teenagers or for how many years they were raised as such. It seems a safe assumption, however, that Catholicism played a reasonably significant role in the earlier lives of many of them. If they had only been "raised Catholic" when they were very young, it is unlikely they would recall it as a significant part of their lives worth mentioning. The language of "being raised" is normally understood as having a significant influence on the way one was reared.[18] Therefore, asking respondents whether they were raised Catholic allows us to identify another significant portion of potential Catholic youth who are usually missed by studies that rely on simpler classification methods.

While being raised Catholic and attending Mass as a second place of worship appear to be useful characteristics for identifying potential Catholics, the same cannot be said for secondary religious self-identification. Very few American youth claim Catholicism as a second or partial religious identification but do not personally attend Mass or self-identify as Catholic or have parents who do so. In our sample, only nine youth can be classified using this secondary self-identification characteristic. Even when we alter the ordering in Table E.1 so that secondary self-identification is accounted for before the second place of worship, only 10 respondents would be classified as Catholic based on their secondary identification. Only 1 percent (n = 125) of the 1,127 potential Catholics mention Catholicism as a secondary self-identification, and Table E.1 shows that only nine of this small subset of youth do not have some other connection to the Catholic Church. Despite the frequently voiced observation (or concern) that youth today are religious omnivores—identifying with multiple religions in order to pick and choose parts as they see fit—it appears that very few youth "borrow" from Catholicism in this way. The vast majority of young people who identify as Catholic consider Catholicism their primary religious affiliation.

Our analysis so far has illustrated the limitations of the typical markers of young people's Catholic affiliation, namely attending Mass and self-identification, as sole indicators of being Catholic. Parents' affiliation, being raised Catholic, and attending Mass as a second place of worship together add substantial numbers of youth who could, and in many analyses arguably *should*, be considered Catholic. Our investigation has also demonstrated the problems with relying on any single characteristic as the sole determinant of who is Catholic. To capture the full range of potential Catholic youth for social scientific analysis, we have argued, it appears necessary to use multiple characteristics.

Using Combinations of Criteria to Identify Catholics

Not only does relying on single indicators of Catholicism seem to exclude an important segment of "legitimate" Catholics, it also poses the opposite risk of including youth as Catholic who should *not* be considered as such. Thus far in this book, we have considered Catholic anyone who reports attending Mass. But note that this includes youth who attend Mass only a few times a year. Some analysts may not consider this occasional attendance enough of a meaningful involvement in the Catholic Church to warrant classification as a Catholic. Including these nominal attendees as Catholic in social science research may bias the results of an analysis of the (bivariate, i.e., focused on only two variables) relationship between being Catholic and a given behavior or outcome of interest.

For example, suppose we compare frequency of personal prayer across religious groups and find that Catholic youth pray less often than evangelical Protestant youth. The low level of prayer among Catholics could be attributed in part to our inclusion of infrequent attendees as Catholics (since they almost certainly would have lower rates of prayer, thereby bringing the entire group's average down).[19] If the motivation of the analysis was to examine the frequency of prayer of all possible affiliates of each religious group, then this lower average would be accurate. But if researchers want to compare more regularly involved members, this analysis would lead to erroneous conclusions.

One way to avoid this problem is to include a measure of strength with each measured characteristic. Following the example above, we could use not only attendance at Mass but some level of frequency of attendance to determine who should be classified as Catholic, depending on the analysis. Doing so, however, requires researchers to somewhat arbitrarily determine a threshold for what counts as sufficient. There are no hard-and-fast rules to follow, standards differ by religious tradition, and whichever point is used in the classification may ex-clude some youth who should be counted as Catholic and include some who should not.

Instead of favoring this standard, strength-based measure, we here introduce and advocate a strategy that we believe more accurately decides which youth should and should not be considered Catholic. This approach accounts for the theoretical concerns discussed previously and is based on the findings from our initial analyses, which showed the variety of characteristics that can identify po-tential Catholics. It is a combinational procedure to categorize youth as Catholic for social scientific analysis, meaning it examines all of the configurations of characteristics that are possible using the traits that may validly identify some-one as Catholic. We first use the presence of any single characteristic included in the combination to determine who might possibly be considered Catholic. We performed this first step above in establishing the "potential Catholic" group, using all eight possible markers of Catholicism. Next, we assess how many youth display particular combinations of the included factors in order to create rele-vant distinctions within that broad category of potential Catholics.

For example, among the youth who attend Mass, some self-identify as Catho-lic, have Catholic parents, and have been raised Catholic; yet others do *not* self-identify as Catholic but have Catholic parents and have been raised Catho-lic. So we might consider the youth who reflect the first combination to be de-finitively Catholic and the latter to be more nominally Catholics (because they do not self-identify as Catholic). We can then investigate the associations be-tween belonging to each group and exhibiting particular behaviors or outcomes of interest. In our hypothetical prayer example, mentioned above, we might find that the potential Catholics pray less frequently than evangelical Protestants. It is possible, however, that the more clearly Catholic youth (as defined by possess-ing particular combinations of characteristics) will report the same average fre-quency of prayer as evangelical Protestants, while the more nominal Catholics will report a much lower frequency. By using a combination of available charac-teristics, we will be able to create a more detailed categorization of affiliation within the broad group of "potential Catholics" that produces more nuanced and accurate analyses.

Two-Way Combinations. Before we examine all of the possible combinations of Catholic indicators, we present in Table E.2 the percent of youth who display each indicator listed in the columns who also exhibit the characteristic listed in each associated row. For example, 76 percent of youth who report attending Mass as a first place of worship also self-identify as Catholic. (Because of the high number of possible combinations, we have simplified the table by combining teens whose parents attend Mass and those whose parents do not attend Mass but self-identify as Catholic—keeping in mind that the majority

Table E.2 Joint Catholic Behaviors and Identities (Percents) (N = 1,127)

Criteria	Primary Mass Attendance	First Self-Identification	Parent Attends Mass or Identifies as Catholic	Parent Spouse/Partner Is Catholic	Secondary Attendance at Mass	Half/Second Catholic Self-Identification	Raised Catholic
Primary Mass Attendance	100	78	71	70	27	23	72
First Self-Identification	76	100	65	68	25	0	82
Parent Attends Mass or Identifies as Catholic	89	86	100	84	32	55	82
Parent Spouse/Partner Is Catholic	63	59	62	100	27	33	55
Secondary Attendance at Mass	4	3	3	4	100	12	4
Half/Second Catholic Self-Identification	1	0	2	2	4	100	2
Raised Catholic	77	92	70	64	29	40	100
n	629	615	797	557	93	27	698

Notes: The 1,127 respondents here are those who fulfilled at least one of the identifiers shown in Figure E.1. This sample represents 36 percent of the total NSYR sample. Percents are calculated as "column" percents, meaning that they illustrate the percentage of the column variable that also exhibits the row characteristic. Percents do not add to 100. Weighted percents are shown.

Source: NSYR Wave 1.

[89 percent] of this combined category is composed of teens whose parents attend Mass.) Even in these basic, two-way combinations, we can start to observe distinctions in types of Catholic youth.

We do see a high level of overlap among the most commonly used indicators of Catholicism. Still, the amount of commonality is lower than some might have expected. For example, on the one hand, 76 percent of youth who attend Mass at least a few times a year self-identify as Catholic, and the majority of Mass attendees also have parents who identify as Catholic. On the other hand, 24 percent of youth who attend Mass do *not* identify as Catholic, a number well shy of the 100 percent we might have expected, if we assumed that youth who attend Mass should in theory also identify as Catholic. Similarly, while 78 percent of those youth who self-identify as Catholic attend Mass, 22 percent of them *never* attend Mass. This suggests that, while attendance at Mass and self-identifying as Catholic tend to go together, neither is a necessary or sufficient condition for the other. Rather, there is a significant number of youth who maintain a Catholic identity without attending Mass, and another set who attends Mass without identifying as Catholic. This again illustrates the usefulness of a combinational strategy for classifying Catholics, since from just these two factors we could create four types of Catholic youth: those who attend Mass and self-identify as Catholic; those who attend Mass but do not self-identify as Catholic; those who do not attend Mass but self-identify as Catholic; and those who do neither but might be considered Catholic by other criteria. Catholics in these different categories could have been influenced by their religion in very different ways, which will affect our social science findings about Catholics.

Another interesting pattern emerges when we examine our youth's parents. Two of the highest percentages across any of the pair-wise combinations are between youth who attend Mass or self-identify as Catholic and having parents who also attend Mass or self-identify as Catholic. Eighty-nine (89) percent of youth who attend Mass and 86 percent of those who self-identify as Catholic have parents who attend Mass or self-identify as Catholic. These high percentages suggest an almost necessary relationship: teenagers who attend Mass or self-identify as Catholic have at least one parent also attending Mass or self-identifying as Catholic. Less than 15 percent of youth who attend Mass or self-identify as Catholic do *not* have such a parent. Still, while seeming almost necessary, attending Mass or self-identifying as Catholic as a parent is not a sufficient condition for "producing" a child who attends Mass or self-identifies as Catholic. When we look in the "Parent Attends Mass or Identifies as Catholic" column in Table E.2, we see that only 71 percent of such parents have youth who attend Mass and even fewer (65 percent) self-identify as Catholic. Taken together, these findings suggest that, in general, most youth will tend to be only as Catholic as their parents, but also that a parent's Catholicism does not guarantee that a child will attend Mass or self-identify as Catholic.

We can thus see how including a third factor adds complexity to the possible distinctions among Catholic youth. Using two factors produced four possible distinctions. By moving up to three factors we create eight possible configurations: each of the four listed above with the additional division of youth in each of the four cells by whether they have a Catholic parent. As a result, in thinking theoretically about the causal mechanisms that might explain why being Catholic could affect different behaviors and outcomes, we can more specifically separate youth who might experience these causal factors in different ways. This combinational approach enables us to distinguish more explicitly between important subgroups of potential Catholics, rather than relying on a crude and perhaps inaccurate single-indicator division between Catholics and non-Catholics.[20]

Still focusing on parents, we see in Table E.2 that Catholic youth often have only one parent who is Catholic. Only 62 percent of parents who attend Mass or self-identify as Catholic report that their spouses or partners are also Catholic. Some of this discrepancy is driven by the existence of single-parent Catholic households, in which there is no spouse or partner present. Still, in another survey question (not shown) focusing on two-parent households, almost 20 percent of surveyed parents who attend Mass or self-identify as Catholic report that their spouses or partners are not Catholic. Comparing youth who have a single Catholic parent to those with two Catholic parents and two parents of different religions may reveal important differences in how these youth construct and maintain (or abandon) their Catholic identity.

Being raised Catholic has virtually the same degree of overlap among teenagers with attendance at Mass and self-identification as those identifiable as Catholic based on indicators measured later in life: 72 percent of youth who report being raised Catholic attend Mass, only six percentage points less than the proportion of youth who currently self-identify as Catholic who attend Mass. Similarly, 82 percent of youth who were raised Catholic currently identify as Catholic, which is 6 points higher than the percent of Mass-attending youth who self-identify as Catholic. Even more strikingly, 92 percent of youth who currently self-identify as Catholic report being raised Catholic. This shows that very few self-identified Catholic teens are converts or new Catholics, with only a small subset of all self-identified youth "brought into the Catholic fold" after being raised in a different religion or a non-religious household. Some of these are likely the result of an earlier parental divorce and remarriage to a Catholic step-parent. This also shows that, regardless of how religiously observant a young person currently is, being raised Catholic tends to have an enduring impact on religious self-identification. These findings highlight the reliability and validity of using the variable of having been raised Catholic as an important but not in itself an adequate factor for determining who should be considered Catholic for social science analyses.

Multiple Configurations of Characteristics. Next we look at various combinations of indicators of being Catholic. A helpful analogy for understanding how these combinations are constructed is to think of a row of light switches. Imagine that each light switch represents one of the characteristics examined above, and it is turned "on" when the youth exhibits the trait and is flipped "off" when he or she does not. Each youth therefore fits into only one possible combination of the many on and off switches. For example, if a teen exhibited every single Catholic factor, he or she would belong to the configuration defined by having every light switch turned on, and thus not belong to any configuration that contained any light switch turned off. Using this image, we can more easily see how youth represent the specific combinations of these potential markers of being Catholic.

Using the seven factors listed in Table E.2, there are 127 possible combinations of characteristics (2^7 minus the single combination defined by not having any Catholic indicators), although only 54 are actually filled by one or more NSYR potential Catholic respondents (73 combinations do not occur in our sample).[21] For example, none of the NSYR respondents fits the combination that includes *not* attending Mass as their first place of worship yet includes all of the other characteristics (self-identifying as Catholic, both parents being Catholic, attending Mass as a second place of worship, and being raised Catholic). Even so, the 54 unique combinations that are present in our data suggest a high level of diversity of life situations within the (potential) Catholicism of American youth. To help simplify the examination of these configurations, Table E.3 presents the 20 most common combinations, which together represent more than 90 percent of potential Catholic youth. Variables listed in capitalized letters are present and those in small-case letters are absent.

One of the most common combinations, not surprisingly, indicates an extremely strong and clear Catholic: these teens attend Mass as their first place of worship, self-identify as Catholic, have two Catholic parents, and were raised Catholic (Configuration 1). They make up 26 percent of all potential Catholics and just more than 9 percent of the total U.S. youth population. Similarly, the next most common combination of characteristics (Configuration 2) is identical to the first, except in it only the parent respondent (but not his or her spouse or partner) attends Mass or self-identifies as Catholic. This configuration would involve youth having two parents with differing religions and those living in single-parent households. In either case, these youth show a high number of the Catholic markers used here. Taken together, these two Catholic configurations represent 37 percent of all Catholic youth (25.9 + 10.8), and 13 percent

Table E.3 **The 20 Most Prevalent Configurations of Catholic Characteristics among Potential Catholic Youth**

	Configuration	Percent of Potential Catholics	Cumulative Percent	Percent Total Sample
1	MASS + ID + PARENT + OTHERPARENT + othermass + otherid + RAISED	25.9	25.9	9.4
2	MASS + ID + PARENT + otherparent + othermass + otherid + RAISED	10.8	36.7	3.9
3	mass + id + parent + OTHERPARENT + othermass + otherid + raised	6.7	43.4	2.4
4	mass + id + PARENT + otherparent + othermass + otherid + raised	6.4	49.8	2.3
5	MASS + id + PARENT + OTHERPARENT + othermass + otherid + raised	5.8	55.7	2.1
6	mass + id + parent + otherparent + othermass + otherid + RAISED	4.8	60.4	1.7
7	mass + id + parent + otherparent + OTHERMASS + otherid + raised	4.7	65.1	1.7
8	mass + id + PARENT + OTHERPARENT + othermass + otherid + raised	3.7	68.8	1.3
9	mass + ID + PARENT + otherparent + othermass + otherid + RAISED	3.0	71.8	1.1
10	mass + ID + PARENT + OTHERPARENT + othermass + otherid + RAISED	2.9	74.7	1.1
11	MASS + ID + parent + otherparent + othermass + otherid + RAISED	2.8	77.5	1.0
12	MASS + id + parent + otherparent + othermass + otherid + raised	2.4	79.9	0.9
13	mass + ID + parent + otherparent + othermass + otherid + RAISED	2.3	82.1	0.8

Table E.3 **(continued)**

	Configuration	Percent of Potential Catholics	Cumulative Percent	Percent Total Sample
14	MASS + id + PARENT + otherparent + othermass + otherid + raised	2.2	84.3	0.8
15	mass + ID + parent + otherparent + othermass + otherid + raised	1.8	86.1	0.7
16	mass + id + PARENT + OTHERPARENT + othermass + otherid + RAISED	1.7	87.8	0.6
17	MASS + ID + PARENT + OTHERPARENT + OTHERMASS + otherid + RAISED	1.4	89.3	0.5
18	mass + id + PARENT + otherparent + othermass + otherid + RAISED	1.3	90.5	0.5
19	MASS + id + PARENT + otherparent + othermass + otherid + RAISED	1.2	91.7	0.4
20	MASS + ID + PARENT + otherparent + othermass + otherid + raised	0.8	92.6	0.3

Note: Capital letters indicate the presence of the factor (listed in the key below), while lower-case letters indicate their absence.

Key:

MASS: Primary Mass Attendance

ID: Self-Identification

PARENT: Parent attends Mass or Identifies as Catholic

OTHERPARENT: Parent Spouse/Partner is Catholic

OTHERMASS: Second Attendance at Mass

OTHERID: Half/Second Self-Identification

RAISED: Raised Catholic

Source: NSYR Wave 1.

of the entire U.S. youth population (9.4 + 3.9). More than one-third of all youth who show any sign of being Catholic are what we might think of as "thoroughly" Catholic, meaning that they attend Mass, profess a Catholic identity, have Catholic parents, and were raised Catholic. That also means that significantly more than half of all potential Catholics are missing one or more of these criteria.

The next four most common combinations (Configurations 3–6), accounting together for 24 percent of potential Catholics and 9 percent of the entire U.S. youth population, represent youth who are, we might say, Catholic "by association." In three of the four combinations, they do not report any indication of currently being Catholic. Rather, they either have a parent who attends Mass or identifies as Catholic or else they say they were raised Catholic. The fourth configuration is similar, except the youth in it attend Mass. Some teens in this category likely attend Mass simply because they have two Catholic parents, since they themselves do not identify as Catholic. These four configurations together highlight youth who are "Catholic" through exposure to the Church, primarily through their parents. They do not express specific indicators of being Catholic personally, but do have links to others who do. It may be reasonable for social scientists to consider these youth as Catholic for certain analyses, as Catholicism likely plays some influential role in their lives—even if only through connections to significant ties who are Catholic.

Our combinational approach here thus not only helps to identify a larger set of youth as potential Catholics—when a significant proportion of them would have certainly been missed with the use of only a single indicator—but also allows us to sub-categorize Catholic youth to include certain types in analyses of behaviors and outcomes of interest that our theories tell us ought to be included.

The next most prevalent combination in Table E.3 (Configuration 7) includes youth who are only attending Mass as a second place of church attendance and exhibit no other markers of Catholicism in their lives. This group represents 5 percent of all potential Catholic teenagers and 2 percent of all youth. The relative prevalence of this configuration speaks to several issues raised in the first half of this chapter. It shows that we must consider second places of religious service attendance when using place of worship as a marker of young people's religion. Nearly one in 50 American youth are attending Catholic Mass as a second place of worship. How attendance at multiple types of religious services is related to the ways social scientists classify youth (and adults) into religious categories, therefore, needs more careful consideration. Scholars may very well be using an instrument far too blunt to measure and analyze religion in the U.S., and our findings as a result may be systematically inaccurate.

Identifying Major Categories of U.S. Catholic Youth

Using 54 different groups of Catholics in any analysis would be impossible. We have therefore condensed these 54 unique configurations into seven major categories of Catholics. Each category is defined by a particular combination of factors that hang together conceptually. To create these categories from all of the possible configurations, we broke the individual characteristics into three primary groups: (1) teens' primary attendance at Mass and self-identification as Catholic; (2) parental attendance at Mass or identification as Catholic and youth being raised Catholic; and (3) secondary church attendance at Mass and secondary identification as Catholic. The seven major categories are then defined by the particular set of indicators that are present among each group. To be clear, these categories are defined by how definitively or by which markers teens can be classified as Catholic, not necessarily by how strong or committed of Catholics those teens may be.

Table E.4 summarizes each conceptual category. The "Completely Catholic" category comprises youth who show the full set of primary Catholic characteristics, including attendance at Mass, self-identifying as Catholic, having Catholic parents, and being raised Catholic. The next three categories are defined by progressively relaxing the number of required primary Catholic characteristics defining them. At the bottom of this range, "Nominal Catholics" must only attend Mass as a primary place of worship *or* self-identify as Catholic but were not raised Catholic and do not have Catholic parents. The remaining three categories, "Family," "Previous," and "Secondary" Catholic, are classified based on the presence or absence of certain characteristics. The "Family" and "Previous" Catholic youth are similar in that they do not attend Mass or identify as Catholic; but "Family Catholic" youth have at least one parent who attends Mass or identifies as Catholic, while the "Previous" Catholic youth were only raised Catholic. The "Secondary Catholic" group is defined by either attending Mass as a second place of worship or identifying as Catholic in addition to another religious tradition.

Table E.5 displays the percent of potential Catholics and all U.S. teens represented by each category. Completely Catholic youth represent the largest single group of potential Catholics (39 percent), followed by youth who have Catholic families but do not express Catholicism themselves (20 percent). The other categories contain fewer U.S. youth.

The last two columns in Table E.5 allow us to come full circle to examine exactly how many U.S. youth can be classified as Catholic in various ways. *Following a strict definition and including only the most distinctively Catholic youth, we see that 14 percent of all American youth are Catholic. Adding in the "Mostly,"*

Table E.4 **Definition of Seven Types of Catholics**

Type	Definition
Completely Catholic	Youth who attend Mass as first place of worship *and* self-identify as Catholic *and* have Catholic parent(s) *and* were raised Catholic.
Mostly Catholic	Youth who possess *all but one* of the primary characteristics: attend Mass as first place of worship, self-identify as Catholic, have Catholic parent(s), and were raised Catholic.
Somewhat Catholic	Youth who attend Mass as first place of worship *or* self-identify as Catholic *and* have Catholic parent(s) *or* were raised Catholic.
Nominally Catholic	Youth who attend Mass as the primary place of worship *or* self-identify as Catholic but do not have Catholic parents and were not raised Catholic.
Family Catholic	Youth who are not personally connected to the Catholic Church but have a Catholic parent(s).
Previous Catholic	Youth who are not personally connected to the Catholic Church but were raised Catholic.
Secondary Catholic	Youth who do not have any of the primary Catholic characteristics or identities, but either attend Mass as a second place of worship or identify as Catholic in addition to another religious affiliation.

"Somewhat," and "Nominally" Catholic groups, however, increases that number to 26 percent. Further including youth who seem connected to the Catholic Church only through their parents increases the total to 33 percent. Thus, depending on how strict or relaxed the criteria are for determining who is Catholic, we can double (or halve) the estimate of how many American youth are in fact Catholic. Using this multi-factor, combinational approach allows for a much clearer interpretation of these numbers, by providing a more detailed and holistic context for what we scholars might mean in our analyses by "Catholic."

As further evidence for the advantage of using this combinational approach, Table E.6 shows the percent of each Catholic category that prays and reads the Bible regularly. We see here how the magnitude of the relationship between being Catholic and these behaviors varies, depending on the different classifications as Catholic. For example, 53 percent of Completely Catholic youth report praying at least a few times a week, compared to less than 40 percent of Nominal

Table E.5 **Percent of Each Type of Catholic**

Major Catholic Type	Percent of Potential Catholics	Cumulative Percent of Potential Catholics	Percent of Total U.S. Youth Sample	Cumulative Percent of Total U.S. Youth Sample
Completely Catholic	39	39	14	14
Mostly Catholic	13	52	5	19
Somewhat Catholic	12	64	4	23
Nominally Catholic	4	68	3	26
Family Catholic	20	88	7	33
Previous Catholic	5	93	2	35
Secondary Catholic	7	100	1	36
N	1,127		3,290	

Notes: Weighted percents are shown.

Source: NSYR Wave 1.

and Family Catholics. Only 19 percent of Nominal Catholic teenagers report reading the Bible at least once a month, a number more than 10 percentage points lower than that of any other group. In a typical study that uses either attendance at Mass or self-identification as the only markers of Catholic affiliation, these "Nominal Catholics" would have been included with all other Catholics, which would substantially decrease the overall estimate of how many Catholics participate in these religious practices. Our combinational strategy disaggregates these different types of Catholics to produce a more accurate view of the proportion of kinds of Catholics who read the Bible and pray frequently.

The following chapters take advantage of this classification system to more thoroughly compare other behaviors and outcomes of interest across these distinct Catholic categories and with other non-Catholic religious groups. We believe this method of categorizing Catholics advances the state of the art in the social scientific study of Catholicism and improves our analytical understanding and explanations of U.S. Catholic youth.

Table E.6 **Percent of Each Catholic Type that Frequently Prays and Reads the Bible**

	Completely Catholic	Mostly Catholic	Somewhat Catholic	Nominally Catholic	Family Catholic	Previous Catholic	Secondary Catholic	All Potential Catholics
Prays a Few Times/Week or More	53	45	50	36	34	48	58	47
Reads Bible a Few Times/Month or More	30	31	37	19	29	40	53	32
N	441	137	128	42	243	54	82	1,127

Notes: Weighted percents are shown.

Source: NSYR Wave 1.

Conclusion

Determining who is Catholic for social science analysis is far more complicated than it first appears. There are many ways that people may be associated with the Catholic faith, and those multiple ways can come in various combinations for different people. We must recognize that *the methods by which scholars include and exclude survey respondents from their Catholic category can have a significant impact on their substantive findings.* That is, our scholarly results can be determined not only by the objective reality of the world we are studying but also by our analytical methods and decisions. If we wish to better understand the reality of Catholics in the U.S. and elsewhere, we need to improve our method for classifying different kinds of Catholics for analysis. This requires asking more and better survey questions. It also requires more conceptual work. Toward that end of better understanding, we propose the combinational method described in this chapter, use it for our analysis in this book, and commend it to other scholars interested in improving research on Catholicism.

Religious Trajectories from the Teenage Years into Emerging Adulthood

One of the most common questions about the religious lives of Catholic youth is what factors most shape their religious trajectories as they transition out of the teenage years into emerging adulthood. For those working with or concerned about youth, this question is a matter of great pragmatic importance. Understanding the characteristics, experiences, and beliefs that tend to lead teens to higher levels of faith and practice during the young adult years can help parents, pastors, catechists, and mentors shape the faith lives of children and teenagers. For social science researchers, who may be less concerned with fostering particular outcomes, investigating factors during adolescence that predict changes in religiosity over time sheds valuable light on the theoretical mechanisms that affect human experience and behavior, both religious and otherwise.

The goal of this chapter is to explore how a variety of aspects of adolescents' lives lead to different religious pathways into emerging adulthood. The uniquely encompassing quantitative data of the NSYR allow that. Because the NSYR surveyed youth and their parents when they were still in adolescence, some as young as age 13, we are not forced to rely on often-flawed retrospective accounts of older respondents. So the reported *youth* behaviors and beliefs that are associated with *emerging adult* behaviors and beliefs are not clouded by the haze of memory, which is susceptible to selective and inaccurate recall. The NSYR's longitudinal data are also ideal for assessing the causal orders and directions of the relationships we test. Without this information representing multiple waves of data collected at different points over many years, it is virtually impossible to know developmentally whether, for instance, involvement in youth group leads to considering faith more important or vice versa. Using the reports of different religious behaviors and beliefs at two points in time allows us to determine which of these causal stories is more accurate.

This chapter analyzes the quantitative survey data from the NSYR and is the most statistically "thick" and consequently probably the most challenging for non-scholarly readers in this book. "Lay" readers who work to follow the arguments and findings of this chapter should be able to understand it all, however, and will be rewarded with several novel insights into the religious trajectories of Catholic youth between the teenage and emerging adult years. To ensure that our findings and conclusions remain accessible to all audiences, we use graphs whenever possible to visually depict the patterns we discuss, and, for readers who are especially wary of statistical figures, we frequently summarize and highlight the most important findings. The latter are also summarized under "Summary Conclusions," located at the end of each section throughout the chapter. Readers who are more concerned with the analytic details of this chapter should study the statistical tables and discussion of our statistical strategies in Appendix A.

Our analysis in this chapter follows a somewhat "cyclical" approach, in which we make initial observations, form ideas about causal relationships based on those observations, and then explore the data in greater depth to assess the validity of these ideas. This approach allows us to take a broad view of the factors that may causally shape young adults' religious faith and practice, instead of being subjected to the constraints of a deductive paradigm more normal in much social science research. Even so, our work here is informed by prior research and theories. We start by presenting information on the pathways that Catholic youth take in their religious journeys into young adulthood, describing how Catholic youth variously increase, decrease, or maintain their same levels of religious faith and practice as they become emerging adults. We then analyze a host of characteristics and beliefs of youth to identify those that seem most influential in leading youth into one of these different religious pathways. Next, we examine unique *combinations* of factors that set youth on different religious trajectories. Finally, we describe the causal mechanisms that seem to explain the relationships we discover.

Patterns of Religious Change

Let us begin by mapping the most common religious pathways from the teenage to the emerging adult years among Catholic youth in the U.S.

Different Levels of Religiousness. One of the most difficult challenges in trying to understand changes in people's religiousness over time is determining exactly what is meant by "religiosity." Entire books discuss the difficult issues involved in trying to measure levels of religiousness. For present purposes, we will use a combination of three different but related measures of religiosity: (1) frequency of Mass attendance; (2) frequency of personal prayer; and (3) self-reported importance of religious faith. These three are standard measures used in sociological research to assess variance in people's religiosity. We selected them because they also capture distinctive dimensions of religiosity. Attendance at Mass reflects respondents' objective, public religious behavior; personal prayer measures their private devotion; and the level of importance they assign to religion reflects a more subjective assessment of their faith's personal significance.

To create a single measure out of these three factors, we use a combinational strategy, similar to the one discussed in the Excursus. Rather than simply summing the scores across the three items, which can easily misrepresent a subject's true level of religiousness, we examine the actual configuration of attendance, prayer, and importance for each young person in our study. Based on that, we classify each into one of four groups: Lowest, Minimal, Moderate or Highest religiousness. These four groups are defined by a specific combination of answers to the three survey measures. For example, youth who said they attend Mass once a week, pray once a day or more, and believe religion is extremely important were placed in the Highest category. The remaining three categories reflect progressively lower levels of Mass attendance, prayer, and self-rated importance of religion. (For a detailed explanation of this procedure, see Appendix A.)

Religious Change over Time. Using the four named categories, we compare stability and change in levels of religiousness between the teenage and emerging adult years. Comparing the percent of respondents in each category at each time period provides a summary picture of the overall change in religiousness in the course of Catholic youth's transition into emerging adulthood. To begin examining these religious trajectories, we first separate the survey respondents by the Catholic categories defined in the Excursus (Completely, Mostly, Somewhat, etc.). The top panel of Figure 5.1 shows the percent of respondents from each Catholic category who belonged to the Highest religiousness group as teenagers and as emerging adults. The dark bars represent the Highest level as teenagers and the light bars the Highest as emerging adults. The two bars on the far right side of this panel represent all non-Catholic youth.

To begin, comparing Catholics of all types to non-Catholics, we see that Catholics are less likely to be in the Highest religiosity group both as teenagers and as emerging adults. Almost 40 percent of non-Catholic teenagers attend worship services very frequently, pray at least once a day, and report that religious faith is very important in their lives. Only one of the Catholic categories, Somewhat Catholic, surpasses even 30 percent. The other Catholic categories are even lower. Similarly, in emerging adulthood, 27 percent of non-Catholics belong to the Highest religiosity group (the light bar on the far right side), while all Catholic types are lower. Non-Catholic American youth decrease in their religiousness between the teenage and emerging adult years, but they remain more religious at the high end than do Catholics. Less than 20 percent of all of the more religious Catholic categories belong to the Highest group as emerging

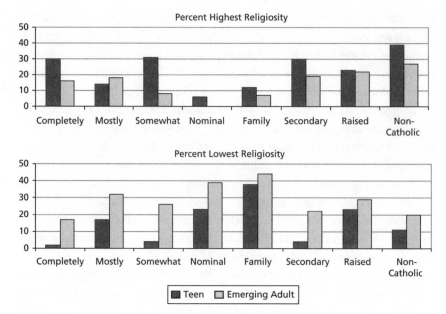

Figure 5.1 Percent of each Catholic category in highest and lowest religiosity group as teens and emerging adults (percents) (N = 2,432) [Weighted].

adults. As a first finding, then, we can say that Catholic teenagers and emerging adults lag behind their non-Catholic peers in being at the very highest levels of religious faith and practice.

The lower panel of Figure 5.1, which focuses on the lowest level of religiousness, demonstrates a slightly different pattern. Here higher percentages indicate more respondents being among the *least* religious. Unlike what we saw in the upper panel, here we observe three Catholic categories that *during the teenage years* have a smaller percentage of youth in this Lowest religiosity group than their non-Catholic peers. Eleven percent of non-Catholic teenagers exhibit very low levels of worship attendance, prayer, and self-reported importance of faith. Comparatively, less than 5 percent of the Completely, Somewhat, and Secondary Catholic categories exhibit these very low levels of religiousness. So during the teenage years, some types of Catholic youth are less likely to be among the least religious than their non-Catholic peers.

That pattern changes dramatically by the time young people reach emerging adulthood. For all but one Catholic type (Completely Catholic), Catholic emerging adults are more likely to be in the Lowest religious category than their non-Catholic peers. This suggests that a sizeable number of Catholic youth from the Somewhat and Secondary categories, especially, significantly decrease their religious practices over time, thereby increasing each of these categories' numbers in the Lowest group. Even the Completely Catholic category (while having a smaller percentage of emerging adults who are in the Lowest religiosity group than non-Catholics) reflects a significant increase in this very low religiousness group. As teenagers, only 2 percent of Completely Catholics were in the Lowest religiosity group, but by emerging adulthood the number increases to 17 percent.[1] Although the number of non-Catholics in this Lowest group nearly doubles between the teenage years and emerging adulthood, even that change is not as dramatic as that of many Catholic types.[2]

In addition to these differences between Catholic and non-Catholic youth, we also see several interesting patterns across Catholic groups. The Completely Catholic teenage type has one of the largest percentages of Highest religiousness and the smallest percentage of Lowest religiosity during both adolescence and emerging adulthood among Catholics. Perhaps surprisingly, the Somewhat Catholic type has a higher percentage of youth who are in the Highest group and a lower proportion in the Lowest group than the Mostly Catholic type. Even though the latter group appears to be more obviously Catholic, they do not express their religiousness at higher levels in this analysis. These differences diminish, and even reverse in some cases, however, in emerging adulthood. That suggests that the Mostly Catholic young people, although somewhat less religious during the teenage years, maintain a higher level of religious faith and practice into emerging adulthood than Somewhat Catholic youth. Finally, the Family Catholic type shows the highest percentage of teens and emerging adults in the Lowest religiosity category. Catholic youth who have religious parents but who do not personally express signs of being seriously Catholic are the least likely to frequently attend Mass and pray and to say that religious faith is very important in their lives.

The first general developmental trend in the lives of Catholic youth, then, is a consistent decrease over time in the proportion of each Catholic category in the Highest religiosity group and an associated increase in the percent in the Lowest religiosity group. The Completely and Somewhat Catholic types provide the clearest demonstrations of this pattern. These two types have a higher percentage of teenagers attending Mass regularly, praying frequently, and reporting that faith is very important than any other Catholic category. Yet both of these types of Catholics see those proportions cut in half by emerging adulthood. The Completely type shows a decline of 15 percentage points, while the Somewhat Catholic type reflects a dramatic 23-point drop. These two Catholic categories also have the sharpest corresponding rise in the percentage of members who move into the Lowest religiosity group by emerging adulthood. Though the Completely and Somewhat Catholic types have the smallest percentage of respondents displaying Lowest religiousness during the teenage years, both show a big increase in that category by emerging adulthood. The Completely and Somewhat Catholic types thus contain the most highly religious teenagers, but also appear to be the most susceptible to a loss of youth into low levels of religiousness by emerging adulthood.

Two Catholic categories do not follow this trend of decreasing Highest religiosity and increasing Lowest religiosity. Teenagers whom we identify as Catholic because they report being raised Catholic are the most stable over time in terms of being in the Highest and Lowest religiosity groups. The Raised Catholic type demonstrates a decrease of only one percentage point in its membership in the Highest religiousness group, and a relatively small six-point increase in the Lowest group between adolescence and emerging adulthood. These changes are less than one-half of that experienced by the other Catholic categories. Raised Catholics do, however, still display a general decline in religiousness over time. In results not presented here, the Raised Catholic category shows a substantial decrease in its membership in the Moderate religiousness group and a concurrent increase of 18 percentage points in the Minimal religiousness group.[3] That tells us that teens who were raised Catholic but then stopped practicing their faith tend to maintain their former level of religiousness as they transition into emerging adulthood, but only when they start at either the highest or lowest level. If they are somewhere in the middle of religious faith and practice as teenagers, they tend to slide to a lower level of religiosity, although usually without abandoning their faith completely.

The other category that shows a somewhat nuanced pattern is the Mostly Catholic type. As noted above, this set of Catholic youth has a smaller proportion of respondents in the Highest religiosity group and a larger proportion in the Lowest religiosity than both the Completely and (surprisingly) the Somewhat Catholic categories. Unlike these other two types, however, the Mostly Catholic youth category actually *increases* its proportion of respondents in the Highest religiousness group by emerging adulthood. It is the only type of youth to show an increase in religiosity over this time. The proportion of Mostly Catholic respondents in the Highest group only grows by four percentage points, admittedly, but when every other Catholic type is losing upwards of 10 percentage points, any increase at all is a substantial move against the norm. The results of other analyses not shown here suggest that Mostly Catholic youth tend to "split" in terms of religiousness as they become emerging adults. While most youth show a general decline, Mostly Catholic youth "migrate" from the two middle levels of religiousness (that is, Moderately and Minimally religious) into either the highest or lowest category. So the Mostly Catholic type does experience a 15-point drop in its membership in the Lowest religiosity group once they reach emerging adulthood. But at the same time, we see an increase in the Highest religiosity group. This suggests that teenagers of the Mostly Catholic type end up either becoming very dedicated to or very detached from religious faith and practice by the time they enter emerging adulthood.

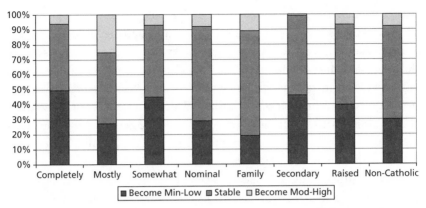

Figure 5.2   Religious trajectories by Catholic categories (N = 2,432) [Weighted]*.
* Stable is defined as staying in the Lowest or Minimum categories of religiousness, or staying in the
Moderately or Highest religiousness groups, meaning that some teens do change religiousness
categories in emerging adulthood but are still counted as Stable. For example, someone who moves
from the Lowest category to the Minimal category is counted as being "Stable" in this figure.

To more directly display the type and level of developmental changes underway, Figure 5.2 shows the percent of each Catholic type that (1) moved from
one of the higher two religiousness groups as teens into the lower two groups as
emerging adults; (2) made the inverse change; or (3) maintained a relatively
stable level of religiousness during the transition into emerging adulthood. (This
figure is different from Figure 5.1 because whereas Figure 5.1 only examined respondents in the Highest and Lowest categories, Figure 5.2 covers all respondents, with "movement" meaning that a respondent crosses the low–high
threshold. For example, someone who moves from the Lowest category to the
Minimal category is counted as "Stable" in this figure.) The most prominent
trend in this graph is the high level of stability across the Catholic types. Approximately half (or more) of every category *maintains* the same high or low
level of religiousness measured during the teenage years in the transition into
emerging adulthood. Despite the popular perception of this transition as an un-
stable time of losing (or perhaps finding) one's religious faith entirely, the majority of American Catholic young people actually maintain similar levels of Mass
attendance, personal prayer, and self-rated importance of faith when they
become emerging adults. Relative *stability*, not dramatic change, is thus the
norm for all Catholic types during these transitional years.

The second clear trend evident in Figure 5.2, reinforcing what we have already noticed, is a substantial movement among those who do change toward
the lower levels of religiousness, with only minimal change in the opposite direction toward becoming more religious. Of the Catholic youth in each category
who do not maintain their level of religiousness across this time period, more

than 75 percent move toward the lower two levels of religiosity. In all but two groups, less than 10 percent of youth move upwardly into the Moderate or Highest religiousness categories. (The two categories that are the exceptions are the Mostly and Family Catholic types.) So when Catholic teenagers do change their religiousness in the transition to emerging adulthood, the substantial majority of them *decrease* their frequency of Mass attendance and personal prayer and rate faith as *less* important, with only a small minority becoming more religious in this transition. The most striking counter-example is the Mostly Catholic type, about one-quarter of whom became more religious. That is likely, we think, because the Mostly Catholic teenagers have enough religion-strengthening factors in their lives to seriously strengthen their Catholic faith and practice, while still being not so strongly Catholic as to have no room for upward movement.

A final item to note in Figure 5.2 is a relatively high degree of similarity with regard to stability and change across Catholic categories, and even with the non-Catholics. Although we see some differences across these types, they are actually quite similar in terms of their overall patterns of change. The Non-Catholic, Completely Catholic, Somewhat Catholic, Nominal Catholic, and Raised Catholic types all show only a six- to eight-point increase in their membership in the two highest levels of religiousness between the teenage and emerging adult years. Non-Catholics show a slightly higher level of stability than these Catholic groups (62 percent compared to between 45 and 55 percent), but their general trend strongly resembles that of Catholics. Only the Mostly Catholic youth and Family Catholic youth stand out as being a bit different. The Mostly Catholic type exhibits the largest increase in the proportion of youth becoming more religious in the transition to emerging adulthood, with more than 25 percent of teenagers in this category moving into the Moderate or Highest religious group as emerging adults. The Family Catholic category, on the other hand, demonstrated the highest level of stability, with 70 percent of youth in this category maintaining their previous level of religiousness, whatever that was, when they became young adults.

Because of this similarity, in the remainder of this chapter we place what we consider to be the most definitively Catholic types into one "big tent" classification of Catholic youth. As we did in a previous chapter, we classify any youth who belongs to the Completely, Mostly, Somewhat, Nominally, and Family Catholic categories as "Catholic" for all of the remaining analyses. Although there are some differences between these categories, this consolidation will ease the interpretability of the following results, and we can keep in mind that our primary conclusions also hold true when the categories are separated.

As a final examination of the general patterns of change in religiosity between the teenage and emerging adult years, Figure 5.3 presents a more direct comparison of this larger Catholic grouping with non-Catholic youth. As already

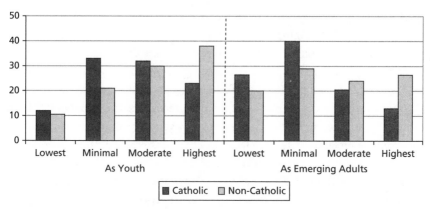

Figure 5.3   Religious trajectories among Catholic and non-Catholic youth (N = 2,432).

noted, both kinds of youth exhibit a decline in religiosity during the transition to emerging adulthood, with a decrease in the proportion of respondents in the Highest religiosity group and an increase in the Lowest religiosity group. Similar proportions of Catholics and non-Catholics are in the Lowest religiousness group at both points in time: about 10 percent of Catholics and non-Catholics are in this group as teenagers, and about 20 to 26 percent by emerging adulthood. Catholics and non-Catholics also have comparable percentages of youth and emerging adults in the Moderately religious group: about 30 percent of respondents as teenagers and just below 25 percent by emerging adulthood.

The biggest differences between the Catholics and non-Catholics appear in the Highest and the Minimal religiosity groups. A significantly larger proportion of non-Catholics than Catholics belong to the Highest religiosity group as teenagers: the gap is more than 15 percentage points. And although the absolute percent of highly religious non-Catholics decreases in emerging adulthood, the difference between non-Catholics and Catholics remains similar. Non-Catholics, therefore, start out with more youth who frequently attend church and pray and who rate religion as more important in their lives than Catholics; and a smaller percentage of non-Catholics than Catholics abandon or less frequently exhibit these behaviors in their transition to emerging adulthood. By contrast, Catholics have more teenagers in the Minimal religious group than non-Catholics by a gap of 12 percentage points. And again, although both groups have significant numbers of respondents move into this lower religious group by emerging adulthood, Catholics remain more likely to belong to the Minimal group than non-Catholics. Overall, non-Catholics are more likely than Catholics to exhibit a high degree of religious devotion both as teenagers and emerging adults.

Summary Conclusions. We can draw several initial conclusions from these findings. First, young non-Catholics surpass Catholics at the highest levels of religiosity, as defined by worship attendance, frequency of prayer, and the self-rated importance of religious faith. And this difference does not change during the transition to emerging adulthood. Based on these three markers of religiosity, Catholic youth are simply not as devoted as non-Catholic youth. However, at the very low end of religiosity, Catholics are comparable to, and perhaps slightly more religious than, non-Catholics both as teenagers and emerging adults. Although Catholics are not as highly devoted overall as non-Catholics, it is not because they are extremely unreligious, but rather because Catholics are more likely to fall somewhere in the middle levels of religiousness. They tend to gravitate more toward moderate levels of religious faith and practice. Second, we have discovered a general trend of religious stability over time among Catholic (and non-Catholic) youth. Most Catholic young people sustain a relatively constant level of Mass attendance, personal prayer, and self-rated importance of faith as they become emerging adults. However, the teenagers who *do* change religiously are more likely to become less religious rather than more so. Very few Catholic teenagers who attend Mass rarely, pray infrequently, and consider religion unimportant in their lives become more religiously devoted by these measures once they enter emerging adulthood. In becoming emerging adults, Catholic teenagers thus appear either to maintain the same level of religious faith and practice or to decline in it, with little chance of significantly increasing their religious faith and observance. In some cases, as mentioned above, the type of Catholic that teenagers are will influence how much religious change they experience.

Factors Shaping Religious Trajectories

Seeing the patterns of religious change (and stability) in Catholic youth as they transition into emerging adulthood raises the key question of what factors causally influence these different trajectories. If we know that a significant portion of Catholic youth show a decline in religious faith and practice over time as they become emerging adults, we should also want to know which features of their lives as teenagers contributed to this drop. Similarly, we can examine the factors associated with maintaining a constant level of religiosity and even those aspects that lead a small number of Catholic youth to become more religious as they enter emerging adulthood. To answer these questions, we will now investigate how different aspects of the lives of Catholic teenagers are correlated with different levels of religiousness in emerging adulthood.

Table 5.1 presents a variety of such relevant factors of teenagers' lives, listed in the column on the far left side, for which we calculated statistical correlations. The other columns list each factor's correlation value (zero-order Pearson's r) with each of the three components of our overall religiousness measure

Table 5.1 **Zero-Order Pearson's *r* Correlations for Three Key Third-Wave Religion Outcome Variables and Multiple First-Wave Variables (N = 670) [Weighted]**

	Attendance at Mass w3	Importance of Faith w3	Frequency of Praying Alone w3	Strength of Correlation
Attendance at Mass w3	1.00			
Importance of faith w3	.56	1.00		strong
Frequency of praying alone w3	.46	.62	1.00	strong
Importance of faith w1	.30	.47	.36	moderately strong
Highly religious parents w1	.36	.36	.23	moderately strong
Frequency of praying alone w1	.24	.35	.46	moderately strong
Personal religious experiences w1	.23	.32	.34	moderately strong
Attendance at Mass w1	.39	.24	.20	moderately strong
Satisfaction with parish w1	.33	.26	.20	moderately strong
Believes in divine miracles w1	.25	.25	.28	moderately strong
Frequency reading scripture w1	.22	.23	.25	moderately strong
Supportive religious adults w1	.21	.26	.25	moderately strong
Frequency of Sunday school attendance w1	.22	.14	.11	moderately strong
Satisfaction with youth group w1	.22	.16	.12	moderately strong
Church has youth minister w1	.21	.16	.12	moderately strong

continued

Table 5.1 **(continued)**

	Attendance at Mass w3	Importance of Faith w3	Frequency of Praying Alone w3	Strength of Correlation
Number of religious friends w1	.15	.24	.23	moderately strong
Frequently teased about religion w1	.15	.18	.22	moderately strong
Employs religious criteria first in moral decision-making w1	.16	.16	.18	weak
Believes in abstaining from sex before marriage w1	.15	.17	.14	weak
Believes other teens look down on religion w1	.08	.09	.09	weak
Has engaged in oral sex w1	−.10	−.04[n.s.]	−.08	weak
Hispanic	.08[n.s.]	.14	.06[n.s.]	weak
Number of extracurricular religious activities w1	.09	.08[n.s.]	.05[n.s.]	very weak
Number of mission trips w1	.04[n.s.]	.01[n.s.]	−.03[n.s.]	very weak
Attends a Catholic high school w1	.05[n.s.]	−.01[n.s.]	.02[n.s.]	very weak
Has doubts about religious beliefs w1	−.00[n.s.]	.05[n.s.]	.06[n.s.]	very weak
Catholic Category as Teen[1]				
Completely	.21	.13	.10	moderately strong
Mostly	−.05[n.s.]	.07[n.s.]	.04[n.s.]	very weak
Somewhat	.03[n.s.]	−.04[n.s.]	−.05[n.s.]	very weak
Nominally	−.09	−.08	−.03[n.s.]	very weak
Family	−.20	−.16	−.10	moderately strong

Note: All correlations are significant at p < .05 level, except when labeled [n.s.] (for "not significant").
[1]Each Catholic type compared to all of the other types combined.

Source: National Survey of Youth and Religion, 2002–2003, 2007–2008.

described above.[4] Values that are closer to 1.0 indicate a very strong positive correlation, meaning that high levels of that characteristic among teens (row) are strongly associated with high levels of the emerging adult outcome (column). Values closer to −1.0 show a strong inverse relationship (that is, high levels of the youth factor are related to *low* levels of the emerging adult outcome). Values close to zero indicate that the given characteristic in the teenage years does not have a strong relationship with the outcome in emerging adulthood: the relationship between the two is weak or non-existent. The teen-era factors are organized from top to bottom according to the strength of their (bivariate) relationships, and the final column on the right provides a description of that strength based on standard criteria for interpreting such correlation values.

Table 5.1 reveals a large number of factors during the teenage years (labeled as w1, since they were measured in the first wave of the NSYR) that have a moderately strong relationship with higher Mass attendance, more frequent prayer, and greater self-reported importance of religious faith in emerging adulthood (labeled w3). Among them, having highly religious parents, praying frequently, having several personal religious experiences (such as having a prayer answered), attending Mass frequently, and being satisfied with one's parish as a teenager stand out as particularly strongly associated with a higher degree of religiousness in emerging adulthood. On the other hand, participation in extracurricular activities sponsored by religious organizations, involvement in mission trips, attending a Catholic high school, and having doubts about one's religious beliefs are very weakly or not at all correlated with greater religious faith and practice during emerging adulthood. Other measured factors fall somewhere in the middle between the seemingly influential and not influential. Finally, the bottom part of the table presents correlations in emerging adulthood religiousness with the different Catholic types that respondents belonged to as teenagers, as described above. The results show only weak relationships between Catholic type and religiosity in emerging adulthood, as even the strongest correlations of Catholic types with the outcome measures are still fairly low, all being below 0.3. (This last finding also validates our decision to continue to analyze the larger Catholic group as a whole, rather than broken down into sub-types, in this chapter.)

Identifying Independent Effects. These correlations are helpful as a starting point, but they cannot tell us much about what actually causes different religious outcomes in emerging adulthood. The weakness of these measures is that they examine the association of each factor with religious outcomes without taking into account many other factors that may affect that correlation. The lives of youth do not consist of a collection of isolated factors. Rather, many of the behaviors and characteristics listed in Table 5.1 are likely related to and exerting influence on others. So looking only at these (bivariate) relationships can cause us to overlook the true causal relationships and so misunderstand the story. Some factors may look more important in Table 5.1 than they really are, because they are actually related to other factors not being taken into account. For example, hypothetically, teenagers' attendance at Mass may not actually be that influential on their religiosity as young adults once we account for how much they like their parish. If this is the case, the only reason Mass attendance seems important when viewed as a simple correlation is that it also reflects how much youth like their parish. Furthermore, some factors may wrongly appear unimportant in isolation, as their actual effects could be "suppressed" in bivariate analysis since it does not account for the influence of other factors. For example, hypothetically, we might discover that the belief that one should abstain from sex is strongly related to emerging adult religiousness only after we account for whether youth have engaged in oral sex.

One way to untangle these complicated relationships is through the use of "multiple regression" statistical techniques. These statistical methods allow us to consider all possibly relevant factors, including demographic variables, at once in one model, and they isolate the specific effect of each variable on emerging adult religiousness, "net of" all of the other factors.[5] After we "control" for the independent influence of all other factors, we can discern which measured factors from the teenage years are actually most important. The statistical results from our series of multiple regression analyses are extensive and complex, not worth showing here in detail. We therefore present only a descriptive summary of our findings in Table 5.2. This table describes the influence of each factor from the teenage years on our combined religious outcome measures (Mass attendance, prayer, and self-reported importance of faith combined).[6]

Like Table 5.1, this table is arranged from top to bottom in descending order of importance, so that factors with the strongest and most consistent influence on Catholics' religiousness in emerging adulthood are presented at the top, followed by factors that either have a weaker association or only show an apparent influence in some analyses. The few factors that show no significant influence on religiosity are listed at the bottom. We see in this table a group of six teenage-era factors that exert a strong and consistently positive impact on emerging adult religiosity: considering faith important, having religious parents, believing in divine miracles, having relational bonds to religious adults, attending a Catholic high school, and frequently reading the Bible. After we controlled for possibly confounding or otherwise associated demographic and religious variables, these are the factors present during the teenage years that seem to matter most for religious faith and practice in the emerging adult years.

The next group of factors, which are somewhat important but consistently so, includes having numerous personal religious experiences (such as having a prayer answered or experiencing a miracle), regularly attending Sunday school

Table 5.2 **Summary of Factors Measured during the Teenage Years Associated Significantly with Higher Religiousness during Emerging Adulthood**

Teenage Period Factors	Description of Teenage Period Factor
Consistently Very Important	
High Importance of Religious Faith	Professed greater importance of religious faith in everyday life
Strong Parental Religion	More religiously committed parents (greater religious service attendance and professed importance of faith)
Belief in Divine Miracles	Believing in divine miracles
Many Supportive Religious Adults	Enjoying more adults in religious congregation to whom youth can turn for support, advice, or help
Catholic High School	Attended a Catholic high school
Frequent Reading Scriptures	Reading scriptures more frequently
Consistently Somewhat Important	
Has Religious Experiences	Making a commitment to God and/or experiencing a miracle, prayers answered, and/or a "powerful spiritual experience"
Frequent Sunday School Attendance	More frequent Sunday school attendance
Frequent Personal Prayer	Greater frequency of personal prayer
Frequent Mass Attendance	More religious service attendance
More Religious Friends	Greater proportion of close teenage friends are religious
Mission Trips[a]	Doing more religious mission trips and service projects (a negative association)
Conditionally Somewhat Important	
Decide Morality by Religion	Reliance for moral guidance on "what God or scripture says is right" (instead of what makes one feel happy, what helps one to get ahead, or the advice of a parent, teacher, or other respected adult)

continued

Table 5.2 (**continued**)

Teenage Period Factors	Description of Teenage Period Factor
Satisfaction with parish	Combined from the teenager reporting that (1) his or her religious congregation is a good place to talk about serious issues like family problems, alcohol, or trouble at school; (2) he or she would attend the same congregation if it was totally up to the teen to choose; and (3) he or she does not think other teenagers in the congregation are hypocrites
Church Has a Youth Pastor	The primary place of Mass attendance has a dedicated youth pastor
Likes Youth Group	Reports liking their religious youth groups
Believing Sex Belongs in Marriage	Believing that people should not have sex until they are married
Made Fun of for Religious Faith	Has been made fun of by peers for religious faith
Few Religious Doubts	Expresses few or no doubts about religious beliefs
Hispanic	Reports being Hispanic or Latino
Not Independently Important	
Number of Religious Activities	Greater participation in activities at religious congregation other than regular Mass attendance
Sexual Chastity	Has not had oral sex or sexual intercourse
Believe Teens Look Down on Religion	Agrees that other students in school look down at people who are religious

Note: Factors are ranked in general order of importance within categories based on the magnitude of their standardized regression coefficients for significant variables. [a] Taking more religious mission trips as a teen has a *negative* impact on emerging adult religiosity.

Source: National Survey of Youth and Religion 2002–2003, 2007–2008.

(which would also include classes prior to receiving confirmation), praying alone frequently, attending Mass often, having more friends who are religious, and participating in short-term religious mission trips. Interestingly, this final factor, taking mission or service trips, is *negatively* associated with emerging adult religiousness. Although mission trips are typically considered a mechanism increasing commitment to religious faith, once we control for other religious characteristics, they appear to be related to *decreases* in religiosity by emerging adulthood. The finding about mission trips is unexpected, and we cannot fully explain it with the current data. More research ought to be conducted to better understand the long-term impact of youth mission/service trips, particularly among Catholic teens.[7]

The next eight factors are only marginally influential, and the final three show no signs of significantly affecting Catholics' religiosity as emerging adults.[8] Of the factors related to religious practice, having highly religious parents, believing in divine miracles, having ties to religious adults, attending a Catholic high school, and reading scriptures are the most influential. Other characteristics play some role in determining the religiosity of Catholic emerging adults, but not as large a role as these top six.

Stepping back to examine the full list of factors, we can make a broader assessment of what affects Catholic emerging adults' religiosity. In order for Catholic teenagers to maintain or achieve a high level of religious commitment and practice as they become emerging adults, three primary factors are key. First, teens must have strong *bonds to religiously committed and supportive family and friends*. Parents are the most important, but knowing supportive non-parental adults in one's parish and having friends who are religious also increase the level of religiosity in emerging adulthood. Second, *internalizing Catholic beliefs* is also crucial for teenagers to become highly religious Catholic emerging adults. Considering faith important for shaping everyday life is the single strongest predictor of religious devotion in emerging adulthood. Believing in divine miracles as a teen and having personal religious experiences—either "cognitive" experiences, such as making a commitment to live one's life for God, or powerful "spiritual" experiences—also associate with high religiosity in emerging adults. These factors all show that Catholic teenagers have accepted the importance and truth of their religious faith to the point that it has become an integral part of how they think about and experience the world. The third and final set of influential factors is *regular religious behaviors and practices*. Not only must Catholic teenagers have close relationships with religious people and believe in their religion, but they also must engage in spiritual and liturgical practice to sustain or reach high levels of religious commitment in emerging adulthood. Reading the Bible, attending Sunday school or confirmation classes, attending Mass, and praying frequently are the most influential of religious behaviors and practices.

Later in this chapter we will examine how these factors together operate to lead to higher or lower levels of religious faith and practice among Catholic emerging adults, and we will explore why these factors may exert the causal impact they do. For now, we can conclude that Catholic teenagers who enjoy strong relationships with religious friends and family members, who develop and personally internalize the Catholic faith such that it is important in their lives, and who participate in basic Catholic devotional and sacramental practices are the most likely to be strong Catholics in emerging adulthood.

Noticeably absent from the previous discussion was the factor of attending a Catholic high school. As Table 5.2 shows, this factor has one of the stronger associations with greater emerging adult religiosity.[9] It is interesting to discover this association given that the in-depth interviews, discussed in Chapter 4, did not reveal a substantial, positive influence of attending a Catholic high school. This finding illustrates the utility of a mixed methods approach, as the quantitative analysis, which can use a greater sample of Catholic youth, has revealed a potentially important relationship that may have been obscured when relying on the smaller interview population (and the even smaller subsample of Catholic interviewees who attended such a high school).

Trying to classify it with the other important factors, however, is challenging. Teenagers attend Catholic high schools for different reasons. One could argue that it is another sign of the importance of relational bonds to other religious people. It is safe to assume, all else being equal, that youth who attend Catholic high schools have more chances to develop strong relationships with highly religious adults and peers. But it could also be an indicator of frequent participation in Catholic devotional practices, as many Catholic high schools deliberately set time aside during the school day for the study of scriptures or personal prayer. Of course, it may be a qualitatively different type of influence. Because of this complexity and the larger interest in how attending Catholic high schools affects the lives of Catholic youth, we devote a full chapter (Chapter 7) to more detailed analysis of this subject and leave it out of the remaining discussion in this chapter.

We are confident in the statistical analyses that we have used to generate these findings, but a word of caution on interpreting their meaning is in order. The effects that we have identified apply to the majority of Catholic youth, to the "typical" Catholic youth, if there is such a thing, but definitely not to each particular Catholic. For a factor to be judged significantly related to stronger emerging adult religiosity it must show that relation for a major portion of Catholic youth. We are talking about probabilities, not determinants. It is therefore entirely possible that several of the factors that we have claimed are extremely influential on religiosity may not matter at all for some Catholic youth. There are certainly Catholic teens with highly religious parents, for example, who end up showing no signs of religiosity as emerging adults. Still, if more Catholic youth with highly religious parents end up being highly religious as emerging adults than youth without religious parents, we can safely say that the religious commitments and practices of parents significantly associate with and likely causally influence emerging adult religiousness. It is even more important to highlight this aspect of statistical methods with regard to the factors that appear *not* to impact emerging adult religiosity. For example, participating in religiously spon-sored extracurricular activities during the teenage years has no effect on the reli-gious observance of the majority of Catholics as emerging adults. But that does not negate the (positive) influence that these activities may have for some Cath-olic youth. These findings are not "one size fits all" or deterministic in the case of any particular young Catholic. They speak about probabilities operating among Catholic teens as a population. So seemingly unimportant factors can dramati-cally shape the religious lives of some Catholic youth, even if that influence does not show up in statistical analysis of the entire population. None of our findings is necessarily determinative in any given case; rather, our conclusions describe probabilities and tendencies applying to groups.

Similarly, we must remember the age range with which we are dealing when thinking about how these teenage-era factors shape religious trajectories. The analysis we present here can only speak to the influence that characteristics and behaviors from the teenage years seem to exert as these youth reach early emerg-ing adulthood, ages 18 to 23. It is quite possible that several of the most influen-tial factors identified here will stop mattering past this age range. And some of the factors that appear less influential for this stage in life could prove very im-portant in shaping Catholics' religious lives in later adulthood. Furthermore, the current analysis is not able to speak to what factors lead to certain Catholic teens exhibiting the characteristics and behaviors we measured. That is, because our survey began with teenagers between the ages of 13 and 17, we cannot identify what childhood characteristics encourage some Catholic teens to consider reli-gion very important or attend religious services frequently. Even though we be-lieve these teen-era factors have emergent properties that influence religiousness during young adulthood (net of the properties that produced them), under-standing the preceding link in the causal chain clearly would be important. While we can learn a lot from NSYR data, then, we must also be aware of the limits of our findings reveal. The factors may work differently in the case of any given Catholic youth than they do for the majority. And the time in life when these factors seem to have most influence is limited by our data not extending earlier into childhood or later into adulthood.

Magnitude of Effects. Merely identifying the most significant independent as-sociations does not tell the whole story. More important is assessing the magni-tude of the influence of these factors. Not only do we want to know which fac-tors during the teenage years are likely to increase or sustain Catholic faith and practice in emerging adulthood, but we also want to see the extent to which these factors influence that outcome. Figure 5.4 provides a visual depiction of the size of the influence of each factor, displaying the predicted level of religious-ness in emerging adulthood based on the level of the stronger factors identified in Table 5.2 (with the exception of attending a Catholic school). The X-axis

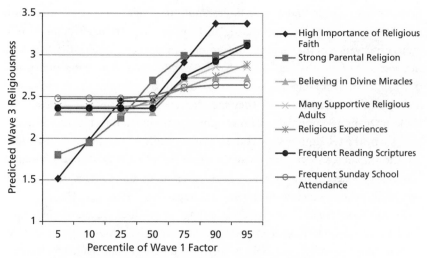

Figure 5.4 Predicted value of level of emerging adult (wave 3) religiousness as influenced by important first-wave factors in full ordered logistic regression (N = 661). Source: National Surveys of Youth and Religion 2002–2003, 2007–2008. Note: The Y-axis scores (1–4) are the predicted outcome score in terms of the logit function; the values are calculated by first multiplying each estimated coefficient by its variable's mean, except for the variable of interest which varies by percentile value. These products are then summed, producing a predicted outcome for that level of the variable of interest, with all other variables set at their mean (this method is similar to the calculation of a predicted value in OLS regression, but the estimation of an ordered logistic regression model transforms the dependent variable into a log odds through the use of a logit function, a transformation that eliminates the direct comparability of these predicted values to the original scale of the dependent variable). Attended Catholic high school has been omitted from the figure and will be dealt with in Chapter 7. Because believing in divine miracles is a dichotomous variable (i.e., yes or no), only two predicted values are calculated.

(horizontal, ranging from 5 to 95) shows the level of each factor during the teenage years. The height of the line on the Y-axis (vertical, ranging from 1 to 3.5) shows the predicted level of religiousness in emerging adulthood. The steepness of each line, moving from left to right, indicates how strongly the given factor influences religiosity during emerging adulthood—the steeper the line, the stronger the association; the flatter, the weaker.

This graph dramatically illustrates the major influence of the importance of faith in Catholic teenagers' lives and the religious commitment of their parents on their religious lives as emerging adults, which are denoted by the lines with diamond and square markers respectively. They show the strongest effects. When Catholic teenagers report their faith is not at all important in their lives and have parents who are not very religious (the far left of the graph), their religiousness in emerging adulthood is predicted to be very low. As each of these two factors increases, we see a steep rise in the predicted level of emerging adulthood religiousness. We expect teenagers who consider their faith very important and who have strongly religious parents to be among the most highly religious as emerging adults. The other factors that we have identified (belief in miracles, etc.) also show a substantial influence on emerging adult religiousness, although not to the degree of the self-reported importance of faith or parents' religiosity. Those appear to be the two most important factors.

An interesting finding among the remaining factors concerns reading the Bible. This practice shows a flat line for each level below the 50th percentile— the left half of the graph representing the one-half who read the Bible least frequently. When Catholic teenagers read scripture more frequently, we see a sharp increase in their predicted level of emerging adulthood religiousness. On the right side, reflecting more frequent reading of the Bible, this increase actually parallels the large effect of having highly religious parents. Reading scriptures *in*frequently, therefore, does not seem to hinder emerging adults' religiousness as severely as believing one's faith is unimportant to life or having minimally religious parents. But reading scriptures above the average frequency increases the likelihood that a Catholic teenager will become a highly religious emerging adult as much as having highly religious parents does.

Table 5.3 provides an even more definitive assessment of these differences. The columns in this table show the percent of Catholic teens who end up in the Highest religiousness category as emerging adults, based on the level of each factor shown in the rows.[10] For example, only 5 percent of Catholic teenagers who ranked at or below the 25th percentile on the importance-of-faith variable (that is, who said that religion is not very or not at all important in their lives) went on to be in the group of Highest religiousness in emerging adulthood. Comparatively, 26 percent of Catholic teenagers who were at or above the 75th percentile on that variable (who said their religious faith was very or extremely important in their daily lives) end up in the Highest level of religiousness as emerging adults. In other words, teens who consider religion quite important are *five times* more likely to be very religious as young adults than teens who consider faith unimportant. Comparing other rows and columns in this table tells us how likely (or unlikely) Catholic teenagers are to be highly religious as emerging adults, given the level of various other factors measured during their teenage years.

It is important to remember that only 13 percent of all Catholic emerging adults belong to the Highest religious group. So even though only about 20 to 25 percent of teens in the highest quartile of each factor ends up being in the Highest religiousness group, those percentages are almost double what we would expect by chance. For instance, Catholic teenagers in the highest category of enjoying supportive religious adults in their lives have an almost one-in-four chance of being in the Highest religiosity group as emerging adults (24 percent). This may seem low, but again, this probability is nearly twice that of the one-in-eight

Table 5.3 Percent of Emerging Adults in the Highest Level of Third-Wave Religiousness by Teenage Years Factors (percents) (N = 661) [Weighted]

Teenage Years (Wave 1) Factors	25th Percentile and Lower of Wave 1 Factor Distribution	Middle 50 Percent of Wave 1 Factor Distribution	Greater than 75th Percentile of Wave 1 Factor Distribution
Importance of Religious Faith	5	5	26
Parental Religion	3	14	24
Believes in Divine Miracles	9	---[b]	18
Supportive Religious Adults	8	13	24
Attended Catholic High School	13	---[b]	16
Frequency of Reading Scriptures	11	9	20
Religious Experiences	7	8	20
Attendance at Sunday School	12	11	19
Combined: Importance of Religious Faith + Parental Religion + Supportive Religious Adults in Congregation + Believe in Divine Miracles[a]	0	---[b]	48
Combined: Frequency of Reading Scriptures + Religious Experiences + Attendance at Sunday School[a]	8	28	31

Note: [a] Indicates percent of cases that score in the given percentile group on *all* variables listed who at Wave 3 are at the highest religion level. [b] The variables related to believing in miracles and attending a Catholic high school are coded dichotomously (yes/no), so no middle percentile category exists in those variables or the combination that includes one of them.

Source: National Surveys of Youth and Religion 2002–2003, 2007–2008.

chance (13 percent) that teenagers in the middle 50 percent (between the 25th and 75th percentile) on this factor have of ending up there; and it is three times the one-in-twelve chance (8 percent) that teenagers have who come from the lowest quartile of this factor. So while reporting that religious faith is very important in everyday life and having highly religious parents and strong ties to other religious adults does not guarantee that Catholic teenagers will five years later be highly religious emerging adults, they are more than three times more likely to be highly religious than Catholic teenagers who lack these factors in the teenage years. In short, the odds are low that *any* given Catholic teenager will be among the most highly religious adults as an 18- to 23-year-old, but the odds are even more greatly diminished for those for whom faith is not important and who do not have highly religious parents and other adults in their lives.

The other factors in Table 5.3 show similar patterns, though less dramatic ones. Catholic teenagers who do not read the Bible frequently, do not believe in divine miracles, and do not attend Sunday school or confirmation classes have slightly greater chances (compared to those who lack the crucial factors above) of still becoming a highly religious emerging adult. Teenagers in the lowest quartile on these characteristics have approximately a 10 percent chance of ending up in the Highest group as emerging adults. Still, that likelihood is almost one-half that of teenagers who are in the highest quartile on these factors, again demonstrating the importance of these factors in setting teenagers on a trajectory toward higher religiosity. (Again, we will discuss the question of attending a Catholic high school in another chapter.)

Of course, many Catholic teenagers belong to the highest and lowest percentile groups on several factors together. These variables usually overlap and reinforce each other. Catholic teenagers who report that faith is very important in their lives are also likely to have highly religious parents and believe in divine miracles. And teens who score highly on all three factors should have an even greater chance of ending up in the Highest religious group as emerging adults. Likewise, teenagers in the lowest quartile on these factors in combination should be especially unlikely to end up in the Highly religious group. The bottom two rows of Table 5.3 show two examples of these combinations. The first combination shows the extreme unlikelihood of Catholic teenagers becoming highly religious emerging adults if they begin in the lowest quartile of self-rated importance of faith *and* religious parents *and* supportive religious adults *and* religious experiences.[11] No such Catholic teenagers in our sample (0 percent) later become emerging adults who frequently attend Mass and pray and say that their religious faith is very important in their lives. By contrast, Catholic youth who are in the highest quartile on all three of these factors have a 48 percent chance of ending up in the Highest religiousness group as emerging adults. The difference is obviously massive. This nearly 50–50 chance may seem low for such strongly religious teenagers. But given the overall paucity of very religious Catholic emerging adults (13 percent), a one-in-two chance of being highly religious as an emerging adult is quite elevated. The combination of the other three factors (in the bottom row) shows a similar, although not quite as strong, pattern. Catholic teenagers who do *not* believe in divine miracles *and* who read scriptures *infrequently and* who attend Sunday school *infrequently* have merely an 8 percent chance of becoming highly religious emerging adults. But the Catholic teenagers in the top quartile of these three factors have a 31 percent chance of doing so. We see then that these factors are statistically significant when taken alone, but when operating in reinforcing combinations they even more substantially increase or decrease the chances of Catholic teens sustaining high levels of faith and practice during emerging adulthood.

Summary Conclusions. Our analyses have identified several important factors that appear to influence the religious trajectories of Catholic teenagers into emerging adulthood. We have found three primary domains of Catholic teenagers' religious lives that seem crucial to the development of highly religious emerging adults. First, Catholic youth who have strong relational bonds with highly religious parents, other adults, and friends are more likely to maintain or increase their religious faith and practice when they transition into early emerging adulthood. Second, developing an internalized belief system involving a faith that is personally important, belief in divine miracles, and spiritual experiences also helps teens to sustain religious faith and practice into emerging adulthood. Finally, Catholic teenagers who live out their faith through certain religious practices, especially reading the Bible and frequently attending Sunday school, are more likely to become highly religious emerging adults. These factors dramatically influence the likelihood of youth becoming highly practicing and faithful Catholic emerging adults. Catholic teenagers who are in the bottom quartile on any of these factors typically have less than a one-in-ten chance of becoming highly religious emerging adults, whereas those in the top quartile during the teen years have upwards of a one-in-five chance of being a highly religious emerging adult.

Causal Combinations and Religious Trajectories

Our analysis to this point has illustrated what we might call "net effects." The regression-based techniques reveal how much each factor correlates with Catholic emerging adults' religiousness when all other factors are set at their average level of influence. It holds all the other control factors at a constant value to see how a change in the variable of interest associates with variance in emerging adults' religious faith and practice. This type of analysis is beneficial for identifying the independent importance of each particular characteristic or belief. It is not, however, well suited for examining how multiple factors may combine in particular patterns to lead to various religious trajectories.[12] Doing that requires a different conceptual and analytic approach, which we take in what follows.

The bottom of Table 5.3 demonstrated that when different factors are jointly operating, they combine to have a unique influence—seemingly more than just the sum of their individual influences—on the level of religiousness of Catholic emerging adults. Having a faith that is very important in one's daily life, highly religious parents, and ties to supportive religious adults during the teenage years all had a positive influence on Catholic youths' religious trajectories. But when these three factors occurred at high levels *together*, Catholic teens were especially likely to become highly practicing and faithful emerging adults. It is possible, and even likely, that such combinational experiences or conjunctural causes drive most patterns of religiousness during the transition to emerging adulthood.

As an analogy we can think about the factors that make a running back in football have a successful game. Independently, possessing speed, agility, large stature, a sure understanding of the plays, and a good knowledge of the opposing team would all help a running back accumulate many yards in a game. Although each of these factors may be useful individually, none of them alone would be enough to make an extremely successful player. Rather, the way that these factors come in *combinations* determines who ends up in the Hall of Fame versus who doesn't make the team. Switching to a combinational perspective also allows us to discover potentially surprising combinations of relevant factors, some of which may actually require that certain factors exist at *low* levels. Extending the football analogy, under certain conditions an effective running back may possess large size, agility, and knowledge of the plays but lack speed. This type of player, although possessing a factor (running slowly) that typically hinders success as a running back, is particularly useful in situations where a team is very close to the end zone and needs a chugging but powerful runner to drive the ball in for touchdowns. Similarly unexpected patterns might be relevant when it comes to religion. Catholic youth who have parents who are not very religious, for instance, but who attend Mass frequently themselves and believe religion is very important may become highly religious emerging adults—precisely because they have developed an independent, maybe even rebellious, religious posture in contrast to their lukewarm parents. Employing a combinational approach to analysis allows us to discover such unexpected pathways.

Table 5.3 also highlighted another interesting relationship between the most important variables during adolescence and religion in emerging adulthood. Certain factors appear to be nearly *necessary* conditions for a high level of religious faith and practice in emerging adulthood. For example, only 3 percent of Catholic youth who do not have at least moderately religious parents end up being highly religious as emerging adults. Without religious parents, Catholic teens today have almost no chance of ending up in the highest religiosity group as early emerging adults. Necessary conditions are like keys to a door with many locks: if one is missing one of the keys, it is impossible to unlock the door. Conversely, no single factor appears to be *sufficient* for producing highly religious emerging adults by itself. Even when Catholic young people experience the influential characteristics at the highest levels, the chance that they will become highly religious emerging adults is 50–50, at best. Having highly religious parents or considering religious faith extremely important as a teenager does not guarantee strong religiosity in emerging adulthood. It is theoretically possible, however, that when we consider complex combinations of factors, some sufficient pathways will actually emerge. In the analysis that follows, we investigate how unique combinations of important factors identified above seem to affect religious faith and practice in early emerging adulthood, searching in particular for factors and combinations of factors that are necessary or sufficient for producing strong religiosity among emerging adults.

The following results are based on an analytical technique called Qualitative Comparative Analysis (QCA).[13] QCA places survey respondents into groups based on the unique combinations of their religious beliefs and behaviors. For example, one group may include youth who have very religious parents, say their faith is very important, and read scriptures frequently, while another group would comprise youth who have very religious parents but do *not* consider faith important and do *not* read scriptures frequently. The total number of possible combinations depends upon the number of causal factors that are included. We then determine what percentage of youth who belong to each combination goes on to belong to the group exhibiting high religiosity in emerging adulthood (fitting our categories of Moderate or Highest religiousness, meaning they attend Mass frequently, say that their religious faith is at least somewhat important in their daily lives, and personally pray often).[14] If any group, defined by a combination of factors at high or low levels, has more than half of its members end up in this high religiosity group as emerging adults, it is considered a "true" causal combination, meaning that those youth are more likely to be a highly religious emerging adult than not. Then, having identified all of those "true" causal combinations, we eliminate certain factors if they are present at high and low levels in similar combinations. For example, if we find that Catholic teens who have highly religious parents and read the Bible frequently as well as those who have highly religious parents but do not read the Bible frequently are both likely to become highly religious emerging adults, we can conclude that the decisive factor is having highly religious parents—since whether the teens read the Bible or not, they are still likely to be highly religious as emerging adults.

To determine which factors to examine in this analysis, we first included the five factors that were identified above by our regression analyses as consistently very important, shown in Table 5.2 (considering faith important, having religious parents, believing in divine miracles, having ties to supportive religious adults, and reading the Bible; again we omit attending Catholic high school from the current investigation and devote Chapter 7 to that topic). As one would expect, combinations of these factors at high levels make Catholic teenagers more likely to become highly religious emerging adults. Our analysis reveals that only three of the five factors need to be present for Catholic youth to become highly religious as emerging adults. But one of those three factors always has to be having highly religious parents. That is, having highly religious parents appears to be a necessary condition for Catholic youth to become highly religious as emerging adults.

But this initial qualitative comparative analysis does not fully take advantage of the added possibilities of a combinational approach. One of the primary benefits of using QCA is finding novel, unexpected combinations that produce a given outcome. It is not surprising that when we include the most consistently influential factors, we find a fairly straightforward set of combinations leading to our outcome of interest. We already knew that these central factors markedly increase the likelihood of Catholic teens becoming highly religious emerging adults. The next set of factors, however, was shown to matter but to less consistently increase the probability of teenagers becoming highly religious emerging adults. Factors from this second tier, therefore, appear to be the most likely to be effective among youth when operating in certain combinations and contexts—in tandem with specific combinations of other factors. To investigate this possibility, we altered some of the factors that are included in the QCA combinations. First, we added having many religious experiences and attendance at Sunday school and confirmation classes. We chose these two factors from the set of "Somewhat Consistently Important" factors in Table 5.2 because they bring in slightly different aspects of Catholic teens' lives not captured by the first five factors. Religious experiences should reflect the more spiritual aspect of some teens' faith that may not be fully captured by how they rate the general importance of faith. Attending Sunday school and confirmation classes is a more public display of faith (beyond Mass attendance) than a behavior like reading scripture. We omitted belief in divine miracles from this second analysis, because it seems to overlap (both in theory and in our respondents) with the variable about religious experiences.

Changing the factors that are included in various combinations reveals new findings, shown in Figure 5.5. Displayed there are the combinations of factors from the teenage years, displayed in the boxes to the left, that will produce emerging adults in the higher religiosity groups more than 50 percent of the

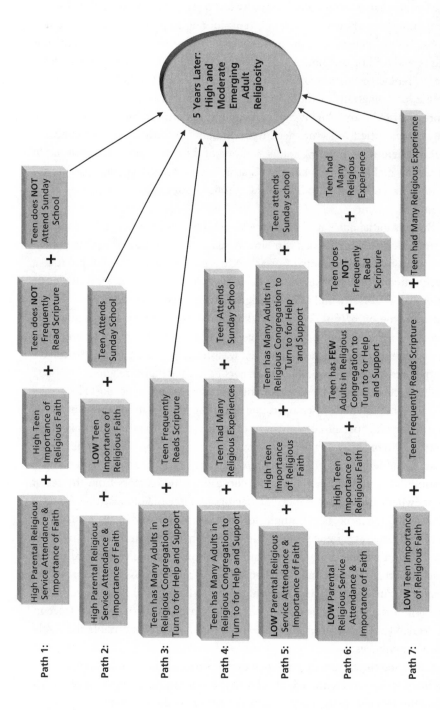

Figure 5.5 Qualitative comparative analysis showing combinations of teenage-era causal factors most likely producing highest emerging adult religiosity.

time. That is, if Catholic teens experience one of these seven combinations of factors, there is a greater than 50–50 chance they will become highly religious as emerging adults. Most of the factors here must be present at high levels, although a few actually need to be present at *low* levels to lead to high religiousness in emerging adulthood. Keep in mind that these seven combinations are not the only ones that lead some teens into high religious faith and practice in early emerging adulthood. Other pathways, however, do not consistently produce high religiousness among emerging adults (they produce high religiosity less than 50 percent of the time). While some Catholic youth from other combinations become highly religious emerging adults, it is more likely that they will not.

To simplify the analysis of the seven possible "true" pathways to high religiousness, we have sorted them into three distinct groups. The first group contains two unique combinations and is defined by the common factor of having highly religious parents. One combination includes Catholic teenagers who have highly religious parents *and* say religious faith is very important in their lives but do *not* read scriptures frequently and do *not* attend Sunday school frequently. The second combination again includes having highly religious parents, but in this pathway Catholic youth actually do *not* find faith important, although they do attend Sunday school frequently. It may seem odd that some normally important religious factors are *absent* in some pathways leading to higher religiousness in emerging adulthood. But therein lies an advantage of this analytic approach: rather than detecting various probabilities based on individual factors, it examines actual teens and discovers the specific combinations of factors most likely to turn teens into highly religious emerging adults.

These results allow for a more qualitative, theoretical interpretation of the causal mechanisms leading Catholic youth into particular religious trajectories. The first combination seems to show Catholic youth who have solid religious backgrounds and support systems (highly religious parents) and believe their faith is very significant in their lives. These teens, however, do not practice their faith privately by reading scripture or publicly by attending Sunday school. These Catholic teenagers *may* represent the much-discussed "over-programmed" youth, whose intense extracurricular schedules have pushed out time for religious activities (here we speculate but do not have the data to establish this possibility). Their low level of participation in certain religious practices as teenagers may actually be an important aspect of why they become highly religious as emerging adults. As they leave adolescence and their high school–based activities end, their strong family and personal religious background may lead them to fill that void with greater religious faith and practice: as emerging adults, they continue to consider faith important, they attend Mass frequently, and they pray regularly.

The second pathway here shows a slightly different type of Catholic youth. This combination involves highly religious parents and frequent Sunday school attendance but a *lack* of deeming faith important. These teens have a strong religious support system and are engaged in religious practices, but they appear not to have made a personal cognitive commitment to religious faith, or at least they have not figured out how it relates to their everyday lives. Perhaps these youth were "forced," by their highly religious parents, to attend Sunday school, even though they do not completely see its value. Having a strong religious foundation in terms of ties to religious people and practices, even if perhaps not by their own choice, allows them to develop this internalized and "personalized" faith as they transition into emerging adulthood.

These first two combinations demonstrate yet again the *importance of having highly religious parents* as a crucial basis for Catholic teens to become highly religious emerging adults. With that parental foundation, Catholic youth must *either* personally internalize the importance of faith (but not necessarily practice that faith in private ways) *or* engage in an important religious practice (Sunday school or confirmation classes) in order to have more than a 50 percent chance of becoming highly religious emerging adults. These findings point to a "substitutability effect," such that Catholic youth who have highly religious parents and are either subjectively religious or behaviorally religious, but not necessarily both, are among the most likely to end up as highly religious emerging adults. These two combinations account for the largest portion of Catholic youth who in fact end up being highly religious emerging adults. More than 15 percent of all highly religious emerging adults come from one of these two combinations of factors (with 45% of all highly religious adults coming from one of the top seven pathways in Figure 5.5).

The next group of sufficient combinations comprises youth who have many supportive, religious *non-parental* adults in their lives, but who do not necessarily have religious parents. These three combinations show another form of "substitutability," such that other adults take the place of highly religious parents. Added analysis (not presented here) revealed that these other adults are often extended family members, such as grandparents[15] or aunts and uncles. The first two combinations in this set illustrate again that merely having strong relational religious supports does not guarantee that a Catholic teen will be religious as a young adult. That relational foundation must be buttressed either by religious practices (reading the Bible or attending Sunday school) or personal religious experiences. In fact the second of these combinations, which includes many supportive adults and many religious experiences and frequent Sunday school attendance, is the pathway that most consistently produces highly religious Catholic emerging adults: fully 80 percent of teens in this category later become highly religious young adults. When Catholic youth combine at least one factor from each of the primary influential domains we have identified (supportive religious relationships, internalized faith, and religious practices) it is very likely that they will be set on a high religious trajectory into emerging adulthood.

The third combination in this set is somewhat surprising because it involves Catholic youth with parents who are less religious. However, the absence here of what has been shown to be an almost necessary condition must be compensated for by rating faith as personally important, knowing many supportive religious adults, and frequently attending Sunday school. These youth seem to be establishing religious identities independent of and perhaps in contrast to their parents. They might see their religious faith as a way to distinguish themselves from their parents. To succeed, however, these teenagers must have a strong support system of religious adults, internalize the importance of faith, and consistently engage in religious practices. So it is possible for a Catholic teen with parents who are not very religious to become a highly religious emerging adult, but it is unlikely, and it requires just the right combination of other factors.

The final set of variable conjunctions includes two unique combinations. Both paths include the *absence* of factors that generally increase religiosity in emerging adulthood. What these combinations illustrate is the power of religious experiences. Catholic youth in both categories have experienced a miracle, committed their lives to God, had prayers answered, and/or had a moving spiritual experience. These personal religious experiences appear capable of pushing Catholic youth into a trajectory of high religious observance. The first of these combinations appears to be highly spiritual, but possibly isolated, Catholic youth. They have had numerous religious experiences and say faith is very important in their lives, but they have less religious parents and few or no ties to other religious adults, and they do not read scripture frequently. Like the teens discussed above, these teens could find the distinctiveness of being religious among non-religious parents and acquaintances to be a motivating factor leading to higher religious commitment in early emerging adulthood. The second path is slightly more difficult to interpret, as it includes Catholic teenagers who have had several religious experiences and read scriptures frequently but do not say that faith is very or extremely important in their lives. It may seem hard to imagine that any Catholic youth fit this combination. They are a definitely a small minority, accounting for only 2 percent of highly religious emerging adults, but these Catholic youth might be what many call "spiritual seekers." With survey data, it is hard to tell. But they may have encountered powerful religious experiences and devoted themselves to reading the Bible as a way to understand them, even though they seem not to have fully internalized the importance of faith for everyday life.

The seven distinct pathways shown in Figure 5.5 account for 45 percent of all highly religious emerging adults. And overall, 62 percent of the Catholic teenagers in these seven combinations become highly religious emerging adults. Though these seven pathways account for less than half of all highly religious emerging adults, they are the only combinations that are more likely to produce highly religious emerging adults than not, that beat the 50–50 odds. Numerous other combinations of variables can produce Catholic youth who become highly religious as emerging adults, but they only do so in a minority of cases. These seven combinations are the most consistent paths by which Catholic youth become highly religious emerging adults.

Summary Conclusions. This analytic focus on combinations of variables has provided several important insights. First, it underlined the crucial importance of ties to supportive adults (both parents and other religious adults) for most teens. The vast majority of pathways that consistently lead Catholic youth to become highly religious emerging adults involve either religious parents or ties to highly religious non-parental adults. Catholic teenagers can't do it on their own. To maintain or increase their religious faith and commitment into emerging adulthood, Catholic youth must have a significant religious support system during the teenage years. Second, strong relational religious support systems need to be paired with either strong internalized faith or frequent engagement in religious practices. These two factors appear to be "substitutable" (or inter-changeable) for leading to high religiosity in emerging adulthood. Just as Catholic youth can't do it on their own, in other words, parents and other supportive adults can't by themselves set Catholic teenagers on religious trajectories either. In most cases, Catholic teenagers must have some personal attachment to or experiences of religion, either through practice, particularly frequent attendance at Sunday school or confirmation classes, or by expressing that faith is very important in their daily lives. Finally, personal religious experiences, such as having prayers answered or witnessing a miracle, appear to be a crucial factor for those few Catholic youth who become religious emerging adults *without* strong relational religious support systems.

Pathways to Religious Decline. The analyses above investigated factors that together lead Catholic teenagers to be highly religious as emerging adults. Although this chapter has shown that the majority of teens follow relatively stable religious trajectories across the transition into emerging adulthood, the most common pathway of change for Catholic teenagers is religious decline. Most Catholic youth do not end up in the two highest religious categories. So we can flip the previous question on its head to ask which factors, in combination, most consistently lead to the more common religious trajectory of a decline in religious faith and practice. The combinations may not be just the opposite of those identified above—and in fact our data show that they are not such. To explore this question, we repeated the analyses from above, except we changed the outcome. Rather than examining the more religious Catholic emerging adults, we looked at Catholics who were in the Moderate or Highest religiosity groups during their teenage years, but then declined into the Minimal or Lowest categories as emerging adults.[16] These respondents were religiously strong as teenagers, but by emerging adulthood they attended Mass infrequently, said that religious faith is only minimally important in their lives, and did not pray frequently. For this analysis we used the same teen-era factors from the second of the two analyses above: rating faith as (un)important, having religious parents, having ties to other supportive religious adults, reading scripture, attending Sunday school or confirmation classes, and having religious experiences. We searched for which combinations of these factors are more likely to produce the low-religion outcome than not (combinations in which at least 50 percent of members end up exhibiting low religiosity in emerging adulthood). Figure 5.6 displays the results of this analysis.

The findings show that Catholic teens who are already on the margins in their religious behaviors and belief are the most likely to slip into very low religiosity by emerging adulthood. They also contradict the sometimes-voiced concern about a "rebellion effect," which posits that Catholic youth who are extremely involved and invested in the Church during the teenage years may be more likely to rebel or burn out and shed their religious faith and practice as they age.[17] Our analysis finds little evidence of that type of pathway. Rather, most of the Catholic youth who end up in the lower categories of religiosity in emerging adulthood only experienced one of the five important factors at high levels during their teenage years. The analysis also supports several of our conclusions above about religious emerging adults. The importance of a strong relational religious support system, for instance, remains evident. Four of the five combinations of factors most likely to lead to low religiosity in emerging adulthood involve the absence of religious parents or other ties to religious adults. Without highly religious parents or numerous close ties to other religious adults during the teen years, Catholic youth are likely to display very little religious faith and practice as emerging adults. Lacking bonds to religious adults is a path to low religiosity even for youth who believe that religion is very important, read the Bible frequently, or report having had several religious experiences. While the absence of relational ties is almost a necessary condition for low religiosity, however, it is not sufficient. It must be combined with either minimal faith practices (not reading the Bible and not attending Sunday school or confirmation classes) or not having personal religious experiences. It is this joint absence of bonds to religious others *and* religious practices or experiences that makes it most likely that a Catholic teenager will end up in one of the two less religious categories in early emerging adulthood.

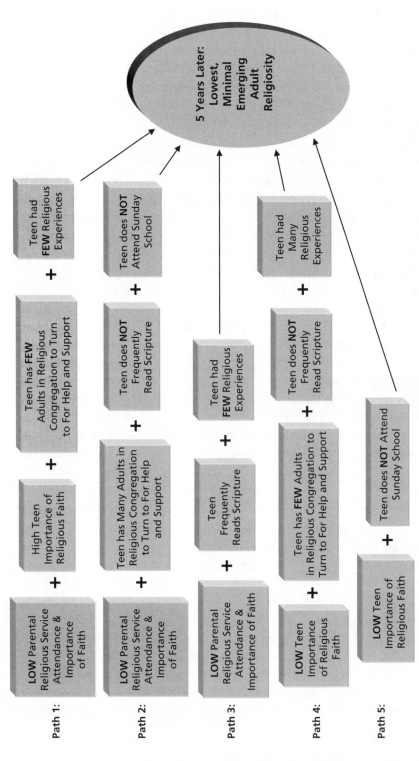

Figure 5.6 Qualitative comparative analysis showing combinations of teenage-era causal factors most likely producing a decline into minimal or lowest emerging adult religiosity.

However, one combination is an exception to this general trend. The final combination in Figure 5.6 involves Catholic youth who do not say that religion is important and who do not attend Sunday school or confirmation classes. Lacking both factors—regardless of religious ties—is alone enough to put Catholic youth on a path of low religiousness into emerging adulthood. As much as 77 percent of Catholic teens who experience this combination end up in the low-religiosity categories as emerging adults, and the combination accounts for 22 percent of all emerging adults in those categories. We here see the vital impact of teenagers considering faith very important in life and attending Sunday school or confirmation classes. When Catholic youth lack these two factors, they are unlikely to sustain high levels of religiousness into emerging adulthood, even though they started off in the higher religious groups as teenagers.

Summary Conclusions. Our analysis of the combinations of factors that lead Catholic teenagers into lower levels of religiosity as emerging adults supports the primary findings of the previous analysis. Bonds to religiously committed parents and other religious adults are a crucial factor shaping the religious trajectories of Catholic youth. The absence of these ties is a crucial element in the major pathway into lower religiosity among emerging adults. The lack of these ties, however, is not the only element on this pathway: to be highly probable to decline in religiosity, teens must also perceive faith as unimportant, attend Sunday school infrequently, or have few personal religious experiences. The other finding from our analysis here was the additional pathway involving only a low perceived importance of faith and infrequent Sunday school or confirmation classes—regardless of relational ties to religious adults. The combination of these two factors is sufficient to lead Catholic youth away from religion in the transition to emerging adulthood. Not developing some personal relationship with their faith *or* the Church, in short, makes it quite likely that Catholic youth will fall away from the faith of their upbringing as early emerging adults.

Theorizing the Causal Mechanisms

In this chapter we have used different analytic strategies to understand the key factors that associate with the religious trajectories of Catholic youth. These analyses have identified three major domains of Catholic teens' lives that exert the greatest influence on their religious pathways as they transition into emerging adulthood. Having bonds to religious parents or other adults, internalizing a religious belief system, and engaging in religious practices are the factors during the teenage years that most consistently affect faith and practice in emerging adulthood. What this quantitative analysis so far has not addressed, however, is *why* and *how* these factors have such an impact. Here we depart from a purely empirical approach to discuss the causal mechanisms that we have good reason to believe give rise to the associations we have found in the preceding quantitative analyses. Identifying statistical correlations does not itself explain why some Catholic teens remain religious and others do not. We need to dig below the visible surface to understand the causal processes that drive these observed relationships.[18] The interpretations we offer next are not proven by direct observation; no such causal influences could be. Still, we have good reason to believe that they are the most likely explanations, given our accumulated knowledge about how social life and religious faith work.

Bonds to Religious Parents and Other Adults. Catholic youth who have highly religious parents or ties to other religious adults, we have seen, are much more likely to sustain or increase their religiosity in the transition to emerging adulthood than youth without such bonds. What underlies the connection between these types of ties and higher religious faith and practice later in life? Although there are numerous potential mechanisms, two stand out as the most prominent: *religious socialization* and *the avoidance of relationship breakdown* (see Table 5.4). Socialization is the general process of transmitting values, behaviors, beliefs, habits, and norms from one generation to the next. Religious socialization, therefore, involves parents or other adults training young people how to be religious. This training can come in the form of direct and explicit teaching, but much of it occurs through modeling (by the adults) and imitation (by the youth). As a result of such socialization, teens are more likely to accept the religious worldview of their parents or other important adults, understand the necessary behaviors and norms of a given community, and embody a similar set of priorities that leads to a continuation of religious behaviors.

The avoidance of relationship breakdown as a second causal mechanism involves the importance of relationships to all normal humans' lives. People generally value their relationships with family and friends, and therefore tend to act in ways that maintain those relationships. If one partner in a relationship begins to act in ways that directly contradict central values of the other partner, the relationship can become strained. It can be difficult to maintain relationships in which the partners do not agree on important issues. Thus, most people, especially those in subordinate roles (like teens in relation to parents), adapt their beliefs and behaviors in ways that help sustain valued relationships. In this way, Catholic youth with highly religious parents or close ties to other religious adults understand discontinuing their religious behaviors or disavowing central Catholic beliefs comes with a "penalty." The desire to avoid damaging or losing these relationships, which youth typically value, makes teens more likely to continue attending Mass, praying, and cultivating religious faith as an important part of their lives.

Table 5.4 Summary of Theoretical Mechanisms Leading to Higher Religiosity in Young Adulthood among Catholic Youth

Theoretical Mechanism	Description	Significant Variables Supporting Operation
Socialization	Values, behaviors, and beliefs are transmitted from important others to teens through formal teaching and informal modeling.	Strong Parental Religion Supportive Religious Adults
Avoidance of Relationship Breakdown	Youth act in ways toward shared agreement to maintain valued relationships.	Strong Parental Religion Supportive Religious Adults
Enjoyment of Participation	Intrinsically rewarding activities are more likely to be continued and to have their messages internalized.	Supportive Religious Adults
Belief and Desire Reinforcement	Cognitively and emotionally fortifying one's moral beliefs about what is true, good and right in life	High Importance of Religious Faith Having Many Religious Experiences Frequently Reading Scriptures Attending Sunday School/Confirmation Classes
Drive for Identity Continuity	Desire to maintain one's sense of who one is and presentation of that self to others	High Importance of Religious Faith Having Many Religious Experiences Frequently Reading Scriptures Attending Sunday School/Confirmation Classes
Conserving Accumulated Capital	Investment in activities and communities accrues potential benefits, which discontinuing participation would eliminate.	Frequently Reading Scriptures Attending Sunday School/Confirmation Classes

Religious socialization and the avoidance of relationship breakdown are causal mechanisms that shape the trajectories of youth across all religious groups.[19] Several unique aspects of the Catholic faith, however, make religious socialization a particularly influential factor in the lives of Catholics. First, Catholicism involves many rituals, sacraments, and sacramentals. Catholics need to participate in and (ideally) understand these rituals and practices to live in full communion with the Catholic Church. Parents and other important adults (such as extended family members) are the most immediate sources of this information for teens. Said differently, Catholic youth who do not have highly religious parents or other accessible religious adults must seek out and learn this knowledge and these practices independently. Few teens are apt to undertake this activity on their own, which is why relational ties to faith are a virtually necessary factor in the development of highly religious Catholic emerging adults. Second, Catholicism in the U.S. still has strong connections to ethnicity and immigration, which makes Catholicism a central part of many families' identities. Although Catholics in the U.S. are not as literally segregated from non-Catholics as in the past (see Chapter 1), this cultural-historical framework continues to influence American Catholics. To many Catholic youth, being a part of their family and being Catholic are synonymous. Catholic teens who come from families in which the Catholic faith is taken seriously are less likely to decrease their religious faith and practice, because doing so would threaten not only their connection to the Church but their relationship with their family as well. Catholicism's central place in some teens' religious and family identity amplifies the negative consequences of abandoning the Church and increases the incentives for continued participation.

Another mechanism that seems to drive the connection between having such valued relational bonds, especially to non-parental adults, and maintaining religiousness in emerging adulthood is *heightened enjoyment of participating in a religious congregation*. People are more likely to continue participating in an activity or behavior if they enjoy it. But many youth do not find Mass fun or even very enjoyable. When teens do not feel that they have any real, personal connections with people in their congregation, attending Mass is even less likely to be a rewarding experience. They may feel that they are alone in a crowd. But if they can socialize and connect with important adults via Mass, Sunday school, and other religious activities, then these events become more rewarding. This straightforward mechanism of enjoyment may explain in part why youth with such relational ties are more likely to maintain their religiousness, especially as it is exhibited in continued church attendance, during their transition to emerging adulthood.

Before going much further, we acknowledge the limitations of these causal mechanisms. Catholic youth are, of course, active participants in their own lives, and they often make choices that directly contradict the lessons imparted by their parents. Also, many parents, even highly religious ones, actively promote an environment of choice, encouraging teens to seek out their own path. There is the additional possibility that rifts in the youth–parent relationship actually spur on the child's exit from the Church, as an explicit break from the family. We are in no way positing these mechanisms, or the ones we detail below, as universal, "covering" laws that operate in a uniform fashion in every case. Rather, we believe the mechanisms of religious socialization, avoidance of relationship breakdown, and enjoyment of religious congregation participation help explain the strong empirical relationship between bonds to religious parents and other adults and high religiosity in emerging adulthood.

Internalized Beliefs. The second domain of teens' lives that has the most significant impact on their religious trajectories is the development of an internalized Catholic belief system. Catholic teens who claim religion is very important in their daily lives and believe in divine miracles display greater religious devotion as early emerging adults. Similarly, a Catholic young person who has had several personal religious experiences—such as having prayers answered, witnessing miracles, or making a personal commitment to live for God—is also likely to be more religious as an emerging adult. But how exactly do these internalized belief systems and personal experiences causally influence young Catholics' later Mass attendance, prayer, and perception of the importance of religious faith? *Religious belief and desire reinforcement* coupled with a *drive for identity continuity* seem to be the most directly responsible mechanisms. Both of these mechanisms share the basic idea that people, even young people, generally exhibit consistency in their lives. Both through active choices and structural constraints, most people follow relatively stable paths over time; they do not move chaotically from one worldview or set of priorities to another. Furthermore, some degree of inertia operates in most people's lives that keeps their beliefs, morals, and identities pretty constant. Much research has shown that people are unlikely to abandon beliefs or practices that are central to their identities.[20] Even though the transition to emerging adulthood can involve identity exploration, it is not the "free-for-all" transformation of morals and identities that pop culture often depicts.[21] Catholic youth who consider religion very important in their lives, who believe in divine miracles, and who have had religious experiences are more likely to see being Catholic as a significant component of their personal identities. Doing so involves embracing and investing in a particular worldview and life practices. Once they establish this outlook and set of habits, youth are more likely to see the world in a way that confirms their perspective and to discount or ignore aspects that may contradict it or call it into question. Abandoning a belief system means incurring social and psychological costs (e.g., having to find a new worldview) that most people normally try to avoid. Therefore, religiously observant Catholic youth are very likely to continue acting and thinking in ways that support their beliefs and allow them to maintain identity continuity, even as they transition into emerging adulthood.

Belief enforcement and identity continuity also operate generally across denominations, but particular aspects of Catholicism make these mechanisms especially important. Although most religions involve a very specific set of beliefs, in practice many liberal churches and denominations today focus more on general attitudes and morals (such as being nice to one another). Relative to these churches, at least officially, the Catholic Church still maintains an explicit set of beliefs to which members are expected to adhere. While such an elaborate belief system may "turn off" some youth, Catholic teenagers who experience their faith as very important in their lives are likely to internalize these beliefs as a way of organizing their larger worldview. Holding these beliefs, such as the Church's teachings on abortion and contraception, may make youth feel like they are part of a cultural minority. Rather than pushing them to abandon their controversial beliefs, this perceived opposition may actually strengthen some Catholic young people's investments in their faith.[22] That is, committed adherence to certain beliefs demarcates an "us" and a "them," which further embeds the beliefs in Catholics' lives. Cultural and cognitive commitment solidifies the centrality of these beliefs, thereby making them difficult to abandon, meaning youth who "buy into" the system are unlikely to give it up.

Catholic teens who say their religious faith is very important to their lives, who have committed their lives to God, and who believe in divine miracles would also seem to have made being Catholic a significant part of their personal identity (though there is no definitive marker for such an interior dimension of life). Further, as noted above, for Catholics this religious identity is often intertwined with family and even national identities. Faith cannot be easily separated from these other identities and relationships, which makes Catholic young people even less likely to discard it. In addition to being shaped by the desire for consistency of identity, the average person is unlikely to alter a central component of his or her personal identity when doing so would require a major alteration of his or her way of life (for example, of friends, daily schedule, central values and morals, and so on). Because being Catholic can be so deeply rooted in other key identities, youth who internalize it as their own identity are more likely to maintain it across the transition to emerging adulthood.

While belief reinforcement and identity consistency apply to all factors within the domain of internalized belief, the aspect of religious experience may be especially important for Catholic youth. Religious experiences (such as having committed their lives to God, having experienced a miracle, and having a prayer answered) may be critical components in allowing Catholic teens to connect in a personal way to their religious faith. Relative to evangelical Protestant churches, Catholicism can seem to youth to involve a more distant and inauthentic spirituality. In a culture that valorizes individual subjective experience, Catholicism's focus on historical saints, a (distant) pope, and routinized rituals may inhibit many teens' personal connection to their faith. In such a situation, experiencing a divine miracle or answered prayers may help young people to internalize what they might otherwise perceive as an ethereal and external spirituality. And when this happens, they are more likely to make being Catholic an important aspect of their identity, which increases the chances that they will maintain their religious commitment into the future.

Religious Practices. The third and final domain most influential in helping Catholic youth to maintain or increase their religiousness across the transition to emerging adulthood is frequent religious practices during the teen years—most importantly, reading the Bible and attending Sunday school or confirmation classes. The reasons these practices matter are similar to several that we have already described, but they probably operate slightly differently in this domain. One of the primary mechanisms driving the relationship of both religious practices and internalized belief systems with continued religiousness is *religious belief and desire reinforcement.* For religious practices, however, this mechanism is more interactive or circular. Catholic youth who read the Bible and attend Mass are likely to learn and become committed to a particular perspective on life. They then may draw upon this outlook when they encounter everyday life challenges and decisions. When they find their religious worldview helpful in addressing life issues, they are more likely to see the value in continuing to read scripture or attend Sunday school, which then reinforces their commitment to these beliefs and ideas, and so on. Religious practices can thus give Catholic youth a set of tools to use in their daily lives, and when these tools prove useful, youth will be more likely to want to hone their use of the tools or acquire new tools, which promotes the maintenance or growth of religious devotion across the transition to emerging adulthood. This developmental process does not seem to happen for most Catholic youth, but it does for some.

These frequent religious practices are also likely part of the *drive for identity continuity.* Unlike internalized beliefs, religious practices not only signal and contribute to the individual youth's Catholic identity, but also constitute a public expression of that identity. Reading the Bible and especially attending Sunday school and Mass show others that they are indeed at least somewhat seriously Catholic. As much as people strive for identity continuity for internal reasons, there are also social consequences for disrupting or contradicting one's professed identity. When a young person's friends and peers know him or her as "a Catholic" (or any other identity), it is easier for the young person to interact with those individuals while maintaining their Catholic identity. For example, their friends know they can (or perhaps cannot) talk to that Catholic young person about religious topics. If the youth then abandons that religious identity, these social relations have to be reorganized and modified, and they can potentially be lost. By attending Sunday school and Mass and reading scripture frequently, youth are likely to become known as committed Catholics, which makes it is easier for them to maintain the behaviors necessary to support that identity over time.

The transition to emerging adulthood is a time when most youth undergo major upheavals in their social relations—moving away to go to college, starting new jobs, and so on—which would seem to allow for or even promote significant changes in identity. But most people's life courses are structured by a process termed "reciprocal continuity."[23] That means that even in times of transition, people seek out new institutions or social relations that support and enhance their previously established identities. For example, many American teenagers move away from home to attend college, but those with strong Catholic identities are more likely than others to attend a Catholic college or join a Catholic student group. These new institutions essentially replace or update their previous social relations and are partly dependent upon their ongoing Catholic identity status. These new relations and institutions then further bolster their Catholic identity and overall religiousness. Hence, the Catholic identity that is shaped and projected by reading the Bible and attending Sunday school as a teenager often directly leads to heightened religiousness in emerging adulthood.

Attending Sunday school or confirmation classes is particularly important in this process for Catholic youth. According to survey data on youth from different religious denominations, Sunday school attendance is a rather weak predictor of religiousness in emerging adulthood. But for Catholic youth, it proves important. This difference most likely stems from the heightened internal and public signaling of a Catholic identity that occurs through the sacrament of confirmation. Not receiving confirmation also likely signals a lack of parental investment in the child's Catholic faith. Many other religious denominations have processes similar to confirmation. Catholic confirmation is more central to believers' faith and a more ritualized event, however, than many of these. Confirmation is also something that most outsiders know about and recognize as a significant aspect of Catholic faith. So in addition to signaling commitment to other Catholics, receiving the sacrament of confirmation is a public way that youth can define their Catholic identity, which reinforces the mechanism of identity continuation.

The final process by which engagement in religious practices may lead to maintaining religiousness during the transition to emerging adulthood is the drive to *conserve accumulated "religious capital."*[24] Religious knowledge and faith can be seen as a resource or even an investment, analogous to being able to play an instrument, fix computers, or play a sport. By reading the Bible and attending Sunday school, Catholic youth are investing in and accumulating religious capital. People who have amassed a greater amount of a particular resource are less likely than people with less of that resource to remove themselves from contexts in which that capital is valuable. Catholic youth who have devoted a great deal of time to reading scripture and attending Mass and Sunday school will have a larger store of religious capital than those who have not. If these teens were to abandon their faith, then that religious capital would no longer be very useful in their lives. To maintain the benefits that stem from the accumulation of this resource, such youth need (and are therefore likely) to maintain high levels of religiousness into emerging adulthood.

A related aspect of this mechanism is acquiring more religious skills. As with other types of knowledge-capital (such as knowing how to play musical instruments), the more youth participate in their faith, the better they get at it. Reading the Bible and attending Sunday school and confirmation classes are ways to become "better" Catholics, by learning and understanding more about the rituals, history, beliefs, and nuances of the faith. As people become better at a given skill or behavior, they tend to enjoy it more. And when people enjoy a certain activity more, they are more likely to continue participating in it. So just as a youth who spends a great deal of time becoming a proficient pianist is more likely to enjoy playing the piano and therefore to continue playing the piano more, Catholic youth who become more adept at being Catholic will like attending Mass or Sunday school more and will continue to engage in these behaviors during the transition to emerging adulthood.

Conclusion

The goal of this chapter has been to examine and understand the religious trajectories of Catholic teenagers as they enter early emerging adulthood. The different analyses we have used have helped us map those diverse pathways and understand the factors that influence youth in each pathway. The first major conclusion from this investigation concerns the primary patterns of religiousness that occur during this transition. On average, Catholic youth exhibit lower religiosity—based on attendance at religious services, prayer, and self-rated importance of faith—than non-Catholic youth. This gap does not diminish when these teens become emerging adults. Instead, over this transition the primary religious trajectory is one of great stability. While Catholic youth may adjust their individual behaviors or beliefs as they age, most remain at the same level of religiousness or move to only a slightly different level from the teen years to emerging adulthood. Therefore, the religious views, experiences, and practices of Catholic teenagers are extremely consequential for how Catholic they are five years later. Among those youth whose religiosity does change significantly, the most common path is to decrease in religious faith and practice. A substantial group of Catholic teens moves from the highest to the lowest levels of religiousness as they enter emerging adulthood. Conversely, only a small minority of Catholic youth dramatically increases their religious faith and practice over this stage in the life course.

We have discovered three major domains of teens' lives that influence their religious trajectories. The first is close relational ties to religious adults. Parents, relatives, and other adults help socialize youth into the faith and practices of the Church; form relationships with teens that most teens will try to maintain through continued participation in faith; and make attending church and Sunday school a more meaningful and rewarding experience. The second influential domain is internalized religious beliefs, which are manifested by viewing one's faith as important in daily life, believing in divine miracles, and experiencing an answer to prayer. These factors are central to the formation of a Catholic world-view and identity, which, once established, are likely to be sustained, both due to the costs of abandoning them and the benefits of sustaining them. Having prayers answered or experiencing miracles may help youth go beyond intellectual belief and external rituals to connect on a personal level with the spiritual, intangible aspects of the Catholic faith. Third, religious practices are likewise an important factor in whether youth maintain or increase their religiousness in the transition to emerging adulthood. Not only do these practices make Catholicism more central to teens' identity (leading again to higher religious devotion), but they also become something like a "capital investment" or a valuable resource. Once youth have built up religious capital through going to Mass and similar practices, they will be more likely to take advantage of its rewards by continuing to participate in the Catholic Church and believe its teachings.

Worth emphasizing once more is the necessity of *relational ties* to religious adults, both parents and other adults (such as relatives and youth ministers), for fostering high religiosity among emerging adult Catholics. A few Catholic youth do become very religious emerging adults without such bonds, but they were a small minority. In almost all cases, having strong relational ties to the faith is a necessary condition of becoming a strong Catholic emerging adult. Although having these ties does not guarantee that a teen will be a highly religious Catholic as an emerging adult, in their absence the likelihood of Catholic youth increasing or maintaining their religious faith and practice across this life transition is extremely low. For those who are invested in forming faithful Catholic youth, this causal connection is crucial to understand. And for academic religion researchers, studying how and why adult ties are so central to this process can provide key insights into questions of religious socialization more generally. The results of this chapter validate a key insight of sociology: significant social relationships are the channels of the most causally important forces in human life. Sociologically speaking, religious institutions, programs, and practices matter because they foster and guide these relationships. In the absence of such relationships, the institutions, programs, and practices can feel empty to teens and thus become almost totally ineffective. But when they succeed in cultivating healthy relationships that foster religious faith and human flourishing, they can be very powerful indeed in passing on the Catholic faith.

Chapter Appendix

Table 5.A **Descriptive Statistics Comparing Religious Levels and Change between Survey Waves 1 and 3 (percents) (N = 2,432) [Weighted]**

Levels of Religiousness	Teenage Catholic Type							Non-Catholic	Total Sample
	Completely	Mostly	Modestly	Nominal	Family	Secondary	Raised		
As Emerging Adults									
Lowest	17	32	26	39	44	22	29	20	22
Minimal	45	31	41	39	35	37	43	28	32
Moderate	22	19	26	22	14	22	6	25	23
Highest	16	18	8	0	7	19	22	27	22
As Teenagers									
Lowest	2	17	4	23	38	4	23	11	11
Minimal	27	44	34	36	35	21	25	21	25
Moderate	41	25	31	35	16	46	30	29	30
Highest	30	14	31	6	12	30	23	39	34
% of "eligible" wave 1 to *more* religious group[a]	16	26	10	8	11	9	17	19	17
% of "eligible" wave 1 to *less* religious group[a]	28	22	31	48	26	24	15	16	20

Note: [a] Eligible defined as cases who had the opportunity to move in the given direction. For example, the percentage moving *higher* is based on cases who were Lowest, Minimal, or Moderate during wave 1 because youth in the Highest group could not have possibly moved higher.

Source: National Survey of Youth and Religion, 2002–2003, 2007–2008.

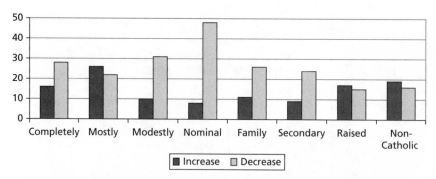

Figure 5A.1 Percent of eligible[a] in each Catholic category that increase or decrease religiosity between teen and emerging adult (percents) [Weighted]. [a] Eligible defined as respondents who had the opportunity to move in the given direction. For example, the percentage moving higher is based on respondents who were Lowest, Minimal, or Moderate at wave 1 because youth in the Highest group could not have possibly moved higher.

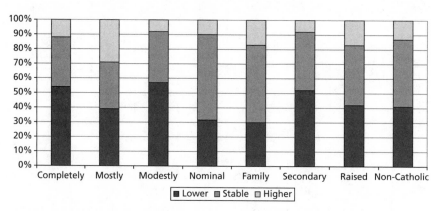

Figure 5A.2 Religious trajectories by Catholic categories (N = 2,432) [Weighted]*.
* This figure is similar to Figure 5.2, but here change is defined as any change in religiousness categories. Stable is defined as staying in the exact same religiousness group. For example, someone who moves from the Lowest category to the Minimal category was counted as being "Stable" in Figure 5.2, but would be counted as Lower in this figure.

‖ 6 ‖

Catholic Faith and Life Course Outcomes

This chapter examines a variety of Catholic emerging adult life experiences and outcomes. We ask whether the religious faith and practice of emerging adult Catholics makes any difference in the quality of their day-to-day lives. Does regularly practicing one's faith matter for familial relationships, civic engagement, moral beliefs, outlook on life, risky behavior, mental and physical health, life satisfaction, self-efficacy, educational attainment, attitudes about consumerism, and sexual behavior? This chapter addresses these life outcomes by using measures from the third wave of the NSYR survey. We find that practicing Catholic emerging adults are distinct from non-practicing ones on many, but not all, of these experiences and outcomes.

Catholic Religious Ideal Types for Comparative Analysis

Before we can examine emerging adult life outcomes, we need to explain how we divide up our sample of Catholic emerging adults into groups for comparison based on measures of religious practice and salience. Readers of *Soul Searching* and *Souls in Transition* may already be familiar with this strategy of religious "ideal types." Briefly put, we pull together various dimensions of religiousness into meaningful categories. Instead of assessing the influences of Mass attendance, self-rated importance of faith, and frequency of private prayer individually, we combine them to form three distinct categories of Catholics that we describe below. Both practical and theoretical concerns made us choose this strategy. Practically, this chapter is already heavy on data. Analyzing all of the outcomes by each religious variable would vastly multiply the amount of information presented, making it difficult to come away with a "big picture" assessment of the impact of Catholic faith and practice on the life outcomes of emerging adults. Theoretically, it is artificial to statistically pull apart various dimensions of religious faith and practice that actually cluster together quite meaningfully in the experiences of real Catholic emerging adults. So we work here with an ideal-type strategy of analysis.

We developed our Catholic ideal-type variable through a two-stage process. In the first stage we used a statistical technique known as "latent class analysis"[1] to group respondents into three categories[2] using our full sample of Catholics.[3] After inspecting each of these subgroups, we labeled them "Practicing," "Sporadic," or "Disengaged," based on how they ranked on our measures of religion. The second step involved revising the group membership for certain respondents based on our judgment about particular important aspects of their lives. Specifically, if respondents in an extreme subgroup (Practicing and Disengaged) exhibited inconsistencies between the three indicators of religious faith and practice, we moved them to the medium subgroup (Sporadic). We changed the categories for 41 cases (less than 6 percent of the Catholics in our sample). In our final groupings of emerging adults we have 110 Practicing Catholics (16 percent), 396 Sporadic Catholics (57 percent), and 216 Disengaged Catholics (27 percent).[4] All Catholic respondents in our sample are included in one of the three categories, which is a bit different from how ideal types were analyzed in previous NSYR books.[5] In order to assess the strength of our newly constructed variable, we examined how well our subgroups differentiated between the categories of other measures of religious practice and belief in the NSYR. We also compared this variables performance against two other measures: (1) An ideal-type variable constructed without the aid of latent class analysis, and (2) an ideal-type variable constructed *only* using latent class analysis method. The results clearly favored our two-step variable over the other variables, so we proceeded on that basis.

Some of the decisions we made in constructing the ideal types were driven by practical considerations related to sample size. When dividing Catholics into meaningful subgroups, we had to make certain that we had enough individuals in each group to provide reliable estimates of the true population values, as well as to find any statistically significant differences between groups. Ideally, we would like to slice the groups even finer than we have in this chapter. For example, if we tighten the requirements for belonging to the Practicing Catholic group to include only those who attend Mass weekly, who say their faith is very or extremely important, and who pray at least a few times a week, then we find many of the differences between Practicing Catholics and Disengaged Catholics to be considerably more pronounced. The trouble is that, under these more stringent requirements, the Practicing category shrinks from 110 to 51 cases (only 7 percent of emerging adult Catholics in our sample). At the very least, it is important to recognize that it matters where we draw the line between different types and groups. The Practicing Catholics, as we have categorized them in this chapter, are not "super Catholics." On the whole, they are Catholics who take their faith seriously and practice it both publicly (in Mass attendance) and privately (in prayer). A bit less than half of them might be considered "super Catholics," as described above.

Table 6.1 **Religious Service Attendance, Frequency of Prayer, and Importance of Faith of Catholic Emerging Adults, Ages 18 to 23, by Ideal Types (Percents)**

	Catholic type		
	Practicing	*Sporadic*	*Disengaged*
Religious service attendance			
Never	0	28	91
A few times a year	0	34	8
Many times a year	0	13	1
Once a month	13	13	1
Two to three times a month	29	7	0
Once a week	65	5	0
More than once a week	11	0	0
Frequency of private prayer			
Never	0	6	73
Less than once a month	1	19	12
One or two times a month	10	23	10
About once a week	13	14	5
A few times a week	21	16	1
About once a day	27	16	0
Many times a day	29	7	0
Importance of religious faith in daily life			
Not important at all	0	1	51
Not very important	0	11	40
Somewhat important	0	61	9
Very important	50	23	0
Extremely important	50	4	0

Note: Percentages are rounded to the nearest whole number and may not add to 100.

Source: National Survey of Youth and Religion, 2007–2008.

Table 6.1 shows how the three ideal-type categories—Practicing, Sporadic, and Disengaged—score on the three variables we used to construct the categories. Practicing Catholics attend Mass at least once a month, and the majority attend Mass weekly. The overwhelming majority (91 percent) of Disengaged Catholics never attend Mass, and the few that do only attend occasionally.

Sporadic Catholics fall between those two groups, with most attending Mass only occasionally. A similar pattern is evident for private prayer. Almost all Practicing Catholics pray weekly or more often (and over one-half pray at least once a day), while a sizable majority (72 percent) of Disengaged Catholics never prays. Again, most Sporadic Catholics fall somewhere between these two extremes. Lastly, Practicing Catholics all report that their faith is extremely or very important in their daily lives, while no Disengaged Catholics claim the same. Most Sporadic Catholics claim their faith is just somewhat important in shaping their daily lives. Even though these three categories provide only a rough division of emerging adult Catholics, then, it is clear that the differences between them on religious measures are big. They can thus allow us to compare other differences in life outcomes by differences in Catholic faith and practice.

Catholic Religious Ideal Types and Life Outcomes

We now turn to the main question of this chapter: Does believing and practicing the Catholic faith make any difference in the day-to-day life experiences and outcomes of U.S. emerging adults? And if so, how much difference? The remainder of this chapter explores these questions by analyzing the non-religious experience and outcome variables measured in the third wave of the NSYR. In every table that follows, we display life-course experiences and outcomes for each of the Catholic religious ideal types described above. We used multivariate regression statistical models for each measure to control for the influence of age, sex, race/ethnicity, region of residence, parents' education, parental income, and parental assistance with expenses, as these variables can affect the relationship between religious ideal type and the experience or outcome in question. Why might this be necessary? To take one example, the group of Disengaged Catholics is 61 percent male, while females make up a slight majority of the other two groups. Since the gender of respondents is often associated with different life experiences or outcomes, raw percentages (like those in the below tables) that don't account for gender might misrepresent the actual relationship between the ideal type and any given outcome. Our multivariate models help to reveal the true relationship between religious ideal types and various life-course experiences and outcomes. When statistically significant differences exist (with 95 percent confidence) between the Disengaged category and either of the other two categories, the relevant percentages appear in bold type in the tables. The leftmost column in each table provides the national average on each measure for all U.S. emerging adults (Catholic and non-Catholic combined) for comparison.

Quality of Parental Relationships. Table 6.2 displays the quality of respondents' relationships with their parents for each Catholic ideal type. For some measures,

Table 6.2   **Quality of Parental Relationships of Catholic Emerging Adults,
Ages 18 to 23, by Ideal Types (Percents)**

	U.S.	Catholic type		
		Practicing	Sporadic	Disengaged
Still in contact with mother	98	98	100	99
Feels extremely or very close to mother	76	**88**	74	74
Gets along extremely or very well with mother	74	81	74	74
Talks to mother about personal subjects very often	26	**36**	23	18
Feels mother understands them very much	46	**57**	44	42
Still in contact with father	94	98	97	94
Feels extremely or very close to father	56	**73**	**60**	49
Gets along extremely or very well with father	64	67	66	64
Talks to father about personal subjects very often	9	18	9	7
Feels father understands them very much	34	**44**	36	28
Parental breakups				
None	58	**65**	**67**	56
2+ times	15	13	**11**	16

Note: Percentages are rounded to the nearest whole number. Differences that are statistically significant at the 0.05 level from the Disengaged category after controlling for age, sex, race, region of residence, parental education, individual income, and parental assistance with expenses are in bold.

Source: National Survey of Youth and Religion, 2007–2008.

such as being in contact with one's mother or father, the vast majority of Catholics respond similarly and there are no differences across categories. For most measures, however, Practicing Catholics are slightly to moderately more likely to have a close relationship with both their mother and father than Sporadic or Disengaged Catholics. Practicing Catholics are more likely to feel close to both their mother and father (88 percent feel close to their mother compared to 74 percent of Disengaged Catholics, and 73 percent feel close to their father compared to 49 percent of Disengaged Catholics), get along better with their mothers (81 percent compared to 74 for Disengaged Catholics), talk to both their mother and father about personal subjects often (36 percent versus 18 percent of Disengaged Catholics to their mother, and 18 percent versus 7 percent of Disengaged Catholics to their father), and feel that their mother and father understand them very well (57 percent compared to 42 percent of Disengaged Catholics for mother and 44 percent versus 28 percent of Disengaged Catholics for fathers). Many of these differences remain statistically significant after we control for a number of possible confounding factors, as described above. Additionally, the parents of both Practicing Catholics and Sporadic Catholics are slightly more likely to never have broken up (65 and 67 percent respectively) than the parents of Disengaged Catholics (56 percent), and Sporadic Catholics are less likely than Disengaged ones to have experienced two or more parental breakups (11 percent versus 16 percent). On no measure do the Disengaged emerging adult Catholics have stronger relationships with their parents than the Practicing, even by a margin too small to be statistically significant. On many of these measures, the Practicing Catholics have stronger relationships with parents than the average emerging adult in the U.S.

We do not believe that there is a simple, one-way causal influence from practicing Catholicism to achieving the outcomes related to parental relationships. It is likely that family stability and closeness to parents help instill the Catholic faith in young people and make it important enough to them that they will continue practicing their faith during the transitional period of emerging adulthood. The causal direction almost certainly runs in both directions here, reciprocally. The larger point is that practicing the Catholic faith and enjoying better relationships with parents seem frequently, although not inevitably, to come linked together.[6] On the one hand, being a stronger Catholic tends to help one have better relationships with parents. On the other hand, having better relationships with parents tends to make emerging adults stronger Catholics. The differences are not enormous, but they are often significant, and any real differences in such outcomes are worth understanding. So either or both of those conclusions—whichever it is in fact—is important to know.

Giving, Volunteering, and Involvement in Organized Activity. Table 6.3 compares the Catholic ideal types' rates of financial giving and volunteering rates. Here we find some pronounced differences. Practicing Catholics are nearly twice as likely as Disengaged Catholics (40 versus 23 percent) to have given away more than $50 of their own money in the past year, and almost two-thirds more likely to volunteer for community service (49 versus 31 percent). These differences remain statistically significant after controlling for other factors. Although not statistically significant, Practicing Catholics appear to be slightly more likely to volunteer frequently (10 or more times in the past year) and more

Table 6.3　**Giving and Volunteering Behavior of Catholic Emerging Adults, Ages 18 to 23, by Ideal Types (Percents)**

	U.S.	Catholic type		
		Practicing	*Sporadic*	*Disengaged*
Gave more than $50 to organizations or causes in last year	34	**40**	31	23
Volunteered for community service that was not required	40	**49**	**41**	31
Frequency of volunteer activities in past year				
10 or more times	15	20	16	16
1–2 times	13	14	12	10
Helped homeless or needy independently				
A lot	12	19	7	9
A little or none	59	49	60	64
Proportion of five closest friends who volunteer / do community service				
None	50	**45**	56	57
Less than half	31	32	28	31
Half or more	18	**22**	14	11

Note: Percentages are rounded to the nearest whole number. Differences that are statistically significant at the 0.05 level from the Disengaged category after controlling for age, sex, race, region of residence, parental education, individual income, and parental assistance with expenses are in bold.

Source: National Survey of Youth and Religion, 2007–2008.

likely to help the homeless or the needy directly, not through a program (19 percent claim they do this frequently, versus 7 percent of Sporadic Catholics and 9 percent of Disengaged Catholics). One probable cause of Practicing Catholics' higher rates of volunteering and community service is that their friends are more likely to be doing the same. Twenty-two percent of Practicing Catholics report that half or more of their closest friends engage in volunteer work, whereas 14 percent of Sporadic Catholics and 11 percent of the Disengaged report the same.

Another explanation for emerging adults' low levels of civic engagement, according to many scholars, is the low levels of formal organizational involvement

Table 6.4 **Organized Activity Involvement and Online Social Networking of Catholic Emerging Adults, Ages 18 to 23, by Ideal Types (Numbers, Percents)**

	U.S.	Catholic type		
		Practicing	Sporadic	Disengaged
Total number of organized activities involved with	1.6	**2.1**	**1.6**	1.3
Number of organized activities sponsored by a religious organization (not including worship or youth group)	0.3	**0.4**	0.1	0.0
Number of organized activities not sponsored by a religious organization	1.2	**1.6**	**1.5**	1.3
Member of a social networking website (percent)	76	77	81	79
Visits a social networking website once a day or more (members of website only) (percent)	53	51	56	59

Note: Percentages are rounded to the nearest whole number. Differences that are statistically significant at the 0.05 level from the Disengaged category after controlling for age, sex, race, region of residence, parental education, individual income, and parental assistance with expenses are in bold.

Source: National Survey of Youth and Religion, 2007–2008.

and membership during this period of the life course. Organizations provide the opportunity and often help supply the motivation to volunteer and give. Table 6.4 presents the organizational involvement of Catholic emerging adults by religious ideal type. Perhaps unsurprisingly, Practicing Catholics participate in more organized activities (an average of 2.1) compared to both Sporadic Catholics (1.6) and Disengaged Catholics (1.3). These differences are statistically significant after the use of controls. One might suppose that this is entirely due to different levels of participation in religiously sponsored activities, but this is not the case. While Practicing Catholics do participate in more religiously sponsored activities (0.4 versus 0.1 and 0 for Sporadic and Disengaged Catholics, respectively), they also participate in more activities sponsored by non-religious organizations (1.6 versus 1.5 and 1.3 for Sporadic and Disengaged Catholics, respectively). While these differences are not huge, they are statistically significant and meaningful. This also tells us that participating in religious activities does not appear to come at the expense of non-religious organized activities for those practicing their Catholic faith. Stronger Catholics are more involved in both religious and non-religious organizations. On some but not all of these measures, the Practicing Catholics are slightly more civically engaged than the average emerging adult in the U.S.

Also shown in Table 6.4 is online social networking activity. The differences between ideal types in "offline" organizational involvement do not translate to clear differences in online social networking activity. This suggests to us that it is not just general sociability that explains why Practicing Catholics are more likely to be involved in organized activities. Sociable individuals would be expected to be more sociable both online and in local organizations than the less sociable. Rather, it is more likely that regularly participating in Mass increases through a variety of causal mechanisms young people's opportunities and motivation for being involved in other organizations, both religious and secular.

Moral Orientation. We shift gears a bit in Table 6.5 to analyze the moral beliefs and orientations of emerging adult Catholics. Perhaps somewhat surprisingly, we find no substantial differences between the ideal types in the belief that it is okay to break moral rules if doing so offers an advantage and one can get away with it. This is a minority position for all Catholics—only about one-fifth affirm the statement, while four-fifths disagree with it. Other indicators of moral orientation and concern, however, do reveal differences by ideal type. Practicing Catholics are considerably less likely to believe that morals are relative (42 percent) than Disengaged Catholics (63 percent). Sporadic Catholics fall in between (54 percent), and both Sporadic and Practicing Catholics are significantly different from Disengaged Catholics. The final measures in this table ask respondents to indicate how much they care about the following three social issues: (1) equality between different racial groups, (2) the needs of the elderly, and (3) the needs of the poor. In each case, Practicing Catholics are more likely than other Catholics to affirm that they personally care very much about these issues; however, the magnitude of the gap varies. In caring about equality between racial groups, the difference between Practicing and Disengaged Catholics is 12 percentage points (51 percent versus 39 percent). Yet there is a much bigger difference when it comes to the elderly (66 percent of Practicing Catholics care very much about them versus 35 percent of the Disengaged) and the poor (72 percent of the Practicing care and 32 percent of the Disengaged). The differences between Practicing Catholics and Disengaged Catholics are statistically significant for both caring about the elderly and caring about the poor (and the Sporadic Catholics are statistically different on the measure of caring about the elderly). On most of these measures of morality, the Practicing Catholics, at least, appear somewhat stronger than the average emerging adult in the U.S., although the differences may not be statistically significant.

Risk Behaviors. Does being Catholic affect whether emerging adults in the U.S. engage in behaviors like binge drinking, smoking cigarettes or marijuana, and fighting? Table 6.6 reports the answer to this question. Practicing

Table 6.5 **Moral Orientation of Catholic Emerging Adults, Ages 18 to 23, by Ideal Types (Percents)**

	U.S.	Catholic types		
		Practicing	*Sporadic*	*Disengaged*
Believes that it is okay to break moral rules if it offers you an advantage and you can get away with it	16	18	20	21
Believes that morals are relative, that there are no definite rights and wrongs for everybody	46	**42**	**54**	63
Personally cares very much about equality between different racial groups	46	51	39	39
Personally cares very much about the needs of the elderly	53	**66**	**48**	35
Personally cares very much about the needs of poor people in the United States	51	**72**	46	32

Note: Percentages are rounded to the nearest whole number. Differences that are statistically different at the 0.05 level from the Disengaged category after controlling for age, sex, race, region of residence, parental education, individual income, and parental assistance with expenses are in bold.

Source: National Survey of Youth and Religion, 2007–2008.

Catholics are somewhat less likely to drink alcohol frequently than other Catholics: 30 percent report drinking at least weekly, while 43 percent report drinking a few times a year or never. This pattern is reversed for Disengaged Catholics. Forty-five percent report drinking at least weekly and 22 percent report drinking a few times a year or never. Sporadic Catholics are nearly identical to Disengaged Catholics on this measure. Even after controlling for other variables, Practicing Catholics are significantly different from Disengaged Catholics in reporting drinking seldom or never. A similar pattern emerges for binge drinking, which is defined as four or more drinks on a single occasion for a woman, or five or more for a man. Nearly twice the proportion of Disengaged Catholics report binge drinking three or more times in the last two weeks compared to Practicing Catholics (24 percent versus 13 percent). Practicing Catholics are more likely to report never engaging in this practice (57 percent) than other emerging adult Catholics (43 percent for Sporadic Catholics and 42 percent for Disengaged Catholics). These

Table 6.6   **Risk Behavior of Catholic Emerging Adults, Ages 18 to 23, by Ideal Type (Percents)**

	U.S.	Catholic types		
		Practicing	*Sporadic*	*Disengaged*
Drinks alcohol				
Weekly or more	35	30	45	45
A few times a year or never	37	**43**	26	22
Frequency of alcohol binge drinking				
Three or more times in the last two weeks	17	13	22	24
Never	53	57	43	42
Smokes cigarettes				
Weekly or more	24	15	22	27
Never	67	**76**	68	67
Smokes marijuana				
Weekly or more	12	**3**	12	17
Never	70	**83**	71	63
Has been in a serious fight more than once in the last two years	26	27	23	22
Likes to take risks	72	72	73	78
Percent of five closest friends who do drugs or drink a lot of alcohol	40	**31**	41	49

Note: Percentages are rounded to the nearest whole number. Differences that are statistically different at the 0.05 level from the Disengaged category after controlling for age, sex, race, region of residence, parental education, individual income, and parental assistance with expenses are in bold.

Source: National Survey of Youth and Religion, 2007–2008.

differences are not statistically significant, however, after controlling for the demographic variables named above.

Similar overall patterns emerge regarding smoking marijuana and cigarettes. Practicing Catholics are less likely to smoke in general, but particularly less likely to smoke pot frequently (3 percent do so weekly versus 17 percent of Disengaged Catholics). These differences remain when we control for the effects of a number of demographic influences in our statistical models. Somewhat surprisingly, a higher proportion of Practicing Catholics report being in a serious fight recently (27 percent in the past two years versus 23 percent for Sporadic Catholics and 22 percent for Disengaged Catholics). The differences are small, though, and not statistically significant. On many of these measures, the Practicing Catholics engage in fewer risk behaviors than the average emerging adult in the U.S.

Lastly, one survey question in Table 6.6 directly asks respondents whether they agree with the statement "I like to take risks." While the Disengaged Catholics are slightly more likely than others to agree with this statement (78 percent versus 72 percent for the Practicing Catholics and 73 percent for Sporadic Catholics), the differences are small and not statistically significant in our multivariate models with controls. However, we do find differences in the composition of friendship networks. Practicing Catholics have fewer close friends who do drugs or drink a lot of alcohol (on average, 31 percent of their five closest friends do these things, versus 49 percent for Disengaged Catholics). In sum, Practicing Catholic emerging adults are somewhat more likely to avoid alcohol and smoking—especially smoking marijuana—but this is not because they are particularly risk averse, by their own account. It is more likely the result of being embedded in friendship networks and communities of faith that provide fewer opportunities to engage in these behaviors and that enforce informal sanctions against them.

Physical Health, Mental Health, and Subjective Well-being. Table 6.7 reports that emerging adults we label as Practicing Catholics both perceive themselves to be in better health than other Catholics (72 percent report being in excellent or very good health compared to 60 percent of Disengaged Catholics) and score better on the body mass index ratio of height to weight (67 percent report being in the normal range, compared to 52 percent for Sporadic Catholics and 53 percent for Disengaged Catholics)—differences that may be due to Practicing Catholics' lower levels of alcohol use and smoking. However, BMI differences do not reach statistical significance in our multivariate models that control for related demographic factors. Despite their better overall health, the differences between Practicing Catholics and other Catholics in feelings of happiness about their own physical appearance are quite small (78, 74, and 70 percent feel very or somewhat happy, for Practicing, Sporadic, and Disengaged Catholics, respectively). None of these differences reach statistical significance.

Table 6.7 also includes two general measures of personal well-being. The first asks respondents how often they think about and plan for the future. Being "planful" in adolescence and emerging adulthood is linked, according to many other studies, to successfully adjusting to adulthood and new responsibilities later in life.[7] Most Catholic emerging adults report that they engage in this type of planning very or fairly often. However, a higher proportion of Practicing Catholics report this (91 percent compared to 83 percent for Sporadic Catholics

Table 6.7 **Health and Subjective Well-being of Catholic Emerging Adults, Ages 18 to 23, by Ideal Types (Percents)**

	U.S.	Catholic type		
		Practicing	*Sporadic*	*Disengaged*
Physical health is excellent or very good	63	**72**	63	60
BMI categories				
Normal	56	67	52	53
Overweight	27	17	33	27
Obese	13	14	12	13
Feelings about own body and physical appearance				
Very or somewhat happy	73	78	74	70
Very or somewhat unhappy	18	14	19	21
Thinks about and plans for the future				
Very or fairly often	82	**91**	83	80
Rarely or never	4	3	2	5
Thinks about the meaning of life				
Very or fairly often	44	**55**	38	34
Rarely or never	24	**21**	**22**	39

Note: Percentages are rounded to the nearest whole number. Differences that are statistically different at the 0.05 level from the Disengaged category after controlling for age, sex, race, region of residence, parental education, individual income, and parental assistance with expenses are in bold.

Source: National Survey of Youth and Religion, 2007–2008.

and 80 percent for Disengaged Catholics), a difference that we can confidently say is real, even after controlling for other factors. Last in this table is a measure of how often emerging adult Catholics report thinking about the meaning of life. A slight majority of Practicing Catholics claims that they think about this very or fairly often (55 percent), while only approximately one-third (34 percent) of Disengaged Catholics report doing the same. On the other end of the spectrum, nearly twice the proportion of Disengaged Catholics (39 percent) report rarely or never thinking about the meaning of life compared to Practicing Catholics (21 percent) or Sporadic Catholics (22 percent). These differences are statistically significant. On many of these measures, the Practicing Catholics appear healthier than the average emerging adult in the U.S.

Continuing with this theme of a healthy interior life for emerging adult Catholics, Table 6.8 covers measures of depression and social acceptance. According to our findings, emerging adults who believe and practice their Catholicism more are no more protected against depression (63 percent rarely or never feel depressed) than other Catholics (65 percent of Sporadic Catholics and 67 percent of the Disengaged rarely or never feel depressed). When we examine feelings of meaninglessness we see something similar. Although few respondents report frequently feeling that life is meaningless, there are no substantial differences between groups. (The only statistically significant difference is between the 82 percent of Sporadic Catholics who report rarely or never feeling this compared to 75 percent of Disengaged Catholics.) However, Practicing Catholics report modestly higher levels of social support, which may help them cope with feelings of depression or meaninglessness. Eighty-seven percent of Practicing

Table 6.8 **Mental Health and Social Relationships of Emerging Adults, Ages 18 to 23, by Religious Ideal Types (Percents)**

	U.S.	Catholic type		
		Practicing	*Sporadic*	*Disengaged*
Rarely or never feels sad or depressed	63	63	65	67
How often life feels meaningless				
Very or fairly often	6	4	5	7
Rarely or never	80	82	**82**	75
Feels loved and accepted a lot	73	**87**	73	73
Never feels alone and misunderstood	42	**53**	40	41
Never feels invisible	69	69	67	67
How often feels guilty about things in life				
Very or fairly often	21	27	18	19
Rarely or never	41	36	43	48
Has experienced a traumatic event in the last 2 years	48	55	46	43

Note: Percentages are rounded to the nearest whole number. Differences that are statistically different at the 0.05 level from the Disengaged category after controlling for age, sex, race, region of residence, parental education, individual income, and parental assistance with expenses are in bold.

Source: National Survey of Youth and Religion, 2007–2008.

Catholics report feeling loved and accepted a lot for who they are, compared to 73 percent of both Sporadic and Disengaged Catholics. Similarly, a little more than one-half (53 percent) of Practicing Catholics report never feeling alone and misunderstood. Sporadic and Disengaged Catholics report 40 and 41 percent respectively. In both cases, Practicing Catholics are statistically significantly different from the Disengaged Catholics. Still, about two-thirds of all Catholics report never feeling invisible, regardless of whether they are Practicing, Sporadic, or Disengaged.

Although most emerging adult Catholics do not feel guilty about things they have done in their lives, slightly higher proportions of Practicing Catholics report experiencing guilt frequently (27 percent report feeling guilty very or fairly often versus 18 percent of Sporadic Catholics and 19 percent of Disengaged Catholics), and a lower proportion report rarely or never feeling guilty (36 percent of Practicing Catholics, compared to 43 percent of Sporadic Catholics and 48 percent of Disengaged Catholics). However, our multivariate statistical analyses, which report no statistically significant differences, suggest we cannot be highly confident that these differences are real in the Catholic emerging adult population.[8] Lastly, one measure inquires whether the respondent has experienced a traumatic life event, such as the death or serious illness of someone close to the respondent, in the past two years. Although these differences do not reach statistical significance, a slightly higher percentage of Practicing Catholics report having such an experience (55 percent, versus 46 percent of Sporadic Catholics and 43 percent of the Disengaged). It is certainly plausible that in experiencing such an event, some young people turn to the Catholic faith they were raised in to help cope. It is also possible that Practicing Catholics have larger and more extensive social networks, increasing the likelihood that someone close to them will be in an accident, become seriously ill, or die. But the lack of statistical significance for these differences means we should not read too much into variability in the reported percentages. On only a few of these measures, the Practicing Catholics appear to be healthier than the average emerging adult in the U.S.

Purpose, Gratitude, Locus of Control, and Life Satisfaction. The next four tables, Table 6.9 through Table 6.12, report on several psychological constructs included in the NSYR. In each table we include the individual components of the construct as well as an additive index. The first of these, Table 6.9, includes items measuring emerging adults Catholics' sense of purpose in life. Practicing Catholics have modestly higher scores overall, indicating a greater sense of purpose. Practicing Catholics are particularly distinct from others on the first two items. They are less likely to say that their life lacks clear goals or directions (21 percent compared to 29 percent for Disengaged Catholics) and that they do not have a good sense of what they want to accomplish in life (11 percent versus 21 percent

Table 6.9 **Sense of Purpose of Catholic Emerging Adults, Ages 18 to 23, by Ideal Types (Percents)**

	U.S.	Catholic type		
		Practicing	*Sporadic*	*Disengaged*
Life often seems to lack clear goals or directions	25	**21**	24	29
Does not have a good sense of what he or she wants to accomplish	21	**11**	23	21
Not someone who wanders aimlessly through life	82	80	81	82
Average purpose scale score	11.4	**12.1**	11.4	11.3

Note: Percentages are rounded to the nearest whole number. Differences that are statistically different at the 0.05 level from the Disengaged category after controlling for age, sex, race, region of residence, parental education, individual income, and parental assistance with expenses are in bold.

Source: National Survey of Youth and Religion, 2007–2008.

for Disengaged Catholics). These differences shown in bold are statistically significant in models that control for other variables. There were not clear differences in the third item, which asked respondents whether they agree that they are not someone who wanders aimlessly through life. Most of the differences between the Practicing Catholics and all U.S. emerging adults are modest.

The next table, Table 6.10, includes items designed to measure respondents' feelings of gratitude. The first item, which asks whether long amounts of time can go by before the respondent feels grateful to something or someone, shows the least agreement among Practicing Catholics (29 percent answered in the affirmative). Forty-six percent of both Sporadic and Disengaged Catholics report agreeing with the same statement. This difference is statistically significant. However, there are no clear differences between Catholic emerging adults on the other two measures of gratitude. Very few Catholics—between 5 and 7 percent—say that there is not much in the world to be grateful for, and nearly all Catholics agree that they have so much to be thankful for in their own lives (99 and 100 percent). It appears that most U.S. emerging adult Catholics recognize that they have people or material blessings in their lives for which they ought to be grateful. However, nearly half of Sporadic and Disengaged Catholics do not always express this gratitude. Practicing Catholics are somewhat more likely to report feeling grateful. The composite index of gratitude indicates that Practicing Catholics are significantly more likely to be grateful than Disengaged Catholics. Table 6.11 includes three measures of "locus of control"—the degree

Table 6.10 **Feelings of Gratitude of Catholic Emerging Adults, Ages 18 to 23, by Ideal Types (Percents)**

	U.S.	Catholic type		
		Practicing	*Sporadic*	*Disengaged*
Long amounts of time go by before feeling grateful to something or someone	41	**29**	46	46
Does not see much to be grateful for in the world	5	5	6	7
Has so much in life to be thankful for	98	100	99	99
Average gratitude scale score	12.0	**12.7**	11.9	11.7

Note: Percentages are rounded to the nearest whole number. Differences that are statistically different at the 0.05 level from the Disengaged category after controlling for age, sex, race, region of residence, parental education, individual income, and parental assistance with expenses are in bold.

Source: National Survey of Youth and Religion, 2007–2008.

Table 6.11 **Locus of Control of Catholic Emerging Adults, Ages 18 to 23, by Ideal Types (Percents)**

	U.S.	Catholic type		
		Practicing	*Sporadic*	*Disengaged*
Feels they have little control over things that happen	27	27	29	24
Feels there is no way to solve some personal problems	27	29	28	26
Feels there is little one can do to change many of the important things in life	23	21	25	22
Often feels helpless when dealing with problems of life	23	23	24	19
Average locus of control scale score	14.8	15.1	14.6	15.0

Note: Percentages are rounded to the nearest whole number. Differences that are statistically different at the 0.05 level from the Disengaged category after controlling for age, sex, race, region of residence, parental education, individual income, and parental assistance with expenses are in bold.

Source: National Survey of Youth and Religion, 2007–2008.

to which respondents feel self-empowered and in control of their lives—as well as its composite index. There are no substantive or statistically significant differences between Catholics on any of these items. Attending church frequently, praying often, and claiming that faith is important do not seem to affect how much control emerging adult Catholics feel over the circumstances of their lives. In fact, these Catholics feel about the same as all U.S. emerging adults, meaning their faith does not seem to make a difference in their locus of control.

Table 6.12 includes four measures related to overall life satisfaction as well as the composite index of satisfaction. On two of the measures, there are moderate differences between Practicing Catholics and other Catholics, and on two others there appears to be little to no difference. Practicing Catholics are more likely to agree that their lives are close to ideal (76 percent versus 60 percent of Disengaged Catholics) and that they have gotten the important things in life (80 percent versus 68 percent of Disengaged Catholics). These differences remain statistically significant in our multivariate models. However, Practicing Catholics are only slightly more likely to say that the conditions of their lives are excellent (78 percent compared to 72 percent of Disengaged Catholics), and virtually no different in feeling satisfied with their personal lives (87 percent compared to 86 percent of Disengaged Catholics). Overall, this produces a modestly higher, as well as statistically significant, score on the composite index for life satisfaction for Practicing Catholics. Sporadic Catholics are also different from Disengaged Catholics to a statistically significant degree on the overall index. Differences between Practicing Catholic emerging adults and all U.S. emerging adults are modest and sometimes non-existent.

Table 6.12 **Life Satisfaction of Catholic Emerging Adults, Ages 18 to 23, by Ideal Types (Percents)**

	U.S.	Catholic type		
		Practicing	*Sporadic*	*Disengaged*
Feels that life is close to ideal	68	**76**	**71**	60
Feels that the conditions of life are excellent	74	78	74	72
Feels satisfied with personal life	87	87	87	86
Have gotten the important things in life	70	**80**	73	68
Average life satisfaction scale score	14.6	**15.5**	**14.7**	14.1

Note: Percentages are rounded to the nearest whole number. Differences that are statistically different at the 0.05 level from the Disengaged category after controlling for age, sex, race, region of residence, parental education, individual income, and parental assistance with expenses are in bold.

Source: National Survey of Youth and Religion, 2007–2008.

Table 6.13 **Education, Employment, and Debt of Catholic Emerging Adults, Ages 18 to 23, by Ideal Types (Percents)**

	U.S.	Catholic type		
		Practicing	Sporadic	Disengaged
Highest level of education completed some college or more	66	73	71	70
Unemployed	13	**11**	**13**	16
Average work hours (among those not enrolled in school)	30	33	28	29
Level of credit card debt:				
In dollars	1,244	1,135	1,053	1,207
As a percentage of income	17.3	8.8	25.7	12.8

Note: Percentages are rounded to the nearest whole number. Differences that are statistically different at the 0.05 level from the Disengaged category after controlling for age, sex, race, region of residence, parental education, individual income, and parental assistance with expenses are in bold.

Source: National Survey of Youth and Religion, 2007–2008.

Education, Employment, Debt, and Attitudes about Consumerism. Moving away from the psychological state of emerging adult Catholics, we now turn to measures of educational attainment, employment, and debt in Table 6.13. Overall, Catholics appear slightly more likely than all U.S. emerging adults to have completed at least some college, but there are not clear and statistically significant differences between types of emerging adult Catholics. Seventy-three percent of Practicing Catholics, 71 percent of Sporadic Catholics, and 70 percent of Disengaged Catholics have taken some college classes or gone even further in their education. Turning to work-related outcomes, there are some modest differences in unemployment (actively looking for a job in the past two weeks) between types of emerging adult Catholics. Practicing Catholics and Sporadic Catholics have lower unemployment rates (11 percent and 13 percent respectively) than Disengaged Catholics (16 percent), and these differences are statistically significant. Among those who are working and not enrolled in school, Practicing Catholics work a few more hours per week (33 hours) than either Sporadic Catholics (28) or Disengaged Catholics (29). But these differences are not statistically significant. Finally, we see very few differences in terms of the dollar amount of credit card debt (ranging from $1,053 to $1,207). When translating this debt to a percentage of personal income, Sporadic Catholics have a much greater debt load, but these differences (despite being large) are not statistically significant. Personal income varies widely during the emerging adult

Table 6.14 **Attitudes about Consumerism of Catholic Emerging Adults, Ages 18 to 23, by Ideal Types (Percents)**

	U.S.	Catholic type		
		Practicing	*Sporadic*	*Disengaged*
Would be happier if they could afford to buy more	54	50	54	55
Admires people who own expensive homes, cars, and clothes	37	33	38	38
Feels that things owned say a lot about how well they are doing in life	47	**54**	**51**	42
Shopping and buying things gives a lot of pleasure	66	69	68	62
Average Consumerism Scale Score	12.1	12.2	12.3	12.0

Note: Percentages are rounded to the nearest whole number. Differences that are statistically different at the 0.05 level from the Disengaged category after controlling for age, sex, race, region of residence, parental education, individual income, and parental assistance with expenses are in bold.

Source: National Survey of Youth and Religion, 2007–2008.

years, with many young people having no income because they are not yet working. For these reasons, it will be more instructive to examine personal debt during later emerging adult years, when personal income and spending habits become more stable and clear.

The next table, 6.14, measures attitudes about consumerism among emerging adults. The only substantial differences between Catholic types is about whether the things one owns say a lot about how well one is doing in life. Interestingly enough, the Practicing Catholics (54 percent) affirm this statement more than the Sporadic Catholics (51 percent) and the Disengaged Catholics (42 percent). The differences between the first two groups and the third remain statistically significant in our multivariate models, meaning that socioeconomic status of family of origin cannot explain these differences. However, the composite index of attitudes about consumerism indicates that there are no overall differences between the Catholics groups, nor between Catholics and the general emerging adult population.

Sexual Activity. The final three tables present our findings about the sexual behavior of Catholic emerging adults. The first table deals with a variety of sexual behaviors other than oral sex and vaginal intercourse, the second-to-last table deals with oral sex, and the last with sexual intercourse. We begin with self-reports on the frequency of viewing pornography in the past year in Table 6.15.

Table 6.15 **Sexual Activity of Catholic Emerging Adults, Ages 18 to 23, by Ideal Types (Percents)**

	U.S.	Catholic type		
		Practicing	Sporadic	Disengaged
Frequency of viewing pornography in the last year				
More than five times	16	12	17	22
Never	50	55	48	41
Ever willingly touched private area of another person or been touched by another person (asked only those never married)	85	**74**	91	89
Median number of people ever been physically involved with, more than holding hands and light kissing (only those never married)	3	**2**	3	4
Number of nights in the past 4 weeks spent overnight with significant other (only those never married)				
None	56	64	50	51
1–7	28	30	36	26
8 or more	16	7	**14**	22
Ever cohabited	19	25	23	
Will likely marry person currently in a romantic relationship with (asked only those currently in a romantic relationship)	85	**90**	**89**	78
Have a lot or very many regrets over sexually intimate experiences (asked only those never married and physically involved)	10	11	6	3

Note: Percentages are rounded to the nearest whole number. Differences that are statistically different at the 0.05 level from the Disengaged category after controlling for age, sex, race, region of residence, parental education, individual income, and parental assistance with expenses are in bold.

Source: National Survey of Youth and Religion, 2007–2008.

A smaller proportion of Practicing Catholics reports viewing pornography five or more times in the previous year (12 percent) than Sporadic Catholics (17 percent) or Disengaged Catholics (22 percent). Likewise, a larger proportion of Practicing Catholics reports never viewing pornography (55 percent) than Sporadic Catholics (48 percent) or Disengaged Catholics (41 percent). Still, neither the Practicing Catholics nor Sporadic Catholics are statistically different from Disengaged Catholics in the multivariate models with controls. The next measure concerns the percent of unmarried emerging adult Catholics who report willingly having touched a private area of another person or being touched by another person in this way. While roughly nine out of ten Sporadic Catholics (91 percent) and Disengaged Catholics (89 percent) report having done this, only about three out of four Practicing Catholics claim the same (74 percent). In other words, most emerging adult Catholics have willingly touched or been touched by another person in private areas of the body, though among Practicing Catholics this experience is somewhat less common. Next, looking at the median number (that is, the number at the 50th percentile of each group) of people each respondent reports being physically intimate with, beyond holding hands and light kissing, we find that Practicing Catholics report two, Sporadic Catholics three, and Disengaged Catholics four. The difference between Practicing and Disengaged Catholics is statistically significant.

The next several measures ask about the respondents' romantic and sexual partners. Overall, Practicing Catholics report spending the night with their significant other less frequently than either Sporadic Catholics or Disengaged Catholics. Nearly two-thirds of Practicing Catholics (64 percent) report that they did not spend the night at all with a significant other in the previous four weeks, while approximately half of other Catholics report the same. Significantly fewer Practicing and Sporadic Catholics had spent the night with a significant other eight or more times in the previous four weeks than Disengaged Catholics (at 7, 14, and 22 percent for those groups, respectively). Practicing Catholic emerging adults also spend the night with significant others less frequently than all U.S. emerging adults. A slightly lower percentage (19 percent) of Practicing Catholics than Sporadic Catholics (25 percent) or Disengaged Catholics (23 percent) report having ever cohabited with a significant other. However, the differences in the number of overnight stays and the cohabitation rate between Disengaged Catholics and others are not statistically significant in our full statistical analysis. The next measure is about whether respondents who are currently in a romantic relationship expect to marry this person—not strictly a question about sex. Fully nine in ten Practicing Catholics and Sporadic Catholics (90 percent and 89 percent respectively) believe they will marry their current romantic partner. Among Disengaged Catholics this proportion is closer to three-fourths (78 percent). These differences are statistically significant. Lastly, among those never-married Catholics who have been physically involved, 11 percent of Practicing Catholics report having a lot of or very many regrets over these sexually intimate experiences. Six percent of Sporadic Catholics and 3 percent of Disengaged Catholics report having frequent regrets. As we found with the measure of guilt we mentioned earlier, fewer emerging adult Catholics than all U.S. emerging adults are in any sort of anguish over their past sexual behaviors. Nevertheless, despite not reaching statistical significance, the percentages still suggest that Practicing Catholics tend to experience more of these types of feelings than other emerging adult Catholics.

Table 6.16 reports on the frequency of oral sex among never-married Catholic emerging adults. About half of Practicing Catholics (53 percent) report that they have had oral sex. This proportion is substantially smaller (to a statistically significant degree) than those of both Sporadic Catholics (77 percent) and Disengaged Catholics (84 percent). The remaining items in the table are restricted to unmarried respondents that have engaged in oral sex. Practicing Catholics who have had oral sex report having had it the first time at a slightly older age than the other groups (16.8 versus 16.3 for Sporadic Catholics and 16.1 for Disengaged Catholics) and have had fewer oral sex partners on average (a median of one for Practicing Catholics, two for Sporadic Catholics, and three for Disengaged Catholics). These differences are not statistically significant according to our multivariate models, however, which is probably due to the fairly small sample size of Practicing Catholics who have had oral sex and have never been married (N = 61). Both Practicing and Sporadic Catholics report that fewer of their oral sex partners were in a "casual" relationship with them (26.4 percent and 25.1 percent respectively) compared to Disengaged Catholics (36 percent). However, like the other measures, this one does not reach statistical significance. Among those who have had oral sex, both Practicing Catholics and Sporadic Catholics appear to have done so less frequently than Disengaged Catholics (51 percent of those Practicing Catholics report having had oral sex many times, 47 percent of Sporadic Catholics, and 61 percent of Disengaged Catholics), although almost all Catholic emerging adults who have had oral sex have done so more than once. Only the Sporadic Catholics are significantly different from Disengaged Catholics (once again, most likely due to the low sample size of Practicing Catholics who have had oral sex). When asked how recently they have had oral sex, Practicing Catholics are actually the most likely to report having done so in the past month (64 percent), although they are not statistically different from Disengaged Catholics (60 percent). Lastly, there appears to be no substantial differences between Catholic types in the use of protection against STDs during oral sex. Roughly one in ten Catholics who have had oral sex report using protection every time, and a little more than half report never using protection. Overall, Practicing Catholic

Table 6.16   **Oral Sex Behavior of Never-Married Catholic Emerging Adults, Ages 18 to 23, by Ideal Types**

	U.S.	Catholic type		
		Practicing	*Sporadic*	*Disengaged*
Have had oral sex	71	**53**	77	84
Mean age of first oral sex (if has had oral sex)	16.2	16.8	16.3	16.1
Median number of oral sex partners (asked if has had oral sex)	3	1	2	3
Percent of oral sex partners in "casual" relationship (asked if has had oral sex)	30.4	26.4	25.1	36.0
Frequency of oral sex (asked if has had oral sex)				
Once	4	2	2	2
A few or several times	46	47	**51**	37
Many times	51	51	**47**	61
Recentness of oral sex (asked if has had oral sex)				
Last month	54	64	53	60
More than 1 year ago	9	7	6	9
Used protection against STDs during oral sex (asked if has had oral sex)?				
Every time	14	9	14	8
Never	52	56	53	54

Note: Percentages are rounded to the nearest whole number. Differences that are statistically different at the 0.05 level from the Disengaged category after controlling for age, sex, race, region of residence, parental education, individual income, and parental assistance with expenses are in bold.

Source: National Survey of Youth and Religion, 2007–2008.

emerging adults do not look very different from all U.S. emerging adults on these measures.

The final table, Table 6.17, presents many of these same outcomes for sexual intercourse. First, as with oral sex, unmarried Practicing Catholics are considerably less likely to report having engaged in sexual intercourse. About three out of five Practicing Catholic emerging adults have had sexual intercourse outside of marriage (61 percent), while about four out of five other Catholic emerging

Table 6.17 **Sexual Intercourse Behavior of Never-Married Catholic Emerging Adults, Ages 18 to 23, by Ideal Types (Percents)**

	U.S.	Catholic type		
		Practicing	*Sporadic*	*Disengaged*
Has had sexual intercourse	73	**61**	79	81
Mean age of first sexual intercourse (asked if has had sex)	16.2	17.0	16.4	16.3
Median number of sex partners (asked if has had sex)	3	2	3	4
Percent of sexual partners in "casual" relationship (asked if has had sex)	35.7	27.4	29.0	38.6
Number of times respondent has had sexual intercourse (asked if has had sex)				
Once	2	5	2	1
A few or several times	32	**42**	**37**	20
Many times	64	**49**	**60**	78
Recentness of last sexual intercourse (asked if has had sex)				
Last month	66	60	65	71
More than 1 year ago	6	8	4	5
Used condom to protect against STDs during most recent sexual intercourse (asked if has had sex)	63	**73**	**63**	52
Has been pregnant (asked only of never married females)				
Never	80	80	80	92
Once	13	20	12	6
More than once	6	0	8	2
Has impregnated someone (asked only of never married males)	12	21	12	11
Has had an abortion (asked of all females)	3	4	5	4

Note: Percentages are rounded to the nearest whole number. Differences that are statistically different at the 0.05 level from the Disengaged category after controlling for age, sex, race, region of residence, parental education, individual income, and parental assistance with expenses are in bold.

Source: National Survey of Youth and Religion, 2007–2008.

adults have done the same (79 percent of Sporadic Catholics and 81 percent of Disengaged Catholics). The next outcomes are restricted to this sample of never-married Catholics who have had sexual intercourse. We find virtually the same numbers for sexual intercourse that we find for oral sex on the next few measures. Practicing Catholics waited a little bit longer to have sexual intercourse for the first time (17 years old compared to 16.4 and 16.3 for Sporadic and Disengaged Catholics), have had fewer partners overall (with the median number being two for Practicing Catholics, three for Sporadic Catholics, and four for Disengaged Catholics), and describe fewer of their sexual partners as being in a "casual" relationship with them (27.4 percent for Practicing Catholics, 29 percent for Sporadic Catholics, and 38.6 percent for Disengaged Catholics). None of these differences remain statistically significant after controls are introduced, however.

Within the same restricted sample of Catholics who have had sexual intercourse, there are some notable differences in the number of times they have had sex. Approximately half (49 percent) of Practicing Catholics who have had sex report having had it many times. Three in five (60 percent) Sporadic Catholics and nearly four in five (78 percent) Disengaged Catholics report the same. The differences between the first two groups and the Disengaged Catholics are statistically significant in our full models with statistical controls. In another finding similar to those about oral sex, very few Catholic emerging adults who have had sexual intercourse report having had it only once. When asked about the last time they had sexual intercourse, slightly lower proportions of sexually active Practicing Catholics report having done so recently (60 percent in the past month) compared to Disengaged Catholics (71 percent), but these differences are not statistically significant. Unlike what we found with oral sex, however, Practicing Catholics who have had sexual intercourse outside of marriage are *more* likely to use condoms to protect against STDs than other Catholics (73 percent report using them compared to 63 percent of Sporadic Catholics and 52 percent of Disengaged Catholics). This may be because they are more likely to have sex within a more serious relationship, which we might infer from the statistics on "casual" relationships above.

The final three measures in Table 6.17 examine pregnancy and abortion. Perhaps somewhat surprisingly, never-married Practicing and Sporadic Catholic females report higher rates of pregnancy than Disengaged Catholics (20 percent of both groups report being pregnant at least once, while only 8 percent of Disengaged Catholics report the same). Male Practicing Catholics who have never been married report similar numbers to their female counterparts (21 percent report impregnating someone), while only 12 and 11 percent of Sporadic and Disengaged Catholics report the same. But these differences are not statistically significant after controlling for demographic variables. Lastly, there are no substantial differences in the percentage of female Catholics who have had an abortion (a statistic that includes those who have been married). Four to five percent of all Catholic female emerging adults report having had at least one abortion.[9] Thus, the Practicing and Sporadic Catholics are not statistically significantly different from the Disengaged Catholics on any of the measure about pregnancy and abortion.

Emerging Themes

Taking a step back and surveying the general patterns evident in the tables above, it is clear that the group we labeled Practicing Catholic displays usually modest, but in some cases quite substantial, differences in life experiences and outcomes compared to the other Catholic ideal types, particularly compared to the Disengaged Catholics. We must not overstate the size of these effects. Few are dramatic. Nevertheless, we find fairly consistent evidence that these groups are genuinely different, at least to some modest degree, on many life experiences and outcomes.

For example, on many indicators of involvement in public life and organized activities, it appears that Practicing Catholics have more opportunities to become involved and take advantage of them. Many young people are structurally disengaged from the institutions of public life during this phase of the life course.[10] On the whole, emerging adult Catholics who believe and practice their faith more actively tend to voluntarily donate money more, volunteer more, and participate more in organized activities. One reason we see for this is the composition of their friendship networks. Practicing Catholics are more likely to surround themselves with friends who give, participate, and volunteer as well as friends who avoid deviant activities such as heavy drinking or drug use. But we suspect it is not only their close friends who are influencing these practices. Those who have spent time in a religious congregation know that it makes one more aware of opportunities to give financially, volunteer, and become involved with other organizations. This may be through casual acquaintances in conversation or official organizational recruitment efforts. Not only are opportunities for involvement increased, but people's motivation to serve and give often comes through other parishioners or homilies expounding on Christian service to others. While those who believe and practice the Catholic faith more during emerging adulthood do not automatically give more, volunteer more, or participate more in organized activities, their world is structured in such a way as to make these outcomes more likely.

Also, although Practicing Catholics do not report feeling more self-empowered, they report having more social and community support objectively.

Emerging adult Catholics who are involved with their faith still report feeling depressed, having personal problems that they feel they cannot solve, and feeling helpless or feeling they have little control over parts of their lives at roughly the same rate as other Catholics (and emerging adults more generally). Not only this, but Practicing Catholics are slightly more likely to have experienced a traumatic event in the past two years (such as someone close to them dying, becoming seriously ill, or being in an accident). Regular participation in and identification with the Catholic faith does not prevent these things from happening or prevent the anxiety and depression that can result. Nevertheless, Practicing Catholics report having the social support to help cope with these difficult parts of life. They feel more loved and accepted and less alone and misunderstood than other Catholics. On average, they also have closer relationships with their mothers and fathers. Perhaps it is this social support, and not protection from the difficulties of life as an emerging adult, that leads these Catholics to express more gratitude overall and report a greater general satisfaction with their life.

Furthermore, Practicing Catholics are more purposeful and mindful about their lives and future than other emerging adult Catholics. They are more likely to think about and plan for the future and more likely to express a sense of purpose in their lives. They are considerably more likely to think often about the meaning of life. Catholic faith and practice appear to provide some of the tools that allow emerging adults to take a step back from their immediate circumstances and assess their current station and future trajectory in life. Studying data collected over decades from respondents born in California in the 1920s, one sociologist found this type of mindfulness about one's own life and future (something he calls "planful competence") to be highly predictive of successfully inhabiting future adult roles and life-course transitions.[11] We suspect that the moral framework inhabited by emerging adult Catholics who are more involved in a local parish, who regularly pray, and who report that their faith is important in daily life helps them to better narrate and make sense of their lives and provides directives for the future. Regular involvement in a parish is also likely to have the very practical consequence of exposing emerging adults to responsible older adults who can serve as role models and help them to successfully enter full adulthood themselves.

At the same time, commitment to the Catholic faith during emerging adulthood has little impact on personal attitudes toward consumerism and consumption. Practicing Catholics were no different from other Catholics on these outcomes. As we documented earlier in Chapter 1, American Catholics as a group have moved from a state of ethnic, political, and cultural marginalization and into the American mainstream during the mid–twentieth century. During this process they appear to have rather uncritically embraced middle-class American consumerism. Elsewhere, one of us has written more extensively about the widespread acceptance of consumerism among emerging adults more generally.[12] It is sufficient here to note that American Catholicism, as it is widely practiced and taught to youth, does not seem to have the cultural tools to counter the dominant accounts of the (materialistic) "good life" for most Americans. Nevertheless, Practicing Catholic emerging adults are still more likely to accept the Church's teaching on issues of social justice and responsibilities toward the poor. As far as we can tell from this survey data, however, in the minds of emerging adult Catholics, these teachings have little to do with a general embrace or critique of consumerism and overconsumption.

Lastly, most emerging adult Catholics are not living out the Catholic Church's teaching on sex and sexuality, but neither do all of them completely bracket off their faith from this part of their lives. Some scholars have claimed that Catholic emerging adults' sex lives are almost completely disconnected from matters of faith.[13] From our data this does appear to be true for most emerging adult Catholics. Yet the sexual practices of emerging adult Catholics who are at least moderately committed to their faith are noticeably different. For example, while most unmarried emerging adult Catholics have had sexual intercourse, among those Catholics we labeled "Practicing," only a minority is having frequent sex (about three in 10). This may still seem to some like a large proportion, but it is relatively small compared to the nearly two out of three unmarried Disengaged Catholics who are frequently having sex. Thus, it appears that some Catholics are trying to heed the teachings of the Catholic Church at least somewhat, even if they are a distinct minority. Still, understood from a sociological perspective, such matters are not simply about a conscious decision to follow Church teaching or not. The social environments of Practicing Catholics are also likely to be constructed in such ways as to lessen the opportunities for sex and increase the cost of sex, particularly for men. The sociologists Mark Regnerus and Jeremy Uecker make a strong case that variations in sexual activity among unmarried youth have much to do with the supply of opportunities for sex for men.[14] Despite the "hook up" culture of casual sex among emerging adults, most opportunities for sex still come in the form of committed relationships. We suspect that women who belong to religious communities that proscribe premarital sexual activity, and provide social support to uphold these proscriptions, are able to limit men's access to sexual opportunities in ways that women outside of such communities may be less able to use.

Conclusion

Most accounts of young Catholics today lump all self-identifying Catholics together as a group and compare them to youth in other religious traditions, to the non-religious, or to older Catholics. This is one useful way to get a very broad assessment of Catholics. However, it often overlooks the real diversity within American Catholicism. To take a different approach, in this chapter we divided emerging adult Catholics into three different "ideal types" based on their religious identity and practice. We found that on a variety of measures of life experiences and outcomes, these groups fared differently. Often the differences were small, but sometimes they were moderate or large. The patterns of differences were also fairly consistent: emerging adult Catholics who were more involved in their faith—as measured by Mass attendance, prayer, and self-rated importance of faith—are doing what most people (especially most committed Catholic adults) would consider to be better in life on many outcomes.[15] We do not claim that this difference is produced solely by the personal faith commitments of these emerging adults, as a matter of simple, one-directional causation. But we do note that some positive life-course experiences and outcomes seem more likely to be associated among Catholic emerging adults with more seriously practicing and committing to religious faith.

|| 7 ||

Catholic High School and Religiousness in Emerging Adulthood

We discovered in Chapter 5 that attending a Catholic high school is a significant teenage-era factor associated with increased religiousness in the transition to emerging adulthood. Given its substantive importance to many readers and its potentially complex theoretic underpinnings as a causal mechanism in the transmission of religious faith, we decided to devote additional analysis and discussion to this aspect of some Catholic teenagers' lives. In what follows, we more fully examine the Catholic school effect to discover to what extent, how, and why attending Catholic high school seems to impact religiousness in the transition to emerging adulthood. Our method is similar to Chapter 5 in that it takes a primarily quantitative approach, yet also tries to translate our conclusions and interpretations into clear English for readers who are less interested in the numbers. This chapter also draws upon supplemental data from a sample of college students at the University of Notre Dame.

All of the factors discussed in Chapter 5 are important and arguably warrant additional analyses and explanation. Attending Catholic high school, however, stands out for several reasons. First, as a public issue, Catholic schools are at the center of several social and political debates. Current arguments about the use of public funds for school vouchers intersect with long-standing debates over the role of religion in education to make Catholic schools a prominent issue on the national level and in many locales. Second, the available empirical data about the impact of Catholic schooling on religiousness later in life is murky at best. Early studies were plagued by several methodological challenges. Despite some notable recent studies, there is little consensus on how youth who attended Catholic schools may be different from Catholics who attended Protestant or public schools on a range of outcomes, including religious behaviors and beliefs.[1] Finally, the last section of Chapter 5 summarized the potential mechanisms that explain the relationships between the important teenage-era factors and emerging adult religiousness. Categorizing Catholic school attendance into one of these categories is difficult. As we discuss below, Catholic schools may involve several of the mechanisms we described, including religious socialization, avoidance of relationship breakdown, drive for identity continuity, conserving religious capital, and religious belief enforcement. A more focused analysis of Catholic schooling can help clarify which of these mechanisms seems to be driving the relationship between attending such schools and religiousness in emerging adulthood.

We find below, to anticipate our conclusions, that the effects of attending a Catholic high school and belonging to a youth group on religious faith and practice in emerging adulthood are mixed, modest, and a bit complicated. Readers interested in learning that Catholic schooling and youth group involvement have a strong, consistent, positive impact on the subsequent religiousness of Catholic youth may be disappointed. At the same time, we find that both Catholic high school attendance and youth group participation appear to strengthen the subsequent religious faith and practice of *some* Catholic teens *under certain conditions*—the specifics of which are worth identifying and understanding. But after taking into account differences in the crucial factor of the Catholic faith commitments and practices of parents, we cannot report that Catholic schooling and youth group participation have robust effects on emerging adult faith and practice.

However, everything we report in this chapter has to be read in light of the major limitations on our data's meaning and applicability. Readers need to understand the following. First, we studied young Catholics across a period of only five years between the teenage years (when respondents were between the ages of 13 and 17) and early emerging adulthood (ages 18 to 23). Viewed in the context of the entire life course, this is a brief phase with which to test the possible effects of Catholic schooling. What we report says absolutely nothing about the possible effects of Catholic schooling and youth group involvement in the lives of Catholic adults after age 23. It could well be—future research will have to investigate it—that these factors have significant effects in later emerging adulthood and beyond. We cannot determine that one way or another here. Second, we are not claiming that Catholic youth who attend Catholic high schools and youth group are not different from those who do not. In fact, they are very different in being more committed to and more actively practicing their faith. Our analysis only shows that most of that difference seems to be caused less by the Catholic schools and youth groups themselves than by the more seriously Catholic *families* from which youth who attend Catholic schools and youth groups tend to come. That does not diminish the importance of Catholic schooling and youth groups in the lives of those families, but it does shift our attention back to the families rather than the schools and youth groups per se. Third, our findings cannot predict what would happen if Catholic youth who do *not* attend Catholic high schools or youth groups were to start doing so. They as a population might be influenced in other ways than those revealed in our analysis. In fact, as we will see, we have good reason to believe that Catholic schooling and youth group would have a real impact on such uninvolved teens, likely a larger impact than on those already involved in them. For that matter, it could be that participation in Catholic schooling and youth group by teenagers from less committed Catholic families could actually exert causal effects back onto those families, strengthening the faith and practice of parents in the same ways that it would likely do for their children. That is possible, although beyond our capacity here to determine. The bottom line of all of these cautions and possibilities is simply to remind readers to keep the findings of this chapter in perspective, to take them seriously without making more of them than the data allow.

How and Why Might Catholic Schools Matter

Previous research on the effects of attending a Catholic high school yielded some contradictory conclusions. Early studies showed that teenagers who attended Catholic schools were more religiously committed than those who did not.[2] Subsequent studies concluded that, on the contrary, differences between Catholic-schooled teenagers and others were small and insignificant.[3] All of these early studies were limited by their methodological design, however. Many relied on retrospective reports from self-identified Catholic adults. That type of design limits researchers' ability to control for possible confounding factors, such as parental religion or teenage religious behaviors, due to problems with respondents' recall. These adult samples also partially "select on" the outcome of interest. That is, the Catholic adults who are surveyed are those who have remained committed enough to still self-identify as Catholic, while those who are no longer Catholic are left out. When comparing outcomes within this group of still-Catholic adults, the effect of Catholic school attendance is likely to be minimized because only the most devout Catholics are being studied. The "true" effect of attending a Catholic school may primarily be on maintaining a Catholic affiliation into adulthood, but without including former Catholics who have abandoned that affiliation in a study, it is impossible to make this discovery. Conversely, when such studies compare Catholic adults to non-Catholic adults, the impact of attending a Catholic school may be overstated because only the strongest Catholics are being included. Catholic teenagers who attended a Catholic school but then disaffiliated—most likely lowering the average religious commitment of the whole Catholic school population—are excluded, thereby making the remaining attendees look considerably more religious than they actually are.

Several important recent studies have overcome many of these methodological problems, providing new insight into the potential impact of attending Catholic schools. Jeremy Uecker, for instance, has shown that teenagers who attend Catholic schools attend Mass more frequently and believe religion is more important than public-schooled teenagers. He also found, however, that Catholic-schooled teenagers are not different from their public-school counterparts on any religious outcome once they become young adults *and* once parents' religiousness had been statistically taken into account.[4] That is, Catholic-schooled emerging adults may be more religious because they have more religious parents, not because of any direct effect of Catholic schooling. Uecker's studies also suggest that teenagers who attend Catholic schools may actually be worse than their secular-schooled peers on particular religious behaviors, especially on attending extra-curricular religious activities and classes. Attending Catholic schools may be seen by some students or parents as sufficient religious socialization; in such cases teenagers may not seek out additional religious activities. If such activities are important for religious development, then attending Catholic schools may have an unintended negative effect on later religiousness.

In another study, Paul Perl and Mark Gray found that attending Catholic school prevented disaffiliation from Catholicism, although it had no independent impact on rates of Mass attendance among current adult Catholics.[5] This finding is illuminating because it highlights the importance of clarifying who is being compared to whom and on what specific outcome in studies of the effects of attending a Catholic school. Uecker's studies compared teenagers who attended a Catholic school to all those who did not attend a Catholic school. He did not explicitly compare outcomes for Catholics only by type of school attended. As we demonstrated in Chapter 5, Catholic youth as a whole tend to lag behind non-Catholics religiously, both as teenagers and emerging adults. So attending Catholic school may not be enough to overcome this gap, but it still may be correlated with the highest level of religiousness among Catholics only—in which case we may conclude that Catholic schools are vital among Catholics, even if they do not lead to Catholics being as religious as non-Catholic emerging adults. Currently there exists to our knowledge little to no research that uses adequate samples to address these within-Catholic effects during the teenage years and in the transition to emerging adulthood.

Knowing what topics to consider is only half the battle. There is also the matter of how to think about the outcomes of interest. From previous research and general sociological insight, we expect Catholic schooling to exert different impacts on Mass attendance, personal prayer, and participation in missions because of the importance of differential behavior or belief. But even so, the way we understand these outcomes or even whether or not we see "results" is shaped by whether we and other researchers look at continuous or categorical outcomes. For example, we may be interested in what makes some teenagers attend Mass more frequently than others—a continuous outcome. But just as importantly, we may want to know what leads to teenagers never attending Mass—a categorical outcome. Although they seem similar because they both concern Mass attendance, the former treats differences between attending a few times a month and attending once a week, for example, as important, while the latter focuses on what places people into categorically distinct types. Catholic schooling may not lead to small continuous changes, but may nonetheless be important for grouping youth into categorically different levels of religiousness. Our analyses below will address both types of outcomes. We highlight these distinctions because historical transformations of Catholic schooling in the U.S. may have qualitatively altered the nature of Catholic schools, which in turn may have shifted the ways in which they shape teenagers' and emerging adults' religiousness.

The first way Catholic schools may affect the religious trajectories of Catholic teenagers is through *direct religious socialization*. Catholic schools often have mandatory religious services, religious education and Bible study classes, and times for prayer. Many schools are adorned with religious texts and icons and have classes taught by clergy or men or women religious, who teach religious messages in addition to academic lessons. In these ways, Catholic schools function as a type of religious training. Students who attend these schools should be more active and devout Catholics than those who do not, other things being roughly equal, in the same way that someone who attends a summer band camp should become a better musician than someone else who does not. The influence of this direct socialization may have waned in recent years, however, as some Catholic schools may have shifted their priorities. Some critics have argued that many Catholic schools no longer even intend to be religious training sites, but have instead become primarily elite *academic* schools. If so, this heavier emphasis on academics has come at the expense of time and resources for religious education. One study found that the majority of Catholic school leaders ranked "religious development" as a lower priority than academic development.[6] This move away from direct religious education may not only attenuate the overall influence of attending a Catholic school on students' religiousness, but it also may change the kind of impact it has. Specifically, on the point of direct religious socialization, the existing but less intense religious education may be enough to keep Catholic teenagers from abandoning their faith but not enough to dramatically increase their religiousness, especially into emerging adulthood.

It is also possible that this explicit religious training was never the causal mechanism at work in the first place, but rather religious commitment among Catholic school students came from their being embedded in strong religious *social networks*. Teenagers who attend Catholic schools are more likely than those who do not to develop friendships with other Catholic youth and form strong bonds to Catholic adult mentors, both of which have been shown to strengthen religious faith and practice in teenagers and emerging adults.[7] From this perspective, Catholic schools are primarily facilitating the development of pro-religious networks, which in turn encourage and maintain teenage religiousness. Yet, as noted above, at least some Catholic schools are prioritizing academic achievement over religious formation. To the extent that this is the case, these schools would be likely to recruit students for whom being Catholic is a lower priority.[8] Parents who are focused on doing whatever it takes to help their children succeed in school and subsequent careers would likely be willing to tolerate the "religious dogmas" of a reputable Catholic school in hopes of it propelling their children to the best possible college.[9] If such cases have grown more common at Catholic high schools, as they seem to have done, then Catholic teenagers who attend them would be more likely to form relationships with peers who do not share their own religious beliefs, and the number of Catholic mentors might be reduced as clergy are replaced by more academically focused lay teachers. These reductions in more robustly Catholic social networks present in Catholic schools would limit their ability to increase religiousness of Catholic teenagers. On the other hand, if new students now coming to Catholic schools for academic reasons are more likely to be only nominally Catholic, they may find themselves in relatively more Catholic social networks, which could increase their religiousness, perhaps shifting them from nominal to at least moderately committed Catholics. In short, for strong Catholics, the Catholic networks at Catholic high schools may have weakened; but for nominal Catholics, the Catholic social networks may have strengthened, compared to the public school they may have attended otherwise.

A third possible mechanism linking Catholic school attendance to religiousness is more abstract than the first two. Rather than being a site of direct religious socialization or religious social-network building, Catholic schools may be the foundation of a *general cultural framework*. In part because the more intense Catholic religious education and culture seems to have weakened overall, and since Catholic social networks in Catholic high schools have probably grown thinner as a result, Catholic schools may simply indicate to teenagers that Catholicity is still an important part of personal identity and affiliation. Especially when teenagers transition into emerging adulthood and start making independent decisions about the type of religious person they are going to be, having gone to a *Catholic* high school might signal to them that being Catholic should form some aspect of who they are and become. By analogy, this mechanism would operate like brand loyalty, only applied in this case to religious heritage and identity.[10] It seems reasonable, from a sociological perspective, at least, that this mechanism would not operate with as much strength as the previous two, and therefore while it could prevent a complete abandonment of religiousness or encourage a move to a slightly higher level of religiousness among those who start out at low levels, it likely will not lead to very high levels of Catholic faith and practice.

Who Goes to Catholic Schools

This theoretical discussion should lead us to ask first: who is attending Catholic schools? Figure 7.1 presents descriptive figures comparing teenagers (from the full sample of respondents in the first wave of the NSYR) who attend Catholic schools to those who do not. These percents are based on everyone who reports attending a Catholic school, whether they are classified as Catholic or not. The top half of the figure shows that Catholic-schooled teenagers are different from their peers in terms of socioeconomic status. American teenagers who go to a Catholic school are more likely than those who do not to live with both their biological parents, and their parents make more money and have more education. Nearly 70 percent of Catholic-schooled teenagers have parents who have at least a bachelor's degree, compared to just over 40 percent of non-Catholic–schooled students. This difference may confirm the idea that Catholic schools

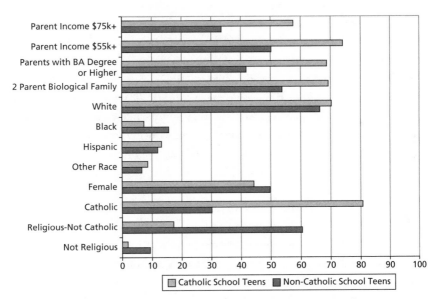

Figure 7.1 Percent of Catholic school attendees and non-attendees by demographic factors (N = 3,290) [weighted]. Note: The percents for Catholic school are based on all respondents who report attending a Catholic school, which includes some who are not identified as Catholic.

have increasingly become elite academic destinations appealing to parents who want to improve their children's chances of going to a prestigious college. This support is not definitive, but highly suggestive, especially when viewed in terms of the longer socioeconomic history of Catholicism described in Chapter 1.

Interestingly, Catholic schools are racially quite similar to their non-Catholic counterparts. Although there is a slightly lower proportion of black students in Catholic schools (just over 7 percent) than non-Catholic schools, there is a slightly higher percentage of Hispanics and students of other races. Catholic schools do not differ substantially in their gender make-up. In terms of religious background, Catholic schools are predominately filled with Catholic teenagers. More than 80 percent of all Catholic school students are Catholic. Still, a substantial minority of students are non-Catholic, with just under 20 percent of students claiming some other religious affiliation and the small remaining percent reporting no religion. A study conducted in 1972 found that more than 95 percent of Catholic school students were Catholic.[11] So although Catholics clearly still dominate Catholic schools, the percent of non-Catholics at these schools has increased significantly from the past.

Although the change from 95 to 80 percent of the Catholic school population being Catholic may seem minor, it has important implications for the types of friendship networks that are available and likely to form. Consider a hypothetical Catholic school with a population of 200 students. In this case, a 95-percent Catholic population would mean the presence of only 10 non-Catholic students, but an 80-percent one would mean 40 non-Catholics, which sharply increases the probability of any given Catholic student becoming friends with at least one non-Catholic student. American teenagers report having between four and five close friends, on average.[12] In our hypothetical school of 200 students, a 95-percent Catholic population would mean 19 Catholic students for each non-Catholic, making the chances very low that any particular friendship group would include a non-Catholic. But an 80-percent concentration of Catholic students produces a ratio of only four Catholic students per non-Catholic, dramatically increasing the natural likelihood that a friendship group will include a non-Catholic student.

To further investigate this trend of non-Catholics sending their children to Catholic schools, Figure 7.2 shows the proportion of Catholic and non-Catholic teenagers who attend each type of school (besides public schools). This figure flips the calculations from Figure 7.1, where we examined the percent *of all Catholic school students* in each demographic group. Figure 7.2 instead displays the percent *of all Catholic* and *non-Catholic teenagers* who attend Catholic schools, other private religious schools, and non-religious private schools. If the aforementioned trends about the changing nature of Catholic schools are true, we might expect the likelihood of Catholic and non-Catholic parents choosing a

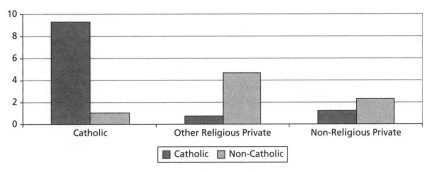

Figure 7.2 Percent of Catholic and non-Catholic teenagers attending each school type (N = 3,290) [weighted]. Note: Percent of each group attending non-private schools not shown. 89% of Catholics and 92% of Non-Catholics attend non-private schools.

Catholic school to be somewhat similar. Further, in some areas a Catholic school may be the only private school available, which could increase its appeal to non-Catholics even if the school itself is very definitively a Catholic institution. In such cases, some non-Catholic parents may be willing to set aside their religious differences in the interest of their children's education. (Whether Catholic schools provide a better education is of course an open and important question; the assumption here is that private schools of all types are perceived by many as superior to public schools, especially for college admission success.) Both of these forces should increase the likelihood of non-Catholics sending their children to Catholic schools. The data in Figure 7.2 contradict this prediction, however. Catholics are still much more likely to send their children to Catholic schools than non-Catholics. Nine percent of all Catholic teenagers attend Catholic schools, while merely 1 percent of non-Catholics do the same. Catholics are very unlikely to send their children to any type of private school that is not Catholic: less than 2 percent of Catholic teenagers attend any type of non-Catholic (whether religious or non-religious) private schools. Non-Catholics also prefer religious private schools, with 4.5 percent of non-Catholics attending a religiously sponsored private school and just over 2 percent attending a non-religious private school. (The remaining Catholic and non-Catholic teens attend public schools.)

How can we resolve these seemingly contradictory results? Figure 7.1 showed a substantial number of non-Catholics attending Catholic schools, while Figure 7.2 suggested that non-Catholics are extremely unlikely to send their children to Catholic schools. The key is each group's relative size in the population—the non-Catholic group being much larger. The rather large increase in the presence of non-Catholics in Catholic schools has resulted from a very small increase, probably of less than half a percentage point, in the likelihood of non-Catholic teens attending Catholic schools. Given that non-Catholics represent a substantial

majority of the population, however, even this small increase in the percent sending their children to Catholic schools has a dramatic effect on the demographic
make-up of these schools. In addition, the typically smaller size of Catholic schools
makes it easier to alter the composition of the schools with only a small number of
non-Catholics in the student body. For example, if everything else stayed the
same, and the proportion of non-Catholic teens going to Catholic schools increased by merely one percentage point, non-Catholics would then represent
more than one-third of the Catholic school population.[13] And in our hypothetical
school of 200 students, there would only be two Catholic students for every non-
Catholic student, making it virtually certain that most friendship groups would
include a non-Catholic.[14]

These initial descriptive analyses reveal several noteworthy patterns. The
average Catholic high school student comes from an economically advantaged
family and has parents with more education than the typical American. These
facts have combined to promote the perception of Catholic schools as elite
academic institutions. While the majority of Catholic students still comes from
Catholic families, substantial numbers of non-Catholics choose Catholic
schools, most likely due to those schools' changing focus from religious training
to academic preparation. This influx of non-Catholics has created more opportunities for Catholic students to form friendships with non-Catholic peers. Still,
non-Catholics are very unlikely to send their children to Catholic schools: they
are more likely than Catholics to select other private school options and far less
likely than Catholics to attend Catholic schools. The increasing number of
non-Catholic students, therefore, has come from a very minor increase in the
percent of non-Catholic teens attending Catholic schools. This pattern suggests
that, given non-Catholics' larger proportion of the population, if even a slightly
greater percentage of non-Catholics start sending their children to Catholic
schools in the future, the schools' overall religious makeup will continue to
drastically change.

An Initial Look: Catholic Schooling and Teenage Religiousness

Now we turn our attention more directly to examining differences in religious
outcomes based on teenagers' attendance at Catholic high schools. Figure 7.3
shows the percent of students at each school type who exhibit different religious behaviors during their teenage years. For example, on the far left, we see
that slightly more than 10 percent of Catholic students who attend Catholic
schools report never attending Mass. This set of bars also shows that Catholic
students attending Catholic schools are the least likely of all groups to never
attend religious services, although the differences are very small (less than five

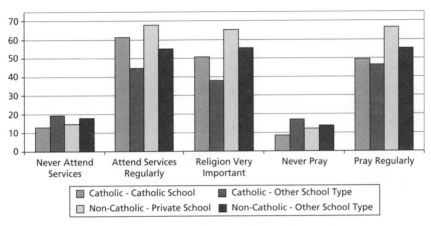

Figure 7.3 Percent of each school type exhibiting religious characteristics in teenage years (N = 3,269) [weighted]. Note: Attend Services Regularly is defined as attending "2–3 times per month" or more often. Praying frequently is defined as praying "many times per week" or more often. Both Other School Type categories include public schools.

percentage points). Overall, Figure 7.3 demonstrates that Catholics who attend Catholic schools are more religiously committed by these measures than their Catholic peers who do not attend Catholic schools. Catholic teenagers attending Catholic schools attend Mass more frequently, say that religion is more important in their daily lives, and are much more likely to pray at least somewhat frequently than Catholic teenagers who attend other types of schools. Catholic teenagers attending Catholic schools are slightly more likely to frequently pray than their Catholic peers in non-Catholic schools, but the difference is small.

Across all of the outcomes, attending a Catholic school is most strongly associated with attending Mass. Catholic teenagers at Catholic schools are the least likely to never attend religious worship services, and they are very close to being the most likely to attend services regularly. One plausible reason for the high rates of reported Mass attendance among Catholic-schooled Catholic teenagers is that their schools have mandatory worship services built into the school day. This interpretation is supported by the fact that the differences between Catholic-schooled teens and other teens are much smaller for the other religious behaviors, and the differences are much greater between Catholics and non-Catholics for these behaviors. While 63% of Catholic high school students report attending Mass "regularly" versus 43% of Catholic teenagers in non-Catholic schools—a difference of 20 percentage points—this gap shrinks to just more than 10 points for considering religion very important and three points for frequent prayer. Only four percentage points more non-Catholic private school teenagers attend religious services frequently than Catholic teenagers in Catholic schools, and the latter are almost 10 percentage points more likely to attend religious services frequently than non-Catholic public school teenagers. Catholic teenagers in Catholic schools are more than 15 percentage points *less* likely, however, to believe that religion is very important and to pray frequently, than non-Catholic private school teenagers.

This analysis generally supports the theoretical predictions noted above. Attending a Catholic school is correlated with greater public religiousness among Catholic teenagers, mainly in areas such as Mass attendance that are typically required by Catholic schools. The gap in religiousness between Catholic-schooled Catholic teenagers and other Catholic teenagers is smaller when it comes to personal religiousness, and the boost Catholic school seems to provide for Catholic teenagers is still not enough to overcome Catholics' lower average level of religiousness.

A Further Look: Catholic School and Religiousness in Emerging Adulthood

Figure 7.4 covers the same school types and religious characteristics as Figure 7.3, except it examines how the type of school respondents attended during the teenage years is related to these religious behaviors five years later, during early emerging adulthood. The first clear finding from this figure is that Catholic emerging adults continue to lag behind non-Catholics in all religious areas measured here. Both groups become less religious during the transition into emerging adulthood, but the differences between the two either remain the same or increase. Having attended a Catholic high school does not appear to do much to

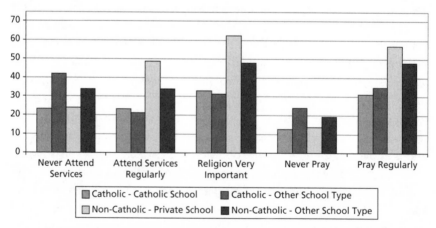

Figure 7.4 Percent of each school type who exhibit religious characteristics in emerging adulthood (N = 2,438) [weighted]. Note: Attend Services Regularly is defined as attending "2–3 times per month" or more often. Praying frequently is defined as praying "many times per week" or more often. Both Other School Type categories include public schools.

limit the drop in religiosity or the religiosity gap between Catholics and non-Catholics. During the teenage years, Catholics attending Catholic high school are almost as likely to attend religious services frequently as non-Catholic private school attendees, and are more likely to do so than non-Catholic public school attendees; however, in emerging adulthood they are less likely than either group to do so (by 25 and 11 percentage points, respectively). This confirms the hypothesis that attending Catholic high school does not help Catholic teenagers close the religious gap with non-Catholics.

What is different during early emerging adulthood is the diminished difference in religiousness among Catholics. During the teenage years, Catholics who attended Catholic schools are more likely to attend services, pray frequently, and report that religion is very important in their lives than their Catholic peers in non-Catholic schools. Yet each of these differences has almost disappeared or even slightly reversed five years later when these Catholics reach emerging adulthood. Once they leave high school, previously Catholic-schooled emerging adults appear no more religious than their Catholic peers. Apparently, any positive impact that attending Catholic schools has on teenagers is not sustained during the transition into early emerging adulthood. This conclusion is tempered, however, when we examine the "never" categories. There we see that Catholic emerging adults who attended Catholic high schools are much less likely to *never* attend Mass and *never* pray than Catholic emerging adults who did not attend Catholic high schools. These differences have increased by emerging adulthood, especially for attendance at Mass, which grows from a small five percentage point gap to a sizable 20-point difference. Emerging adult Catholics who attended Catholic high schools are even less likely to never attend Mass or pray than both non-Catholic groups, although their difference from non-Catholic private-schooled adults is negligible. According to our findings, what Catholic schools (or other unmeasured factors associated with attending Catholic schools) seem to "do," in short, is prevent Catholic teenagers from *completely abandoning* religious practices during the transition to emerging adulthood.

It is worth highlighting that the most substantial effect in this regard concerns Mass attendance. As discussed above, much of Catholic school attendees' higher rates of Mass attendance likely stems from their schools' requirements related to that practice. Some people may discount this attendance as not meaningful or important because it is "forced." Our results suggest, however, that what may have once been mandatory rather than voluntary "sticks" in some ways even when young people have left that institutional requirement behind. Emerging adults who attended Catholic high schools clearly do not attend Mass very frequently, but the vast majority still attends at least occasionally. Mandatory Mass attendance in Catholic high schools thus seems to create a habit or perceived norm among students, which they see as important enough to continue to respect. Skeptics may argue that this infrequent attendance during emerging adulthood is driven by a lingering sense of guilt, which they consider bad. Our answer is, first, that we have already established that there is no "Catholic guilt" among Catholic youth today[15]; and, second, that most Catholic emerging adults are free to never attend Mass if they so choose. So we are not inclined to accept the "lingering guilt" explanation.

Complicating the Picture: Identifying *Independent* Effects

These figures, while helpful, are of limited use, because they do not account for other factors that may drive the apparent relationship between Catholic schooling and religiousness. Earlier, we showed that teenagers who attend Catholic schools are different, on average, from those who do not, in terms of parental income, education, and race. These and other factors may be partly correlated with a relationship between attending Catholic schools and religiousness in emerging adulthood. To address that possibility, we use the multiple regression statistical techniques described in Chapter 5 to isolate the *independent* influence of attending a Catholic school, net of other factors. For the following analysis, as in Chapter 5, we limit our examination to Catholics only, and we include all the potential causal factors listed in Table 5.2 (frequent Mass attendance, having religious parents, etc.).[16] The religion outcome is the same four-level measure of religiousness (Highest, Moderate, Minimal, Lowest) that we created from a combination of Mass attendance, personal prayer, and self-rated importance of faith and used in Chapter 5. The technique we use in these analyses focuses on predicting continuous change in religiousness in emerging adulthood.

What we find is the following. When we examine all of these factors together, we see that attending a Catholic high school as teenagers has a significant and positive influence on increased religiousness among Catholics in emerging adulthood. At the same time, this direct relationship disappears once we statistically control for respondents' religiousness during the teenage years. That is, the reason that teenagers who attended Catholic schools are more religious in emerging adulthood appears to be that they were more religious during the teenage years in the first place. So when we compare teenagers who have a similar level of religiousness, we find that attending Catholic school makes no significant difference in their religiousness as emerging adults. This pattern of findings suggests that attending a Catholic school is perhaps more of a "selection effect" than a true causal factor. That is, Catholic schools do not do anything that *independently* increases religiousness during early emerging adulthood, but rather they appear to attract the most religious teenagers, who proceed in the next five years to be more religious as emerging adults.

We realize that such a conclusion may be surprising to many readers. It seems as though religious institutions, such as Catholic schools, should increase teens' religiousness during the transition to emerging adulthood. Given the importance of this claim, we show additional results to clarify and support it. Table 7.1 presents a more straightforward way of seeing the pattern that the regression results revealed. The first column of numbers shows the average difference in Mass attendance, importance of faith, frequency of prayer, and overall religiousness between Catholics who attend a Catholic high school and those who do not.[17] Each of the individual behavior measures ranges from 0 to 4 (i.e., greatest possible difference would be 5), while overall religiousness ranges from 1 to 4 (i.e., greatest possible difference would be 4). For example, teens who attend a Catholic school have an average level of Mass attendance of about 2.8 (meaning about two to three times per month) and Catholic teens who do not attend a Catholic school have an average level of Mass attendance of about 2.3 (meaning between many times per year and once per month), producing an average difference of just over .5. All of the differences are calculated by subtracting the non–Catholic

Table 7.1 **Average Difference in Level of Religious Characteristics by Catholic School Attendance and Parent Religiousness (N = 661)**

As Teens	*Average Difference between Catholic School—Non-Catholic School*[a]		
	All Catholics	*High Parental Religiousness*	*Low Parental Religiousness*
Attendance at Mass	.505*	.072	.507
Importance of Faith	.349*	.199	.320
Frequency of Prayer	.340*	.107	.472
Overall Religiousness[b]	.354*	.099	.398*
As Emerging Adults			
Attendance at Mass	.421*	.193	.308
Importance of Faith	.177*	.071	−.018
Frequency of Prayer	.259	.101	.284
Overall Religiousness[b]	.274*	.178	.122

[a]The average difference is calculated by taking the average value of the ordinal survey measure for Catholics who do not attend high school minus the average value of the ordinal survey measure for Catholics who attend a Catholic high school on each given measure.

[b]The overall religiousness measure is the variable that is used as the outcome in the regression analyses.

*p<.05. Significance determined by an independent samples t-test.

school average from the Catholic school average, such that positive values mean those who attended(ed) Catholic schools have a higher average on the measure, while negative values would indicate that those who attend(ed) other types of schools have a higher average. Overall, we see that both during the teen years and in early emerging adulthood, the Catholic-schooled teens exhibit a substantially and statistically significantly higher level of all three religious characteristics than their non-Catholic school counterparts.

The next columns make these same comparisons, but restrict the sample to Catholics whose parents show similar levels, high or low, of religiousness. We use parental religiousness as our control factor in this example because it is the least likely, through reverse causation, to be shaped by Catholic school attendance. We think it is safe to assume that parents' level of religiousness was set before their teenagers attended high school. If the original differences by type of school diminish once we account for these pre-existing differences, we can more confidently conclude that the Catholic school effect we initially observed was in fact due to a selection effect.[18] As the table shows, this is indeed the case. In almost every comparison within high and low parental religiousness, the difference in Mass attendance, self-rated importance of faith, frequency of prayer, and overall religiousness between Catholic school and non–Catholic school teenagers is dramatically diminished to the point of non-significance on all measures but one.[19] This diminished relationship is particularly clear in the transition to emerging adulthood (the bottom half of the table). There is little to no sign of increased religiousness for the Catholic school teenagers *within* similar levels of parental religiousness. The reason we initially observed differences between Catholic-schooled and other Catholic teenagers is that the former teens tend to have more religious parents, which increases their teenagers' religiousness. Once we account for the parents' religiousness, the direct relationship between Catholic schooling and religiousness in the teenage years and in emerging adulthood is dramatically weakened. In other words, if we took two groups of Catholic teenagers whose parents were equally religious, we would expect to observe little to no difference in their Mass attendance, self-rated importance of faith, frequency of prayer, and overall religiousness (as teenagers and as emerging adults) even if one group attended a Catholic high school and the other did not.

It is possible, however, that Catholic schools exert an influence on other important religious behaviors or beliefs that are not captured by our outcomes of Mass attendance, self-rated importance of faith, or frequency of prayer. Our measures do not assess teenagers' or emerging adults' views on God or Jesus, which may be more directly altered by lessons learned in a Catholic school. To assess this possibility, we conducted a similar analysis to that in Table 7.1 using the following five questions as outcomes: Do you believe in God? How close do you feel to God? What is your personal view of God? How strongly do you believe that to be truly religious someone must be a part of a congregation? What is your view on Jesus? The results (not shown here) reveal higher levels of traditional religious beliefs among those who attended Catholic schools. Even before accounting for parents' level of religiousness, however, these differences, in both teens' and emerging adults' responses, were minimal. For example, in emerging adulthood, only 12 percentage points more of Catholic-schooled teenagers believe in God than Catholic teens who attended other types of schools. Although clearly a difference, it is not very dramatic on such a central measure of faith. This 12 percentage point difference by school type was the second largest among all of the variables examined.[20] And once we accounted for parents' religiousness, this difference dropped below 10 percentage points (and to non-significance) for all Catholics, whether their parents' religiousness was high or low. This pattern of results confirms our conclusion that the higher levels of religiousness of Catholic-schooled young people, both as teens and in emerging adulthood, are driven more by Catholic schools' selection of highly religious teenagers than by their direct impact on teenage and emerging adult religiousness.

Our analyses above are based on changes in continuous types of variables, investigating how Catholic schooling may increase religiousness in emerging adulthood. We also ran tests of categorical differences. Specifically, we examined the factors that significantly increased the likelihood that a Catholic teenager would enter a higher category of religiousness during emerging adulthood—for example, going from "Minimal" religiousness as a teenager to "Moderate" religiousness as an emerging adult. This type of analysis has two benefits. First, it eliminates the "Highest" religious Catholic teenagers from the analysis, since they have no room to increase, thus shifting our analytical focus to those Catholic teenagers who are not already highly religious. Second, it allows us to investigate meaningful qualitative changes, in that we are not merely looking for factors that increase religion on a numeric scale but those that move Catholic teenagers into substantively different categories of religiousness.

The results of this analysis are presented in Figure 7.5, which shows the predicted likelihood that a Catholic teenager with certain characteristics will rise into a higher religiousness category as an emerging adult, while controlling for the host of teenage-era factors. The steeper a line slopes upward, the stronger the positive effect that factor exerts: a steep upward line represents a more dramatic increase in the likelihood of higher religiousness when the factor in question increases. This figure clearly illustrates the importance of attending a Catholic high school for the probability of later moving into a higher category of religiousness during early emerging adulthood. Catholic teenagers who do not attend a Catholic school (labeled as "Low" here) have a less than 10 percent chance of moving into a higher religiousness category as emerging adults,

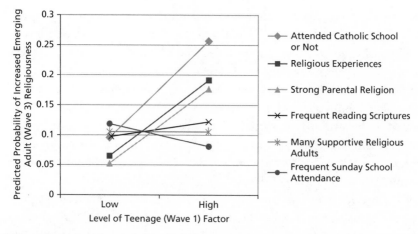

Figure 7.5 Predicted probability of increasing religiousness in the transition to emerging adult (wave 3) as influenced by select teenage-era (wave 1) factors in full logistic regression (N = 526). Source: National Surveys of Youth and Religion 2002–2003, 2007–2008. Note: The n (526) is lower than the full n (661) because teenagers who were classified as being in the Highest religion category as teens could not "increase," and were therefore eliminated from the model. The Y-axis scores (0–1) are the predicted probability of a teenager increasing his or her level of religiousness in the transition to emerging adulthood; the values are calculated by first multiplying each estimated coefficient by its variable's mean, except for the variable of interest which varies by the values on the X-axis; these products are then summed, producing a predicted probability for that level of the variable of interest, with all other variables set at their mean (this method is similar to the calculation of a predicted value in OLS regression, but the estimation of an logistic regression model transforms the dependent variable into a log odds through the use of a logit function). For Attended Catholic School, "Low" represents respondents who did not attend a Catholic school, while "High" represents those who did attend a Catholic school. For all other variables High is defined as the 90th percentile value, while Low is defined by the 10th percentile value.

whereas teenagers who *do* attend a Catholic school (labeled as "High") have a greater than 25 percent chance. This 25 percent chance may still seem low itself; however, considering the fact that only 15 percent of all Catholics increase in religiousness at this stage, attending Catholic school as a teenager *significantly* improves the likelihood of increasing religiosity into emerging adulthood. Stated differently, we can expect only one out of every 10 Catholic teenagers who do not attend a Catholic high school to move into a higher category of religiousness during emerging adulthood, versus one out of every four teenagers who attended a Catholic high school. That is a big difference.

Attending a Catholic school as a teenager is one of the most, if not *the*, most influential teen-era factors for high religiosity in emerging adulthood.[21] As a comparison, teenagers who never read scriptures have a less than 10 percent chance of moving into a higher religiousness category as emerging adults, which is almost exactly identical to the chance of those who do not attend a Catholic high school doing so. Teenagers who read scripture several times a month (in the 90th percentile on this variable) have only slightly more than a 12 percent chance of making this change. Reading scriptures increases teens' chances of becoming more religious by barely three percentage points, a tiny shift compared to the 15-point difference that attending a Catholic school makes. The predictor next most strong to attending a Catholic high school—namely, having several personal religious experiences during the teenage years—produces a predicted 19 percent likelihood of respondents becoming more religious. Note that these relationships exist even after accounting statistically for differences in teenagers' initial personal religiousness and the religiousness of their friends and supportive adults. Therefore, Catholic schools *do* appear to significantly raise teens' chances of moving into a higher religiousness category during emerging adulthood—an impact that is not completely explained by direct religious training or practice (for example, Mass attendance) or enhanced social networks (such as more religious adult mentors). These results indicate the importance of Catholic high school attendance for sustaining and perhaps improving later Catholic religiousness. Attending Catholic schools makes teenagers who are *not* among the most religious significantly more likely to make a categorical improvement in religiousness when they enter emerging adulthood than their Catholic peers who do not attend Catholic schools. Comparing these findings to the previous analyses, we see that the main influence of Catholic schooling appears to be in *categorical* shifts rather than *continuous* increases in religiousness. We have discovered that these categorical shifts seem most likely for teenagers who are less religious to begin with.

Catholic Schooling in Causal Combinations in Religious Trajectories

The analyses above suggest that the effect of attending Catholic schools may differ for different types of Catholic teenagers. Attending a Catholic school may strengthen the future religiousness of Catholic youth to a greater or lesser degree, depending on other religious and family characteristics. This insight calls for another analytic strategy that more directly examines how specific teenage-era factors combine to influence levels of religiousness in emerging adulthood. We again use the method of Qualitative Comparative Analysis (QCA) that we introduced in Chapter 5. The main difference between the current analysis and that of Chapter 5 is that here we include attending a Catholic school among the potential causal combination pathways. In what follows, we examine the likelihood that Catholic teenagers end up as emerging adults in a high religiousness category, based on the type of school they attend as teens, the religiousness of their parents, their reported importance of faith, the number of supportive religious adults to whom they are close, and their frequency of reading scriptures.[22] The results from this analysis are presented in Figure 7.6. Displayed there are the combinations of teenage factors, shown in the boxes to the left, that are more likely than not to produce emerging adults who belong to the Highest or Moderate religiousness group. When Catholic youth experience one of these four combinations of factors, in other words, there is a greater than 50–50 chance they will become highly religious as emerging adults.

The figure shows four potential pathways to higher religiousness in emerging adulthood. The first two include the most important factors found in the analyses presented in Chapter 5. In the first path are Catholic teenagers who have very religious parents, say that religious faith is very important in their lives, and have many supportive non-parental religious adults. The second path does not rely on highly religious parents. Rather, even stronger personal teenage religiousness, as expressed by frequently reading scriptures, combines with the other important factors (high professed importance of religious faith and relationships with supportive religious adults) to produce highly religious emerging adult Catholics. In neither of those combinations does attending Catholic high school figure.

The next and last combinations include the Catholic school factor, which is an important finding. If attending a Catholic high school were not a crucial factor leading to high religiousness in emerging adulthood, it would not have appeared in any of the causal combinations. Yet our findings show that attending a Catholic high school is a key factor in two of four prominent pathways to higher religiousness in early emerging adulthood. The third path, which requires attendance at a Catholic school, confirms several of our previous findings. In this pathway, having parents with *low* levels of religiousness, perceiving faith as very important, knowing *few* supportive religious non-parental adults, and attending Catholic school combine to be likely to produce highly religious Catholic emerging adults. Teenagers in this pathway have few supportive relational bonds to their faith, since their parents are not very religious and they do not have many ties to other supportive adults who are religious. However, they do have the basis of a strong faith, in that they report that their own faith is very important in their lives. When such teenagers also attend a Catholic high school, they are likely to remain or become highly religious as an emerging adult. This could involve teenagers whose not-very-religious parents send them to a Catholic school for purely academic reasons, but after the teens are exposed to Catholic religious practices in their schools, they go on to establish or maintain higher religiousness in emerging adulthood. Catholic schools may thus provide the training necessary for teenagers to become more religious even without highly religious parents, and they may foster a supportive Catholic friendship network that helps teenagers increase in religiousness.

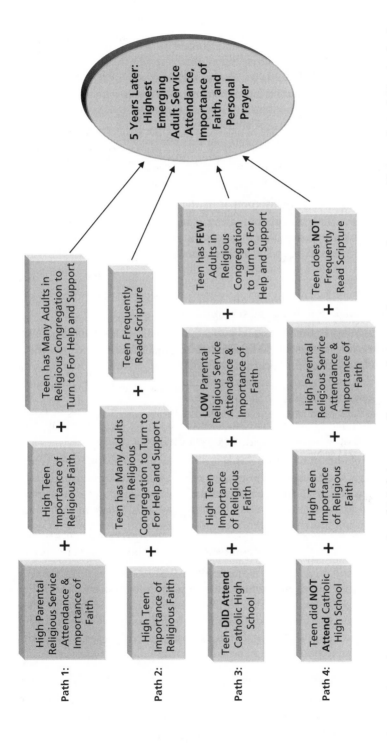

Figure 7.6 Qualitative Comparative Analysis (QCA) showing sufficient combinations of teenage-era factors most likely producing higher levels of emerging adult religiousness.

Interestingly, there is one path to higher religiousness in emerging adulthood—the fourth combination—which actually requires *not* attending a Catholic school. A Catholic teenager who has very religious parents, believes religion is very important, does *not* read scripture frequently, and does *not* attend a Catholic school is more likely to become a highly religious emerging adult than not. This fourth pathway perhaps indirectly validates the importance of Catholic schools as sites of religious training and exposure to religious role models, as we explain next. When Catholic teenagers are not practicing their religion at a high level (not frequently reading scriptures) and lack a primary source of religious training and exposure to religious networks (by not attending Catholic school), then they *must* have highly religious parents *and* a faith they describe as highly important in their lives. Directly comparing these last two combinations helps clarify a key point, since they share the common characteristic of teenagers believing religious faith is very important in their lives. In one path, the Catholic teenagers' religious role models and support networks are weak: their parents are not very religious and they do not know many other adults who are religious. In the other path, personal religious practices (such as the reading of scriptures) and academic religious training and support networks (found in a Catholic high school) are missing. In the former, relationships with religious people are missing and must be replaced by the academic, institutionalized system of attending Catholic school; while in the latter, the academic system is missing and must be replaced by relationships with highly religious parents. Together, these findings support the idea that Catholic schools provide a site of religious training and network development—a role that the home or parish can fill when highly religious parents or other supportive adults are involved.

The results of our combinational analyses reinforce many of our earlier findings. Attending a Catholic high school is most beneficial in promoting religious faith in early emerging adulthood for Catholic teenagers who were not already highly religious. Attending Catholic school can particularly boost the later faith and practice of Catholic young people who do not have highly religious parents or a strong non-parental religious adult support system. Catholic schools can provide religious training, role models, and social networks for such teenagers in ways that lead to higher religiousness in early emerging adulthood.

Conclusion: How and Why Do Catholic Schools Matter?

Our analyses confirm and extend much of the previous research on the religious effects of Catholic schools. First, attending a Catholic school does not eliminate the gap between Catholics and non-Catholics on a range of religious outcomes. Catholics who attend Catholic schools still attend religious services less frequently, say that religion is less important in their lives, and pray less frequently than non-Catholics, especially in early emerging adulthood. When we focus solely on the population of Catholics, however, we see that attending a Catholic school does make a difference, although not a simple, uniform, or direct one. Attending a Catholic school does not change outcomes on *continuous* measures among Catholics once the religious influence of parents is accounted for. Although teenagers who attend Catholic schools are markedly more religious than their peers who attend other types of schools, this difference disappears in the transition to emerging adulthood, so that five years down the road, the two groups are approximately equally likely to attend Mass regularly, pray often, and consider religion very important. Once teenage-era religious characteristics are accounted for statistically, there is no significant direct effect of attending a Catholic school on increased religiousness in emerging adulthood.

However, when religiousness is viewed as a *categorical* measure that frames the comparisons differently, Catholic schools are influential in two important ways. First, they seem to deter Catholic youth from completely ceasing to practice their religious faith during the transition to emerging adulthood. Catholic emerging adults who attended Catholic high schools are less likely to never attend Mass or never pray than those who did not attend Catholic school. We may be setting the bar on religious expectations fairly low, but given the preponderance of Catholics who do not continue strong or at all in the faith as emerging adults, this influence is substantial. Catholic high schools seem to create in students a bond to the Catholic faith, even if they practice that faith at only a minimal level during emerging adulthood. Catholic schools may create a type of loose "brand loyalty" causing emerging adults to feel compelled to keep it as at least a small part of who they are, but not to identify with it so closely that it is a central aspect of their lives, at least during that phase of life. Second, Catholic high schools can significantly increase the religiousness of teenagers who come to them at lower levels of religiousness. Attending a Catholic school may not boost the religiousness of teenagers who are already very religious, especially compared to their very religious peers at other types of schools. But Catholic high schools do seem to increase the likelihood that less religious teenagers—those who do not regularly practice or strongly believe the Catholic faith—will become more religious emerging adults. They serve to buttress fragile, lower religiousness in the teenage years, and encourage continued religious development into emerging adulthood.

Determining *why* Catholic high schools exert these influences is more complicated. At the beginning of this chapter we described three possible causal mechanisms that may explain this relationship: Catholic schools may (1) provide the explicit religious education and training needed to preserve high religiousness in emerging adulthood; (2) foster religious friendship networks among teenagers that help sustain high religiousness five years later; and (3) provide important cultural indicators to teenagers that they are definitely "Catholic," which may cultivate their internal motivation to maintain their faith into the future. Our analyses cannot definitely pinpoint which of these mechanisms is most at work, but they do provide some insight into which may be more important than others.

The first mechanism, religious training, appears to be at work somewhat during the teenage years, but shows only a marginal influence in emerging adulthood. While Catholic-schooled teenagers attend Mass at higher levels than other Catholic teenagers, their attendance and frequency of prayer in emerging adulthood are virtually identical. Any direct, behavioral training that students received at Catholic high schools does not seem to affect their religious observance in early emerging adulthood, especially when we account for the influence of their parents' religiousness. Emerging adults who attended Catholic schools were more likely than others to attend Mass and pray at least occasionally; those who did not attend Catholic schools were more likely to completely abandon them. The religious practices that are often required in Catholic schools thus seem to become habitual to the point that students may greatly reduce their participation in those practices, but still retain some observance of them, when they are no longer mandatory. In short, attending Catholic high school does not make it more likely that young people will practice their faith (attend Mass and pray) at *higher* levels in emerging adulthood; but it does make it more likely that they will practice at *some* level, even if minimal.

Our results also highlight the declining percentage of Catholic students in Catholic schools, which decreases the density of the Catholic friendship networks that teenagers are likely to be able to form in Catholic schools. At the same time, however, our analysis showed that Catholic high schools may successfully compensate for some students' lack of supportive religious adult networks and thereby promote higher religiousness in emerging adulthood. For such Catholic teenagers who are not already embedded in highly Catholic social networks, Catholic high schools may provide an important place to develop social ties to Catholic peers and adults that foster increased religiousness later in life.

Finally, our regression analyses showed that Catholic high school attendance increases religiousness among emerging adults (after accounting for respondents' religious practices as teens and the religiousness of their peers and other supportive adults), especially for teenagers who were on the lower end of the scale of religiousness. These findings suggest that Catholic schools exert some influence that is not tied entirely to their formal behavioral training or ability to foster social ties to religious friends and mentors. This seems to support our belief that the third, *cultural* mechanism may be the most influential of the three mechanisms. Catholic high schools may be doing less than in the past to directly increase students' religiousness, and now may serve more as a cognitive indicator to teenagers that being Catholic is part of who they are and should remain. This possibility is further supported by our results showing that Catholic schools are very effective in preventing a total loss of religiousness in emerging adulthood. Catholic schools may not lead to heightened religiousness; however, they do typically stop teenagers from completely abandoning the Catholic faith.

Chapter Appendix: The Difference of Attending Catholic High School among Students at the University of Notre Dame

This chapter so far has examined findings from nationally representative NSYR data on the effects of attending Catholic high school on Catholic youth. This appendix adds to that discussion by exploring findings about a more specific population that we also surveyed: students at the University of Notre Dame (Notre Dame, IN). Notre Dame students are obviously not nationally representative, but these findings do provide another perspective on the Catholic high school question.

In January 2013, two of us (Smith and Christoffersen) conducted a survey of all Notre Dame undergraduate students who were enrolled in one of the two core theology courses required to graduate. The survey was conducted in every section of these theology classes being offered in the spring semester of 2013. Since these are required courses for all Notre Dame undergraduates, nearly one-quarter of the entire student population is registered in one of them in any given semester. Most of the students enrolled in these classes are first-year students or sophomores. In essence, this survey represents a sample of all underclassmen and women enrolled as undergraduates at Notre Dame. Every instructor of the required theology classes agreed to dedicate 20 minutes of the first class session of the semester for the fielding of the survey. The surveys were in paper-and-pencil scantron form, administered in person by graduate and undergraduate student volunteers, who went to every section of every class, explained and administered the survey, and collected and returned the forms to the Notre Dame Center for Social Research for data reading. Through careful planning, communication, cooperation, and coordination, we obtained an amazing 99.9 percent response rate—essentially, every student enrolled in these classes completed our survey—producing a final N of 1,694 completed surveys. We analyzed the data ourselves and present our results in the figures that follow. The survey itself consisted of a handful of questions testing basic knowledge of the Bible, basic Christian theological knowledge, basic Catholic theological knowledge, respondents' attitudes about Christian theology as a discipline, and respondents' intentions and feelings about the Catholic Church.[23] The survey also asked respondents whether or not they had attended a Catholic high school and, if they had, how many years they attended it. The figures below represent the simple comparison of scores on the questions just mentioned between Notre Dame students who had attended Catholic high school for four or more years versus those who never attended Catholic high school (very few had attended for only one to three years). All of the differences but two are statistically significant at the p>.05 level.[24]

Because we did not collect information in this survey about students' families, their parents' religious beliefs and practices, and other demographic factors, we are not able to employ multivariate statistics to isolate the direct effects of Catholic schooling. It may be, then, that some of the differences observed below reflect selection effects differentiating those (presumably mostly Catholic) families who send their children to Catholic high school from those who do not—a phenomenon we noticed above. However, our analysis significantly compensates for this uncertainty in the following ways. First, Notre Dame undergraduates represent a homogeneous group of college students relative to the entire population of young Catholics: they are more likely to be white, well educated, successful in schooling, and from middle- and upper middle-class families. That itself helps to remove the possibly confounding effects of social class and family background. Second, the sampled population, as noted above, is mostly composed of first- and second-year college students, who have only completed between one and three semesters of college. This means that, in comparison to all college students, they remain close to their high school experience and its residual effects on their lives. Third, we restricted our analysis here to student respondents who reported they are currently Catholic or were raised Catholic, removing any possible influences in the backgrounds of non-Catholic respondents. Fourth, one-half of the students sampled for this survey had already taken and passed the basic "Foundations" theology course required for all Notre Dame undergraduate students. This means that possible differences in knowledge, attitudes, and feelings between students who attended Catholic high school and those who did not had a good chance to be mitigated by their experience in this earlier course. If anything, compared to the differences we might have found had we administered this survey during freshman orientation, say, before students' responses were affected by their college experience, the differences in our findings here are likely muted. At the same time, to properly interpret the figures below we must reiterate that, while the data well may demonstrate that Catholic high schools have significant influence on young Catholics, we cannot isolate that influence in our analyses from possible selection effects, the underlying differences between families who use Catholic schools and those who do not. Nonetheless, our findings, which largely corroborate those presented above, are, we think, interesting and important. So, what did we discover?

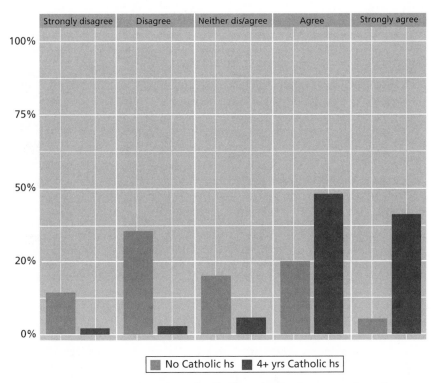

Figure 7.7 Notre Dame undergraduates "well-educated in the doctrines and moral teachings of the Catholic faith" by Catholic high school attended, 4 years vs. none.

Figure 7.6 shows how well educated the surveyed students felt they been in the doctrines and moral teachings of the Catholic faith before coming to Notre Dame. Those who attended Catholic high school for four years were far more likely than those who had not to report that they had been well educated in Catholic doctrine and moral teachings. The vast majority of them agreed or strongly agreed that they came to Notre Dame well educated in Catholicism, whereas most who did not attend Catholic high school disagreed, strongly disagreed, or said they neither agreed nor disagreed. That clearly suggests that, at least among Notre Dame students (and probably also other Catholic college students who are similar to them), Catholic high school makes a big difference in educating students in Catholic beliefs and morality.

Figure 7.8 shifts our attention to students' basic knowledge of the Bible. There we see that Notre Dame students who attended four years of Catholic high school know more about the Bible, on average, than those who did not (even though about one-half of respondents, randomly distributed in this sample, had already taken a beginning theology course that focuses on the Bible). Only on the question about Jesus being born in Bethlehem did the two groups answer

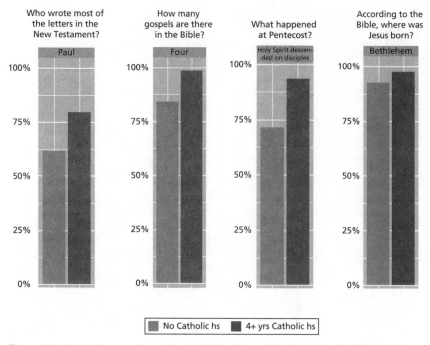

Figure 7.8 Notre Dame undergraduates' biblical knowledge by Catholic high school attended, 4 years vs. none.

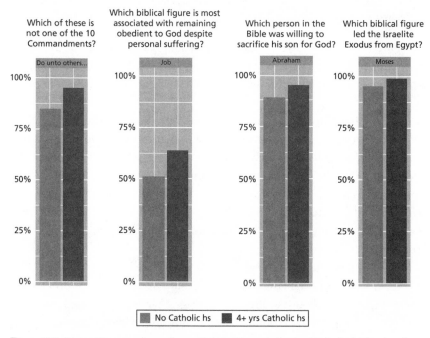

Figure 7.9 Notre Dame undergraduates' biblical knowledge by Catholic high school attended, 4 years vs. none.

correctly at similar rates. The same gap in levels of biblical knowledge can be seen in Figure 7.9, although the differences are smaller than in the previous figure. All, however, are statistically significant.

Figure 7.10 presents comparable findings regarding students' knowledge of basic Christian theology. Once again, Notre Dame students who had attended four years of Catholic high school scored noticeably better—and statistically significantly so—in theological knowledge than those who did not. (An important aside: about 40 percent of respondents did not understand Trinitarian doctrine well enough to know that the Holy Trinity does not have a temporal origin, and about 35 percent did not know that it was the Son of God who, according to Christian doctrine, became incarnate, numbers which—although not directly related to our primary focus on Catholic schools—are surprisingly high.) Figure 7.11 also displays respondents' rate of answering basic theological questions correctly. Here the differences between those who attended Catholic high school and those who did not are extremely modest, but they are still statistically significant.

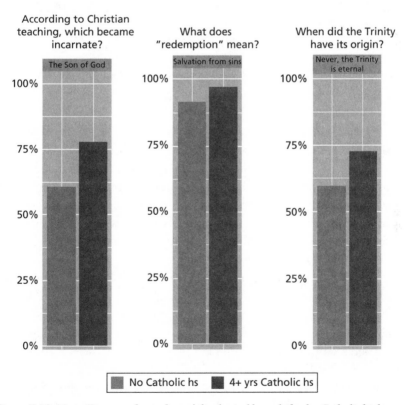

Figure 7.10 Notre Dame undergraduates' theological knowledge by Catholic high school attended, 4 years vs. none.

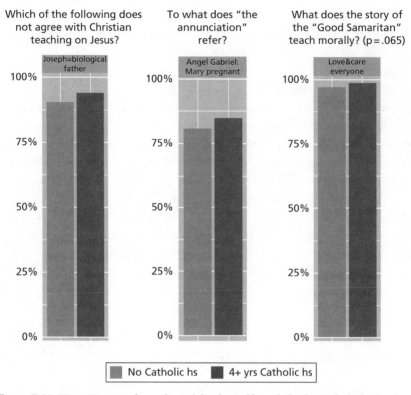

Figure 7.11 Notre Dame undergraduates' theological knowledge by Catholic high school attended, 4 years vs. none.

Figure 7.12 shows more dimensions of Notre Dame students' theological knowledge, but the questions focus on specifically Catholic doctrines. Following the pattern noted above, Catholic students who did not attend Catholic high school were much less likely to know the correct answers than those who attended Catholic high school for four years. The margins of difference are substantial, consistently about 20 percentage points. (Again worth noting, however, are the large minorities of students in both groups who are apparently unfamiliar with these arguably basic elements of Catholic doctrine.)

Figure 7.13 shows Notre Dame students' views about Christian theology as a discipline. Only a minority of respondents strongly agreed that Christian theology is interesting, important, and relevant to their lives. But those who had attended Catholic high school for four years were significantly more likely to strongly agree with these statements than those who did not—about 10 percentage points more likely, on average.

Finally, Figure 7.14 presents data on Notre Dame students' attitudes about their personal relationship to the Catholic Church. High school background made no difference in whether the students felt very positive about the Catholic

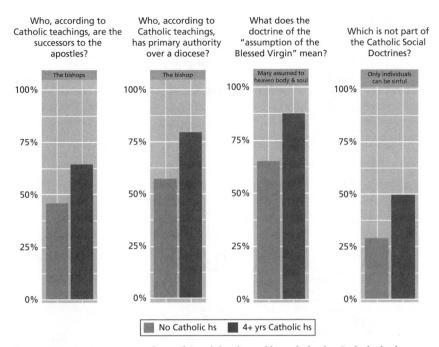

Figure 7.12 Notre Dame undergraduates' theological knowledge by Catholic high school attended, 4 years vs. none.

Church (the chart on the far right-hand side): less than 20 percent of each group was very positive about the Church. But those who had attended four years of Catholic high school were more likely than those who did not to strongly agree both that the future of the Church is very important to them and that they are personally committed to living as faithful members of the Catholic Church. The differences there are not enormous, but they are statistically significant and large enough to notice. (Again, however, only a minority of respondents strongly agree with these statements, regardless of high school, although many more simply agreed—not strongly—with these statements.) Interestingly, we find here that many more Notre Dame students care about the future of the Church and are committed to living as faithful members of it than feel very positive about the Church. Whether one views those differences as good news or bad depends on how one interprets their meaning.

In sum, the data presented in Figures 7.7 to 7.14 tell us that although many Catholic students attending an elite Catholic university such as Notre Dame do not know as much about the Bible and theology as they might and perhaps should, those who attended Catholic high school for four years know significantly more on average than those who did not. Graduates of Catholic high schools also view themselves as better educated in Catholic doctrine and moral teaching; are more likely to believe that theology as a discipline is interesting,

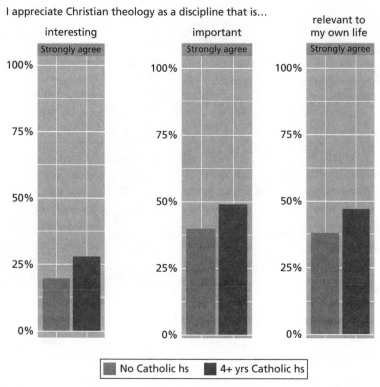

Figure 7.13 Notre Dame undergraduates' theological interest by Catholic high school attended, 4 years vs. none.

important, and relevant; and are more likely to express a commitment to the future well-being of the Catholic Church and their place as members in it. At least among the kind of Catholic emerging adults who attend colleges like the University of Notre Dame, having attended Catholic high school appears to make a sizeable difference in what young Catholics know about the Bible and theology and how much they care about theology and the Church. And for any study of the effects of attending Catholic high school, that seems well worth knowing.

At the same time, having observed these findings, we must issue another caution about their particularities and limits. The differences noted in this appendix do not pertain to a nationally representative sample of Catholic emerging adults, but rather to mostly first-year and sophomore, Catholic (or formerly Catholic) undergraduate college students at an elite Catholic university. Given the particular characteristics of that sample, these findings do not apply to any population except perhaps one very similar to it. Furthermore, it may well be that some of these differences are an artifact of which kinds of Catholic families send their children to four years of Catholic high school. Nevertheless, assuming that the observed differences are not entirely explained by selection effects, these

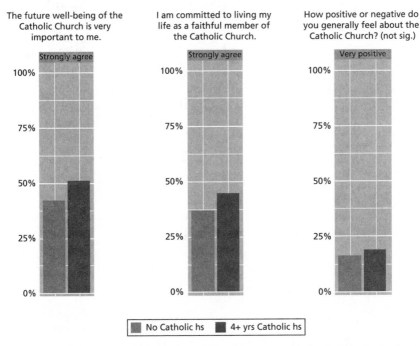

Figure 7.14 Notre Dame undergraduates' church commitment by Catholic high school attended, 4 years vs. none.

findings do show that attending Catholic high school affects the theological knowledge and attitudes about the Church of academically successful Catholic college students in the U.S. today. Further research is needed to better understand the influences of Catholic schooling on Catholic youth from different kinds of family backgrounds as measured at different stages of the life course.

Conclusion

What have we learned in this book and what does it mean? We close here with a brief review of our major findings and themes.

The Light of Historical Perspective

Our first conclusion is that the American Catholic Church is still reckoning with the consequences—particularly among its younger members—of the major demographic and organizational transformations it underwent over the course of the twentieth century. Contemporary commentators on the Catholic Church focus on the dramatic challenges the Church now faces. We suggest, however, that the present situation must be understood in its historical context of many unfolding developments on a long historical trajectory. If the American Church today is confronting major challenges and opportunities, these are not of recent origin. Most have been very long in the making, developing over several generations. On the central question of this book—the character of the faith and practice of contemporary emerging adult Catholics—we have learned that to understand young Catholics and ex-Catholics, one must place them in the context of social, economic, and ecclesial transformations over many previous decades. There is no way to make sense of the situation of Catholic and ex-Catholic emerging adults in the U.S. today without taking into account events from preceding decades: Catholics' socioeconomic upward mobility, suburbanization, and cultural assimilation; the uneven nature of the implementation of the Second Vatican Council in dioceses and parishes; the enthusiasm and subsequent frustration of Catholic liberals; the drastic decline in the number of priests and religious brothers and sisters; the widespread loss of faith in the Church as the final authority in matters of faith and morals; the polarization of many issues in the Church; the dramatic decline in weekly Mass attendance; the deterioration of effective catechesis of Catholic youth; the influence of the cultural and sexual revolutions in American society; and much more.

By our lights, the crucial factor on which many of these forces converged (and which to some extent determined the state of Catholic youth today) was the inability, and sometimes unwillingness, of a critical mass of the parents of the Catholic and ex-Catholic emerging adults we studied—and those half a generation earlier—to model, teach, and pass on the faith to their children. At precisely the same moment, older, more communal, taken-for-granted forms of religious practice and catechesis were eroding and sometimes collapsing in American Catholicism, with the decline of Catholic ethnic neighborhoods in cities and the loss of U.S. Catholics' sense of genuine cultural distinctiveness. Just when the Church and its faithful needed to create new means for propagating the faith better fitted for the circumstances of the late twentieth century, the most important means by which any religion is transmitted to new generations—the investment, modeling, and instruction of parents—was weakened by uncertainty, distraction, and incapacitation. Unsurprisingly, this combination meant a partial breakdown in the effectiveness of religious catechesis. Though these developments were related to many factors, the situation was exacerbated by the dramatic decline in the number of priests and religious women and men who shared the task of forming the faith and religious practices of rising generations of Catholics. The results of these factors and more are what we have described in the chapters above.

Our statistical and historical view of Catholic young adults since the 1970s adds another layer of understanding of these matters. We found that Catholic emerging adults since the 1970s display—with one huge exception—relatively little change in their religious beliefs, attitudes, and practices. Eighteen- to 25-year-old Catholics in the 2000s look very much like 18- to 25-year-olds in the 1970s (and the intervening decades) on a variety of measures. This finding supports our larger conclusion that whatever major changes in beliefs and attitudes happened among Catholic emerging adults on these measures for the most part happened before the 1970s. By then, the transformation had already occurred. The one huge exception, where we do find a divergence in the practices of Catholic and non-Catholic emerging adults over four decades, concerns *Mass attendance*. Catholic emerging adults exhibit a strong decline in church attendance over these four decades, and a sharper decline than their non-Catholic peers. Additional analyses suggest that Catholic youth will not "rebound" to higher levels of church attendance as they grow older, or at least not as much as Protestants likely will. Otherwise, Catholic emerging adults of the past four decades look remarkably similar to non-Catholic emerging adults of the same age during the same time period. Any Catholic distinctiveness among what we now call emerging adults on a variety of measures has in recent decades disappeared. Except for their lower levels of church attendance, Catholic emerging adults basically look like other emerging adults.

Differences among Types of Catholic Emerging Adults

Though young Catholics as a group resemble the larger population of young adults, not all Catholics are identical. Rather, there are many distinctions internal to the Catholic emerging adult population that matter for their religious and spiritual lives. These differences include (1) having multiple overlapping Catholic indicators (measured by our study) or just a few or one; (2) being a white Catholic or a first-, second-, and third-generation (or more) Hispanic Catholic immigrant; (3) growing up with a parent identifying as a traditional, moderate, or liberal Catholic; and (4) having two Catholic parents or only one. These categories' differences are reflected by varying results on most measures of religious practices and beliefs. The differences between groups are usually small to moderate, though sometimes sizable. Emerging adults who display multiple, overlapping indicators of being Catholic practice their faith more and have more traditional beliefs than Catholics who have fewer indicators. The same is true for Catholics raised in homes where both parents are Catholic and those with at least one parent who identifies his or her own Catholic faith as traditional, as opposed to moderate or liberal.

The differences between white Catholics and Hispanic Catholics are more complex. By many measures, though not all, first-generation Hispanic Catholics (the foreign born) are more traditional in their practice and belief. In some instances, white Catholics and first-generation Hispanic Catholics were similar, and it was third-generation Hispanic Catholics (those whose grandparents or earlier were foreign born) who were less religious. Most broadly, among Hispanic Catholic emerging adults, we observed a shift from more religious practice and traditional beliefs to less of the same, the farther the adult is generationally removed from immigration. Even so, we think an important takeaway about Hispanic Catholics is that they cannot be straightforwardly described, and their roles and influences in the Catholic Church are not simple or uniform, but complex. Discussions about the Church and its future sometimes treat Hispanic Catholics as a monolithic group. We find the reality to be more complicated, deserving of more sophisticated research and reflection.

These and other forces at work among Catholic young people give rise to a variety of types of Catholic emerging adults. There is of course more than one way to create a valid and insightful typology of American Catholics. Our own interviews with emerging adult Catholics suggested to us the existence of at least six different major categories. These we called Apostates, Switchers, Estranged Catholics, Nominal Catholics (including a "dormant" subgroup), Engaged Catholics, and Devout Catholics (although none of those we happened to interview qualified as Devout). These types of Catholic and ex-Catholic emerging adults range from embittered youth who scorn the Church to those who attend

Mass regularly, practice their faith consistently, are able to articulate Church doctrine, believe most or all of the Church's teachings, and expect to continue to live as Catholics in the future (some of these latter category are out there, even if they did not end up in our interview sample). No one category of the six dominated in our sample. Rather, significant numbers of the emerging adult Catholics and ex-Catholics we interviewed fell into each.

The Many Ways of Being "Catholic" Today

If there ever was a time in American history when one was simply either Catholic or not Catholic, that day is past. Although many social science studies of Catholicism ignore this fact, there are many ways one can classify respondents as "Catholic" in research. And the way researchers define people as Catholic or not has real consequences for what they find and report about "Catholics" and "Catholicism." Our analysis in this book has explained this problem in detail and used various measures to identify which emerging adults in our sample are "Catholic," as appropriate for the given issue or dynamic under study. The larger point we wish to drive home is that many people in America today, perhaps especially the young, might be Catholic or connected to Catholicism in a variety of ways. What makes anyone a Catholic—at least from the perspective of social science? Going to Mass (even if only on Christmas and Easter, or even less often)? Being "raised" Catholic (regardless of the religious condition of one's family now)? Currently identifying oneself as Catholic (whatever one actually believes and practices)? Having a parent who currently self-identifies as Catholic or attends a Catholic church (regardless of what the parent was or did during one's childhood)? Or something else? Again, different criteria for distinguishing Catholics from non-Catholics will produce at least somewhat different findings. And if research designs set up to answer particular types of questions are not careful about these decisions, the results can be inaccurate and misleading.

Consider, for instance, a study that seeks to assess the impact on youth of attending CCD classes but that only samples self-identifying Catholics. All the people who were raised Catholic but are currently not Catholic, including those who are currently not religious, would be systematically excluded, causing the study's results to be so biased as to be worth little. Yet noting these methodological difficulties is not merely a matter relevant to technical scholarly analyses. They also tell us something larger about the nature of religion and society in America today. The fact that we must confront these methodological difficulties tells us that things are more complicated than they used to be. More Americans today than in the past are not remaining in the faith traditions in which they were raised; are switching religious affiliations; are marrying and having children with people of other religions or no religion; are living in broken, mixed, and refor-mulated (religious) families; are losing their religious faith; and are attending more than one kind of religious service. These changes, which definitely involve American Catholics, present not only measurement challenges for social scientists but also significant pastoral challenges for religious institutions like the Catholic Church.

Religious Changes between the Teenage and Emerging Adult Years

In this study, we examined the changes that take place among Catholic youth as they transition from the teenage to the emerging adult years. We discovered that, as teenagers, Catholics exhibit lower levels of religiousness (as measured by attendance at religious services, frequency of prayer, and self-rated importance of faith) than non-Catholic youth and that these differences do not diminish when the Catholic teens become emerging adults. Across this transition, in fact, the dominant religious trajectory is one of *stability*. Catholic young people may change individual behaviors or beliefs as they age, but most stay in roughly the same category of religiousness from the teenage years to emerging adulthood. The religious experiences, beliefs, and status of Catholic *teenagers* are thus extremely consequential for their religious faith and practice five years later. Stability, as we have noted, is the default; continuity rules. The next most common religious trajectory is to decline in religious faith and practice: a substantial number of Catholic teenagers move into the two lowest levels of religiousness as emerging adults. Those youth who dramatically increase their levels of religious faith and practice over this life-course phase are a small minority in comparison.

Three major domains appear to influence the religious and spiritual lives of Catholic youth during these years of transition. The first is *close relationships to religious adults* who help to form youth in their faith, serve as valuable reference points of belief and participation, and make attending Mass more meaningful and rewarding. The second is *internalized religious beliefs and personal religious experiences,* including having a faith that one finds important in daily life, believing in divine miracles, and experiencing answers to prayer. These factors (beliefs and experiences) often play a central role in forming a Catholic worldview and identity, which, once established, are likely to last into emerging adulthood—in part by helping youth understand the deeper, spiritual aspects of their Catholic faith as authentic life truths. And, note, in most cases this second set of factors is modeled and formed (or not) primarily by those involved in the first domain: adults with whom a teen has close and valued relationships. It all ties together.

Religious practices are the third important component in maintaining Catholic faith and practice during the transition to emerging adulthood. These bolster Catholicism's place as central to a teen's identity and make it a kind of "capital investment" or an accumulating resource with ongoing payoffs, so to speak. Once youth have built up this "religious capital" of know-how in practicing the faith, they are more likely to take advantage of its rewards by continuing to participate in the Church and believe and live out what it teaches.

Most central in this entire process of religious socialization is having *strong relational ties to religious adults, both parents and non-parental adults*. Precious few Catholic youth become highly religious young adults without enjoying such bonds. In nearly all cases, having close relational ties to faith is a *necessary* condition of becoming a strong Catholic emerging adult. Such ties alone cannot guarantee or produce religiousness in young people. But in their absence, the likelihood of Catholic youth increasing or maintaining their religious faith and practice during this life transition is extremely low. It is absolutely crucial for those who are invested in forming faithful Catholic youth to understand this causal connection. And, for academic religion researchers, better understanding how and why adult ties are so central to this process can provide key insights into larger questions of inter generational religious socialization.

Our last conclusion on the subject of Catholic teens' transition to emerging adulthood sheds light on the American Catholic Church's serious discussions about the importance of Catholic schools compared to other ways the Church might invest its resources in forming youth. Our analysis included an exploration of the effects of attending Catholic high school on the subsequent religious and spiritual outcomes of emerging adults. We found that Catholic teenagers who attend Catholic schools exhibit higher levels of religiousness, especially attendance at Mass, than Catholic teens who do not attend such schools. This increased religiousness, however, does not completely close the religiosity gap: even Catholics at Catholic schools are less religious by our measures than non-Catholics, especially non-Catholics who attend private Protestant schools. Further, the differences between Catholic-schooled teens and other Catholic teens nearly disappear in early emerging adulthood, which suggests that any impact of Catholic schooling does not survive this transition—at least during the "college years," the first half of emerging adulthood we focus on here. The one exception to this finding is that attending a Catholic high school is religiously beneficial for Catholic teenagers who are not highly religious. That is, Catholics who are not among the most devout during their teenage years, but attend Catholic high school, appear to be most positively influenced in later religiousness by attending Catholic school. Catholic schools' less dramatic effects on most students may stem from the changing nature of Catholic schools as some prioritize academic success over religious training and thus draw in more nominally religious

Catholic teens. Historical comparisons of the composition of Catholic schools show that this changing emphasis has significantly altered the student population: many Catholic schools are becoming the home of children of academic and financial elites, regardless of their religious affiliation. That state of affairs may have had the unintended consequence of strengthening the religiousness of Catholic teenagers who might not have attended Catholic schools if they were still primarily religious institutions.

Catholic High Schools

We also discovered on closer investigation some additional complicated facts about the effects (or lack thereof) of attending Catholic high school. Catholic teenagers who attend Catholic high school are significantly more religious than those who do not both during their teenage years and five years later during early emerging adulthood. However, again, much of that difference appears to be attributable to the higher religiousness of the families that send their children to Catholic high school, and not so much to the independent effect of the Catholic schooling itself. Catholic families who practice their faith more seriously are more likely to send their children to Catholic high schools, and they typically pass on their higher levels of religiousness to their children. Attending Catholic high school thus appears to be one of many ways that committed Catholic families express their faith, and it no doubt helps to sustain their greater religiousness. Even so, when we statistically control for differences in teens' family backgrounds, we find that Catholic schooling has little to no independent influence five years later on those who attended them. (As always in our analysis, this finding applies not to each individual Catholic teen but to the population as a whole.) That is, the higher religiosity effect we do observe does not appear directly attributable to Catholic schooling. Nevertheless, we do find that such schooling has two noteworthy independent effects. First, youth who attended Catholic high school for four years (whatever their family backgrounds) are significantly less likely than those who did not do so to completely stop practicing their Catholic faith in early emerging adulthood. Even if their religious observance falls to very minimal levels, they tend *not* to entirely abandon attending Mass and praying as emerging adults. Second, again, attending Catholic high school for four years appears to have a religiously beneficial effect on those teenagers who come from less religious families. This particular sub-population of Catholic youth is significantly more likely than other groups to shift from low levels to high levels of religious faith and practice between the teenage years and emerging adulthood. These findings about Catholic schools are intriguing, although they surely require replication before being taken as determined fact. More research on the influence of Catholic schooling is needed to better sort out the effects of these complicated factors on different kinds of Catholic youth.

The Difference Faith Makes in Emerging Adult Life Outcomes

Does being a Practicing Catholic as opposed to a Sporadic or Disengaged Catholic emerging adult make any difference in measurable life outcomes not directly related to religion and spirituality? Our analysis suggests that, yes, it does. On a variety of emerging adult life experiences and outcomes, we found that members of these "ideal type" groups of Catholic youth fare differently. Often the differences are small, but sometimes they are moderate or even large. And the patterns of difference across the outcomes and experiences are fairly consistent. Namely, emerging adult Catholics who are more involved in their faith—as measured by Mass attendance, prayer, and perceived importance of faith—are doing what most people (particularly most committed Catholic adults) would consider to be better on many of the outcomes we measured and tested. The differences are not immense, but they are real and consequential. We do not claim that these differences are produced only by the faith commitments of these emerging adults, as a matter of one-directional causation. Life never operates that simply. But we do think it worth noting that some positive life-course experiences and outcomes are associated among Catholic emerging adults with practicing religion more seriously, which surely contributes in one way or another to those more positive experiences and outcomes.

Conclusion

Before ending, we wish to put our findings into some larger perspective. The National Study of Youth and Religion, the source of the data upon which this book is based, is a big-picture study. It captures and depicts the state of reality of Catholic youth at a *national* level. That is valuable and important. But it also overlooks important differences and details that one can detect with more finely grained analysis. What we report usually concerns the average state of large groupings of Catholic emerging adults. And that means that our findings may not accurately describe life in any *particular* Catholic diocese, parish, school, youth group, or family. Just because we find, for example, that attending Catholic high school has a positive influence *on average* on the later faith and practice of young people does not mean that all or even most Catholic high schools are as effective or impressive as they could be or, from the Church's perspective, should be. Catholic education may have this positive effect on average, yet still have much room for improvement overall and especially in particular schools. By the same token, merely because we found that *on average* participating in mission and service trips as teenagers seems not to associate with stronger faith and practice during Catholics' emerging adult years does not mean that all such trips are useless. Some of them are certainly powerful and life-changing—and that matters, even if it does not show up in national statistical analyses that rely on calculated averages. In short, while we think the findings of this book are interesting, important, and accurate, we want readers to keep in mind our study's broad scope and definite limits. Assessments of the value and impact of Catholic religious education *closer to the ground* will require studies of *particular* parishes, schools, trips, and other programs.

Along similar lines, it is also worth remembering that while the most impressive, committed emerging adult Catholics may not show up in the national sample we analyzed here, we know that they are "out there," living faithful Catholic lives. Given their relatively low numbers and the particularities of our sample, we did not find among our Catholic interview respondents any who qualified as "Devoted" in our scheme of categorization. This is because our study's methodological "net" only "caught" larger groups of Catholics and ex-Catholics. And oftentimes, in the development of social institutions, it is small groups of highly committed people, rather than masses of more loosely affiliated people, who end up making the biggest differences. We also know from our experience with various kinds of students at our own universities and colleges (especially Smith and Christoffersen at the University of Notre Dame) that more than a few such highly committed, seriously practicing Catholic emerging adults exist and are becoming active members and leaders in the Catholic Church. In some cases, they are on the road to becoming clergy and men and women religious. In fact, while sociology has so far done little to investigate this trend empirically, a growing pile of anecdotal evidence suggests at least some rumblings of significant activity for faith and Church renewal springing up among a minority of very serious, highly committed young Catholics. How extensive and influential such movements prove to be will be consequential for the future of the American Catholic Church, for better or worse.

Finally, we close by reiterating the most important themes of our findings. What sociological factors make the biggest difference in the religious and spiritual lives of Catholic young people? *Relationships* with models, mentors, teachers, and friends who are serious about the Catholic faith are paramount. Most crucial are the commitment, intentionality, examples, and encouragement of Catholic *parents*. In most cases, parents with *their own lives and practices* set the standards of faith and practice that determine what their children may achieve or approximate. Beyond parents, and in a few cases substituting for parents, *other Catholic adult role models and mentors*—grandparents, family friends, uncles and aunts, and so on—also often make a big difference in the religious and spiritual lives of Catholic youth. Furthermore, because in these matters stability is the default and "continuity rules," producing the religious fruits that committed Catholics would like to see among Catholic emerging adults requires *active cultivation years before this phase in life*. Everything we have learned over more than a decade of performing and analyzing the National Study of Youth and Religion tells us that committed and practicing Catholic emerging adults are people who were well formed in Catholic faith and practice *as children*, whose faith became personally meaningful and practiced *as teenagers*, and whose *parents* (reinforced by other supportive Catholic adults) were the *primary agents* cultivating that life-long formation. Because (as sociological theories can tell you) it is difficult and unusual to dramatically change religious directions in life, strong trajectories of Catholic faith normally must be launched and guided *early* in life and especially sustained and boosted during the teenage years. If parents and other agents of faith formation wait too long—for example, until confirmation time—to begin deliberate cultivation of young people's religiosity, usually they have waited until it is too late. *Intentional instruction* of and *active investment* in Catholic youth need to start in early childhood and continue all the way through the end of high school and into college, for those who hope to see young adult Catholics carrying on the Church and its faith into the future. Along the way a variety of institutions and programs matter, too, including Catholic schooling, active and robust youth groups, compelling catechetical training, formative faith-deepening retreats, and more. Ultimately, whether such instruction and investment take place is not determined by social forces, but remains an open question in the hands of free, responsible adults who will choose whether to care about them, prioritize them, and act to achieve their realization. Sociology can tell us how human life tends to operate amid various social forces in various societies. But in the end, it is *real, living persons* who actually do or do not make that life happen.

Appendix A

REGRESSION METHODOLOGY
AND FULL RESULTS

We used three measures from the third wave of the National Study of Youth and Religion to create a single measure of religiosity for Chapter 5: attendance at religious services, self-rated importance of faith, and frequency of prayer. We created this measure based on the entire sample (Catholics and non-Catholics). Therefore, the percentages presented for each category are based on this whole sample. The regression results presented below, however, only include our identified sample of Catholics, using their score from this religiosity measure as the outcome.

For attendance, all respondents were asked "Do you attend religious services more than once or twice a year, not counting weddings, baptisms, and funerals?" Respondents who answered yes to this question were then asked "About how often do you usually attend religious services there?," which offered these options as responses: a few times a year, many times a year, once a month, two to three times a month, once a week, and more than once a week. Respondents who said they did not attend religious services were set to "never" on the measure of religious service attendance. Regarding importance of faith, respondents were asked "How important or unimportant is religious faith in shaping how you live your daily life?," which offered the following answers: not at all important, not very important, somewhat important, very important, and extremely important. Finally, respondents were asked "How often, if ever, do you pray by yourself alone?," which had these response options: never, less than once a month, one to two times a month, about once a week, a few times a week, about once a day, and many times a day. Before combining these measures into one index, we had to code them onto similar scales in order to weight their contribution to the resulting index equally. Because importance has five response options, attendance and prayer were recoded from their original seven categories to five (0–4). For attendance, respondents who said "many times a year" and "once a month" were coded into the same category, and respondents who reported attending "once a week" and "more than once a week" were coded into one category. Similarly for prayer, respondents who reported praying "one to two times a month" and "about once a week" were collapsed into one category, and respondents who claimed to pray "a few times a week" and "about once a day" were placed into one category. We based these decisions on the substantive similarity of the relevant answer categories. The new scales also maintain a relatively even distribution of cases across categories on these measures.

A simple way to combine these variables would have been to take individuals' additive or average score across all three. This method, however, does not accurately distinguish between qualitative differences in respondents' overall levels of religiosity. For example, a respondent who attended two to three times per month, said religion was very important, and prayed many times per week would have the exact same average score as someone who only attended a few times per year but thought religion was extremely important and prayed many times per day (they would both have summative scores of nine, or averages of three). Yet these two cases are quite different in their overall expression of religion. To avoid this purely quantitative scoring, we created a single measure to reflect specific combinations of the three variables, based on our informed decisions. The resulting index separates respondents into four categories: Lowest, Minimal, Moderate, and Highest levels of religiosity. We began by categorizing all of the "consistent" cases. All respondents who fell into the two lowest categories on all three variables (that is, all 0's and 1's on our scales of 0 to 4) we put into the Lowest category, and respondents who were in the top two categories on all three variables (that is, all 3's and 4's) we put in the Highest category. Next, respondents belonging to the two middle-lower categories (scoring 1 and 2 on all measures [except for all 1's]) we put into the Minimal group, and respondents scoring only in the two middle-higher categories (all 2's and 3's [except all 2's or all 3's]) we put into the Moderate group. Next we categorized respondents who were inconsistent on only one measure. Respondents who were in the lowest category on two out of three variables, with the third measure not being in the highest category (that is, who reported two 0's and a number no higher than 3 on the third measure), we put in the Lowest group. Respondents in the middle category on two measures with the third measure being in the lowest category (two 2's and a 0) we placed into the Minimal group, two 3's and a 1 in the Moderate group, and two measures in the highest category and the third in the middle category (two 4's and one 2) in the Highest group. This fairly straightforward categorization classified 70 percent of cases that had no missing data on the three component measures. The remaining 30 percent of cases all had slightly ambiguous configurations (e.g., 2 on attendance, 4 on importance, and 1 on prayer). The majority of these combinations, in our studied judgment, however, fell into one of the middle two categories of our overall religiosity index

Table A.1 Ordered Logistic Regression Coefficients Without Lagged Variable on Religiousness at Wave 3 (N = 661) [Weighted]

			Wave 3 Religiousness			
	Model 1	*Model 2*	*Model 3*	*Model 4*	*Model 5*	*Model 6*
Parent Income (Thousands)	−.005	−.005	−.007	−.007*	−.005	−.003
Parent Education	.048	.004	.029	.046	.058	.031
Age (Std)	.067	.076	.111	.150	.115	.141
Two Parent Biological Family	.348	.268	.368+	.382+	.374+	.257
Race (White Ref)						
Black	1.598*	1.448*	1.823***	1.725***	1.776***	1.303*
Hispanic	.335	.196	.471*	.543*	.410+	.191
Other	.126	−.097	.260	.178	.288	−.009
Female	.123	.316+	.302+	.288+	.223	.201
Enrolled in College (Wave 3)	−.039	.137	.123	.156	.115	.037
Attendance at Relig Services	.210*					.007
Importance of Religion	.651***					.466***
Frequency of Prayer	.265*					.127

continued

Table A.1 **(continued)**

			Wave 3 Religiousness			
	Model 1	Model 2	Model 3	Model 4	Model 5	Model 6
Religiosity of Parents		.596***				.464***
Number of Relig Experiences		.264*				.142
Reading Scriptures		.299***				.188*
Decide Morality By Religion		.313				.240
Believes in Divine Miracles		.620*				.411+
Religious Friends			.237*			.067
Pr Supp Rel Adults (Std)			.316*			.195+
Satisfaction w/Congregation			.359***			-.005
Church has Youth Minister			.469*			.240
Number Mission Trips (Std)				-.070		-.122+
Number Religious Acts (Std)				-.055		-.158
In Catholic School				.820*		.263
Satisfaction w/Youth Group				.157*		-.007
Attendance at Sunday School				.183***		.033

continued

Table A.1 (continued)

	Wave 3 Religiousness					
	Model 1	Model 2	Model 3	Model 4	Model 5	Model 6
Doubts abt Religious Beliefs					-.025	-.074
Made Fun of B/C Religion					.617***	-.016
Teens Look Down on Rel					.072	.179
Should Abstain from Sex					.513*	.116
Had Oral Sex					-.122	-.049
Pseudo R-Squared	.0127	.132	.093	.057	.052	.167
BIC	13217221	13138268	13740594	14277115	14353208	12611852

Note: Lagged dependent variables NOT included in all models. Dependent variable contains four categories.

Source: NSYR 2007. [+p < .10 *p < .05, **p < .01, ***p < .001. Two-tailed test.]

Table A.2 **Ordered Logistic Regression Coefficients With Lagged Variable on Religiousness at Wave 3 (N = 661) [Weighted]**

	Wave 3 Religiousness					
	Model 1	*Model 2*	*Model 3*	*Model 4*	*Model 5*	*Model 6*
Parent Income (Thousands)	-.005	-.003	-.005	-.005	-.005	-.003
Parent Education	.048	.019	.058	.062	.057	.031
Age (Std)	.067	.073	.087	.113	.081	.141
Two Parent Biological Family	.348	.253	.349	.352	.342	.257
Race (White Ref)						
Black	1.598*	1.371*	1.545*	1.593*	1.554*	1.303*
Hispanic	.335	.181	.355	.349	.299	.191
Other	.126	-.082	.156	.110	.164	-.009
Female	.123	.210	.150	.112	.107	.201
Enrolled in College (Wave 3)	-.039	.013	-.021	-.031	-.033	.037
Attendance at Relig Services	.210*	.046	.144	.180*	.200*	.007
Importance of Religion	.651***	.475***	.599***	.658***	.643***	.466***
Frequency of Prayer	.265*	.145	.235*	.272*	.256*	.127

continued

Table A.2 (continued)

	Wave 3 Religiousness					
	Model 1	Model 2	Model 3	Model 4	Model 5	Model 6
Religiosity of Parents		.467***				.464***
Number of Relig Experiences		.137				.142
Reading Scriptures		.199*				.188*
Decide Morality By Religion		.211				.240
Believes in Divine Miracles		.389+				.411+
Religious Friends			.048			.067
Pr Supp Rel Adults (Std)			.239*			.195+
Satisfaction w/Congregation			.011			-.005
Church has Youth Minister			.231			.240
Number Mission Trips				-.111*		-.122+
Number Religious Acts (Std)				-.136		-.158
In Catholic School				.502		.263
Satisfaction w/Youth Group				.048		-.007
Attendance at Sunday School				.073		.033

continued

Table A.2 **(continued)**

	Model 1	Model 2	Wave 3 Religiousness Model 3	Model 4	Model 5	Model 6
Doubts abt Religious Beliefs					-.128	-.074
Made Fun of B/C Religion					.173	-.016
Teens Look Down on Rel					.268	.179
Should Abstain from Sex					.117	.116
Had Oral Sex					-.016	-.049
					.268	.179
Pseudo R-Squared	.127	.154	.134	.134	.131	.167
BIC	13217221	12811716	13113170	13117261	13164301	12611852

Note: Lagged dependent variables included in all models. Dependent variable contains four categories.

Source: NSYR 2007. [+p < .10 *p < .05, **p < .01, ***p < .001. Two-tailed test.]

Table A.3 **Logistic Regression Coefficients on Changing from Moderate/Highest Religiousness at Wave 1 to Minimum/Lowest Religiousness at Wave 3 (N = 358) [Weighted]**

	Wave 3 Minimum/Lowest Religiousness				
	Model 1	*Model 2*	*Model 3*	*Model 4*	*Model 5*
Parent Income (Thousands)	.006	.006	.008	.006	.004
Parent Education	−.007	−.031	−.064	−.005	−.005
Age (Std)	.056	.024	−.04	−.027	−.12
Two Parent Biological Family	−.363	−.444	−.437	−.494+	−.379
Race (White Ref)					
Black	−.652	−.932+	−.86	−.883	−.474
Hispanic	.584+	.551+	.546+	.684+	.601+
Other	.725	.471	.307	.434	.919+
Female	.182	.13	.238	.224	.197
Enrolled in College (Wave 3)	.293	.292	.316	.345	.355
Religiosity of Parents	−.456*				−.412*
Number of Relig Experiences	−.223+				−.204+
Reading Scriptures	−.188+				−.187+
Decide Morality By Religion	−.024				.04
Believes in Divine Miracles	−.135				−.181

continued

Table A.3 **(continued)**

	Wave 3 Minimum/Lowest Religiousness				
	Model 1	Model 2	Model 3	Model 4	Model 5
Religious Friends	-.057				-.051
Pr Supp Rel Adults (Std)	-.434*				-.407*
Satisfaction w/ Congregation	.065				.111
Church has Youth Minister	-.251				-.113
Number Mission Trips (Std)		.065			.063
Number Religious Acts (Std)		-.01			.001
In Catholic School		-.316			.003
Satisfaction w/Youth Group		-.027			.021
Attendance at Sunday School		-.137+			-.088

continued

Table A.3 **(continued)**

	Wave 3 Minimum/Lowest Religiousness				
	Model 1	Model 2	Model 3	Model 4	Model 5
Doubts abt Religious Beliefs				.003	-.124
Made Fun of B/C Religion				-.153	.107
Teens Look Down on Rel				.188	.329
Should Abstain from Sex				-.118	-.01
Had Oral Sex				.629	.622
Constant	.760	-.076	.167	-.116	.832
Pseudo R-Squared	.08	.069	.047	.046	.124
BIC	4039387	4085026	4184584	4189272	3846855

Note: Only respondents who were not in the outcome (i.e., not in Minimum or Lowest Religiousness) at Wave 1 are included in the analyses. Because these are "initiation" models, lagged dependent variables cannot be included as predictors.

Source: NSYR 2007. [+p < .10 *p < .05, **p < .01, ***p < .001. Two-tailed test.]

Table A.4 **Logistic Regression Coefficients on Changing from Minimum/Lowest at Wave 1 to Moderate/Highest Religiousness at Wave 3 (N = 303) [Weighted]**

	Wave 3 Moderate/Highest Religiousness				
	Model 1	*Model 2*	*Model 3*	*Model 4*	*Model 5*
Parent Income (Thousands)	−.005	−.005	−.008	−.006	−.009
Parent Education	.022	−.068	.014	.009	.134
Age (Std)	.133	.177	.078	.044	−.142
Two Parent Biological Family	−.860*	−.551	−.401	−.423	−1.150*
Race (White Ref)					
Black	2.446*	2.889***	2.503***	2.563***	2.528*
Hispanic	.624	1.178*	1.253*	1.032*	.527
Other	−.245	−.24	−.044	−.317	.215
Female	1.071*	.748+	.757+	.754+	1.472*
Enrolled in College (Wave 3)	.546	.245	.096	.304	.564
Religiosity of Parents	.649*				.725*
Number of Relig Experiences	.217				.136
Reading Scriptures	.264				.401*
Decide Morality By Religion	.735				1.591
Believes in Divine Miracles	1.312*				1.673*

continued

Table A.4 **(continued)**

	Wave 3 Moderate/Highest Religiousness				
	Model 1	Model 2	Model 3	Model 4	Model 5
Religious Friends		.282			.503+
Pr Supp Rel Adults (Std)		-.178			-.593+
Satisfaction w/Congregation		.182			.17
Church has Youth Minister		.131			-.245
Number Mission Trips (Std)			-.117		-.331+
Number Religious Acts (Std)			-.088		-.221
In Catholic School			1.250+		1.121
Satisfaction w/Youth Group			.272+		.249
Attendance at Sunday School			-.187+		-.353*
Doubts abt Religious Beliefs				-.127	.12
Made Fun of B/C Religion				.382	-.767

continued

Table A.4 **(continued)**

			Wave 3 Moderate/Highest Religiousness		
	Model 1	Model 2	Model 3	Model 4	Model 5
Teens Look Down on Rel				.733	.91
Should Abstain from Sex				.171	-.39
Had Oral Sex				.418	.188
Constant	-3.337*	-2.284***	-1.986*	-2.928*	-2.626+
Pseudo R-Squared	.299	.179	.198	.187	.364
BIC	1625081	1904071	1860293	1885225	1473660

Note: Only respondents who were not in the outcome (i.e., not in Moderate or Highest Religiousness) at Wave 1 are included in the analyses. Because these are "initiation" models, lagged dependent variables cannot be included as predictors.

Source: NSYR 2007. [+p < .10 *p < .05, **p <.01, ***p < .001. Two-tailed test.]

Table A.5 **Logistic Regression Coefficients on Changing into Higher Level of Religiousness at Wave 3 (N = 526) [Weighted]**

			Wave 3 Higher (than Wave 1) Religiousness		
	Model 1	Model 2	Model 3	Model 4	Model 5
Parent Income (Thousands)	-.006	-.008	-.01	-.01	-.010
Parent Education	-.05	-.042	-.055	.007	.022
Age (Std)	-.076	-.044	-.092	-.169	-.223
Two Parent Biological Family	-.247	-.21	-.137	-.15	-.076
Race (White Ref)					
Black	1.636*	1.636*	1.610*	1.721*	1.432*
Hispanic	.384	.451	.428	.345	.3
Other	-.993	-.711	-.722	-.833	-.84
Female	.046	-.023	.047	.043	.17
Enrolled in College (Wave 3)	.352	.428	.291	.477	.356
Religiosity of Parents	.431*				.527*
Number of Relig Experiences	.304*				.408*
Reading Scriptures	.113				.131
Decide Morality By Religion	1.255*				1.299*
Believes in Divine Miracles	.134				.066

continued

Table A.5 **(continued)**

	Model 1	Model 2	Model 3	Model 4	Model 5
			Wave 3 Higher (than Wave 1) Religiousness		
Religious Friends	.15				-.014
Pr Supp Rel Adults (Std)	.098				.003
Satisfaction w/Congregation	-.098				-.313+
Church has Youth Minister	.176				.021
Number Mission Trips (Std)		.005			-.025
Number Religious Acts (Std)		-.032			-.066
In Catholic School		1.088*			1.161*
Satisfaction w/Youth Group		.106			.074
Attendance at Sunday School		-.085			-.085

continued

Table A.5 **(continued)**

	Wave 3 Higher (than Wave 1) Religiousness				
	Model 1	*Model 2*	*Model 3*	*Model 4*	*Model 5*
Doubts abt Religious Beliefs				-.268	-.359+
Made Fun of B/C Religion				.432*	.175
Teens Look Down on Rel				.44	.256
Should Abstain from Sex				.006	-.038
Had Oral Sex				.409	.378
Constant	-2.304***	-1.386*	-1.369*	-1.770*	-1.871*
Pseudo R-Squared	.14	.069	.087	.085	.191
BIC	3278384	3546224	3478387	3487181	3083895

Note: Only respondents who were in Lowest, Minimum, or Moderate level of Religiousness at Wave 1 are included in the analyses. The Moderate group was only counted if they moved into the Highest group, while the Lowest and Minimal counted if they moved into either the Moderate or Highest. Because these are "initiation" models, lagged dependent variables cannot be included as predictors.

Source: NSYR 2007. [+p < .10 *p < .05, **p < .01, ***p < .001. Two-tailed test.]

Table A.6 **Summary of Measures' Influence on Religiousness at Wave 3, Across Model Specifications [Weighted]**

	No LDV	LDV	From Mod/High to Min/Low	From Min/Low to Mod/High	From Mod/Min/Low to Mod/High[a]	Percent Significant[c]
				Wave 3 Religiousness		
Parent Income (Thousands)	B	N	N	N	N	10
Parent Education	N	N	N	N	N	0
Age (Std)	N	N	N	N	N	0
Two Parent Biological Family	B	B	B	B	N	40
Race (White Ref)						
Black	A	A	B	A	A	90
Hispanic	B	N	B	B	N	30
Other	N	N	N	N	N	0
Female	B	N	N	A	N	30
Enrolled in College (Wave 3)	N	N	N	N	N	0
Attendance at Relig Services	B	B	–	–	–	50
Importance of Religion	A	A	–	–	–	100
Frequency of Prayer	B	B	–	–	–	50

continued

Table A.6 **(continued)**

| | No LDV | LDV | From Mod/High to Min/Low | Wave 3 Religiousness | | Percent Significant[c] |
				From Min/Low to Mod/High	From Mod/Min/Low to Mod/High[a]	
Religiosity of Parents	A	A	A	A	A	100
Number of Relig Experiences	B	N	A	N	A	50
Reading Scriptures	A	A	A	B	N	70
Decide Morality By Religion	N	N	N	N	A	20
Believes in Divine Miracles	A	A	N	A	N	60
Religious Friends	B	N	N	B	N	20
Pr Supportive Rel Adults (Std)	A	A	A	B	N	70
Satisfaction w/Congregation	B	N	N	N	B	20
Church has Youth Minister	B	N	N	N	N	10
Number Mission Trips (Std)	B[b]	A	N	B	N	40
Number Religious Acts (Std)	N	N	N	N	N	0

continued

Table A.6 (continued)

			Wave 3 Religiousness			
	No LDV	LDV	From Mod/High to Min/Low	From Min/Low to Mod/High	From Mod/Min/Low to Mod/High[a]	Percent Significant[c]
In Catholic School	B	N	N	B	A	40
Satisfaction w/Youth Group	B	N	N	B	N	20
Attendance at Sunday School	B	N	B	A	N	40
Doubts abt Religious Beliefs	N	N	N	N	B	10
Made Fun of B/C Religion	B	N	N	N	B	20
Teens Look Down on Religion	N	N	N	N	N	0
Should Abstain from Sex	B	N	N	N	N	10
Had Oral Sex	N	N	N	N	N	0
N	661	661	358	303	526	

Note: The first two models are Ordered Logistic Regressions. The final three models are Logistic Regressions and represent "initiation" models, meaning only respondents who were not in the outcome at Wave 1 were included in the analysis.

[a] The Moderate group was only counted if they moved into the Highest group, while the Lowest and Minimal counted if they moved into either the Moderate or Highest.

[b] Term is significant only in Final model and is in opposite direction from expected. Not included in percent calculation.

[c] Percent calculated using A=1; B=.5; N=0.

Source: NSYR 2007.

Key: "A" - Significant in *all* models including Final Model; "B" - Significant only in reduced Block Model; "N" - Never Significant; "—" - Not included in given model specification.

Table A.7 **Summary of Rankings of Influence on Religiousness at Wave 3, Across Model Specifications [Weighted]**

	Wave 3 Religiousness					
	No LDV	LDV	From Mod/High to Min/Low	From Min/Low to Mod/High	From Mod/Min/Low to Mod/High[a]	Average Rank
Attendance at Relig Services	14	N/S	–	–	–	11
Importance of Religion	1	1	–	–	–	1
Frequency of Prayer	11	7	–	–	–	9
Religiosity of Parents	2	2	1	2	3	1.7
Number of Relig Experiences	12	N/S	3	N/S	4	6.2
Reading Scriptures	5	5	4	7	N/S	4.8
Decide Morality By Religion	N/S	N/S	N/S	N/S	1	7
Believes in Divine Miracles	3	3	N/S	1	2	2.6
Religious Friends	13	N/S	N/S	6	N/S	6.8
Pr Supportive Rel Adults (Std)	4	4	2	5	N/S	3.8
Satisfaction w/Congregation	9	N/S	N/S	N/S	7	6.7
Church has Youth Minister	10	N/S	N/S	N/S	N/S	7

continued

Table A.7 (continued)

	Wave 3 Religiousness					
	No LDV	LDV	From Mod/High to Min/Low	From Min/Low to Mod/High	From Mod/Min/Low to Mod/High[a]	Average Rank
Number Mission Trips (Std)	16	6	N/S	8	N/S	7.3
Number Religious Acts (Std)	N/S	N/S	N/S	N/S	N/S	8.2
In Catholic School	6	N/S	N/S	4	2	4.3
Satisfaction w/Youth Group	15	N/S	N/S	9	N/S	7.7
Attendance at Sunday School	14	N/S	5	3	N/S	6.3
Doubts abt Religious Beliefs	N/S	N/S	N/S	N/S	6	7.8
Made Fun of B/C Religion	7	N/S	N/S	N/S	5	6
Teens Look Down on Religion	N/S	N/S	N/S	N/S	N/S	8.2
Should Abstain from Sex	8	N/S	N/S	N/S	N/S	6.7
Had Oral Sex	N/S	N/S	N/S	N/S	N/S	8.2
N	661	661	358	303	526	

Note: The first two models are Ordered Logistic Regressions. The final three models are Logistic Regressions and represent "initiation" models, meaning only respondents who were not in the outcome at Wave 1 were included in the analysis. Rankings are derived from standardized coefficients. Rank is determined first within terms significant in final model, and then within variables only significant in block models. "N/S" - Term never significant in any model (Assigned highest rank value in model +1 for average calculation).

[a] The Moderate group was only counted if they moved into the Highest group, while the Lowest and Minimal counted if they moved into either the Moderate or Highest.

Source: NSYR 2007.

Table A.8 Summary of Measures' Influence on Religiousness at Wave 3, Across Model Specifications

	Wave 3 Religiousness	
	Percent Significant	*Average Rank*
Attendance at Relig Services	50	11
Importance of Religion	100	1
Frequency of Prayer	50	9
Religiosity of Parents	100	1.7
Number of Relig Experiences	50	6.2
Reading Scriptures	70	4.8
Decide Morality By Religion	20	7
Believes in Divine Miracles	60	2.6
Religious Friends	20	6.8
Pr Supportive Rel Adults (Std)	70	3.8
Satisfaction w/Congregation	20	6.7
Church has Youth Minister	10	7
Number Mission Trips (Std)	40	7.3
Number Religious Acts (Std)	0	8.2
In Catholic School	40	4.3
Satisfaction w/Youth Group	20	7.7
Attendance at Sunday School	40	6.3
Doubts abt Religious Beliefs	10	7.8
Made Fun of B/C Religion	20	6
Teens Look Down on Religion	0	8.2
Should Abstain from Sex	10	6.7
Had Oral Sex	0	8.2

Note: Summary measures derived from each measure's coefficient across five model specifications. The first two models are Ordered Logistic Regressions. The final three models are Logistic Regressions and represent "initiation" models, meaning only respondents who were not in the outcome at Wave 1 were included in the analysis.

[a]Percent significant determined by frequency of term's significance across five model specifications.

[b]Rank is determined first within terms significant in final model, and then within variables only significant in block models.

(i.e., they were not representative of the Highest or Lowest levels of religiosity). To distinguish between and categorize the remaining cases, we used the sum of each case's three scores, with cases scoring a total between three and six being placed in the Minimal group, and cases scoring between seven and nine in the Moderate group. Using the sum of the scores to make only these classifications avoids the criticism of this method we noted above, because we used it for a limited group. The sum of these cases' scores provided the best distinction. The Minimal and Moderate groups have significantly more combinations included in their coding, but the majority of these combinations are the aforementioned "inconsistent" configurations, which were far less common among our respondents than the more consistent combinations. By employing this more qualitatively informed method to assess and combine these three measures, we believe we can reflect the real lives of these cases more accurately than a mathematical formula would allow. We are able to distinguish different levels of religiosity based on their overall meaning and typical combinations of these three variables.

NOTES

Introduction

1. The meaning of this term is explained below. Here we wish to say that our use of the word "emerging" is not intended to connect to the movement currently afoot among certain generally younger, mostly evangelical Christians in the U.S. known as the "emerging church" or "emergent church," about which this book takes no particular position.
2. For detailed information about the research methodology used in the first wave of NSYR, see Christian Smith and Melinda Lundquist Denton, 2003, "Methodological Design and Procedures for the National Survey of Youth and Religion (NSYR)," Chapel Hill, NC: The National Study of Youth and Religion; Christian Smith, with Melinda Lundquist Denton, 2005, *Soul Searching: The Religious and Spiritual Lives of American Teenagers*, New York: Oxford University Press, pp. 272–310.
3. Co-authored with Melinda Lundquist Denton, 2005, *Soul Searching: The Religious and Spiritual Lives of American Teenagers*, New York: Oxford University Press.
4. For detailed information about the research methodology used in the second wave of NSYR, see Christian Smith, Lisa Pearce, and Melinda Lundquist Denton, 2006, "Methodological Design and Procedures for the National Study of Youth and Religion (NSYR) Longitudinal Telephone Survey (Waves 1 & 2)," Chapel Hill, NC: The National Study of Youth and Religion.
5. See Christian Smith, Lisa Pearce, and Melinda Lundquist Denton, 2008, "National Study of Youth and Religion Telephone Survey Codebook Introduction and Methods (Waves 1, 2 & 3)," Chapel Hill, NC: The National Study of Youth and Religion.
6. Christian Smith, with Patricia Snell, 2009, *Souls in Transition: The Religious and Spiritual Lives of Emerging Adults*, New York: Oxford University Press.
7. Christian Smith, Kari Christoffersen, Hilary Davidson, and Patricia Snell Herzog, 2011, *Lost in Transition: The Dark Side of Emerging Adulthood*, New York: Oxford University Press.
8. Additional information about empirical data that this book analyzes and interprets, and which serve as the basis of its findings and story, is as follows. The data come, as noted above, from a nationally representative telephone survey of 2,532 18- to 23-year-old Americans, and in-depth personal interviews conducted with a sub-sample of 230 of those survey respondents living in 37 states around the U.S. (all states but Alaska, Hawaii, Tennessee, Arkansas, Iowa, Oklahoma, Kansas, Nebraska, South Dakota, North Dakota, Wyoming, Colorado, and Montana). In addition, Chapter 2 presents findings from analyses of data from the General Social Survey, years 1972 to 2006. Of the 229 interview respondents, 158 had been interviewed before in prior waves of the study, and 71 we interviewed for the first time in this third wave. We introduced the new interviewees in order to refresh our sample and to check through the comparison of their answers with those of prior interviewees for the possible "contamination" or "training" of interview answers in the latter as a result of

their experience of completing prior interviews (our interviews in fact did not suggest that prior interviews biased third-wave answers). All participants in this sample were originally recruited to take part in a nationally representative, random-digit-dial telephone survey first conducted in 2002 and 2003. Those participants were at that time randomly sampled and, as subsequent analyses show, closely represent all American youth of that age group (see Christian Smith and Melinda Lundquist Denton, 2003, "Methodological Design and Procedures for the National Survey of Youth and Religion [NSYR]," Chapel Hill, NC: The National Study of Youth and Religion). Between survey waves, NSYR researchers made every reasonable effort to remain in contact with first-wave respondents and to track down apparently "lost cases." Those efforts met with success. The retention, or response, rate of first-wave participants in this third-wave study is 77.1 percent, which is very high for a study of this age population tracked over that number of years. The third-wave cooperation rate of respondents contacted was a high 87.7 percent. The refusal rate for the third-wave survey was a low 6 percent. In short, the large majority of those who completed the first-wave survey also completed the (second-wave survey and) third-wave survey, and a very large percentage of those we contacted agreed to participate. The vast majority of first-wave survey participants who are not represented in the third-wave study were "lost" between surveys, due mostly to their moving and not sending new contact information to the study tracking supervisors, and to NSYR researchers' inability to track them down.

More important than the calculated third-wave refusal, cooperation, and response (attrition) rates, however, is any possible non-response bias present in the third-wave NSYR data. The issue here is whether those first-wave respondents who did not complete the third-wave survey (i.e., non-responders) are significantly different than those who did complete it. If they were different, then the third-wave data would be biased in the direction of characteristics of those who were disproportionately likely to have completed the survey. If, for example, white or Southern or wealthy youth were more likely to complete the third-wave survey, then that survey's data would be biased toward answers that would be more likely to be given by whites or Southerners or wealthy youth for questions on which their answers would tend to differ. Fortunately, as a result of many factors—including the rigorous contact and tracking methods employed by the NSYR, the generally positive experience enjoyed by respondents of previous NSYR survey waves (as reported to NSYR researchers by many survey and interview respondents), the professional skills of the calling center staff who conducted the surveys (the second and third waves of the NSYR survey were conducted by the Odum Call Center of the Howard W. Odum Institute for Research in Social Science at the University of North Carolina at Chapel Hill, under the gifted leadership of Teresa Edwards, Michelle Temple, Thu-Mai Christian, and Terri Clark), and the financial incentives offered to respondents for completing the survey (third-wave survey respondents were paid $45 to complete the, on average, 52-minute telephone survey)—the third-wave survey data contain no detectable non-response biases. As with the first wave of NSYR data, minor original disproportions are statistically corrected by applying a weight variable that adjusts for slight sample differences in region and income. But analyses comparing the weighted third-wave NSYR data to known population characteristics represented in Census and other highly reliable datasets show that the third-wave NSYR survey data can be taken to be statistically representative of all American 18- to 24-year-olds who are not in prison, serving in the military, or otherwise institutionalized (according to the U.S. Census Bureau's American Community Survey, 1.59 percent of the total U.S. population who were between the ages of 18 and 24 in 2007 were incarcerated that year—specifically, 475,900 U.S. citizens between the ages of 18 and 24 were held in state or federal prisons or in local jails in 2007 [William Sabol and Heather Couture, *Prison Inmates at Midyear 2007: Bureau of Justice Statistics Bulletin*, U.S. Department of Justice, Table 9, page June 7, 2007]. According to the Department of Defense Manpower Data Center 2006 report, 2.7 percent of the same 18- to 24-year-old population [145,774 18- to 24-year-olds] in the U.S. were serving on active military duty in that year [Population Representation in the Military Services 2006, Department of Defense, Defense Manpower Data Center, Washington, D.C.: Department of Defense]). Furthermore— although we used stratified quota sampling to select our third-wave interview respondents— the sub-sample of survey respondents with whom we conducted our 229 in-depth, personal interviews in 2008 proved to be essentially representative of the proportions found in the general population on a set of key demographic variables. That means, in short, that the statistical and interview evidence presented in this book can be assumed with high confidence to accurately represent the entire U.S. emerging adult population about which it intends to speak. Stated even more simply, we can be very confident on social scientific grounds that the evidence upon which this book is based is solid and valid for authorizing the kind of findings and conclusions that we present in this book. Methodologically, the data are sound.

For another longitudinal study of religion over the life course, see Michele Dillon and Paul Wink, 2007, *In the Course of a Lifetime: Tracing Religious Belief, Practice, and Change*, Berkeley, CA: University of California Press.

9. Many major extant scholarly works on emerging adulthood pay relatively little sustained attention to the religious and spiritual lives of emerging adults, such as, for example, Richard Settersten, Frank Furstenberg, and Rubén Rumbaut (eds.), *On the Frontiers of Adulthood*, Chicago: University of Chicago Press; Jeffrey Arnett and Jennifer Tanner (eds.), *Emerging Adults in America: Coming of Age in the 21st Century*, Washington, D.C.: American Psychological Association; Jeffrey Arnett, 2007, *Adolescence and Emerging Adulthood: A Cultural Approach*, Upper Saddle River, NJ: Pearson. One major work on difficulties and solutions during emerging adulthood for socially vulnerable populations appears to make no mention of religion at all: D. Wayne Osgood, E. Michael Foster, Constance Flanagan, and Gretchen Ruth, 2005, *On Your Own Without a Net: The Transition to Adulthood for Vulnerable Populations*, Chicago: University of Chicago Press.

10. Dean R. Hoge, William D. Dinges, Mary Johnson, S.N.D. de N., and Juan L. Gonzales, Jr., 2001, *Young Adult Catholics: Religion in the Culture of Choice*, Notre Dame: University of Notre Dame Press; Patrick McNamara, 1991, *Conscience First, Tradition Second: A Study of Young Catholics*, Albany, NY: State University of New York Press; Robert Ludwig, 1995, *Reconstructing Catholicism for a New Generation*, New York: Crossroads; Nancy McAuley and Moira Mathieson, 1986, *Faith Without Form: Beliefs of Catholic Youth*, Lanham, MD: Sheed & Ward. Also see sections on young Catholics in Jim Davidson et al., 1997, *The Search for Common Ground: What Unites and Divides Catholic Americans*, Huntington, IN: Our Sunday Visitor; D'Antonio, Davidson, Hoge, and Gautier, 2007, *American Catholics Today: New Realities of Their Faith and Their Church*, Lanham, MD: Rowman & Littlefield; James Davidson, 2005, *Catholicism in Motion: The Church in American Society*, Liguori, MO: Liguori.

Colleen Carroll's *The New Faithful: Why Young Adults Are Embracing Christian Orthodoxy* (Chicago: Loyola Press, 2002) tells a different story than those cited above, but it also does not make claims about being representative of any population.

The present study also benefits from and builds upon a number of other very good prior research projects on the religion of American youth not primarily focused on Catholicism (including Robert Wuthnow, 2007, *After the Baby Boomers: How Twenty- and Thirty-Somethings Are Shaping the Future of American Religion*, Princeton: Princeton University Press; Tim Clydesdale, 2007, *The First Year Out: Understanding American Teens after High School*, Chicago: University of Chicago Press; Richard Flory and Donald Miller, 2007, *Finding Faith: The Spiritual Quest of the Post-Boomer Generation*, New Brunswick, NJ: Rutgers University Press; for a view from the British context, see Sara Savage, Sylvia Collins-Mayo, Bob Mayo, and Graham Cray, 2006, *Making Sense of Generation Y: The World View of 15–25 Year-Olds*, London: Church House Publishing; and from an Australian context, see Michael Mason, Ruth Webber, and Andrew Singleton, 2008, *The Spirit of Generation Y: Young People's Spirituality in a Changing Australia*, Mulgrave, Victoria, Australia: John Garratt Publishing). But this book is also unique in certain important ways. The combination of, first, the national scope of its research; second, its mixing of survey and interview methods for gathering its data; and, third, the longitudinal nature of the data collection, which has tracked and studied the same respondents over time in order to follow developmental changes in their lives, together make this study distinctive. Some prior studies of emerging adults offer depth and insight of analysis but are not based on nationally representative samples and so leave us unsure about to whom their findings can actually be generalized. Other previous studies are based on solid, nationally representative survey data but lack in-depth interviews to help contextualize and interpret the meaning of their numbers. That, we think, is a drawback. Still other previous studies nicely combine both survey and interview data but are limited to cross-sectional evidence (data collected at only one point in time), which restricts their ability to speak to ways in which characteristics, influences, and outcomes may change developmentally over time. All of these prior studies are valuable in different ways. But this book's contribution to the conversation combines many strengths that together make it distinctive—a study that we hope greatly enhances readers' knowledge and understanding of the issue in question.

11. For example, Wilde, Melissa J., 2002, "Book Review of *Young Adult Catholics: Religion in the Culture of Choice*," by Dean R. Hoge, William D. Dinges, Mary Johnson, and Juan L. Gonzales, Jr., *Journal for the Scientific Study of Religion*, 41(4): 788–789; Andrew Greeley, 2002, "Book Review of *Young Adult Catholics: Religion in the Culture of Choice*," by Dean R. Hoge, William D. Dinges, Mary Johnson and Juan L. Gonzales, Jr., *American Journal of Sociology*, 107(4): 1141–1142.

12. Patrick McNamara's *Conscience First, Tradition Second* being the exception.

13. This and the following three paragraphs are revised versions of part of a book review essay of mine, Christian Smith, 2007, "Getting a Life: The Challenge of Emerging Adulthood," *Books and Culture*, November/December, pp. 10–13.

14. Jeffrey Arnett, 2006, "Emerging Adulthood: Understanding the New Way of Coming of Age," in Jeffrey Arnett and Jennifer Tanner (eds.), *Emerging Adults in America: Coming of Age in the 21st Century*, Washington, D.C.: American Psychological Association, p. 5.

15. Some of the statistics about emerging adulthood today are not historically unique. For example, young Americans in the nineteenth and very early twentieth centuries, when society was more rural and agricultural, also married later in life than they did in the 1950s. But changes in the larger culture and social order in late twentieth-century America make the experience of emerging adulthood today very different from the young adulthood of a century ago. Today's unprecedented freedom and mobility, available lifestyle options, and greater influence of secular culture make the years between 18 and 29 less orderly and in various ways more risky for most.

16. Robert Schoeni and Karen Ross, 2005, "Material Assistance from Families During the Transition to Adulthood," in Richard Settersten, Frank Furstenberg, and Rubén Rumbaut (eds.), *On the Frontiers of Adulthood*, Chicago: University of Chicago Press, pp. 396–416.

17. Jeffrey Arnett, 2004, *Emerging Adulthood: The Winding Road from the Late Teens through the Twenties*, New York: Oxford University Press.

18. The NSYR is collecting a fourth wave of survey and interview data collection in 2012 and 2013, which should produce empirical data-based answers to questions about the religious and spiritual lives of older emerging adults.

Chapter 1

1. Also see James Davidson, 2007, "The Catholic Church in the United States: 1950 to the Present," in Leslie Woodcock Tentler (ed.), *The Church Confronts Modernity: Catholicism in the United States, Ireland, and Quebec*, Washington, D.C.: Catholic University of America Press, pp. 177–207.

2. Also see Penny Long Marler, 2000, "Young Catholics and Contemporary American Society," in John Fulton, Anthony Abela, Irena Borowik, Teresa Dowling, Penny Long Marler, and Luigi Tomasi (eds.), *Young Catholics at the New Millennium: The Religion and Morality of Young Adults in Western Countries*, Dublin, Ireland: University College Dublin Press, pp. 112–136.

3. Claude Fischer and Michael Hout, *Century of Difference: How America Changed in the Last One Hundred Years*, New York: Russell Sage Foundation, pp. 162–185, especially p. 173.

4. Gerald Gamm, 2001, *Urban Exodus: Why the Jews Left Boston and the Catholics Stayed*, Cambridge, MA: Harvard University Press; James Hudnut-Beumler, 1994, *Looking for God in the Suburbs: The Religion of the American Dream and Its Critics*, New Brunswick, NJ: Rutgers University Press.

5. Mark Massa, 1999, *Catholics and American Culture: Fulton Sheen, Dorothy Day, and the Notre Dame Football Team*, New York: Crossroad.

6. Jay Dolan, 1975, *The Immigrant Church: New York's Irish and German Catholics, 1815–1865*, Baltimore: Johns Hopkins University Press. There was, of course, considerable regional and ethnic variation in many of the dynamics addressed in this chapter, which a more detailed study would certainly reveal.

7. For example, see Robert Orsi, 2002, *The Madonna of 115th Street: Faith and Community in Italian Harlem*, New Haven: Yale University Press. In fact, there was usually more religious diversity than often assumed, but Catholic parishes could so successfully orient residents to Catholic institutions that neighborhoods sometimes seemed more exclusively Catholic than they actually were.

8. That is, when considering Protestantism as one religious bloc, which was not uncommon then, especially when contrasted with Catholicism; however, when focusing on individual denominations, Catholicism became the largest single religious body in the U.S. around 1850.

9. Jay Dolan, 1985, *The American Catholic Experience*, Garden City, NY: Doubleday, pp. 262–293. We mean precisely "normative" here as mandated by clergy, but not universal, since for most of these years, the majority of Catholic children attended non-Catholic schools. Bryan T. Froehle and Mary L. Gautier, 2000, *Catholicism USA: A Portrait of the Catholic Church in the United States*, Maryknoll, NY: Orbis, pp. 68–73; also see Notre Dame Task Force on the Participation of Latino Children and Families in Catholic Schools, *To Nurture the Soul of a Nation: Latino Families, Catholic Schools, and Educational Opportunity*, Notre Dame, IN: Alliance for Catholic Education Press, 2009. Although pre-Vatican II American Catholicism was male-centered in certain visible ways, in fact women tended to rule the schools, colleges, and hospitals that powerfully defined Catholic culture.

10. See, for example, R. Scott Appleby, 1989, "The Era of the Ombudsman, 1930–1954," in Jay Dolan, R. Scott Appleby, Patricia Byrne, and Debra Campbell (eds.), *Transforming Parish Ministry: The Changing Roles of Clergy, Laity and Women Religious*, Chestnut Ridge, NY: Crossroad, pp. 7–23; James O'Toole, 1993, *Militant and Triumphant: William Henry O'Connell and the Catholic Church in Boston, 1859–1944*, Notre Dame, IN: University of Notre Dame Press; Carol Coburn, 1999, *Spirited Lives: How Nuns Shaped Catholic Culture and American Life, 1836–1920*, Chapel Hill, NC: University of North Carolina Press; John Fialka, 2004, *Sisters: Catholic Nuns and the Making of America*, New York: St. Martin's Press. Arguably, American Catholicism before Vatican II suffered from institutional hypertrophy, with many bishops exercising relatively untrammeled authority over their dioceses, with more control than in much of European Catholicism and more parishioner obedience than later emerged. When the larger forces described in this chapter then altered the context, the pendulum swung in the opposite direction of relative institutional atrophy, as described below.

11. Joseph Gremillion and Jim Castelli, 1987, *The Emerging Parish*, New York: Harper and Row, pp. 12–14; James Hunter, 1991, *Culture Wars*, New York: Basic Books, pp. 35–37; Philip Jenkins, 2003, *The New Anti-Catholicism*, New York: Oxford University Press, pp. 30–40.

12. James O'Toole, 2008, *The Faithful: A History of Catholics in America*, Cambridge, MA: Harvard University Press, pp. 142–143.

13. Massa 1999, p. 227; John McGreevy, 1997, "Thinking on One's Own: Catholicism in the American Intellectual Imagination, 1928–1960," *The Journal of American History*, 84(1): 97–131. American Catholicism had also long wrestled with positively appropriating some of the liberal freedoms deep in American culture, to the extent that in 1899 Pope Leo XIII (in *Testem Benevolentiae Nostrae*) condemned "Americanism" as a dangerous form of modernism. (Pope Pius X echoed this condemnation in 1907 in *Nostra Charge Apostolique*.) See R. Scott Appleby, 1992, *Church and Age Unite!: The Modernist Impulse in American Catholicism*, Notre Dame, IN: University of Notre Dame Press; Jay Dolan, 2002, *In Search of American Catholicism: A History of Religion and Culture in Tension*, New York: Oxford University Press; R. Scott Appleby, 1995, "The Triumph of Americanism," in Mary Jo Weaver and R. Scott Appleby, 1995, *Being Right: Conservative Catholics in America*, Bloomington, IN: Indiana University Press, pp. 37–62; David O'Brien, 1989, *Public Catholicism*, New York: Macmillan Publishing Company.

14. Massa 1999, pp. 5–6; Jay Dolan ibid., pp. 357–362; Andrew Greeley, 1959, *The Church and the Suburbs*, New York: Sheed and Ward, p. 52.

15. Lisa Keister, 2007, "Upward Wealth Mobility: Exploring the Roman Catholic Advantage," *Social Forces*, 85(3): 1195–1225; Dolan 1985, p. 426; Stephen Steinberg, 1974, *The Academic Melting Pot*, New York: McGraw-Hill, p. 21; Hennesey 1981, p. 314; Greeley 1989, *Religious Change in America*, Cambridge: Harvard University Press, pp. 78–79; Massa 1999, pp. 4–10; Greeley 1979, pp. 92–95; John Kosa, 1970, "The Emergence of a Catholic Middle Class," in William Liu and Nathaniel Pallone (eds.), *Catholics/U.S.A.*, New York: Wiley, pp. 15–24.

16. Philip Gleason, 1995, *Contending with Modernity: Catholic Higher Education in the Twentieth Century*, New York: Oxford University Press, pp. 261–304. This liberal Catholicism was in many ways similar to the movement of Catholic "Americanism" of the late nineteenth century.

17. Richard Alba, 1981, "The Twilight of Ethnicity among American Catholics of European Ancestry," *Annals of the American Academy of Political and Social Science*, 454: 86–97; Noel Ignatiev, 2008, *How the Irish Became White*, New York: Routledge; David Roediger, 2006, *Working Toward Whiteness: How America's Immigrants Became White*, New York: Basic Books. At the same time, a new demographic trend in Catholicism toward a more "brown" (mostly Latino) Catholic population was getting underway.

18. Massa 1999, p. 5. Dean Hoge, "Interpreting Change in American Catholicism: The River and Floodgate," *Review of Religious Research*, 27(June 1986): 289–300.

19. Even as, complicating this picture, certain Cold War forces—such as anti-communist McCarthyism in the 1950s—exerted strong constraining forces on tolerance and civil rights.

20. Howard Schuman, Charlotte Steeh, Lawrence Bobo, Maria Krysan, 1998, *Racial Attitudes in America: Trends and Interpretations*, Cambridge, MA: Harvard University Press; Charles Glock, 1993, "The Churches and Social Change in the Twentieth Century," *Annals of the American Academy of Political and Social Science*, 527(1): 67–83. Also see John McGreevy, 1998, *Parish Boundaries: The Catholic Encounter with Race in the Twentieth-Century Urban North*, Chicago: University of Chicago Press.

21. Will Herberg, 1955, *Protestant-Catholic-Jew: An Essay in American Religious Sociology*, New York: Doubleday. Herberg judged Catholicism an "over–all American religion" (p. 87).

22. Frank Coppa, 2002, "Pope Pius XII and the Cold War: The Post-War Confrontation Between Catholicism and Communism," in Dianne Kirby (ed.), *Religion and the Cold War*, New York: Palgrave Macmillan, pp. 50–66. Hennesey ibid., pp. 261, 270, 276, 281–289.

23. William D'Antonio, James Davidson, Dean Hoge, and Katherine Myer, 2001, *American Catholics: Gender, Generation, and Commitment*, Walnut Creek, CA: Alta Mira Press, p. 4; Theodore Caplow, Louis Hicks, and Ben Wattenberg, 2000, *The First Measured Century*, Washington, D.C.: American Enterprise Institute, pp. 110–111.

24. Steven Avella calls American Catholicism of this era (1940–1965) the "confident Church." Avella, 1992, *This Confident Church: Catholic Leadership and Life in Chicago, 1940–1965*, Notre Dame, IN: University of Notre Dame Press.

25. D.J. O'Brien, 1972, "American Catholicism and American Religion," *Journal of the American Academy of Religion*, 40: 36–53; James Davidson and Andrea Williams, 1997, "Megatrends in Twentieth-Century American Catholicism," *Social Compass*, 44: 507–527.

26. For example, Mark Massa, 2010, *The American Catholic Revolution: How the Sixties Changed the Church Forever*, New York: Oxford University Press; John O'Malley, 2008, *What Happened at Vatican II*, Cambridge, MA: Harvard University Press; Helen Rose Ebaugh, 1991, *Vatican II and U.S. Catholicism*, Greenwich, CT: JAI Press; Colleen McDannell, 2011, *The Spirit of Vatican II: A History of Catholic Reform in America*, New York: Basic Books; Joseph Gremillion, 1985, *Church and Culture Since Vatican II: The Experience of North and Latin America*, Notre Dame: University of Notre Dame Press; Dean Hoge and Jacqueline Wenger, 2003, *Evolving Visions of the Priesthood: Changes from Vatican II to the Turn of the New Century*, Collegeville, MN: Liturgical Press; John O'Malley, Joseph Komonchak, Stephen Schloesser, Neil Ormerod, and David Schultenover, 2007, *Vatican II: Did Anything Happen?*, New York: Continuum; Joseph Chinnici, 2003, "The Reception of Vatican II in the United States," *Theological Studies*, 64: 461–494; Adrian Hastings (ed.), 1991, *Modern Catholicism: Vatican II and After*, New York: Oxford University Press; Ormond Rush, 2004, *Still Interpreting Vatican II: Some Hermeneutical Principles*, Mahway, NJ: Paulist Press; Ladislas Orsy,

2009, *Receiving the Council: Theological and Canonical Insights and Debates*, Collegeville, MN: Liturgical Press.

27. See, for example, Timothy Kelly, 2009, *The Transformation of American Catholicism: The Pittsburgh Laity and the Second Vatican Council, 1950–1972*, Notre Dame: University of Notre Dame Press.

28. Thomas Woods, 2004, *The Church Confronts Modernity: Catholic Intellectuals and the Progressive Era*, New York: Columbia University Press; William Halsey, 1980, *The Survival of American Innocence: Catholicism in an Era of Disillusionment, 1920–1940*, Notre Dame, IN: University of Notre Dame Press.

29. Langdon Gilkey, 1975, *Catholicism Confronts Modernity*, New York: Seabury. Gilkey here exaggerates some but his essential point is correct. Philip Gleason provides a more nuanced account in his *Contending with Modernity* (Oxford, 1995).

30. Joseph Chinnici, "The Catholic Community at Prayer, 1926–1976," in James O'Toole (ed.), 2004, *Habits of Devotion: Catholic Religious Practice in Twentieth-Century America*, Ithaca, NY: Cornell University Press, pp. 9–88; O'Toole ibid., pp. 145–198; Dolan 2002, pp. 154–155; Dolan 1985, pp. 408–409; Dennis Robb, 1972, "Specialized Catholic Action in the United States, 1936–1949: Ideology, Leadership, and Organization," PhD dissertation, University of Minnesota.

31. Philip Gleason, 1995, *Contending with Modernity: Catholic Higher Education in the Twentieth Century*, New York: Oxford University Press.

32. Massa 1999, pp. 7–8; Robert Handy, *Undermined Establishment: Church-State Relations in America, 1880–1920*, Princeton, NJ: Princeton University Press; Christian Smith (ed.), 2003, *The Secular Revolution: Power, Interests, and Conflict in the Secularization of American Public Life*, Berkeley: University of California Press; George Marsden, 2006, *Fundamentalism and American Culture*, New York: Oxford University Press.

33. Massa ibid. Massa places particular emphasis on the shock of a new outlook of historicism, as opposed to timeless truths, that gripped the Church: "Between 1907 [when Pope Pius X condemned 'Americanism'] and 1965 historical consciousness had grown to be the eight-hundred-pound gorilla in the chapel" (156).

34. Gilkey, 1975, pp. 34–35; Massa 2010. For instance, while Protestantism had for centuries (for better or worse) considered personal experience a theological category and not simply an existential fact, neo-scholastic Catholicism had long denounced "personal experience" as quintessentially "modernist" (for example, see Pope Pius X's *Pascendi Dominici Gregis*, 1907—see Halsey ibid.). In post-Vatican II American Catholicism, however, the pendulum swung far in the other direction: Many prized "experience" as a theological category, which opened numerous doors to arguably problematic elements of individualistic, experience-based American culture.

35. For analyses of how this played out among American Jesuits, for example, see Peter McDonough and Eugene Bianchi, 2003, *Passionate Uncertainty: Inside the American Jesuits*, Berkeley: University of California Press; Peter McDonough, 1994, *Men Astutely Trained: A History of the Jesuits in the American Century*, New York: Free Press.

36. John Tracy Ellis, 1956, *American Catholicism*, Chicago: University of Chicago Press; Ellis, 1955, "American Catholics and the Intellectual Life," *Thought*, 30: 351–388; Thomas O'Dea, 1958, *American Catholic Dilemma: An Inquiry into the Intellectual Life*, New York: Mentor; Commonweal, 1954, *Catholicism in America: A Series of Articles from the Commonweal*, New York: Harcourt, Brace; Robert Cross, 1958, *The Emergence of Liberal Catholicism in America*, Cambridge: Harvard University Press.

37. Philip Gleason, 1995, *Contending with Modernity: Catholic Higher Education in the Twentieth Century*, New York: Oxford University Press, p. 294.

38. Thomas O'Dea, 1958, *American Catholic Dilemma: An Inquiry into the Intellectual Life*, New York: Mentor, pp. 43–44, 102, 136. The overall impression, Gleason observes, "was that practically everything historically associated with American Catholic life, intellectual and otherwise, would have to be scrapped" (p. 292) and that "this degree of alienation from—not to say contempt for—preconciliar Catholic culture was by no means rare in the late 1960s" (294).

39. Gleason, p. 304.

40. Dolan, 1985, p. 430; Joseph Komonchak, 1995, "Interpreting the Council: Catholic Attitudes toward Vatican II," in Mary Jo Weaver and R. Scott Appleby, 1995, *Being Right: Conservative Catholics in America*, Bloomington, IN: Indiana University Press, pp. 17–36; R. Scott Appleby, 2007, "Decline or Relocation?: The Catholic Presence in Church and Society, 1950–2000," in Tentler (ed.) ibid., p. 216.

41. See, for example, Daniel Callahan, 1965, *Generation of the Third Eye*, New York: Sheed and Ward. In Latin America, movements as radical as the theology of liberation were set into motion and, for a time, given seeming permission to thrive. Christian Smith, 1991, *The Emergence of Liberation Theology*, Chicago: University of Chicago Press.

42. See, for example, Eugene Kennedy, 2001, *The Unhealed Wound: The Church and Human Sexuality*, New York: St. Martin's Press.

43. See Mary Jo Weaverand R. Scott Appleby, 1995, *Being Right: Conservative Catholics in America*, Bloomington, IN: Indiana University Press.

44. Froehle and Gauthier ibid., pp. 128–133. In 1945, women religious represented 74 percent of the entire ordained and vowed pastoral labor force of the American Catholic Church. Froehle and Gauthier ibid., p. 127. Also see Dennis Castillo, 1992, "The Origin of the Priest Shortage: 1942–1962," *America*, October 24, 302–304.

45. Froehle and Gauthier ibid., p. 128.

46. Dolan ibid., pp. 436–438; O'Toole ibid., p. 237; Froehle and Gautier ibid., pp. 109–123; Richard Schoenherr and Lawrence Youth, 1993, *Full Pews and Empty Altars: Demographics of the Priest Shortage in United States Catholic Dioceses*, Madison: University of Wisconsin Press; Margaret Mary Modde, O.S.F., "Departures from Religious Institutions," *New Catholic Encyclopedia*, 17: 570–571; Hennesey ibid., pp. 329–330; Peter Steinfels, 2003, *A People Adrift: The Crisis of the Roman Catholic Church in America*, New York: Simon and Schuster, pp. 29, 30; Richard Schoenherr with David Yamane, 2004, *Goodbye Father: The Celibate Male Priesthood and the Future of the Catholic Church*, New York: Oxford University Press; Ann Carey, 1997, *Sisters in Crisis*, Huntington, IN: Our Sunday Visitor.

47. Froehle and Gauthier ibid., p. 128.

48. Christian Smith, Michael Emerson, with Patricia Snell, 2008, *Passing the Plate: Why American Christians Don't Give Away More Money*, New York: Oxford University Press; Greeley, 1989, pp. 67–75. Explaining well why this is the case is a task beyond the scope of this chapter, unfortunately, but one that merits further consideration. But see Charles Zech, 2000, *Why Catholics Don't Give: And What Can be Done About It*, Huntington, IN: Our Sunday Visitor.

49. Smith, Emerson, with Snell ibid., p. 30.

50. Greeley ibid., p. 70.

51. Smith, Emerson, with Snell, ibid., p. 50.

52. Catholic orphanages also play an important role in the larger story, which we, however, cannot adequately address here. But see Mary Oates, 1995, *The Catholic Philanthropic Tradition in America*, Bloomington, IN: Indiana University Press; Matthew Crensen, 2001, *Building the Invisible Orphanage: A Prehistory of the American Welfare System*, Cambridge, MA: Harvard University Press; Dorothy Brown, 2000, *The Poor Belong to Us: Catholic Charities and American Welfare*, Cambridge, MA: Harvard University Press.

53. Joseph Claude Harris, 1996, *The Cost of Catholic Parishes and Schools*, New York: Sheed and Ward.

54. Steinfels ibid., p. 212; James Youniss and John Convey (eds.), 2000, *Catholic Schools at the Crossroads*, New York: Teachers College Press.

55. James Davidson, 2005, *Catholicism in Motion: The Church in American Society*, Liguori, MO: Liguori Press, p. 76. The number of Catholic diocesan and parochial high school students declined by 21 percent between 1960 and 2001, from 520,128 to 375,125 (Davidson ibid., p. 76). These changes were also taking place at a time when governments were investing massive resources into public schooling, which Catholic schools could not match.

56. Dolan ibid., p. 442; Hennesey ibid., pp. 323–324; Margaret Brinig and Nicole Garnett, 2010, "Catholic Schools, Urban Neighborhoods, and Education Reform," *Notre Dame Law Review*, 85(3): 887–954. Also see Andrew Greeley et al., 1976, *Catholic Schools in a Declining Church*, New York: Sheed and Ward.

57. Steinfels ibid., p. 213.

58. Fraser Field, 2001, "How Catholic Are Our Catholic Schools?," *Catholic Exchange*, December 26. Also see Cornelius Riordan, 2000, "Trends in Student Demography in Catholic Secondary Schools, 1972–1992," in James Youniss and John Convey (eds.), *Catholic Schools at the Crossroads*, New York: Teachers College Press, pp. 33–54; Frances Plude, 1974, *The Flickering Light: What's Happening to Catholic Schools?*, New York: Sadlier; C. Albert Koob and Russell Shaw, 1970, *S.O.S. for Catholic Schools*, New York: Holt, Rinehart, and Winston.

59. David Baker and Cornelius Riordan, 1998, "The 'Eliting' of the Common American Catholic School and the National Educational Crisis," *Phi Delta Kappan*, September, pp. 16–24; Christian Smith, with Melinda Denton, 2005, *Soul Searching: The Religious and Spiritual Lives of American Teenagers*, New York: Oxford University Press, pp. 211–214; David Gonzalez, 2007, "Frustration over a $25,000 Catholic School," *New York Times*, September 29, p. 1.

60. For example, see Patrick McCloskey, 2009, *The Street Stops Here: A Year at a Catholic High School in Harlem*, Berkeley: University of California Press.

61. Philip Gleason, 1995, *Contending with Modernity: Catholic Higher Education in the Twentieth Century*, New York: Oxford University Press.

62. Philip Gleason, 1995, *Contending with Modernity: Catholic Higher Education in the Twentieth Century*, New York: Oxford University Press; James Burtchaell, 1998, *The Dying of the Light: The Disengagement of Colleges and Universities from Their Churches*, Grand Rapids, MI: Eerdmans, pp. 557–716; Jo Ann Tooley, 1993, "Struggling to Keep the Faith: In the Face of Potent Cultural Forces, Regional Liberal Arts Colleges Affiliated with the Roman Catholic Church Seek to Hold onto Their Heritage," *U.S. News and World Report*, October 4, 115(13): 122–124. See Christopher Jencks and David Riesman, 1969, *The Academic Revolution*, Garden City, NY: Anchor Books, pp. 334–405.

63. Bernard Häring, 1968, "The Encyclical Crisis," *Commonweal*, September 6, 588; Avery Dulles, S.J., 1993, "'Humanae Vitae' and the Crisis of Dissent," *Origins*, April 22, 774–777; Peter Steinfels, 1993, "Vatican Watershed—A Special Report: Papal Birth-Control Letter Retains Its Grip," *New York Times*, August 1. To be sure, the Catholic bishops of Vatican II themselves had modeled dissent within the Church by refusing to proceed with the proposal for the council initially advanced by the Vatican Curia. Dolan ibid., p. 426; Melissa Wilde, 2007, *Vatican II: A Sociological Analysis of Religious Change*, Princeton: Princeton University Press, pp. 14–26.

64. For the larger history, see Leslie Tentler, 2009, *Catholics and Contraception: An American History*, Ithaca, NY: Cornell University Press.

65. Andrew Greeley, 2004, *The Catholic Revolution: New Wine, Old Wineskins, and the Second Vatican Council*, Berkeley: University of California Press.

66. Andrew Greeley, 1989, p. 20; Greeley 1979, p. 97; also see Michael Hout and Andrew Greeley, 1987, "The Center Doesn't Hold: Church Attendance in the United States, 1940–1984," *American Sociological Review*, 52: 325–345.

67. O'Toole ibid., p. 242; Andrew Greeley, 1997, *The Catholic Myth: The Behavior and Beliefs of American Catholics*, New York: Touchstone, pp. 91–105; William D'Antonio, James Davidson, Dean Hoge, and Ruth Wallace, 1996, *Laity: American and Catholic Transforming the Church*, Kansas City: Sheed and Ward, p. 33.

68. See, for example, Alan Petigny, 2009, *The Permissive Society: America—1941–1965*, Cambridge: Cambridge University Press. On Catholicism specifically, see James Fisher, 1989, *The Catholic Counterculture in America, 1933–1962*, Chapel Hill, NC: University of North Carolina Press.

69. Doug McAdam, 1982, *Political Process and the Development of Black Insurgency*, Chicago: University of Chicago Press; McAdam, 1990, *Freedom Summer*, New York: Oxford University Press.

70. Hunter Davies, 2010, *The Beatles*, New York: W. W. Norton, p. lxxiii.

71. Daniel Yankelovich, 1981, *New Rules: Searching for Self-Fulfillment in a World Turned Upside-Down*, New York: Bantam Books; Maurice Isserman and Michael Kazin, 2007, *America Divided: The Civil War of the 1960s*, New York: Oxford University Press; John Blum, 1991, *Years of Discord: American Politics and Society, 1961–1974*, New York: Norton; Hugh McLeod, 2008, *The Religious Crisis of the 1960s*, New York: Oxford University Press.

72. Davidson, 2005, p. 12.
73. Bruce Schulman, 2001, *The Seventies: The Great Shift in American Culture, Society, and Politics*, New York: The Free Press; Robert Ellwood, 1994, *The Sixties Spiritual Awakening: American Religion Moving from Modern to Postmodern*, New Brunswick, NJ: Rutgers University Press; Mark Massa, 2000, *How We Got Here, The 70s, The Decade that Brought You Modern Life—For Better or For Worse*, New York: Basic Books; Edward Berkowitz, 2006, *Something Happened: A Political and Cultural Overview of the Seventies*, New York: Columbia University Press.
74. Philip Gleason, 1972, "Catholicism and Cultural Change in the 60s," *Review of Politics*, 34: 91–107.
75. David Carlin, 2003, *The Decline and Fall of the Catholic Church in America*, Manchester, NH: Sophia Institute Press, p. 65.
76. William Prendergast, 1999, *The Catholic Voter in American Politics*, Washington, D.C.: Georgetown University Press, pp. 23–24; Dolan ibid., p. 426. See, however, George Marlin, 2006, *The American Catholic Voter: Two Hundred Years of Political Impact*, South Bend, IN: St. Augustine Press.
77. We (with the help of Missy Petrelius) calculated these numbers by pooling GSS data from 1972 to 1978, selecting only respondents reporting (a) being Catholic at age 16 or (b) Catholic at the time of the survey, stratifying that sample by birth-year decade, and calculating percent totals of respondents who were previously divorced or currently divorced or separated. The percent divorced for each birth-year cohort by decade is as follows: before 1900 = 5.7 percent, 1900–1909 = 13.5 percent, 1910–1919 = 15.3 percent, 1920–1929 = 15.9 percent, 1930–1939 = 19.5 percent, 1940–1949 = 18.6 percent, 1950 and later = 14.7 percent. Note that older respondents had had more years in which to get divorced, which helps to explain the lower divorce rates in the last two age cohorts.
78. A substantial number, as shown by William Sander, 1995, *The Catholic Family: Marriage, Children, and Human Capital*, Boulder, CO: Westview Press, pp. 13–14.
79. Andrew Greeley, 1990, *The Catholic Myth: The Behavior and Beliefs of American Catholics*, New York: Touchstone, p. 99; James McCarthy, 1979, "Religious Commitment, Affiliation, and Marriage Dissolution," in Robert Wuthnow (ed.), *The Religious Dimension: New Directions in Quantitative Research*, New York: Academic Press, pp. 179–195; Sander ibid., pp. 15–20; Dolan ibid., p. 433; George Gallup and Jim Castelli ibid., p. 6; Tim Heaton and Kristen Goodman, 1985, "Religion and Family Formation," *Review of Religious Research*, 26(4): 343–359. Also see Coombs and Zumeta, 1970, "Correlates of Marital Dissolution in a Prospective Fertility Study," *Social Problems*, 18: 94; Tim Heaton, Stan Albrecht and Thomas Martin, 1985, "The Timing of Divorce," *Journal of Marriage and Family*, 47(3): 631–639. Note that not all of these percentages reported in the text here are entirely comparable across time (in that some include only Catholics currently divorced at the time, while others add in those previously divorced and remarried and possibly even divorced ex-Catholics), so they must be viewed as representing a real general trend, but not specifically accurate increases measured between time periods. For the years 1971 to 2000, by comparison, Michael Hout uses General Social Survey data to show that in between 1971 and 1979 8 percent of current (but not raised then defected) U.S. Catholics were divorced or separated and 6.5 percent were remarried, meaning that a total of 14.5 percent of Catholics then had been divorced at least once (also, 11.6 percent of "lapsed" Catholics were divorced or separated and 11.9 percent were remarried); while between 1998 and 2000, 15.6 percent of U.S. Catholics were divorced or separated and 9.4 percent were remarried, meaning a total of 25 percent of Catholics had then been divorced at least once (20 percent of "lapsed" Catholics in 1998–2000 were divorced or separated and 13 percent were remarried, totaling to 33 percent divorced at least once) (Hout, 2000, "Alienation Among Divorced and Remarried Catholics in the United States," Berkeley: Survey Research Center Research Report).
80. Dolan ibid., p. 436; Melissa Wilde, 2001, "From Excommunication to Nullification: Testing and Extending Supply-Side Theories of Religious Marketing with the Case of Catholic Marital Annulments," *Journal for the Scientific Study of Religion*, 40(2): 235–249; Tim B. Heaton, Stan L. Albrecht and Thomas K. Martin, 1985, "The Timing of Divorce," *Journal of Marriage and Family*, 47(3): 631–639.
81. Greeley, 2004, p. 39.

82. Joan Fee, Andrew Greeley, William McCready, and Teresa Sullivan, 1981, *Young Catholics in the United States and Canada*, New York: William Sadlier, p. 18. Survey data on the same question are not available for the decades prior to Vatican II, to our knowledge.

83. Gallup and Castelli ibid., p. 182.

84. Greeley, 2004, p. 39.

85. Calculated by the authors using 1978 General Social Survey data, with the variables "relig" and "premarsx."

86. George Kelly, 1979, *The Battle for the American Church*, New York: Basic Books, p. 188; Andrew Greeley, 1977, *The American Catholic*, New York: Basic Books, pp. 142–150; Dolan ibid., p. 435; O'Toole ibid., p. 242; Charles Westhoff and Elise Jones, 1977, "The Secularization of U.S. Catholic Birth Control Practices," *Family Planning Perspectives*, 9: 203–207; Charles Westhoff and Larry Bumpass, 1973, "The Revolution in Birth Control Practices of U.S. Roman Catholics," *Science*, 179: 41–44; also see McCarthy ibid., p. 181.

87. Charles Westhoff and Elise Jones, 1979, "The End of 'Catholic' Fertility," *Demography*, 16(2): 209–217; Sander ibid., pp. 43–61.

88. Gallup and Castelli ibid., pp. 6–7.

89. Dean Hoge and Kathleen Ferry, 1981, *Empirical Research on Interfaith Marriage in America*, Washington, D.C.: United States Catholic Conference; Darren Sherkat, 2004, "Religious Intermarriage in the United States: Trends, Patterns, and Predictors," *Social Science Research*, 33: 606–625; O'Toole ibid., p. 257; for background, see Claude Fischer and Michael Hout, *Century of Difference: How America Changed in the Last One Hundred Years*, New York: Russell Sage Foundation, pp. 201–202. D'Antonio and colleagues summarized matters this way: "The American Catholic laity is evolving a new sexual morality, much of it without benefit of the Church's teaching authority. This morality is consonant with the moral norms that have been evolving with the majority of Americans as attested by surveys and reports throughout the past thirty years." D'Antonio, Davidson, Hoge, and Wallace ibid., p. 62. Also see Ann Rose, 2001, *Beloved Strangers: Interfaith Families in Nineteenth Century America*, Cambridge: Harvard University Press.

90. Massa ibid., p. 5.

91. "For the first time in modern history, Catholics no longer agreed on the answer to the question of what it meant to be Catholic." Dolan 1985 ibid., pp. 427–428.

92. Carlin ibid., p. 25.

93. Massa ibid., pp. 9–10.

94. Dolan ibid., pp. 433–434; Greeley ibid., pp. 123, 127; Gallup and Castelli, 1987, *The American Catholic People: Their Beliefs, Practices, and Values*, Garden City, NY: Doubleday, p. 27. Gallup polls showed a somewhat more gradual decline, from 74 percent of American Catholics attending Mass regularly in 1958 to 60 percent in 1970, 53 percent by the mid-1980s, and between 30 and 40 percent by the 1990s—O'Toole ibid., p. 222. Gallup's measure (having gone to church during the previous week), however, is known to over-estimate the percent of Americans attending church. Kirk Hadaway, Penny Marler, and Mark Chaves, 1993, "What the Polls Don't Show: A Closer Look at U.S. Church Attendance," *American Sociological Review*, 58: 741–752.

95. William D'Antonio, James Davidson, Dean Hoge, and Katherine Myer, 2001, *American Catholics: Gender, Generation, and Commitment*, Walnut Creek, CA: Alta Mira Press, pp. 7–16.

96. Compare, for instance, analysis of the pre–Vatican II, Vatican II, and post–Vatican II generations in D'Antonio, Davidson, Hoge, and Meyer ibid., especially pp. 37–66. Also see William D'Antonio and Anthony Pogorelc, 2007, *Voices of the Faithful: Loyal Catholics Striving for Change*, New York: Crossroad, pp. 76–78.

97. Chinnici ibid., pp. 9–88; Maurer ibid.

98. See Davidson 2005, pp. 170–175.

99. William Portier, 2004, "Here Come the Evangelical Catholics," *Communio*, 31: 35–66.

100. Smith with Denton ibid., Christian Smith with Patricia Snell, 2009, *Souls in Transition: The Religious and Spiritual Lives of Emerging Adults*, New York: Oxford University Press.

101. Smith with Denton ibid., p. 57.

Chapter 2

1. The GSS has only consistently measured race/ethnicity by interviewer identification. Unfortunately this method can be fraught with error, particularly when it comes to identifying GSS respondents of Hispanic origin. For further information regarding potential problems with interviewer identification of race/ethnicity, see Sapersteirn (2006) and GSS Methodology Report #89 (Smith 1997) and #93 (Smith 2001).
2. Greeley and Hout (1999).
3. Hout and Fischer (2002) make the argument that the increase in "no religion" is largely due to a symbolic change in self-labeling by "unchurched believers" who are political moderates and liberals and are trying to differentiate themselves from the Religious Right.
4. When we take recent cross sections of the GSS, we also find that younger Catholics pray less frequently and affiliate with their own tradition more weakly when compared to older Catholics; however, as we argue below, these facts are due less to generational differences in religious commitment than to the cultural and life-course influences of emerging adulthood.
5. The original survey question wording was highly general: "Would you be for or against sex education in the public schools?"
6. Although we are not experts in Catholic medical ethics, it is our understanding that certain cases of a pregnancy endangering a mother's health—when the principle of "double effect" comes into play—that the Catholic Church does not oppose procedures that would end the life of an unborn baby—for example, if a pregnant woman has uterine cancer, it might still be morally acceptable for her to have surgery that results in the death of the child so long as that death was not the reason she obtained the surgery.
7. See Table 7.3 in Smidt et al. (2008). It should also be noted that 79 percent of Catholics who attend Mass regularly and have traditional Catholic theological beliefs voted for Republican George W. Bush in 2004, and 71 percent voted for him in 2008.
8. For a summary and defense of this position, see chapter 4 of Hunter (2010).
9. We think it is important to register an important caveat to our claims against the decline narrative. The GSS data only take us as far back as 1972 (and sometimes not even that far). Therefore, our critique of the narrative of Catholic decline only extends this far. We acknowledge that it is quite possible, perhaps quite likely, that 18- to 25-year-olds prior to the Second Vatican Council could be quite distinct religiously, socially, and politically from this same age group after the council.
10. For example, D'Antonio et al. (2007) find substantial differences between Millennials (those born between 1979 and 1987) and post-Vatican II Catholics (those born between 1961 and 1978) in Catholic identity and level of religious commitment. We question the authors' assumptions that these differences are primarily due to birth cohort effects as opposed to aging effects associated with life-course transitions.
11. We recognize that we are simplifying our analysis of aging and cohort effects. The final patterns of religious participation for Catholics and Protestants will be determined not only by aging patterns among birth cohorts, but also the relative size of particular birth cohorts, the changing meaning attached to self-identifying as Catholic and Protestant over time, and the possibility of period effects that influence the average level of attendance of all birth cohorts. Nevertheless, our own analysis of these patterns suggests that aging differences generally drive Protestant religious participation while cohort differences generally drive Catholic religious participation. These Catholic/Protestant life-course differences hold up when we restrict our sample to those born in the U.S., and even when we restrict our sample to those whose parents were born in the U.S. Also, separating Protestants into evangelicals and mainline Protestants does little to alter anything here—both primarily exhibit aging effects. It is clear that the differences are primarily between Catholics and Protestants.
12. Hout and Greeley (1987) make precisely this case, arguing that *Humanae Vitae* caused a short-lived downward trend in religious participation among Catholics. We believe the continuing decline in Catholic religious participation casts doubt upon this explanation, however.
13. Bahr (1970); Mueller and Cooper (1986); Myers (1996); Roozen et al. (1990); Stolzenberg, Blair-Loy, and Waite (1995).

14. We have pooled data on religious service attendance across waves for respondents of the same age in different years. For example, data for 19-year-olds is collected and pooled from the 2000 through 2004 waves of data (all of the years that have data for 19-year-old respondents). This method allows us to use as much data as is available in the NLSY97.

15. Similar results can be found in the NSYR data between the first and third waves. The proportion of evangelical Protestants and mainline Protestants attending church frequently (once a week or more) in wave three had dropped 31 percentage points from its Wave 1 level. The equivalent drop for Catholics is 26 percentage points.

16. The 2000 follow-up question contains a coding error in the available data from the Bureau of Labor Statistics. We are confident that the data we present here are accurate. More information is available from the authors upon request.

17. As with the NLSY97 in Figure 2.15, we pool data across waves for respondents of the same age in the NLSY79 to use all available data.

18. We immediately suspected that Catholics were more likely than Protestants to continue to identify with their tradition despite ceasing to regularly practice. If this is the case, the apparent Protestant "rebound" would be caused by less religiously observant Protestants removing themselves from the Protestant sample over time. However, this theory cannot explain the findings in Figure 2.16 because the sample is restricted to respondents who identified as Catholic or Protestant in 1979 and still identified as such in 2000.

19. We also found similar results using the Youth-Parent Socialization Panel Study, a national sample of high school seniors in 1965 (and followed up in 1973, 1982, and 1997). Catholic Mass attendance stabilized in adulthood while Protestant church attendance steadily increased.

Chapter 3

1. Readers interested in a comparison of Catholics with non-Catholics on a number of religious dimensions should consult Chapter 4 of Christian Smith with Patricia Snell, *Souls in Transition: The Religious and Spiritual Lives of Emerging Adults*, New York: Oxford University Press, 2009.

2. The Nominally Catholic category is the smallest group and most respondents in it were not asked these Catholic-specific questions (only 13 to 17 respondents depending on the question). Because of this low number, we have refrained from including them in Figure 3.1. Nevertheless, consistent with our expectations, Nominal Catholics were the least likely to report these practices, on all six measures, of any of the Catholic types.

3. We recognize that some of the Catholics in the first wave of the NSYR were too young to have received confirmation. This, however, does not significantly influence our analysis because age varies little between the Catholic groups (the mean age varies from 15.37 to 15.66 between groups). Moreover, we control for age in our multivariate analysis and still find significant differences between the Nominal and Family Catholics and the other categories.

4. Smith with Snell, 2009.

5. Robert D. Putnam and David E. Campbell, 2010, *American Grace: How Religion Divides and Unites Us*, New York: Simon & Schuster, p. 10.

6. Robert Wuthnow, 2007, *After the Baby Boomers: How Twenty- and Thirty-Somethings Are Shaping the Future of American Religion*, Princeton: Princeton University Press.

7. Because the U.S. Census does not collect information on religion, it is difficult to estimate the exact percentage. Most estimates are based on multiplying the proportion of all Hispanics who are Catholic by the number of Hispanics in a given age range. For example, the Fe y Vida Institute estimates that 52 percent of 20- to 29-year-old Catholics in 2011 are Hispanic using this method (see http://www.feyvida.org/research/fastfacts.html). We think this figure is too high, but the proportion is probably between 40 and 50 percent. Reviewing multiple surveys, scholars have found that around 70 percent of American Hispanics are Catholic (see Perl, Paul, Jennifer Z. Greely, and Mark M. Gray, "What Proportion of Adult Hispanics Are Catholic? A Review of Survey Data and Methodology," *Journal for the Scientific Study of Religion*, 45: 419–436). The Fe y Vida estimate puts this figure closer to 80 percent.

8. We generated a weight that inflated the count of Hispanics to match the Census figures and deflated the count of non-Hispanic Catholics. We then compared the frequency distribution of a large number of variables of interest using the new weight and the standard survey weight. Most categories of interest were only altered by a percentage point or two at most. Further information is available from the authors upon request.

9. This is the smallest Catholic group in our data, comprising only 30 respondents in the third wave of the NSYR. For this reason, we extend some caution in interpreting the final proportions reporting various beliefs and practices in this group.

10. For example, sociologist Will Herberg predicted that second-generation immigrants would be less religious than their parents (the first generation) as part of their assimilation to mainstream society. However, he expected that this drop in religious identity and practice would not last. He believed that the third generation would be more religious than the second generation because they would need to distinguish themselves socially and ethnically from the dominant society. Will Herberg, 1956, *Protestant, Catholic, Jew: An Essay in American Religious Sociology*, New York: Doubleday.

11. In other words, Herberg's prediction that the third generation would return to religion does not seem to be the story our data tell.

12. For a summary of this research, see Wendy Cadge and Elaine Howard Ecklund, "Immigration and Religion," *Annual Review of Sociology*, 33(2007): 359–379.

13. Smith with Snell, 2009; Smith with Denton, 2005.

14. In the first wave of the NSYR, when the respondents were adolescents, one parent of each respondent also completed a survey about themselves and their child. If the parent respondent was Catholic, he or she was asked to self-identify as either a "traditional" Catholic, a "moderate" Catholic, or a "liberal" Catholic. While clergy, religious organizations, and sociologists regularly use these labels to identify distinct movements within the Catholic Church, recent research suggests that the laity may use these terms differently when they describe themselves on surveys. Nevertheless, these labels act as meaningful qualifiers to Catholic identity—a way that Catholics place themselves in the larger Catholic landscape. Traditional Catholics can be expected to have a different orientation to the Church and on certain contentious social issues (abortion, homosexuality, birth control, female priests, etc.) than liberal Catholics. See Brian Starks, "Self-Identified Traditional, Moderate, and Liberal Catholics: Movement-Based Identities or Something Else?" *Qualitative Sociology*, 32(2009): 1–32.

15. In the first wave of the NSYR, the parent respondent was asked whether his or her spouse or partner (1) shares their same faith, (2) adheres to a different religious faith, or (3) is not religious. We treat those parents who report that their spouse or partner is of the same faith as constituting a religiously homogamous household.

16. The strategy we employ helps us to isolate the direct impact of each factor. Of course, factors often influence outcomes indirectly through other factors. For example, traditional Catholics are more likely to be married to another Catholic than liberal Catholics. One of the ways that having a traditional Catholic parent influences the religious lives of emerging adults, then, is through religious homogamy in the household. Alternatively, sometimes factors work together to produce an outcome in a unique way. Their collective influence is greater than the sum of their individual influences. In a later chapter we use methods that are better suited to finding these combinations. For now, we simply want to isolate which factors most dramatically shape the religious outcomes of Catholic adolescents and emerging adults.

17. For the sake of presentation, we describe the outcomes of our statistical analyses as opposed to presenting the individual findings. Specific results are available from the authors upon request.

18. Effect size is different than statistical significance. Statistical significance specifies whether, by studying just a sample from a population, we can be confident that the effect really exists in the population as a whole. Statistically significant findings can have a negligible overall effect (especially with large samples), and non-statistically significant findings can have a large overall effect (especially with small samples).

Chapter 4

1. For a fuller explanation, see the Excursus concerning our definitions of "Catholic."
2. Of the 41 Catholic or ex-Catholic emerging adults we interviewed, 27 are male and 14 are female. Twenty-three are white, 11 are Hispanics, and the remaining seven either refused to answer our survey race question or are a different race than white or Hispanic (that is, are black or mixed race).
3. For a similar analysis using a smaller sample and fewer categories, see Penny Long Marler, 2000, "Young Catholics and Contemporary American Society," in John Fulton, Anthony Abela, Irena Borowik, Teresa Dowling, Penny Long Marler, and Luigi Tomasi (eds.), *Young Catholics at the New Millennium: The Religion and Morality of Young Adults in Western Countries*, Dublin, Ireland: University College Dublin Press, pp. 112–136.
4. We asked him if there were any social causes in particular that appealed to him. "My sister does social work in Africa and she's started an organization there. She just graduated from college, she started it with a friend of hers their junior year, so it's only been about two years now. Definitely I would see what they needed resource-wise, what they were doing, help her out because I know that's something that's so important to her. And I would want to support her in that. And then I'd have to look into it, what else I really wanted to help out. I mean medicine, I want to be a doctor, so that's something that's also really important to me, see what I can do around here using that money to help under-privileged people here, too."
5. He reports: "When I was going through that whole Christian period, we [Steve and his sister] had some pretty heated debates about things and we still do now because I'm still not on the same page with her. That's kinda the way my family is. My mom was talking to one of her friends and she was laughing at us that me and my sister have arguments about religion and politics and her kids are fighting about, like, who gets to watch TV. So my family's a little weird in that sense that we have very deep arguments and people get angry, but it's all in good fun, we're fine a half an hour later."
6. As a larger context for this, Steve feels very blessed in his life, after having gone on many service trips on which he saw, "the situations, like that these people in Mexico are living in, just like, wow, your house is half the size of my garage, and I complain when the cable goes out, which is just ridiculous really. When I look around and realize that most Americans live in the top 95 percent, like the 95th percentile of wealth in the world. Someone, I think one of my professors, told me that the average American lives like a king in the 17th century or something like that, and how great that we really have it and we just take it for granted, and in terms of everything really, I feel like I'm blessed." He also thinks of his family and friends as a blessing.
7. Specifically, according to orthodox (i.e., Nicene, Chalcedonian) Christology, Jesus did not stop being God or somehow become less "one with God" as a result of his incarnation (becoming human); nor did he become more "one with God" after his ascension into heaven. In addition, according to either orthodox Protestantism or Catholicism, salvation is not achieved by "being a good person," but rather by the saving merits of the person and work of Jesus Christ alone.
8. Furthermore, we cannot determine to what extent Catholic emerging adults' common focus on premarital sex is the "real" reason why so many of them remain distant from the Church, versus the possibility that this issues serves as a convenient rationalization or additive explanation for what are really many other reasons for that distance—all we can analyze are our interview data, in which this issue comes up recurrently.
9. Renee's biological parents have divorced, which is another factor associated with reduced involvement with the religious faith in which a person is raised.

Excursus

1. This lack of research on categorizing Catholics is surprising, given the extensive study of the characteristics that should be used to identify affiliates of other religious groups, especially conservative Protestants (e.g., Conrad Hackett and Michael Lindsay, "Measuring Evangelicalism:

Consequences of Different Operationalization Strategies," *Journal for the Scientific Study of Religion*, 47(2008): 499–514.

2. Christopher D. Bader, F. Carson Mencken, and Paul Froese, "American Piety 2005: Content and Methods of the Baylor Religion Survey," *Journal for the Scientific Study of Religion*, 46(2007): 447–463; Kennon Sheldon, "Catholic Guilt? Comparing Catholics' and Protestants' Religious Motivations," 16(2006): 209–223; Jeremy Uecker, "Religion, Pledging, and the Premarital Sexual Behavior of Married Young Adults," *Journal of Marriage and Family*, 70(2008): 728–744.

3. William C. Rinaman, Matthew T. Loveland, Robert F. Kelly, and William R. Barnett, "Dimensions of Religiosity among American Catholics: Measurement and Validation," *Review of Religious Research*, 50(2009): 413–440; James Davidson et al., 1997, *The Search for Common Ground: What Unites and Divides Catholic Americans*, Huntington, IN: Our Sunday Visitor Press.

4. Schwadel, Philip, "Age, Period, and Cohort Effects on U.S. Religious Service Attendance: The Declining Impact of Sex, Southern Residence, and Catholic Affiliation," *Sociology of Religion*, 71(2010): 2–24. James Davidson et al., 1997, *The Search for Common Ground: What Unites and Divides Catholic Americans*, Huntington, IN: Our Sunday Visitor Press.

5. For example Christian Smith, with Melinda Lundquist Denton, 2005, *Soul Searching: The Religious and Spiritual Lives of American Teenagers*, New York: Oxford University Press.

6. See Christian Smith, with Melinda Lundquist Denton, 2005, *Soul Searching: The Religious and Spiritual Lives of American Teenagers*, New York: Oxford University Press, for a review.

7. Allesandra Chan and Francois Poulin, "Monthly Changes in the Composition of Friendship Networks in Early Adolescence," *Merrill-Palmer Quarterly*, 53(2007): 578–602.

8. Christian Smith, with Melinda Lundquist Denton, 2005, *Soul Searching: The Religious and Spiritual Lives of American Teenagers*, New York: Oxford University Press; Christian Smith, with Kari Christoffersen, Hilary Davidson, and Patricia Snell Herzog, 2011, *Lost in Transition: The Dark Side of Emerging Adulthood*, New York: Oxford University Press.

9. Jean M. Twenge, 2007, *Generation Me: Why Today's Young Americans Are More Confident, Assertive, Entitled—and More Miserable than Ever Before*, New York: Free Press; Jeffrey Arnett, 2004, *Emerging Adulthood: The Winding Road from the Late Teens through the Twenties*, New York: Oxford University Press.

10. Tim Clydesdale, 2007, *The First Year Out: Understanding American Teens after High School*, Chicago: University of Chicago Press.

11. For example, Mark Regnerus and Jeremy Uecker have shown that evangelical Protestant adolescents abstain from sexual intercourse longer than adolescents belonging to other denominations, yet these same evangelical youth are less likely than their peers to use contraception when they do engage in sexual intercourse (*Premarital Sex in America: How Young Americans Meet, Mate, and Think about Marrying*, New York: Oxford University Press, 2011).

12. Mark Chaves, "Rain Dances in the Dry Season: Overcoming the Religious Congruence Fallacy," *Journal for the Scientific Study of Religion*, 49(2010): 1–14; Christian Smith, "Theorizing Religious Effects among American Adolescents," *Journal for the Scientific Study of Religion*, 42(2003): 17–30.

13. Having direct measures of these mechanisms (i.e., exposure to Catholic beliefs or number of valued Catholic ties) would be ideal, but generally this type of information is not available in nationally representative survey data, so we must rely on proxy measures such as the strength of parents' affiliation as Catholic.

14. Darren Sherkat, "Religious Intermarriage in the United States: Trends, Patterns, and Predictors," *Social Science Research*, 33(2004): 606–625.

15. Nicholas H. Wolfinger and Bradford W. Wilcox, "Happily Ever After? Religion, Marital Status, Gender and Relationship Quality in Urban Families," *Social Forces*, 86(2008): 1311–1337; Lori Baker-Sperry, "Passing on the Faith: The Father's Role in Religious Transmission," *Sociological Focus*, 34(2001): 185–198.

16. See Bader et al., "American Piety 2005," for review of categorization criteria.

17. The 32 youth that are classified based on a parent who self-identifies as Catholic, without attending Mass, remains the same even if this variable is placed after youths' second attendance and identification.

18. Additional analyses (not shown here) show that, among respondents who did not have a direct, current connection with the Catholic Church, older youth were more likely to report being raised Catholic than younger youth. This suggests that the reason these young people are no longer connected to the Catholic Church is because, having grown older, they decided to leave the Church. Most likely when these youth report being raised Catholic, they mean that Catholicism played a significant role in their childhood, but once they were allowed to choose for themselves, they opted out of the Church. This interpretation supports the argument for using this characteristic to classify emerging adult Catholics. If we had asked these almost-emerging adults about their religious affiliation when they were 12 or 13 years old, they very likely would have said outright that they were Catholic.

19. The identified group of evangelical Protestants would most likely not suffer from this problem (i.e., inclusion of infrequent church attendees) because researchers often identify evangelicals using several different markers, such as claiming to be "born again" and believing the Bible is accurate in all its teachings (Hackett and Lindsay, "Measuring Evangelicalism").

20. For example, if we were interested in seeing how having important relational ties to Catholic adults affects frequency of prayer differently from simply identifying as Catholic, we can distinguish youth who self-identify as Catholic but neither attend Mass nor have Catholic parents from those youth who attend Mass and have Catholic parents but do not self-identify as Catholic. We might even then compare these two groups to youth who exhibit all three markers and to those who do not exhibit any. While this level of distinction is not necessary for many analyses, using this approach can allow researchers and readers to better understand what exactly is meant by "Catholic" and how the method of categorization may affect the relationships, associations, and causal dynamics that are discovered in analyses.

21. While the total, logically possible number of combinations here is 127, several combinations should never be present empirically, especially any combination that involves both attending Mass as a first and second place of attendance, which should not occur. Similarly, one's primary and secondary identification should be able to both be Catholic. If we removed configurations that involved these combinations, there are fewer possible combinations.

Chapter 5

1. Some readers may be surprised that Completely Catholics can be in the Lowest religiousness group, given that the former categorization required teens to be attending Mass. The categorization of Completely Catholic only required teens to be attending Mass as their first place of attendance (in addition to other factors), regardless of how frequently they attended. For example, a teen who attends Mass as their first place of attendance but only does so a few times a year would still be classified as Completely Catholic if they also identify as Catholic, have Catholic parents, and were raised Catholic (see Chapter 4 for more details on this classification process). The religiousness outcome categorization is based on a combination of frequency of attendance, prayer, and importance of faith, meaning teens or emerging adults could be in the Lowest religiousness group even if they attend Mass sometimes, as long as they pray infrequently and do not believe faith is important. Therefore it is completely plausible that a Completely Catholic teen could be in the Lowest religiousness group, and the fact that only 2 percent are is an interesting and important finding.

2. The Catholic categories (e.g., Completely, Mostly, Nominal) are based on teenage factors. We then examine how teens in each of these groups experience and practice religion as emerging adults (i.e., we do not reclassify Catholic types in emerging adulthood).

3. These and other supplementary results can be found in Appendix A.

4. That is, not controlling through more complex regression techniques for the possible effects of other related variables.

5. Our analyses in this chapter control for parent income (w1), highest parent education in household (w1), family structure (w1), age of youth, race of youth, sex of youth, and whether the emerging adult was in college (w3).

6. Readers who are interested in the full statistical output that was used to construct this summary table can find it in Appendix A.

7. We conducted several additional analyses to further investigate this unexpected relationship. First, we examined the influence of short-term missions in the entire NSYR sample. In the majority of our tests, these mission trips did not show a substantial relationship with religiousness in emerging adulthood. Although in some of the final tests the relationship was negative, the magnitude was essentially null. The significant, negative influence of short-term missions on emerging adult religiousness, therefore, appears to be particular to Catholic youth.

Second, the distribution of the number of mission trips teens have taken is skewed, with only a few Catholic youth reporting six or more missions. This distribution could create analytic and conceptual problems. To address this issue, we tested several different alterations to the original variable, in which we grouped the few youth who had taken several missions into one larger group (e.g., capping the variable at four or more missions). In all of these tests the significant, negative relationship remains. We also altered the variable from a count of the number of missions to a dichotomous indicator, which differentiated simply between Catholic youth who had taken at least one mission trip versus those who had not. In these tests the significant relationship is not present, which suggests that the negative influence stems from differences among Catholic youth who take several short-term missions. Using basic cross-tabulations (which do not control for other pertinent variables), there appears to be a curvilinear influence, such that Catholic youth who do not participate in any mission trips and those who participate in several are less likely than those who participate in only a few missions to be more religious in emerging adulthood.

Third, a more detailed examination of the regression tests shows that the influence of short-term missions is stronger and more consistently statistically significant when the lagged dependent variables (i.e., religious service attendance, importance of religion, and personal prayer during the teen years) are not included in the tests. This pattern of findings could indicate that the negative relationship is created by a "regression to the mean" effect. That is, if two teens both attend religious services very frequently but one goes on more missions than the other, the "extremely religious" teen is a bit more likely to decline in overall religiosity over time (partly because there is nowhere to go but down).

Fourth, the survey question for this measure asks teens how many times they have participated in a short-term mission or a "service project," meaning the activities teens are reporting may not all involve traveling abroad to perform religious evangelization. Further analysis of the in-depth interviews revealed that several teens were thinking of their volunteer efforts at local shelters or food banks when responding to this question. Of course we would expect this type of volunteer work to be associated with increased religiousness over time, but many of the Catholic youth who appear to be extremely involved in these efforts could be résumé-building, meaning they are only doing these projects to bolster their college applications. When these Catholics enter college they may be less motivated to continue in these types of efforts and decline in their religiousness.

Finally, while this is an exploratory and speculative theory, there could be an interesting and important difference between Catholic youth and the rest of the population. Some of the Catholic youth who report numerous short-term missions might be the children of missionaries. Their decline in religiousness during emerging adulthood, therefore, could stem from a rebellion or burnout effect. Or it might be only the transition from a very intensive religious environment to a more balanced environment leading to a decline in religiousness. Again, the clear finding is that this relationship deserves further investigation.

8. We have placed being Hispanic in the Conditionally Somewhat Important category because there does not appear to be a substantial or significant difference between non-Hispanic Catholics' and Hispanic Catholics religiousness in emerging adulthood. But we must again be careful not to place too much importance on this finding given the relatively small Hispanic Catholic population included in the NSYR.

9. The actual importance of attending a Catholic high school was not apparent in zero-order, bivariate correlations shown in Table 5.1.

10. Because believing in miracles and attending a Catholic high school are dichotomous variables (yes/no), no numbers can be reported for the middle 50 percent; nor can they be reported in the second, combined variable that uses both factors. Those cells have dashed lines in them.

11. We were not able to calculate percents for the combination of all eight variables in Table 5.3 since only 11 respondents in the entire sample scored in the top quartile in a measure that included all eight factors.

12. Charles Ragin, 2000, *Fuzzy-Set Social Science,* Chicago: University Chicago Press.

13. Charles Ragin, 1994, "Introduction to Qualitative Comparative Analysis," in Thomas Janoski and Alexander Hicks (eds.), *The Comparative Political Economy of the Welfare State,* Cambridge: Cambridge University Press; Charles Ragin, 1995, "Using Qualitative Comparative Analysis to Study Configurations," in Udo Kelle (ed.), *Computer-Aided Qualitative Data Analysis,* London: Sage.

14. The exact process for creating these categories is discussed in Appendix A.

15. See Vern Bengtson, 2001, "Beyond the Nuclear Family: The Increasing Importance of Multigenerational Bonds," *Journal of Marriage and Family,* 63: 1–16; Vern Bengtson, Joan Bengtson (eds.), 1985, *Grandparenthood,* Beverly Hills: Sage; Casey Copen and Merril Silverstein, 2008, "Intergenerational Transmission of Religious Beliefs to Young Adults: Do Grandmothers Matter?" *Journal of Contemporary Family Studies,* 38: 497–510.

16. The process for creating these categories is discussed in Appendix A.

17. For examples see Charles W. Peek, Evans W. Curry, and H. Paul Chalfant, "Religiosity and Delinquency over Time: Deviance Deterrence and Deviance Amplification," *Social Science Quarterly,* 66(1985): 120–131; Mark Regnerus, "Linked Lives, Faith, and Behavior: Intergenerational Religious Influence on Adolescent Delinquency," *Journal for the Scientific Study of Religion,* 42(2003): 189–203.

18. Philip Gorski, 2009, "Social 'Mechanisms' and Comparative-Historical Sociology: A Critical Realist Proposal," in Björn Wittrock and Peter Hedström (eds.), *The Frontiers of Sociology,* Leiden: Brill; Douglas Porpora, 2008, "Recovering Causality: Realist Methods in Sociology," in A. Maccarini, E. Morandi, and R. Prandini (eds.), *Realismo Sociologico,* Genova-Milano: Marietti; Jose Lopez and Garry Potter (eds.), 2005, *After Postmodernism: An Introduction To Critical Realism,* New York: Continuum; Andrew Bennett, 2008, "The Mother of All 'isms': Organizing Political Science around Causal Mechanisms," in Ruth Groff (ed.), *Revitalizing Causality: Realism about Causality in Philosophy and Social Science,* New York: Routledge, pp. 205–219; Douglas Porpora, 2008, "Sociology's Causal Confusion," in Ruth Groff (ed.), *Revitalizing Causality: Realism about Causality in Philosophy and Social Science,* New York: Routledge, pp. 195–204; also see Peter Hedström and Richard Swedberg (eds.), 1998, *Social Mechanisms: An Analytical Approach to Social Theory,* Cambridge: Cambridge University Press.

19. Christian Smith, with Patricia Snell, 2009, *Souls in Transition: The Religious and Spiritual Lives of Emerging Adults,* New York: Oxford University Press; Christian Smith, with Melinda Lundquist Denton, 2005, *Soul Searching: The Religious and Spiritual Lives of American Teenagers,* New York: Oxford University Press.

20. Leon Festinger, 1957, *A Theory of Cognitive Dissonance,* Stanford, CA: Stanford University Press.

21. Tim Clydesdale, 2007, *The First Year Out: Understanding American Teens after High School,* Chicago: University of Chicago Press.

22. This perspective borrows heavily from Smith's (1998) Subcultural Identity Theory. Although he applies it directly to Evangelicals, the principles seem to apply also to Catholics for whom religion is a central component of life.

23. Avshalom Caspi, 1987, "Personality in the Life Course," *Journal of Personality and Social Psychology,* 53: 1203–1213.

24. See Laurence Iannaccone, 1990, "Religious Practice: A Human Capital Approach," *Journal for the Scientific Study of Religion,* 29(3): 297–314.

Chapter 6

1. Latent Class Analysis (LCA) uses observed variables to infer unobservable (i.e., latent) subgroups. LCA is conceptually similar to factor analysis and other traditional latent variable methods, except that LCA assumes a categorical as opposed to continuous latent variable. Alternatively, one can conceptualize LCA as a method of classifying cases into a finite number of unobserved subgroups based on observed data.

2. The statistical analysis was run on the software program Mplus. Using observed indicators of frequency of prayer, frequency of religious service attendance, and self-reported importance of faith, we found that goodness-of-fit indices suggested a three-class solution. In other words, three distinct unobserved subgroups were likely producing the observable patterns of religious behavior for the Catholic population.

3. Readers will recall that the groups of Catholics analyzed most frequently in this book are those that we labeled Completely, Mostly, Moderately, Nominally, and Family Catholics in the first wave of the NSYR.

4. The N reported for each group is the actual number of cases in the NSYR, while the parenthetical percentages come from the distribution of these categories using survey weights.

5. A caution, therefore, for readers familiar with the religious ideal types from *Soul Searching* and *Souls in Transition*: the methodology we used to construct the religious ideal types of Catholics is different, and the categories themselves are not comparable with those of the previous books. One of the primary advantages of the current method is that we are able to categorize *all* of the Catholic emerging adults in our sample. Instead of creating a "mixed" category for individuals who do not fit well in any group, we put everyone into the best-fitting category, even if the fit was not perfect. In some ways this makes the categories in this book messier than the ideal types of the previous books.

6. It is not necessary to make strong claims about causality in these findings for them to be meaningful. Along with many other sociologists of religion, we find good reason to conclude that religious identity, beliefs, and practices influence how people think, behave, and live their lives; a strong version of this case need not be made here. Influence could also run in the opposite direction: for example, frequent binge drinking or sexual intercourse outside of marriage could lead some young people to avoid attending Mass or to distance themselves from their Catholic faith in other ways. This reverse causation seems perfectly plausible, but in the end it makes little difference to our primary findings, because we are not claiming that religious faith is the sole, originating source of the observed associations. For an extended discussion of this issue, see Christian Smith with Melinda Denton, 2005, *Soul Searching*, New York: Oxford, pp. 233–240.

7. For example, John Clausen, 1993, *American Lives: Looking Back at the Children of the Great Depression*, New York: The Free Press.

8. For more on "Catholic guilt," see Steve Vaisey and Christian Smith, 2008, "Catholic Guilt among U.S. Teenagers—A Research Note," *Review of Religious Research*, 49(4): 415–426.

9. The actual percentage of women in all categories here, including Catholics, who have had an abortion is likely actually higher than reported here, the difference being probably due to social-desirability bias in survey responses. Among American emerging adults, the peak age for abortions appears to be in the early to mid-20s; when grouped by five age years, the 20–24 group has a higher rate than either the 15–19 or the 25–29 age range, so our reports here are likely low. See Rachel K. Jones and Kathryn Kost, 2007, "Underreporting of Induced and Spontaneous Abortion in the United States: An Analysis of the 2002 National Survey of Family Growth," *Studies in Family Planning*, 38(3): 187–197; Radha Jagannathan, 2001, "Relying on Surveys to Understand Abortion Behavior: Some Cautionary Evidence," *American Journal of Public Health*, 91(11): 1825–1831.

10. Smith with Kari Christoffersen, Hillary Davidson, and Patricia Snell Herzog, 2011, *Lost in Transition: The Dark Side of Emerging Adulthood*, New York: Oxford University Press, pp. 195–225.

11. Clausen, *American Lives*

12. Christian Smith with Patricia Snell, 2009, *Souls in Transition: The Religious and Spiritual Lives of Emerging Adults*, New York: Oxford University Press, pp. 66–67; Smith, *Lost in Transition*, pp. 70–109.

13. See, for example, Donna Freitas, 2008, *Sex and the Soul: Juggling Sexuality, Spirituality, Romance, and Religion on America's College Campuses*, New York: Oxford University Press.

14. Mark Regnerus and Jeremy Uecker, 2011, *Premarital Sex in America: How Young Americans Meet, Mate, and Think About Marrying*, New York: Oxford University Press, pp. 52–61.

15. We recognize that while there may be broad agreement on the desirability of some life-course outcomes during emerging adulthood, not all readers will agree upon what behaviors, attitudes, beliefs, and practices are best for today's emerging adults. For our normative account of what is good for emerging adults, see Smith, *Lost in Transition*, pp. 8–11.

Chapter 7

1. See Jeremy Uecker, 2009, "Catholic Schooling, Protestant Schooling, and Religious Commitment in Young Adulthood," *Journal for the Scientific Study of Religion*, 48(2): 353–367; Paul Perl and Mark M. Gray, 2007, "Catholic Schooling and Disaffiliation from Catholicism," *Journal for the Scientific Study of Religion*, 46(2): 269–280.

2. Andrew Greeley and Peter Rossi, 1966, *The Education of Catholic Americans*, Chicago: Aldine; Andrew Greeley, William McCready, and Kathleen McCourt, 1976, *Catholic Schools in a Declining Church*, Kansas City: Sheed and Ward; Joan Fee, Andrew Greeley, William McCready, and Teresa Sullivan, 1981, *Young Catholics: A Report to the Knights of Columbus*, Chicago: Sadlier.

3. William D'Antonio, James Davidson, Dean Hoge, and Ruth Wallace, 1989, *American Catholic Laity in a Changing Church*, Kansas City: Sheed and Ward; William D'Antonio, James Davidson, Dean Hoge, and Ruth Wallace, 1996, *Laity: American and Catholic: Transforming the Church*, Kansas City: Sheed and Ward; James Davidson et al., 1997, *The Search for Common Ground: What Unites and Divides Catholic Americans*, Huntington, IN: Our Sunday Visitor Press; Thomas O'Connor, Dean Hoge, and Estrelda Alexander, 2002, "The Relative Influence of Youth and Adult Experiences on Personal Spirituality and Church Involvement," *Journal for the Scientific Study of Religion*, 41(4): 723–732.

4. Jeremy Uecker, 2009, "Catholic Schooling, Protestant Schooling, and Religious Commitment in Young Adulthood," *Journal for the Scientific Study of Religion*, 48(2): 353–367; Jeremy Uecker, 2008, "Alternative Schooling Strategies and the Religious Lives of American Adolescents," *Journal for the Scientific Study of Religion*, 47(4): 563–584.

5. Paul Perl and Mark Gray, 2007, "Catholic Schooling and Disaffiliation from Catholicism," *Journal for the Scientific Study of Religion*, 46(2): 269–280.

6. David P. Baker and Cornelius Riordan, 1998, "The 'Eliting' of the Common American Catholic School and the National Education Crisis," *Phi Delta Kappan* (September): 16–23.

7. Christian Smith, with Patricia Snell, 2009, *Souls in Transition: The Religious and Spiritual Lives of Emerging Adults*, New York: Oxford University Press; Christian Smith, with Melinda Lundquist Denton, 2005, *Soul Searching: The Religious and Spiritual Lives of American Teenagers*, New York: Oxford University Press, 2005.

8. As we show below this change may not be as drastic as some suppose, but there is still enough evidence to suggest that studies address the difference between Catholic students at Catholic schools and non-Catholic students at those schools when examining its impact.

9. Allison Pugh, 2009, *Longing and Belonging: Parents, Children, and Consumer Culture*, Berkeley: University of California Press.

10. Stephen Vaisey, 2009, "Motivation and Justification: A Dual-Process Model of Culture in Action," *American Journal of Sociology*, 114(6): 1675–1715.

11. Cornelius Riordan, 2000, "Trends in Student Demography in Catholic Secondary Schools, 1972–1992" in *Catholic Schools at the Crossroads: Survival and Transformation*, edited by J. Youniss and J.J. Convey, pp. 33–54. New York: Teachers College Press.

12. Elizabeth Vaquera and Grace Kao, 2008, "Do You Like Me as Much as I Like You? Friendship Reciprocity and Its Effects on School Outcomes," *Social Science Research*, 37(1): 55–72.

13. As a simple example, assume a population of 1,000 teenagers. Based on our data, approximately 30% of teens are Catholic (see Chapter 4 Excursus, Table E.5). Under this assumption and the current rates of attending Catholic high schools, approximately 27 Catholic teens would attend Catholic high school (300*.09) and 7 non-Catholics would do so (700*.01), making the total Catholic high school population about 80% Catholic (27/34), which matches with Figure 7.1. If the percent of non-Catholics who attend Catholic high schools were to increase to 2%, however, 14 non-Catholics would be attending Catholic high schools,

making the total Catholic high school population about 65% Catholic (27/41). This figure may actually be conservative, as we assumed that the overall size of Catholic schools also increased. If non-Catholic students end up "pushing out" Catholic students, then the change would be even more dramatic.

14. We recognize that our sample was not taken from Catholic schools, meaning we cannot be sure that our data is representative at the Catholic school level. Our sample of U.S. teenagers is nationally representative, however, which leads us to be confident that it is also representative of the Catholic school population as a whole.

15. Steve Vaisey and Christian Smith, 2008, "Catholic Guilt among U.S. Teenagers—A Research Note," *Review of Religious Research*, 49(4): 415–426.

16. Our analysis in this chapter also controls for parent income (Wave 1), highest parent education in household (Wave 1), two biological parent family structure (Wave 1), age of youth, race of youth, sex of youth, and emerging adult in college or not (wave three).

17. We also ran analysis excluding all teens and emerging adults who attended non-Catholic private schools, making the comparison directly between Catholic and public school. The results supported our conclusions.

18. Because parents' religiousness and school attendance were measured at the same point in time, we cannot clearly establish the causal direction between these variables. We recognize the possibility that sending a child to a Catholic school may increase parents' religiousness, perhaps through parents' attendance at the child's events at school or through proximity to and friendship with other religious parents. If this were the causal relationship, then our findings would support a mediation or intervening relationship: the impact of Catholic schooling would operate through its ability to increase parents' religiousness, which in turn leads to increased teen and emerging adult religiousness. Although we are unable to completely rule out this possibility, we feel justified in our assumption that in the majority of families, parents' religiousness is likely to have a greater impact on school choice than the inverse, which is why we interpret our results as a selection effect rather than an intervening one.

19. We recognize that Catholic-schooled teenagers whose parents are not very religious score noticeably higher on these characteristics than teens who do not attend Catholic school and whose parents are not very religious, although the difference does not reach the point of statistical significance. We return to this potential unique impact of Catholic schooling on teens without a strong religious background in the next section.

20. The largest difference came from the question in emerging adulthood about respondents' view of God. About 14 percentage points more of those who had been Catholic-schooled than not reported believing God was a personal being, involved in the lives of people today. This gap does not dramatically diminish among emerging adults who had highly religious parents. This one finding provides some evidence for a direct impact of Catholic schooling. We note, however, that the majority of Catholics who did not attend a Catholic school reported the same view, and the second most popular choice among these Catholics was to see God as a cosmic life force rather than a personal being. Thus, both Catholic-schooled and public-schooled teens were equally likely to believe God was involved in people's lives, the small difference hinging on whether they thought he was personally involved or a more abstract force. Given that this small theological discrepancy was in fact the largest empirical difference between the two groups, we believe our overall conclusion is supported.

21. It is somewhat difficult to compare across factors because Catholic school attendance only has two levels, whereas the other factors contain numerous levels. For this figure, however, we compare the likelihood of movement based on a change from the 10th to the 90th percentile of the other factors, which makes the predicted changes fairly comparable.

22. The other factors included in these combinations were based on the analyses in Chapter 5. These are factors that were found to be consistently important in leading to higher religiousness in emerging adulthood (see Table 5.2).

23. The exact questions on the survey were: 1. According to the Bible, where was Jesus born? ○ Jerusalem ○ Tarsus ○ Jericho ○ Galilee   ○ Bethlehem; 2. Who wrote most of the letters in the New Testament? ○ Peter ○ Luke ○ Paul ○ John ○ Jesus; 3. How

many Gospels (books of scripture recounting the life and teachings of Jesus) are there in the Bible? ○ One ○ Three ○ Four ○ Five ○ Zero; 4. What happened at Pentecost? ○ The first five of Jesus's disciples were chosen ○ The Holy Spirit descended upon the disciples ○ The angels announced Jesus's birth to the shepherds ○ Jesus ascended up to heaven ○ The Israelites burned five Canaanite cities to the ground; 5. Which of these is not one of the Ten Commandments? ○ Do unto others as you would have them do unto you ○ Do not commit adultery ○ Keep the Sabbath Day ○ Do not worship idols ○ Do not give a false witness (lie); 6. Which biblical figure is most associated with remaining obedient to God despite personal suffering? ○ Job ○ Elijah ○ Moses ○ Abraham ○ Samuel; 7. Which biblical figure led the exodus of the Israelites from Egypt? ○ Job ○ Elijah ○ Moses ○ Abraham ○ Samuel; 8. Which person in the Bible was willing to sacrifice his son for God? ○ Job ○ Elijah ○ Moses ○ Abraham ○ Samuel; 9. According to Christian teaching which of the following became incarnate? ○ The Holy Trinity ○ The Son of God ○ The Holy Spirit ○ God the Father ○ The Virgin Mary; 10. What does "redemption" mean? ○ The communion of saints ○ Buying back time from Purgatory with good works ○ Compassion for the poor and sick ○ Salvation from sins ○ The real presence of Christ in the Eucharist; 11. Which of the following does *not* agree with Christian teaching on Jesus? ○ His biological mother was Mary ○ His biological father was Joseph ○ He died on the Cross for our sins ○ He had a divine nature ○ He had the power to forgive sins; 12. When did the trinity have its origin? ○ At the birth of Jesus ○ At the descent of the Holy Spirit ○ At the creation of the world ○ Never, because the trinity is eternal ○ Never, because the trinity is only a symbol; 13. What does the story of "the good Samaritan" teach morally? ○ Our righteousness needs to exceed even that of the Samaritans and Pharisees ○ The poor we will always have with us ○ Different laws may apply to Samaritans than to Jews ○ We are to love and care for everyone, including those who are different from us ○ We must forgive others even up to ninety-nine times; 14. To what does "the annunciation" refer? ○ Jesus rising on a cloud to heaven ○ Mary visiting her cousin Elizabeth while pregnant ○ The angel Gabriel telling Mary that she would become pregnant with Jesus ○ The heavenly host of angels singing "Glory to God in the highest!" to the shepherds ○ The Apostle Paul's first sermon in Antioch; 15. Who, according to Catholic teaching, are the successors to the apostles? ○ The martyrs ○ The bishops ○ Priests ○ The crusaders ○ The Vatican; 16. Who, according to Catholic teaching, has primary authority over a Catholic diocese? ○ The Pope ○ The parish priest ○ The Bishop ○ The college of Cardinals ○ U.S. Conference of Catholic Bishops; 17. What does the doctrine of the "Assumption of the Blessed Virgin" mean? ○ The assumption that Mary is a virgin all of her life ○ The assumption that Mary is "blessed" because she is a "virgin" ○ Mary was assumed, or taken up, into heaven body and soul ○ Mary is assumed into Purgatory as consolation for those being purified ○ Mary is assumed to be the Mother of Jesus; 18. Which of the following ideas is *not* part of Catholic Social Doctrines? ○ That all persons have the right to own property (right of private property) ○ That the rights and goods of human persons must be protected (inviolable human dignity) ○ That only individuals and not institutions or societies can be sinful (the personal reducibility of sin) ○ That the earth's resources are given for the benefit of all humanity (the universal destination of goods) ○ That labor unions have the right to organize (right to collective bargaining); How much do you personally agree or disagree with the following statements? 19. I appreciate Christian Theology as a discipline that is *interesting.* ○ Strongly disagree ○ Disagree ○ Neither disagree nor agree ○ Agree ○ Strongly agree ○ Do not know; 20. I appreciate Christian Theology as a discipline that is *important.* ○Strongly disagree ○ Disagree ○ Neither disagree nor agree ○ Agree ○ Strongly agree ○ Do not know; 21. I appreciate Christian Theology as a discipline that is *relevant to my own life.* ○ Strongly disagree; ○ Disagree; ○ Neither disagree nor agree; ○ Agree; ○ Strongly agree; ○ Do not know; 22. The future well-being of the Catholic Church is very important to me. ○ Strongly disagree ○ Disagree ○ Neither disagree nor agree ○ Agree ○ Strongly agree ○ Do not know; 23. I am committed to living my life as a faithful member of the Catholic Church. ○ Strongly disagree ○ Disagree ○ Neither disagree nor agree ○ Agree ○ Strongly agree ○ Do not know; 24. How positive or negative do you generally feel about the Catholic Church? ○ Very negative

○ Negative ○ Neither negative nor positive ○ Positive ○ Very positive ○ Do not know; 25. Do you agree or disagree with the following statement?: Before coming to ND, I was *well educated* in the doctrines and moral teachings of the Catholic faith. ○ Strongly disagree ○ Disagree ○ Neither disagree nor agree ○ Agree ○ Strongly agree ○ Do not know; 28. How many years, if any, did you attend a *Catholic high school?* ○0 ○1 ○2 ○3 ○4 ○5.

24. The two questions whose differences did not reach statistical significance concern the Good Samaritan in Figure 7.10 (p = .07) and how positive or negative students felt about the Catholic Church in Figure 7.13 (p = .68).

INDEX